what social workers do

Margaret Gibelman

NASW PRESS

National Association of Social Workers
Washington, DC

Jay J. Cayner, ACSW, LSW, President
Robert H. Cohen, JD, ACSW, Executive Director

Linda Beebe, *Executive Editor*
Nancy A. Winchester, *Editorial Services Director*
Fran Pflieger, Maben Publications, Inc., *Copy Editor*
Louise Goines, *Proofreader*
Annette Hansen, *Proofreader*
Oneida Indexing Services, *Indexer*

© 1995 by NASW Press

Library of Congress Cataloging-in-Publication Data
Gibelman, Margaret.
    What social workers do / Margaret Gibelman.
    p. cm.
    Includes bibliographical references and index.
    ISBN 0-87101-242-1
    1. Social service—United States. 2. Social sevice—Vocational guidance—United States. 3. Social workers—United States.
I. Title.
HV91.G447 1995
361.3'2'02373—dc20   95-25498
                      CIP

Printed in the United States of America

what social workers do

contents

PART VI   Substance Abuse

PART VII   Other Areas of Service

preface

During the preparation of *Who We Are: The Social Work Labor Force as Reflected in the NASW Membership* (Gibelman & Schervish, 1993), which I coauthored with Phil Schervish, the breadth of the roles carried out by social workers, the diversity of their work settings and auspices of practice, and the heterogeneity of the social work population itself became clear. The statistical approach to understanding the people who make up the social work profession provided a natural spring board, as well as kindled my interest, in exploring further what it is that social workers do. This volume attempts to address that issue.

In undertaking an effort that spans the breadth of the social work profession, there is a certain amount of anxiety about the selection of what to include and what to exclude. These choices are solely those of the author. Exclusion of some areas of service does not suggest that they are unimportant. However, the focus is on those areas of service in which the majority of social workers, as reflected in the NASW membership, actually work. Since the earliest days of social work, there have been debates about how to conceptualize the profession. The decision to follow the NASW classification system in regard to areas of service is one of expediency; some framework is necessary and many have merit.

The source materials used in this volume come primarily, but not exclusively, from publications of the National Association of Social Workers, thus suggesting a slant toward viewpoints and information considered to be newsworthy and of priority by this professional association. This bias is acknowledged. I also acknowledge a special interest in macro practice, reflected in the decision to devote a section to this subject even though it is not an area of service as are the other sections. The relationship between social work and the society in which it is practiced at any point in time has become even more clear to me during the course of preparing this book. The imperative to influence the direction of that society seems equally apparent in a political environment in which the terms "social work" and "undesirable" sometimes appear to be used together by elected leaders.

As with any project of this scope, many people provided invaluable assistance. Laura Kuzma spent the greater part of a year as my research assistant, and without her help this book would not have happened, at least not in this decade.

The vignettes that appear throughout this volume are based on countless conversations with social work colleagues about the nature of their practice and represent composites of actual or typical situations. Several of the vignettes represent real people and events and are so noted. Susan Hoechstetter, Cheryll Schram, and Mildred Reynolds set aside time for interviews and ensured the accuracy of the content. Other vignettes were drawn from stories that have appeared over the last 12 years in the *NASW News* or are adaptations of events or situations described in major national newspapers.

Several people loaned their substantive knowledge of areas of service to fill in the gaps. Susan Kleszewski, my sister, provided her expertise in mental health, and Susan Safranski, immediate past president of the National Association of School Psychologists and director of special education, Birmingham Michigan Public Schools, stretched the boundaries of her profession to consider the role and function of her social work colleagues. Laura Kuzma loaned her knowledge and creativity throughout the preparation of this book, particularly to the chapter on aging. Steve Kraft shared his knowledge of substance abuse issues, programs and practice, collegiality, and support, all of which are deeply appreciated. Leila Whiting read every word of this manuscript and provided comments and practical help.

Linda Beebe, executive editor of the NASW Press, noting my reluctance to exclude some areas of practice or some literature as yet unread or undiscovered, ultimately defined the boundaries of this book. "Stop," she said; reluctantly, I did. It has been and continues to be a pleasure to work with Linda and the NASW publications staff. I was fortunate to have a second opportunity to work with Fran Pflieger, copy editor of this volume. Nancy Winchester, Editorial Services Director, reviewed proofs. And Sarah Parker and Alina Martinez, librarians at the NASW Library, provided much-needed last-minute assistance in locating the references I omitted or lost. Finally, Sheldon Gelman, dean, Wurzweiler School of Social Work, Yeshiva University, and my colleagues at WSSW provided me with a long-term home in a supportive environment and the peace of mind to pursue this effort.

The world keeps changing and the pace of change continues to accelerate. Each change brings new issues and problems that confront our society and its citizens and, consequently, new opportunities and challenges for social workers. Thus, the profession continues to evolve and no volume about what social workers do will ever be a finished tale.

Margaret Gibelman, DSW
Silver Spring, Maryland

Reference

Gibelman, M., & Schervish, P. (1993). *Who we are: The social work labor force as reflected in the NASW membership.* Washington, DC: NASW Press.

what's it all about?

What do social workers do? Ask this question of a group of social workers and you are likely to get a broad range of responses:

- a request to repeat the question

- a description of the organization or agency in which they work

- a description of the client population—"I work with homeless people"

- a job title—"I'm a case manager" or "I'm a therapist"

- a broad brush—"I'm a social worker"

- a description of rank—"I'm executive director"

- a description of interventions—"I perform psychotherapy."

Why do social workers have a difficult time answering this question? One explanation is that social work, unlike most other professions, has few boundaries. Thus, the practice configuration is affected by setting of practice, area, and auspice of practice; characteristics of clients; presenting problems of clients; level of practice; and methodologies used in practice. The configuration may vary from one social worker to another and change for any one social worker over the course of his or her career. Because of the many variables that define social work practice, it is often easier to explain where one works and with whom rather than what one does.

But the question remains: What do social workers actually do? This book examines what social workers do in their day-to-day work across the broad range of social work settings, levels of practice, and fields of practice (for example, aging or child welfare). I focus on the roles and functions social workers perform in various areas of service. Approaching the subject this way avoids the concern with types of intervention modalities used in practice and the skill requirements for different types of practice. Furthermore, an exploration of social work activities highlights the dynamism and vitality of the profession.

Social workers provide services in a variety of practice settings and at various levels. For example, social workers deliver services in private practice, institutions, hospitals, school systems, clinics or centers, and correctional facilities. The range of practice settings is broad. In these diverse practice settings, social workers carry out a series of functions, each of which is composed of a set of distinctive tasks. *Functions* are major groupings of tasks and activities.

Social work is a diverse profession with fluid boundaries. It is carried out, for example, in medical, legal, and school settings as well as in state governments and proprietary agencies. Social workers intervene with individuals, groups, and communities and provide preventive and ameliorative services. Social work clients represent all populations of society: children, families, and individual adults who have problems that run the gamut of the human condition, from substance abuse to developmental disabilities. Other professions, such as law and medicine, have specialized areas of practice and there is greater public understanding of what physicians, nurses, lawyers, and even psychologists do than is the case with social workers. This phenomenon results in part from the expansive and expanding boundaries of social work and the difficulty of providing succinct, encapsulated descriptions of a complex and multifaceted profession.

Despite the long history of social work in the United States, there is a scarcity of information devoted to the spectrum of career options in the field. In part, this is because social workers do so many different things in so many places. Although attorneys may specialize in tax law or family law, they tend to work in a firm, small group practice, or independent practice. Social workers, on the other hand, may specialize in one of many practice areas and practice their specialization in an even larger array of sites under public, for-profit, or nonprofit auspices.

Social work is becoming increasingly specialized and people considering a career in social work or students enrolled in social work education programs may be confused about career options. Baccalaureate (BSW) and master's (MSW) students frequently ask for information about the range of opportunities within social work. Students know they want to be social workers, but generally do not know where the social work jobs are and what different kinds of things social workers do in the variety of settings. In addition, those currently practicing social work may wonder what options they have in their social work careers.

This book seeks to fill the void about the profession of social work by (1) providing a panoramic view of the profession in action, (2) offering practical information about the current status of the different service areas and the types of jobs available in them, (3) making extensive use of case studies, and (4) bringing together in one volume a discussion of practice functions (such as direct practitioner, supervisor, manager, or policy analyst), practice settings (such as schools, courts, hospitals, or private practice), and practice areas (such as child welfare, mental health, substance abuse, or employment). This approach demonstrates the unity of the profession and shows the connections among seemingly diverse specializations.

Purposes and Uses of This Book

What Social Workers Do provides responses to questions posed by people interested in a career within one of the helping professions, by students enrolled in social work programs, by practitioners in the field interested in knowing more about career paths, and by policymakers and government agencies responsible for establishing standards of care and requirements for professional credentialing and licensing. Questions include

- Where do social workers work?

- What are the clients like?

- What kinds of problems do clients bring to social workers?

- What are the different levels of social work practice?

- What is a "typical" day in the life of a social worker?

- What kinds of technology do social workers use?

- How fluid are social work careers, both vertically and horizontally?

- What about collegial and interdisciplinary relationships?

- What are the long-term career opportunities?

- What distinguishes social work from other helping professions?

I address these questions with case vignettes that highlight what social workers do across settings, areas, and levels of practice. This book will provide a useful reference guide in high school and college libraries to assist students who are deciding on their careers. It can serve as an introductory text in BSW and MSW programs, particularly in courses that provide an overview of the profession and the characteristics of practice. It will be of interest to social work students and practitioners as a reference manual to guide career development. Social work educators will find the case studies useful in stimulating class discussion about situations that arise in practice. The National Association of Social Workers (NASW) and other professional organizations will have a ready, comprehensive resource available to respond to frequent requests for information about the profession.

Organization

Most social workers who are members of NASW, and from whom routine data are collected, work in the following areas:

- mental health

- health

- family and children's services

- aging

- schools

- substance abuse.

NASW has struggled for years to classify the social work labor force in a way that is easy to understand and that accurately reflects the totality of the profession. Given the complexities of this task, any effort to organize and categorize what social workers do is to some extent arbitrary. For example, social workers with a primary service area of substance abuse may work in a school setting (another service area) and provide mental health services (yet another service area). Thus, any discussion of the nature of social work roles and functions in regard to substance abuse invariably overlaps with mental health and school-based practice issues.

This book is organized to reflect the major service areas delineated by NASW. An additional chapter focuses on other service areas that constitute long-standing, important areas of practice but in which a relatively small number of social workers practice. One chapter is devoted to the cross-cutting area of macro practice and focuses on social workers whose functional responsibilities are related to community organization; policy development, implementation, and evaluation; politics (including advocacy and holding office); and organizational consultation.

There are many ways by which the organization of social work can be conceptualized:

- field of practice (health, mental health)

- practice setting (community mental health, schools, courts)

- agency type (nonprofit, government)

- function performed (direct service, supervision)

- client population served (homeless people, children with learning disabilities, chronically mentally ill people)

- methods used (social group work, casework, community work)

- practice goals (prevention, problem resolution, symptom alleviation)

- services provided (marital therapy, case management, discharge planning)

- type of presenting problem (marital discord, depression, unemployment).

Because the social work profession is so broad, classification has inherent limitations. The service areas NASW uses to classify its membership and the literature of the profession (exemplified in *Social Work Abstracts*) also have limitations. Is homelessness, for example, a mental health problem, a problem affecting families and children, or a community organization–housing problem? Are employee assistance programs a component of mental health services, substance abuse services, or occupational social work?

The system NASW uses to classify areas of service highlights some of these dilemmas. For example, "aging" is considered a service area, but it is also a population group. Thus, in part V, Aging, the subject area *is* the population. A notable exception is the area of family and children's services, but here the family unit may include multiple generations, including elderly people. Another service area is schools, but this is also a setting for social work practice. Mental health, or mental illness, refers to a population, a range of social problems, and settings in which social workers practice. Areas of service are most notable for their overlap with practice settings, populations, and social problems. Thus, there is constant fluidity in conceptualization and categorization.

Within each service area listed above, social workers occupy positions in direct services, supervision, and management. Also within each service area, social workers may concentrate on certain targeted population groups, such as chronically mentally ill people or homeless people. Thus, an individual social worker may have a service area of mental health, occupy a supervisory position, and work on problems related to homeless people. And, to add to the complexity, some service areas actually are special populations (for example, elderly people) and other service areas, such as schools, are also settings of practice.

Working in these defined areas of service, social workers deal with social issues that cut across the broad spectrum of problems that affect individuals, groups, and communities. These problems include civil and legal rights, economic status and poverty, employment, rural and urban issues, and problems unique to special populations.

Each chapter includes a discussion of the range and types of practice areas and problems addressed in the particular area of service. Case vignettes illustrate the functions social workers carry out as these are affected by the type and auspice of the employing agency, the position held by the social worker, and the characteristics of the clients served. As appropriate, background information about the service area, agency context, or presenting problem is provided. The range of employment opportunities is presented in sample classified advertisements abstracted from major national newspapers and the *NASW News* during 1994 and the first six months of 1995. The concluding chapter discusses the trends evident in social work employment.

Sources of Information

Information was derived from a number of sources. NASW publications reflected the pulse of the profession's development. The *NASW News* provided a particularly rich source of material about what social workers do and the context in which they practice. To gain a perspective on the growth and change experienced by the profession, all issues of the *NASW News* and *Social Work* published between 1984 and June 1995 were reviewed, as well as the 18th and 19th editions of the *Encyclopedia of Social Work*. Other references include the textbooks and major social work journals used in graduate and undergraduate social work education programs, again with the emphasis on publications released within the last 10 years. Definitions were for the most part drawn from the third edition of the *Social Work Dictionary* (Barker, 1995).

The case vignettes were drawn from interviews, general circulation newspaper articles (*New York Times, Chicago Tribune, Washington Post, Los Angeles Times*), and the *NASW News*. Many of the vignettes are composites of real people and events. In the few instances in which they portray actual people and events, this is noted.

All references were selected because of their relevance to an understanding of what social workers do and the types of issues they confront, including issues that affect job conditions and job security. Therefore, generally not referenced is literature pertaining to diagnosis and assessment; treatment approaches and modalities; dynamics of interventions, social programs, or program development; staff development; the nature of social problems and policy or practice options; special populations; evaluation of services; or theoretical constructs. The exception is literature pertaining to social work functions that may also touch on some or all of the areas mentioned above.

The sequence of the chapters reflects the primacy of each service area within the social work profession as reflected in the NASW membership. "Mental Health" is the first chapter because the largest proportion of NASW members work in this area. Similarly, "Other Areas of Service" appears toward the end of the volume, as the service areas reflected in this catch-all category represent only a very small proportion of the NASW membership. Statistics regarding the proportion of NASW members in each service area are drawn from *Who We Are: The Social Work Labor Force as Represented in the NASW Membership* (Gibelman & Schervish, 1993).

It is not possible in this one book to touch on all the functions social workers perform. Rather, this volume is a sampler of what social workers do and the multiplicity of their diverse settings. The goal is to portray the breadth of the social work profession and the richness of opportunities available.

Terminology

Each profession has its own vocabulary. Gibelman and Schervish (1993) found that the vocabulary social workers use to describe their profession and their practice is by no means standard. For example, NASW members were not found to distinguish accurately between private nonprofit and private for-profit auspices (Gibelman & Schervish, 1993). The language of social work continues to expand and become more complex and refined. Given the broad range of specialties within the profession, it is not surprising that clear communication within the profession and across professions remains a challenge.

The confusion is understandable. In addition to the overlap among terms to describe areas of practice and settings (for example, "school social work"), the social work vocabulary has changed. In 1961, "caseworker" was the term used to describe social workers engaged in direct practice. Now they are termed "clinical social workers" or "clinicians."

Issues of vocabulary may also relate to a general lack of consistency in describing professional identity. For example, clinical social workers frequently identify themselves as "psychotherapists" or "clinicians." Bogo, Raphael, and

Roberts (1993) found that self-identification significantly correlates with preferred client group, practice activity, and interest in private practice. The definitions that follow are offered to establish a common base of understanding of professional "language."

Social Work

The following definition of social work was adopted by the NASW Board of Directors in 1970 and has become generally accepted: "Social work is the professional activity of helping individuals, groups, or communities enhance or restore their capacity for social functioning and creating societal conditions favorable to this goal" (NASW, 1973, p. 4). Other definitions have been offered and debated over the years. For example, Crouch (1979) identified the need for a concise definition of social work built around the profession's diverse fields and specialties. He offered the following definition: "Social work is the attempt to assist those who do not command the means to human subsistence in acquiring them and in attaining the highest possible degree of independence" (p. 46). Barker (1995) offered a succinct definition of social work as the "applied science of helping people achieve an effective level of psychosocial functioning and effecting societal changes to enhance the well-being of all people" (p. 357). Some definitions are narrow, others broad.

Social Work Practice

The definition of social work NASW adopted in 1970 includes clarification about the nature of social work practice:

> Social work practice consists of the professional application of social work values, principles, and techniques to one or more of the following ends: helping people obtain tangible services; counseling and psychotherapy with individuals, families, and groups; helping communities or groups provide or improve social and health services; and participating in legislative processes. The practice of social work requires knowledge of human development and behavior; of social, economic, and cultural institutions; and of the interaction of all these factors. (NASW, 1973, pp. 4–5)

Virtually all professions include specialties within professional training and practice. The legal profession, for example, includes members who are specialists in tax, criminal, or family law. Medicine has a wide range of specialty areas, and the social work profession is equally complex and broad.

As the profession has evolved, the definitions of the profession and its practice have been subject to periodic debate, reexamination, and change. As a profession that interrelates with and seeks to have an impact on the larger socioeconomic and political environment, it is not surprising that the definition of social work would be dynamic in nature rather than rigid and static.

In 1981 the NASW Board of Directors accepted the *Standards for the Classification of Social Work Practice* (NASW, 1981) developed by the NASW Task Force on Labor Force Classification. The intent of the standards is "to identify the specific social work content of social service employment and to provide a basis for differentiating among levels of practice" (p. 3). As defined by the NASW task force, social work practice

> consists of professionally responsible intervention to (1) enhance the developmental, problem-solving, and coping capacities of people, (2) promote the effective and humane operation of systems that provide resources and services to people, (3) link people with systems that provide them with resources, services and opportunities, and (4) contribute to the development and improvement of social policy.
>
> The interventions are provided to individuals, families, small groups, organizations, neighborhoods and communities. They involve the disciplined application of knowledge and skill to a broad range of problems which affect the well-being of people, both directly and indirectly. They are carried out at differentiated levels of knowledge and skill, through an organized network of professional social workers within the boundaries of ethical norms established by the profession and the sanction of society. Within these norms, the interventions may be carried out in cooperation with other helping disciplines and organizations as part of any human service enterprise. (NASW, 1981, p. 6)

Human Services

Human services are services oriented toward the prevention, amelioration, or resolution of health, mental health, social, or environmental problems that afflict individuals, families, specific groups, or communities (Gibelman, 1995). Barker (1995) further delineated human services as programs and activities designed to enhance people's development and well-being. Included is planning, developing, and administering programs for and providing direct services to people unable to provide for their own needs. The term "human services" has been used synonymously with "social services" and "welfare services." However, the term human services has less a negative connotation and also reflects the trend to include the full range of professions involved in the delivery of health, economic, and social services (Barker, 1995).

Human services organizations, the vehicle through which most human services are provided, are those organizations that assist in the growth and development of individuals and families (Wellford & Gallagher, 1988). They may be public (government), at the federal, state, or local level; proprietary (for-profit); or nonprofit. No one sector has a monopoly on the provision of a particular type of service. However, the largest proportion of social workers deliver services through nonprofit organizations (Gibelman & Schervish, 1993). The services offered by human services organizations typically are "uniquely intimate and personal in nature" (Wellford & Gallagher, 1988, p. 49).

Auspices

The aegis under which social workers work is known as the *auspice* of practice. Lowenstein (1964) stated that auspice differentiates between the private provision of a service and the provision of that service by an organization set up by the community at large, either through government or voluntary association, with accountability for, and control over, the service resting with the community at large. Such control and accountability are in contrast to the private control of the contractual relationship mutually exercised by a private practitioner and his client. (p. 4)

The practice of social work has traditionally been carried out in organizational settings. Throughout the profession's history, these settings have basically been of two types: public and private. Public agencies are generally associated with bureaucracies, such as large public assistance or child welfare agencies. Distinctive characteristics of these agencies include clearly defined rules; a vertical hierarchy with power centered at the top; formal channels of communication; and selection, promotion, compensation, and retention based on technical competence (Barker, 1995). Social workers who work for the federal government typically must adhere to civil service rules and regulations.

Public agencies may operate at the federal, state, or local level. For example, the network of Department of Veterans Affairs hospitals, a major employer of social workers, is under federal auspices even though the hospitals themselves are based in communities across the country. Public child welfare and aging services are typically under the jurisdiction of state agencies, although a sizable proportion of the budget for these services comes from the federal government.

The private sector includes both nonprofit and for-profit agencies. Within the nonprofit sector, there are two types of agencies: sectarian and nonsectarian. Sectarian agencies either originated under the auspices of or with the financial support of religious organizations or they are oriented toward providing services primarily to members of a specific religious group. Examples include Catholic Charities USA and its affiliates across the country, Jewish social agencies, LDS Social Services, Lutheran Social Services, and the Salvation Army (Barker, 1995). Nonsectarian agencies are independent of a religious affiliation.

Private social welfare agencies may be under a national rubric, such as the affiliates of the Child Welfare League of America or Family Services America, but these agencies are located in communities and attempt to be responsive to community needs within the parameters of their national standard-setting organizations. The largest proportion of social workers deliver services through nonprofit organizations. In 1991, 38.9 percent of NASW members indicated that they worked in nonprofit organizations, both sectarian and nonsectarian (Gibelman & Schervish, 1993).

The National Taxonomy of Exempt Entities (National Center for Charitable Statistics and The Foundation Center, 1993) considers nonprofit organizations in the human services to be

Organizations or programs that promote or provide a broad range of social or human services to individuals or families, even though specific programs operated within those agencies may be classified elsewhere, i.e., American Red Cross, YM[CAs], YWCAs, YM[HAs],

YWHAs, etc.; family service agencies, including shelters and after-care programs for victims of domestic violence; organizations that provide direct social services to children and adolescents (e.g., adoption and foster care services, child day care, etc.); personal social services for individuals (e.g., credit-counseling, personal enrichment, self-help services, travelers' aid, etc.); residential, custodial care facilities and services for individuals unable to live independently due to developmental disabilities, age or physical infirmity; and programs that promote general independent functioning and living of individuals (e.g., retarded citizens associations; guide dog services for the disabled; etc.). (p. 93)

Nonprofit human services organizations are based in local communities and are governed by volunteers. Sources of revenue include contributions, donations, grants, purchase of service, and fees for service. Most traditional social services and social change organizations are nonprofit (Barker, 1995). A nonprofit agency is accountable to its board of directors, which sets overall policy. The bylaws of the agency explicate the clients to be served, the problems on which the agency should focus its attention, and the methods to be used in providing services (Barker, 1995).

Setting

Social workers provide services in a variety of practice settings, also referred to as fields of practice, that include institutions, hospitals, school systems, private practice, clinics or centers, and correctional facilities. The range of practice settings is broad.

Levels of Practice

Social workers practice in direct service, supervision, management, policy development, research, planning, and education and training capacities. These levels of practice typically are distinguished by their skill and experiential requirements. For example, social workers in management positions tend to have several years of direct service or supervisory experience. In an agency setting, there are typically three major levels of practice: direct service, supervision, and administration. Some agencies, however, may have additional levels, such as paraprofessional or case aides. And within administration, there may be middle-level managers who occupy program management positions and upper-level managers who carry overall responsibility for the operations of the agency.

Barker (1995) listed some administrative functions as

- determining organizational goals

- acquiring and allocating resources

- coordinating activities to achieve selected goals

- monitoring, assessing, and making necessary changes in processes and structures to improve effectiveness and efficiency of operations and services.

The term "administrator" is often used synonymously with "manager."

Another way to conceptualize levels of practice is to look at direct and indirect practice. *Direct practice* refers to the range of professional activities used by social workers on behalf of clients in which goals are reached through personal contact with and immediate influence of the social worker (Barker, 1995); in *indirect practice*, the activities are oriented to achieving social goals or developing human opportunities.

The levels of social work practice have also been distinguished as micro, mezzo, and macro (Barker, 1995). *Micro* practice refers to professional activities that address the problems faced primarily by individuals, families, and small groups. Most of the functions performed take the form of direct intervention on a case-by-case basis. *Mezzo* practice is the level concerned primarily with families and small groups. Related activities include facilitating communication, mediating, negotiating, educating, and linking people together. *Macro* practice is oriented to bringing about change and improvement in the general society. The functions performed in this regard include political action, community organizing, and agency administration.

All social workers engage in all three levels of practice to some extent, even though the major focus of their attention may be at one or two of the levels. Social workers have in common their commitment to help people increase their capacities to solve problems and cope with life. They do this through such means as helping clients (who may be individuals, families, groups, communities, organizations, or society in general) obtain needed resources, facilitating interactions between individuals and between people and their environments, making organizations responsible to people, and influencing the development and implementation of social policies (Barker, 1995).

Functions

In diverse practice settings, social workers carry out a series of functions, each of which is composed of a set of distinctive tasks. The relationship between the goals of social work practice, the objectives related to the particular goals, and the functions and tasks involved is illustrated in Table 1. *Functions* are major groupings of tasks and activities that, when performed by social workers, meet the four practice goals identified in the table.

The functions performed by social workers often overlap with the functions carried out by other helping disciplines. Our claim, as Stewart (1984) noted, is not to a monopoly of functions, but "to uniqueness and distinctiveness in our view about human problems and their solutions and in our particular value and practice orientation" (p. 2).

The ability to carry out these functions is predicated on the use of social work knowledge and skills in ways that are consistent with social work values. Social work practice is oriented to remediating or eliminating existing personal or social problems; habilitating or rehabilitating those whose social functioning has been impaired; and preventing problems before they develop, thus enhancing the possibility for social well-being (Barker, 1995).

Table 1

Summary of Social Work Functions

Goal	Goal	Goal	Goal
To enhance problem-solving, coping, and development capacities of people	To link people with systems that provide resources, services, and opportunities	To promote effective and humane operations of systems	To develop and improve social policy

Functions	Functions	Functions	Functions
Assessment	Referral	Administration/management	Policy analysis
Diagnosis	Organizing	Program development	Planning
Detection/identification	Mobilization	Supervision	Policy development
Support/assistance	Negotiation	Coordination	Reviewing
Advice/counseling	Exchange	Consultation	Policy advocacy
Advocacy/enabling		Evaluation	
		Staff development	

Source: National Association of Social Workers. (1981). *NASW standards for the classification of social work practice* (p. 12). Silver Spring, MD: Author.

In the performance of social work roles, NASW (1981) identified 12 essential skill areas, including the ability to

1. listen to others with understanding and purpose

2. elicit information and assemble relevant facts to prepare a social history, assessment, and report

3. create and maintain professional helping relationships

4. observe and interpret verbal and nonverbal behavior and use knowledge of personality theory and diagnostic methods

5. engage clients, including individuals, families, groups, and communities, in efforts to resolve their own problems and to gain trust

6. discuss sensitive emotional subjects supportively and without being threatening

7. create innovative solutions to "clients" needs

8. determine the need to terminate the therapeutic relationship

9. conduct research or interpret the findings of research and professional literature

10. mediate and negotiate between conflicting parties

11. provide interorganizational liaison services

12. interpret and communicate social needs to funding sources, the public, or legislators. (pp. 17–18)

Practice Areas

Social work practice can also be distinguished on the basis of primary practice area. Primary practice areas reported by NASW in 1991 are shown in Table 2.

Factors Affecting What Social Workers Do

What social workers do depends in part on their age, level of experience, highest degree, and gender. A study of the NASW membership (Gibelman & Schervish, 1993) revealed that the overwhelming majority of members have a primary function of direct services. In 1991, 68.5 percent of respondents indicated that their primary function was direct services. The second-ranked category was management, representing 16.2 percent of respondents.

The study revealed some important differences in what social workers do on the basis of their highest degree. For example, direct service was the primary function of 72.1 percent of members with BSWs, 69.7 percent of members with MSWs, and 39.1 percent of members with PhDs or DSWs. The second largest proportion of doctoral-level members identified education as their primary function. Across the three educational levels, those with doctorates were more likely to identify research as their primary function than were those with BSWs or MSWs.

Not surprisingly, more doctoral- and MSW-level social workers than BSW-level social workers were found to occupy management positions. The findings reveal that 17.3 percent of doctoral level members have a primary function of management, compared to 16.4 percent of MSWs and 9.3 percent of BSWs.

Table 2
Primary Practice Areas of Working NASW Members

Primary Practice Area	1988		1991	
	n	%	n	%
Children	11,165	16.3	14,256	16.3
Community organization–planning	913	1.3	976	1.1
Family services	8,422	12.3	9,860	11.3
Corrections	899	1.3	1,025	1.2
Group services	351	0.5	399	0.5
Medical clinics	9,005	13.2	10,926	12.5
Mental health	21,431	31.3	28,545	32.7
Public assistance	613	0.9	695	0.8
School social work	2,918	4.3	4,083	4.7
Aged	3,227	4.7	3,970	4.5
Substance abuse	2,731	4.0	4,031	4.6
Mental–developmental disabilities	2,038	3.0	2,356	2.7
Other disabilities	364	0.5	460	0.5
Occupational social work	527	0.8	711	0.8
Combined	3,339	4.9	4,836	5.5
Other	522	0.8	136	0.2
Total respondents	68,465		87,265	

Source: Gibelman, M., & Schervish, P. H. (1993). *Who we are: The social work labor force as reflected in the NASW membership* (p. 79, Table 5.1). Washington, DC: NASW Press.

Experience is also a significant factor affecting what social workers do. The study revealed a decided shift in function that occurs between two and five years of practice and between six and 10 years of practice. The proportion of NASW members reporting supervision as their primary function increases sharply at two to five years of experience. Similarly, the proportion of members reporting management as a primary function increases at 11 to 15 years.

NASW members tend to assume the primary function of supervision after working in the field for several years. The same pattern holds true for management and consultation. In the study, NASW members with these primary functions tended to be those who earned their highest degree between 1976 and 1980 or earlier. Those with a primary function of policy or education also earned their highest social work degree 20 or more years ago.

Gender is an extremely important factor. The study showed a higher proportion of women than men in direct service. The proportion of men is higher when the primary function is supervision, management, or education.

It is not unusual for social workers to carry out multiple functions either within the same job (such as supervising and providing direct services) or in two different settings. Thirty-seven percent of the employed NASW members in the study indicated that they had a secondary practice area. Some social workers hold a full-time job and an additional part-time job; some have two part-time jobs. A typical pattern is for social workers to work in an agency as their primary job and then engage in part-time private practice. There are monetary incentives involved, but another motivating is a desire to fulfill occupational interests. Also, the mobility that is possible within the profession may encourage social workers to develop expertise in a new area through part-time employment while they remain in their primary practice setting (Gibelman & Schervish, 1993).

Preparing for Social Work Practice

Formal training and subsequent experience prepare social workers for their professional roles. In 1970 the BSW degree was recognized by NASW as an entry-level professional social work degree, and in 1971 the Council on Social Work Education (CSWE) established a review process to approve BSW programs (Frumkin & Lloyd, 1995). The BSW is a baccalaureate degree awarded to qualified students who majored in social work in a college or university accredited by CSWE. NASW established the Academy of Certified Baccalaureate Social Workers (ACBSW) in 1991 to evaluate and certify the practice competence of baccalaureate social workers. Those who have obtained a BSW from an accredited school of social work are eligible for the ACBSW after they complete two years of full-time or 3,000 hours of part-time postgraduate employment, adhere to the NASW Code of Ethics (NASW, 1994), and complete a certification process composed of a written exam, supervisory evaluations, and professional references (Barker, 1995). The MSW is awarded by accredited schools or programs of social work to students who have completed the required number of academic hours (usually 60), including field placement, and have, when required, completed a research project or thesis (Barker, 1995).

A social worker, then, is a graduate of a social work education program at the baccalaureate or master's level who uses his or her knowledge and skills to provide social services for clients. These clients may be individuals, families, groups, communities, organizations, or society in general (Barker, 1995). Social workers are not a homogeneous group. Although they share in common a belief in and commitment to the principles of the profession's code of ethics, their personal beliefs and values are as varied as the population as a whole. Many social workers are politically liberal, but some are conservative. Some social workers identify with the socialist tradition, whereas others have strong convictions about the merits of free enterprise (Ginsberg, 1983). Some favor a one-on-one approach to helping, whereas others believe that social action is the only viable means of effecting change.

Credentialing

There are several types of credentialing in social work, all designed to assure the profession, clients, and the public that a practitioner has entry-level competence for safe practice (Biggerstaff, 1995). The primary credential is the basic academic qualification. Beyond that, there are a variety of voluntary professional credentials as well as those that a state may require.

One form of credentialing is the voluntary certification program. Whereas state licensing or registration establishes minimum criteria for entry-level practice, voluntary professional certification identifies specialty areas of practice (Biggerstaff, 1995).

Voluntary certification programs have been developed by NASW and other professional organizations. For example, NASW established the Academy of Certified Social Workers (ACSW) in 1962 to evaluate and certify the practice competence of social workers at the master's level. Social workers are eligible for ACSW membership after they have obtained an MSW or doctorate in social work from an accredited school, have two years of supervised full-time or 3,000 hours of part-time practice experience, have passed a written examination, and have provided three professional behaviorally anchored rating references. NASW membership is required for admission to and continued participation in the academy. However, NASW membership is not required for ACBSW certification.

Another example of voluntary certification is the Diplomate in Clinical Social Work. The Diplomate is now used as a credential to distinguish advanced-level professional clinical social workers who meet specified qualifications of the sponsoring organization. There are two sponsoring organizations: the American Board of Examiners in Clinical Social Work (ABE), which sponsors the Board Certified Diplomate in Clinical Social Work, and NASW, which sponsors the Diplomate in Clinical Social Work. Criteria for diplomate status typically include a graduate degree, postgraduate supervision, at least 7,500 hours of direct practice experience within a five-year period, fulfillment of requirements for state licensing, and successful completion of an advanced examination (Barker, 1995).

In recent years, the proportion of NASW members seeking or maintaining their ACSW status has decreased. In 1988, 50.7 percent of NASW members reported having an active ACSW status, compared to 42.5 percent in 1991 (Gibelman & Schervish, 1993). In part, this decrease can be attributed to the licensing and certification options now available to social workers. Every state and the District of Columbia, Puerto Rico, and the U.S. Virgin Islands has some form of legal regulation for social work practice. These laws control who can practice social work, the services they can provide, the methods they can use, and the titles they can present to the public (Biggerstaff, 1995). Of the over 150,000 members of NASW, more than half currently hold at least one credential (Biggerstaff, 1995). Many public and private social services agencies now require licensing or registration, or at least eligibility for same, as a prerequisite for employment.

A licensing law is protective regulatory legislation implemented through state agencies. These laws regulate the interactions between consumers and providers of services by establishing minimum standards for entry into the profession, including education, training, experience, and supervision (Biggerstaff, 1995). A *licensed clinical social worker* (LCSW) is a professional social worker who has been legally accredited by a state government to practice clinical social work in that state (Barker, 1995). Qualifications for the license vary from state to state, but typically include an MSW from an accredited school of social work, several years of supervised professional experience, and successful completion of a social work licensing exam. A *licensed independent clinical social worker* (LICSW) is the designation used by some state licensing bodies and some third-party financing institutions to indicate those practitioners deemed qualified for independent practice (Barker, 1995).

Registration laws and statutory certification, also forms of legal regulation, are voluntary statutes that apply only to social workers who wish to use a particular title. These laws also specify minimum requirements for social workers. Such title protection often can limit certain areas of professional practice, such as private practice, to those who meet the minimum requirements (Biggerstaff, 1995).

Any effort to define what social workers do must indicate the limitations of that endeavor. The social work profession is broader than most professions in regard to types of problems addressed, types of settings, levels of practice, interventions used, and populations served. This professional diversity and complexity was made clear by Senator Daniel Inouye (D-HI), a long-time friend and ally of social work. Seeking to enhance the understanding of the profession, Senator Inouye made the following statement to Congress:

> The scope of social work practice is remarkably wide. Social workers practice not only in the traditional social service agency, but also: in elementary schools; in the military; in businesses, factories, and offices; in federal, state, and local government agencies and

legislative bodies; in private practice—as individual, family, and marriage therapists; in hospitals and in mental health facilities; in courts and correctional settings; in home health care; and in services to the elderly. In fact, social workers can be found anywhere and everywhere there are people who need the help of a professional to alleviate personal or social problems. ("Going on Record," 1986, p. 8)

References

Barker, R. (1995). *Social work dictionary* (3rd ed.). Washington, DC: NASW Press.

Biggerstaff, M. (1995). Licensing, regulation, and certification. In R. L. Edwards (Ed.-in-Chief), *Encyclopedia of social work* (19th ed., Vol. 2, pp. 1616–1624). Washington, DC: NASW Press.

Bogo, M., Raphael, D., & Roberts, R. (1993). Interests, activities, and self-identification among social work students: Toward a definition of social work identity. *Journal of Social Work Education, 29,* 279–292.

Crouch, R. C. (1979). Social work defined. *Social Work, 24,* 46–48.

Frumkin, M., & Lloyd, G. A. (1995). Social work education. In R. L. Edwards (Ed.-in-Chief), *Encyclopedia of social work* (19th ed., Vol. 3, pp. 2238–2247), Washington, DC: NASW Press.

Gibelman, M. (1995). Purchasing social services. In R. L. Edwards (Ed.-in-Chief), *Encyclopedia of social work* (19th ed., Vol. 3, pp. 1998–2007). Washington, DC: NASW Press.

Gibelman, M., & Schervish, P. H. (1993). *Who we are: The social work labor force as reflected in the NASW membership.* Washington, DC: NASW Press.

Ginsberg, L. (1983). *The practice of social work in public welfare.* New York: Free Press.

Going on record about social work. (1986, April). *NASW News,* p. 8.

Lowenstein, S. (1964). *Private practice in social casework.* New York: Columbia University Press.

National Association of Social Workers. (1973). *Standards for social service manpower.* Washington, DC: Author.

National Association of Social Workers. (1981). *NASW standards for the classification of social work practice.* Silver Spring, MD: Author.

National Association of Social Workers. (1994). *NASW code of ethics*. Washington, DC: Author.

National Center for Charitable Statistics and The Foundation Center. (1993). *The national taxonomy of exempt entities* (rev. ed.). Washington, DC: Independent Sector.

Stewart, R. (1984, November). From the president. *NASW News*, p. 2.

Wellford, W. H., & Gallagher, J. G. (1988). *Unfair competition: The challenge to charitable exemption*. Washington, DC: National Assembly of National Voluntary Health and Social Welfare Organizations.

the context of social.work practice

Bob Dylan wrote, "The times they are a-changin." And as the times change, so does the profession of social work. What social workers do in the 1990s is different in many ways from what they did in the 1960s. The sociopolitical and economic environment at any given point in time has always influenced the goals, priorities, targets of intervention, technologies, and methodologies of the social work profession (Schneiderman, 1983). At the same time, the mission of the profession, the motivations and characteristics of the social work labor force, and changes in methodology and technology also serve to expand or contract the roles social workers play.

One of the characteristics that sets social work apart from other helping professions is its views that behavior is a function of the relationship between the person and his or her environment. Within this framework are the reciprocal relationships between an individual, relevant others, and the physical and social milieu. The centrality of the client (be it an individual, group, community, or society as a whole) and the client's interaction with the environment is echoed in the relationship of the social work profession to the larger society. The types of jobs available, the priority afforded particular problem areas or populations, the predominant intervention modalities, and the settings in which social workers practice are all affected by the prevailing sociopolitical philosophy and culture.

The person-in-environment perspective has gained legitimacy among the helping professions, and its influence is reflected in the fourth edition of the *Diagnostic and Statistic Manual of Mental Disorders* (DSM-IV) (American Psychiatric Association [APA], 1994). In weighing the impact of psychosocial and environmental factors on the mental health of clients, DSM-IV uses concepts similar to the person-in-environment (PIE) evaluation guidelines developed by NASW to help social workers describe the social-functioning problems of clients. DSM-IV lists psychosocial and environmental problems that may bear on diagnosis and treatment of mental disorders ("DSM-IV Revises

Psychosocial Axis," 1994). In earlier DSM editions, clinicians were able to rate the severity of psychosocial problems. DSM-IV replaces the rating scale with a checklist of specific problems, thus making greater use of the language of social work. The psychosocial categories include primary support group, social environment, education, occupation, housing, income, access to health care, legal system or crime, and other problems.

Changes in the social work profession are driven by both internal and external forces (Walz & Groze, 1991). The role and function of social workers are, for example, affected by both the larger environmental context in which the profession functions (the economy, social need, culture, political preferences, and so on) and the stage of development of professional thought, leadership direction, technology, and mission and goals. In fact, the multiple missions of the profession and the nature of social work practice reflects this dual focus. As Hopps and Pinderhughes (1987) commented, "the uniqueness of the social work approach lies in its expertise in acknowledging the interface between intrapersonal and environmental forces" (p. 353).

The course and direction of the profession's development can also be seen as a reflection of social work's location in the social structure. Rosenfeld (1983) maintained that the domain of the profession is defined, in part, as the gap between the well-being of people at a particular time and place and the spheres of well-being of individuals for which adequate provision is not provided; dealing with the discrepancies between needs and resources is the specialty of social work. In fact, Rosenfeld contended that the very purpose of social work is to reduce such incongruities. However, because the incongruities change over time, the focus of social work will change in response to the changing human condition in the context of the larger environment. Nevertheless, the expertise of social work remains rooted in the discrepancies between need and need fulfillment, no matter what the nature of the need may be at a given time.

The breadth of social work's domain depends, in part, on the availability of other professions and institutions to provide needed resources. Social workers may assume roles and functions because no other profession is ready to deal with prevailing needs (Rosenfeld, 1983). Any attempt to "fix" the boundaries of the profession is likely to be unsuccessful, given the constantly changing societal environment and prevailing ideologies. Thus, the domain of social work today is likely to be somewhat different tomorrow; it is a dynamic and evolving profession. The evolution of the profession is also rooted in changing technology and intervention methodology; as the knowledge base grows, theories undergo more rigorous testing.

Certain themes reverberate in regard to the boundaries of the social work profession. Debates that Minahan listed in 1982 are ongoing, such as

- appropriate emphasis on social work on behalf of all people versus a focus on special population groups or special social problems

- application of diverse theoretical orientations to understand people and guide interventions

- choice of methods of practice

- role and place of generalist and specialist practitioners

- role of social work in certain areas of service, such as public welfare.

The relative emphasis given to these areas of debate are frequently defined by the prevailing cultural, political, social, and organizational environment. Within this context, social work has also been described as "a residual institution with boundariless areas of concern" (Bar-On, 1994, p. 53). Bar-On argued that the role of social work can only be deduced from the particular context in which it is practiced; the range of the profession's concerns is reflected in the needs not being met by primary need-meeting institutions. Thus, the boundaries of professional concern are defined within the here and now.

Political Ideology and Social Work

Government's prevailing views about its role in human services financing and delivery have a profound impact on the profession of social work. Ginsberg (1988) noted that "social work has been tied to government and politics since its beginning as a profession" (p. 245).

The nature of clients' problems—poverty, homelessness, single parenthood, lack of job skills or education, and poor health, to name just a few—are of such magnitude that only government has the resources and authority to address them in any significant way. Thus, what happens to social programs depends on government ideology and political preferences. In turn, the job market for social workers is affected by the size and type of social programs to which government currently gives priority.

Stewart (1984a) aptly described the relationship between the economy, government ideology, and social work:

> Our profession went through a "clinical depression" beginning in 1981 and gaining full force in 1982, as a result of general economic conditions in our country and profound changes in federal policy and federal spending patterns. The pursuit of "New Federalism" goals such as diminution of the role of government, decentralization, and private/public partnership resulted in significant changes in the funding and delivery of social services in this nation.
>
> As many social workers lost jobs due to these changes and the future of many social programs became in doubt, there developed a parallel mythology, one depicting social work as a "declining profession." . . . But about 10 or 11 months ago, I began to notice a change in mood . . . renewed energy and optimism were evident. With great resourcefulness, social workers found new ways to practice social work—a boom in occupational social work in its variety of forms, shifts to entirely different types of agencies, consultation, private practice, etc. New strategies for the funding of social services began to emerge. . . . Some of our old jobs are gone, yes, but new challenges and positions are unfolding. (p. 2)

The War on Poverty during the 1960s is an example of externally driven change. Although social work theory and practice have always had an advocacy component, the War on Poverty provided an unprecedented opportunity for those wishing to practice advocacy as a primary function. But the strategies of confrontation and change are less effective today; the issues have changed, as has the sociopolitical environment.

"Reaganomics" posed a new set of challenges for the profession. In the early years of the first Reagan administration, the social work literature reflected concern about the potential impact of the president's agenda, an agenda that is being echoed and reemphasized in 1995. "Social work's future appears precarious," wrote Getzel (1983, p. 235). Others offered suggestions about how social agencies might do more with less and develop strategies to deal with retrenchment in human services funding and programs (Turem & Born, 1983). Adaptability was urged. Austin (1984) argued that managing cutbacks involved new role requirements for agency administrators, including strategic planning and "cheerleading" (for example, increasing staff involvement in all levels of decision making). Others cautioned that social workers should not be sanguine about the impact of doing more with less. Taubman (1985), for example, concluded that "minimizing the negative effect of massive budget cuts may lull the profession and its communities and legislatures into the complacency of thinking that less is more" (p. 180).

Anne Minahan (1982), then editor-in-chief of *Social Work*, commented that the Reagan period represented one of the worst of times for social work and our society. She noted, however, that "a time of societal crises can create a common recognition of the shared social work perspective, values, and purpose that shape social workers' view of the world" (p. 291). Taubman (1985) similarly noted that a silver lining may shine through the withdrawal of human services resources. In his view, "the profession may come out of the crisis with a clearer definition of priorities, better monitoring and evaluation mechanisms, and more effective and efficient human service organizations" (p. 181). Nevertheless, the posture of the profession during the Reagan years was largely reactive and incremental; social work fought to maintain the status quo and protect programs and professional status, with modest successes (Schorr, 1988).

But different times called for different strategies. During the Bush administration, an increasing number of Americans began to identify the greed of government, Wall Street, and private industry as an unacceptable phenomenon (Schorr, 1988). The election of Bill Clinton in 1992 was, at least in part, a repudiation of the exercise of power by elites in their own self-interest. Social work was, after 12 years, in a position to be heard and to influence. Social workers mobilized to have a say in the development of new social policies. NASW, for example, drafted a proposed health care reform plan to cover all Americans through a single, publicly financed and administered national health care system, the "National Health Care Act of 1992." Senator Daniel K. Inouye (D-HI) introduced the bill into Congress (Hiratsuka, 1992), and NASW staff and members across the country worked tirelessly to influence passage of the legislation (Ewalt, 1994). This high level of social work participation and the ensuing debate marked a milestone in the profession.

Social work's sanction comes from society. Society recognizes that there are disparities between what is and what should be, and that there is a need to rectify this condition (Rosenfeld, 1983). Society's recognition that it is flawed should not be taken for granted. Social work simply does not exist, or is not allowed to exist, in some contemporary societies because there is no sanction to address societal incongruities. Simply put, recognition that all is not well with some components of a society is prerequisite to the development of a systematic and professional response to the perceived problems. The degree to which society is willing to identify such incongruities depends on the sociopolitical context of the times.

Identifying the discrepancy between what is and what should be leaves unanswered how to fill the gap. For example, there is widespread agreement in the United States that something must be done about crime. Public demands center on "getting tough" on criminals, and these sentiments have found expression in the Crime Bill of 1994. In earlier years, society tolerated, if not encouraged, a more rehabilitative approach for criminals. Patuxent Institution, a state prison in Jessup, Maryland, for example, practiced a psychotherapeutic approach and relied heavily on social workers to implement treatment programs (Hiratsuka, 1989). In 1989 a furloughed inmate on work release fled and allegedly committed rape, an incident that led state legislators to limit Patuxent's authority to grant paroles and furloughs. Social workers on staff feared that the changes would reduce the effectiveness of the rehabilitation program. Prospective inmates were subject to an extensive preadmission evaluation and, once accepted, could be sent back to other "traditional" prisons if their progress was not satisfactory. Hiratsuka (1989) quoted a social worker at Patuxent, who described the approach this way:

> The emphasis is on present behavior and how it relates to patterns that led to criminality. We teach communication skills. We want them to learn about themselves, their crime and the impact on their victims, to look at their own family structure and how families communicate, and look at their antisocial lifestyle. We talk about drug and alcohol abuse, since 95 percent of them are substance abusers. We have Alcoholics Anonymous and Narcotics Anonymous. (p. 3)

Following growing public sentiment for longer sentences—including mandatory sentences and "three strikes and you're out" laws that mandate life imprisonment—and impatience with furlough and work-release programs, Maryland sharply curtailed the rehabilitative focus of the Patuxent Institution. In its place came limits on the prison board's ability to grant leave, work release, and parole and a mandate for the secretary for public safety and corrections to review such decisions. This trend toward "getting tough on crime" alters, and in some cases severely limits or eliminates, the psychotherapeutic role of social workers in prisons.

Social workers carry out the practical work that society requires. As the United States emerged as an information society with a service economy, major transformations occurred in the workplace. The result is underemployment or unemployment for some who lack the skills that are now required. A new underclass has emerged, one of displaced workers. As society has grown more complex, specialized, technical, and fragmented, people's coping abilities are taxed. Social work is the profession that deals with the human impact of these changes, with social workers serving as "professional bridges between people and institutions, people and policies, and people and people" (Stewart, 1985, p. 2).

Impact of Republican Domination

The 1994 midterm elections signify a new bent on the perception that all is not well in society, but this time the system itself is seen as a root cause of the problems. Opposing ideologies have always characterized the American political system, with the pendulum swinging back and forth. Nevertheless, the 1994 election results were a manifestation of a growing distrust in the very institutions of society, Congress included. Distrust in government is widespread. Congress is attempting to respond by decreasing government's role and its costs, so a request by any interest group for more funds, programs, or services is now looked on with suspicion if not disfavor.

Dear (1995) listed the following opposing forces that characterize the political system in the mid-1990s:

- the need for more government and more centralized decision making versus less faith in government and opposition to national government

- the need for a more equitable distribution of income versus growing inequality

- the need for more higher education versus the slow, neutral, or negative growth in state funding of higher education

- the need for a more communitarian, cohesive society versus escalating fragmentation resulting from the power of specialized interests

- the need to bring population growth in check versus individuals' rights to procreate and to decide on the size of their family

- the need for rapid public response to worsening social crises versus demosclerosis and policy gridlock. (p. 235)

Dear contended that these opposing forces constitute the parameters in which social welfare policy decisions will be made now and into the foreseeable future, affecting the breadth, content, and form of the programs and services for which social workers are responsible.

Although the nature and scope of desired societal changes is less clear than the demand for change, the Republican-controlled House of Representatives is, at the time of this writing, seeking to implement with all due haste its "Contract with America," which gives shape and form to the immediate and perhaps longer-term social welfare system. Social workers have quickly and loudly voiced their opposition to this contract, because of its potential impact on the most vulnerable populations and its likely effect on the provision of services by social workers and other helping professionals. For example, NASW maintained that welfare reform measures proposed under the Personal Responsibility Act will "place this nation's most precious resource, its children, in great jeopardy" ("'Contract' Draws Condemnation," 1995, p. 1). Initial proposals would have allowed states to use federal funds to establish and operate orphanages for children whose parents were not successful in leaving the welfare rolls.

The extent to which the components of the "Contract" are enacted and successfully implemented will have a significant impact on the breadth and nature of human services in the coming years. Proposals such as prohibiting welfare benefits to minor mothers, cutting Aid to Families with Dependent Children, requiring work for welfare, eliminating the social spending provisions of the Violent Crime Control and Law Enforcement Act of 1994 (P.L. 103-322) to fund prison construction, strengthening parents' rights in educating their children, and raising the social security earnings limit ("Enacting the 'Contract,'" 1995) suggest a desire to profoundly alter the role of government in the provision of human services and society's responsibility to protect and promote the well-being of its citizens. It seems clear that some of these proposals will succeed, with profound implications for current and potential social services clients and the professionals who deliver services to them.

Social workers have experienced large-scale assaults on social welfare funding before, most notably during the Reagan and Bush administrations. The philosophy of the Reagan administration in the 1980s was that the private rather than the public sector should plan, administer, and provide social services. The Bush administration extended Republican control of government (Hopps & Collins, 1995), and "do more with less" became a rallying cry. The social work literature reflected a concern with survival strategies, cutback management, holding the line, advocacy, and hope for the future (for example, Kahn, 1984; Weatherley, 1984).

Social workers took an active role in educating decision makers about the impact of budget cuts ("Congressional Committee Staffs Briefed," 1987). Social work did indeed survive, finding ways to stem the tide of cuts and reaching out to embrace new areas of practice to augment or replace the ones hit hardest by retrenchment. Today's political currents, however, suggest even more formidable challenges for the profession. The simultaneous actions of the federal, state, and local governments to curtail social services spending and the punitive climate toward social services in general suggest profound implications for the nature of social work practice.

What's different now? Feldman ("Social Work Deans," 1995) put it this way:

> For the first time in recent memory, three crucial "planets" (the federal, state and city governments) are aligned simultaneously against the interests of social work clients, professionals and educators. In previous eras, social workers in the City [New York] were

able to gain support from one or the other of these entities even if the others were hostile. Hence, it would be foolhardy for social workers to underestimate the long-term adverse consequences of the recent election. . . . If the next Congress is able to implement the major features of the so-called "Contract with America," public expenditures for social work and social welfare will erode greatly. . . . New problems will emerge and old ones will rise again to afflict vulnerable populations. Indeed, orphanages could be resurrected for youngsters whose sole sin is that they were born to young, poor unwed mothers. (p. 1)

The conservative bent of the mid-1990s suggests that areas of social work practice that were perceived as deeply entrenched and perhaps sacrosanct are indeed vulnerable. In April 1995, New York Governor George E. Pataki announced plans to eliminate the requirement for social work departments at urban hospitals. Instead, hospitals would be held to "clear standards of performance for the provision of social services" (Fisher, 1995, p. B4). The rationale for this move was that regulations had "gone too far" and that it was time to make government less burdensome. Cost savings were also cited as a rationale, and the reduction in paperwork and reporting would, in the governor's view, allow hospitals and nursing homes to become more efficient, which would lead to better patient care.

But as in other eras of constricted social welfare funding and programming, the adage "what goes around comes around" seems to apply. Feldman ("Social Work Deans," 1995) forecast that as social needs go unattended, a pent-up demand for services will develop in the long run. The likely result is a resurgence of social services and of increased employment opportunities for social workers. Social workers will, more than ever before, be asked to document and prove the quality and cost-effectiveness of the services they provide and to demonstrate that these services are effective in changing people's lives. The profession will need to find ways to fulfill its mission with greater independence from government, strengthening and diversifying its resource base and collaborating more effectively with allied professions and other constituencies. Social workers will be called on to increase lobbying and social advocacy efforts toward the goal of ensuring more humane social policies and programs ("Social Work Deans," 1995).

Social workers continue to influence their environment, not just respond to it. The movement to control health care costs has implications for the quality of health and mental health services, as well as access to care and clients' freedom to choose their providers. Social workers have had to learn quickly the business of managed care, including its technicalities, reimbursement systems, and legal and regulatory requirements. Gary Gould, who chaired NASW's Managed Health Care Task Force, cautioned that social workers must learn to work effectively within this system and influence its direction. "Social workers can influence the future of managed health care," said Gould, "or they can have it happen to them and suffer the consequences" (Hiratsuka, 1990, p. 3).

Even if the political climate becomes more favorable to human services, the availability of funds may be curtailed because of unanticipated events. The experience of several southwestern states in the 1980s, including Texas, Louisiana, New Mexico, Oklahoma, and Colorado, exemplifies the close relationship between social services and states' financial situation. In 1986, falling oil prices severely limited state revenues. As a result, state officials cut back on social services funding at the same time that rising unemployment and recession-related family stress, crime, and domestic violence were on the upswing ("Oil Price Plunge," 1986).

Social workers are mobilizing to deal with the most recent assault on human services. Strategies include educating decision makers by emphasizing the successful outcomes of social services interventions and highlighting areas of unmet need; creating partnerships with clients, allied professionals, and concerned citizens; and refining skills to enhance effectiveness (Shepherd, 1995).

Regardless of the strategy used, social workers must help "jumpstart" the nation into action, creating a new wave of caring and hope (White, 1993). White saw the challenge in this way:

> To dream *possible* dreams. Also, we must dream with the full knowledge that most of society does not yet hold the homeless, the disadvantaged, the mentally distressed or the disabled in the same high regard that we do. So we still have challenges. But we have something else. It does not matter what it is called—purpose, legacy, dream, goal or vision. All those words signal the same intent: to inspire ourselves and to empower others toward possible dreams. (p. 2)

Beneficiaries of Public Policy

Although the current political environment suggests that the profession may experience some selective diminution of its roles and boundaries, at least in the short term, social work has also been the beneficiary of public policy. For example, during the 1960s social workers were active and successful in pressing state legislatures to enact consumer choice legislation, which recognizes social workers as qualified providers of mental health services and makes them eligible for insurance and other third-party reimbursement for services rendered (Whiting, 1995). These laws stipulate that consumers have the freedom to choose any qualified mental health care provider, of which social workers are one category, if the client's health insurance provides mental health coverage. As a precursor to such legislation, social workers were also successful in gaining legal recognition, in the form of licensing and registration laws now operative in all 50 states and the District of Columbia. Legal regulation of social work is almost always a requirement for eligibility under state consumer choice or vendorship laws (Whiting, 1995).

Federal policy has also contributed to the expanding boundaries of social work practice. The Omnibus Budget Reconciliation Act of 1989 (P.L. 101-239) included provision for clinical social workers to join the limited class of mental health professionals eligible for reimbursement under Medicare. More recently, final regulations for the Family and Medical Leave Act of 1993 (P.L. 103-3) include clinical social workers as health care providers. Clinical social workers were added to the definition of "health care providers" in this act following active lobbying by more than 400 practicing social workers, five members of Congress, and 14 organizations ("Family-Leave Regs Revision," 1995). Earlier regulations issued by the U.S. Department of Labor did not include clinical social workers as eligible providers to certify and treat the serious health conditions that might trigger employees' eligibility for family and medical leave.

Many federal policies that have expanded the boundaries of social work's domain concern the establishment of policies and programs to meet the needs of specific populations. In these instances, social workers are responsible, in whole or part, for planning, implementing, and administering the programs. For example, with the enactment of such national social welfare policies as the Stewart B. McKinney Homeless Assistance Act of 1987 (P.L. 100-77), the first major federal initiative to approach the problem of homelessness from a multiple problem framework; the Adoption Assistance and Child Welfare Act of 1980 (P.L. 96-272), which ushered in an emphasis on permanency planning and family preservation; the Americans with Disabilities Act of 1990 (P.L. 101-336); and the Anti–Drug Abuse Act Amendments of 1988 (P.L. 100-690) came new and expanding roles for social workers. These and other laws provided a new conceptualization of social problems and the financial incentive for new programs.

Interpreting Who We Are

Part of a professional social worker's job is to consistently interpret for the public who we are and what we do. The same socioeconomic and political factors that affect the boundaries of the profession and the psychosocial conditions of clients also play a role in defining the general public's view of our work. The image of social workers has not always been positive.

During the summer of 1994, major television networks broadcast a paid political announcement that featured noted actor and political conservative Charlton Heston. Speaking against the Omnibus Crime Bill and on behalf of the National Rifle Association, Mr. Heston asked if citizens wanted crime control to be turned over to "social workers instead of cops." The crime-prevention programs proposed in that bill, including midnight basketball programs to get kids off the streets, were labeled "wasteful social spending" and the number of social workers who might be hired was ridiculed ("Gun Groups' Crime Ads," 1994). Just one month earlier, then House Republican Whip (now Speaker of the House) Newt Gingrich praised efforts to block the Omnibus Crime Bill, saying the bill meant "that if you call 911, you get a social worker instead of a cop" (Moss, 1994, p. 1). NASW and the social work profession were put on the defensive. No matter how misleading and inaccurate the messages, they no doubt lingered in people's minds.

Such attacks are neither unusual nor surprising. When the word "liberal" is branded as bad, social work inevitably suffers by association. Social workers have also been branded as "bleeding hearts" and "do-gooders." Stewart (1984b) suggested that the values and practice commitments of the profession, which include respect for and protection of the dignity of all people, can place social workers out of the mainstream of public sentiment. Social work client populations are the "unwanted" in American society, those who are weak, sick, unproductive, or unappealing. By association, Stewart suggested, social workers become identified with these populations and are themselves objects of public avoidance, anger, and scorn.

The more the public knows about the nature and value of social work services, the less likely it is that misinformation can be communicated successfully. This is not an easy task. In part through the efforts of NASW, the profession has sought to influence the public's perception of social work. In June 1985, the NASW Board of Directors approved a three-year plan to develop a communication program to educate the public about the nature and practice of social work ("Profession Gets Higher Profile," 1987). The result has been a significant expansion of major articles about social work in the top newspapers in the country. In 1985 the *New York Times* carried an article called "Social Workers Vault Into a Leading Role in Psychotherapy," the content of which reflected information supplied by NASW (Goleman, 1985). This article generated similar stories in other major newspapers. For example, a 1987 *Business Week* supplement, *Business Week Careers*, published a lengthy article titled "Social Work: Beyond the Stereotype." The author wrote that "As people become more aware of the variety of settings in which social workers are found, as well as their expanded job functions, we can move beyond the stereotype in our perceptions of them" (quoted in "Profession Gets Higher Profile," 1987, p. 7).

The NASW Communications Network compiled a list of several hundred social workers representing 41 areas of practice expertise to serve as technical advisers to production companies focusing on social issues ("Image-Building Plan Under Way," 1988). The goal "is to help shape the portrayals of social issues and social workers as early in the creative process as possible, from script through production" (p. 8).

The substantial change in social workers' functions over time relates to social work's integral relationship with society. The traditional emphasis on practical problems, concrete tasks, and the provision of resources has changed to a focus on more clinical concerns, or a change from "hard" to "soft" social work functions (Davis, 1988). This shift in focus toward clinical social work is evident in the growing proportion of social workers in private, psychotherapeutically oriented practice (Gibelman & Schervish, 1993).

Value judgments are inevitably applied by commentators on the status of the profession. For example, the shift in focus toward the provision of soft services has been labeled as negative for psychiatric patients when social workers are reluctant to perform some of the more concrete service tasks, such as discharge planning, that are essential to clients' well-being. Davis (1988) concluded that this "current mind-set should be challenged and practical functions should be reincorporated into the social worker's repertoire" (p. 373).

Similarly, Specht and Courtney (1994) unequivocally viewed the movement toward a clinical, private practice emphasis within the profession as negative when they wrote: "We believe that social work has abandoned its mission to help the poor and oppressed and to build communality" (p. 4). In their view, community problems are increasing while social work is devoting itself more and more to "the psychotherapeutic enterprise." They claim the profession now seeks overridingly to "perfect the individual" rather than acting on a belief in the "perfectibility of society." This argument is not new; it resurfaces as the profession's boundaries change and expand and the traditional concepts of what constitutes social work are scrutinized. Debates about the appropriate direction and emphasis of the profession will continue. Such dialogue helps crystalize the issues and fosters knowledge and informed decision making among social workers.

Change comes from both the preferences of the professional social work labor force and the response of social workers to external change. In both the United States and Great Britain, for example, professional roles and relationships have undergone substantial transformation, largely because of a political environment that is hostile toward the profession and those it serves. Media perceptions and political rhetoric, perhaps fueling each other, raised questions about the legitimacy of the profession and left social work without a clear sense of direction (Jones & Novak, 1993). At the same time, social workers exercise their own preferences in regard to areas of practice and specializations, as evidenced in the dramatically decreasing number of professionals in public welfare and the equally dramatic increasing number of social workers in private practice.

Withdrawal from Public Service Role

In 1961, government at the federal, state, or municipal level was the major employer of NASW members. The 1961 *Study of Salaries of NASW Members* (Becker, 1961) found that "contrary to the long-held belief that the most highly trained social workers tend not to favor employment in the public services, the survey of NASW members shows that more than 52 percent work for federal, state, county, and municipal governmental agencies" (p. 5).

Over a 30-year period, this situation has changed significantly. Declassification, defined as the reduction in standards of professional education and work-related experience for public social services jobs, has been identified as a formidable challenge facing the social work profession (Pecora & Austin, 1983). In 1981, the NASW Delegate Assembly adopted a policy statement ("Declassification," 1991) on declassification, which noted that

> Public social service departments have failed to recognize the profession of social work as a major contributor to effective social services and advocacy for the welfare movement in this country. This lack of recognition is evident in the trend toward eliminating social workers from policymaking, supervision, and direct services. (p. 202)

Among the reasons cited for this state of affairs were

- the unavailability of baccalaureate (BSW) and master's-degree (MSW) social workers, due to disinterest or too few numbers, to fill the positions needed to expand the staffing of public programs

- the assumption that on-the-job training could and would compensate for professionally earned social work degrees

- the emphasis of unions, representing state, county, and municipal employees, to promote staff on the basis of agency experience and seniority rather than professional education

- the emphasis on quantitative rather than qualitative accountability among public agencies

- the undifferentiated use of BSWs and MSWs, resulting in the assumption that a master's degree is superfluous to service provision

- the proliferation of legislation and administrative rules that allow equivalences to social work education

- the lowering of standards for hiring due to dwindling resources. ("Declassification," 1991, p. 202)

These factors, when combined, have resulted in a redefinition of functions associated with public-sector social services provision in a manner no longer congruent with social work practice.

The phenomenon of declassification, however, may include a backlash component against social workers. Disenchantment with the social advocacy movement of the 1960s, spiraling public welfare and social services costs attributed to the War on Poverty, and passage of Medicare and Medicaid and other (liberal) changes in entitlement programs have been seen as contributing factors to the conservatism of the 1970s and removal of public welfare from the domain of social workers. Walz and Groze (1991) noted that during the 1970s social work professionals were transferred from management and policy positions to service units or other positions with limited policy influence. They contend that these changes resulted in social work's virtual abandonment of public welfare.

Cutbacks in federal training funds, which during the 1960s supported many public welfare employees through master of social work programs, also reduced the number of graduates entering or returning to public social services employment (Gibelman, 1983). Meanwhile, other social work specialties, especially private practice, were gaining ground. The growth in private practice was also attributable to external forces, such as third-party reimbursement made possible by the increasing number of states offering licensure to social workers. The role of social workers, then, in public social services was affected by the de-emphasis on social work intervention in the public sector and the concurrent increase of professional opportunities in the for-profit sector. These shifts had the longer-term effect of altering the demographics of the traditional social work clientele—poor and disenfranchised people.

In spite of these forces, recognition of the real and potential role of social workers at all levels of government has been promoted. For example, the Federal Social Work Consortium, composed of social workers within the federal system, was recognized in 1987 by then Health and Human Services Secretary Otis R. Bowen. In an address to a large gathering of federal government social workers, Dr. Bowen said:

> Trained caseworkers, experienced clinicians, and social workers trained to manage health and social programs are essential to the management and delivery of services through all HHS programs. We should all take pride in your public service careers, and continue your good work. Together, we can provide opportunities for many people to achieve a life of self-sufficiency, independence, productivity, accomplishment, dignity, and purpose. ("HHS, NASW Commend Federal Social Workers," 1987)

But the times keep changing. With "Reinventing America," President Clinton's proposal to curb the size and scope of the federal bureaucracy, and concurrent retrenchments in state and local governments, social work opportunities in government service may well be diminishing. This time, declassification is not the issue. Instead, social work practice in the public sector is threatened by the overall trend to reduce the size and role of government.

Private Practice

Social work has traditionally been practiced in organizational settings. The history of the profession has been marked by a consistent and dual tension between a focus on the individual and a focus on the environment. This dynamic tension can be construed, in practice terms, as a blend of individually focused and advocacy interventions. Hopps and Pinderhughes (1987), however, noted that the tension often reaches such levels that choices must be made:

> The profession is anchored on one side by service to and empowerment of those in acute need, and on the other by the dominant segment of society that controls the resources and sharing of power essential to meeting that need. . . . In its more expansive cycles, society tends to view social work as a mirror of its own openhandedness and optimism. However, in times of stasis, contrived shortage, or divisiveness . . . the values of practitioners of social work become unwelcome reflections on societal priorities and injustices. At such times, the profession's members face difficult choices about the extent to which they serve as arms of the institutional structures or as advocates of the excluded. Consequently, more than any other profession, social work tends to be vulnerable to shifts in the social climate. The profession's fluctuating emphases on cause and function and on environmental reform and individual change have all reflected the boundaries of the profession and its responsiveness to milieu. (p. 353)

One means of resolving this tension may be evident in the trend toward independent practice. Data reveal that private practice has become an increasingly important alternative for the provision of social work services (Gibelman & Schervish, 1993). The proportion of NASW members engaged in private practice has steadily increased. Disillusionment with agency-based practice, economic need, desire to gain control over working conditions, and social worker interest in concentrating on clinical work with particular populations or types of presenting problems have been cited as reasons for this growth (Abramovitz, 1986; Jayaratne, Davis-Sacks, & Chess, 1991; Saxton, 1988).

Although the merits and pitfalls of the private practice of social work have been debated for years, the debate should now logically focus on the implications of private practice along a number of dimensions. These include the consequences of private practice for the profession and for service delivery: who gets served, with what types of interventions, for how long, and with what outcomes, and, as private practice takes on a distinctly individual-oriented nature, how the profession reconciles its role in and commitment to advocacy, social policy development, and management of service delivery systems (Gibelman & Schervish, 1993).

The nature of social work practice thus mirrors the values, priorities, and technologies of American society at any given point in time. At various times in modern history, this societal context has stimulated an expansion of professional boundaries; at other times, social workers have had to advocate for and create opportunities in spite of prevailing politics and ideology.

But the reality of human need remains constant. Social work roles and functions may shift, but the profession remains rooted in American society. Stewart's (1984a) commentary on the future of the profession, written during the Reagan era, holds true today:

> Social work, a growth profession, has an important future in this nation. It is precisely social work's diagnostic and practice orientation, its focus on persons in relation to their environments, that makes its knowledge and skills so vital today. Our people are experiencing major disruptions and displacements because of revolutionary and public social policy changes. Inherent in those changes is an increased need for professionals best equipped to help persons cope with significant shifts in their lives and environments. That is social work's forte. (p. 2)

Although the profession has needed to adapt to internal and external forces, social work has remained committed to its enduring mission, values, and ethics. As articulated in the preamble of the NASW Code of Ethics (NASW, 1994), the fundamental values of the social work profession include the worth, dignity, and uniqueness of all people, as well as their rights and opportunities. Social work fosters the individual, group, community, and societal conditions that promote these values.

An Ongoing Search for Clarity

Some of the debates over how the profession defines itself and the boundaries of what constitutes social work practice have been waged since the earliest days of the profession. As far back as 1915, Flexner raised the question of whether social work is a profession, and Richmond (1917) sought to identify the skills required for work with individuals and families. The 1959 Curriculum Study of the Council on Social Work Education (Boehm, 1959) pointed to "the lack of a single, widely recognized, or generally accepted statement . . . of the aims and purposes of social work" (p. 40). This landmark study concluded that the core activities of social work have not been authoritatively differentiated (Boehm, 1959).

In 1973, NASW sought to explicate levels of practice and develop a classification structure through the promulgation of *Standards for Social Service Manpower* (NASW, 1973). Refinements to definitions and concepts were incorporated into the *Standards for the Classification of Social Work Practice* (NASW, 1981).

Changes in definition of the profession and the characteristics of professional practice are reflective of the evolving and dynamic nature of social work. Hopps and Pinderhughes (1987) saw such changes as positive: "Because social work continues to be seen as emerging and developing, it is important that the profession constantly defines and clarifies itself over the years" (p. 352).

Social work has been hampered throughout history by the ambivalence of society. In prosperous times, society regards social work as openhanded and optimistic, but in hard times sees it as an unwelcome reflection of society's injustices (Hopps & Collins, 1995). As the political and economic environment shifts, maintaining professional boundaries and identity become extremely important tasks. However, social work is sustained in times of flux by its own values and ethics. Respect for human dignity, recognizing the individual's right to self-determination, and empowering those in need are building blocks of the profession that stand firm even in times of change and uncertainty (Hopps & Collins, 1995).

The context for social work will reflect societal trends such as a growing aging population, increasing numbers of people (especially children) in poverty, and an educated public that is less willing to relinquish control and material resources to provide social services to people in need (Hopps & Collins, 1995). Therefore, social workers must become a diverse and talented group who can think critically, deal with pressure, and continue to be committed to serving clients in the best possible manner (Hopps & Collins, 1995).

From its beginnings in the 19th century, social work has maintained a dual focus. One stream has emphasized the personal needs of individuals, families, and groups and the other has emphasized social reform and social justice—the common collective good (Falck, 1988). Stewart (1984b) noted that

> The reason we are called "social workers" is because our practice is distinctly social in nature. People are social beings, living in a social context that profoundly influences their lives, for better or worse. No other profession has understood or employed that focus more consistently or effectively than social work. (p. 2)

References

Abramovitz, M. (1986). The privatization of the welfare state: A review. *Social Work, 31*, 257–264.

Adoption Assistance and Child Welfare Act of 1980, P.L. 96-272, 94 Stat. 500.

American Psychiatric Association. (1994). *Diagnostic and statistical manual of mental disorders* (4th ed.). Washington, DC: Author.

Americans with Disabilities Act of 1990, P.L. 101-336, 104 Stat. 327.

Anti–Drug Abuse Act Amendments of 1988, P.L. 100-690, 102 Stat. 4181.

Austin, M. J. (1984). Managing cutbacks in the 1980s. *Social Work, 29*, 428–434.

Bar-On, A. A. (1994). The elusive boundaries of social work. *Journal of Sociology & Social Welfare, 21*, 53–67.

Becker, R. (1961). *Study of salaries of NASW members*. New York: National Association of Social Workers.

Boehm, W. (1959). *Objectives of the social work curriculum of the future* (Social Work Curriculum Study, Vol. 1). New York: Council on Social Work Education.

Congressional committee staffs briefed on service cuts' impact. (1987, April). *NASW News*, pp. 1, 14.

"Contract" draws condemnation. (1995, February). *NASW News*, pp. 1, 14.

Davis, S. (1988). "Soft" versus "hard" social work. *Social Work, 33*, 373–374.

Dear, R. N. (1995). Social welfare policy. In R. L. Edwards (Ed.-in-Chief), *Encyclopedia of social work* (19th ed., Vol. 3, pp. 2226–2237). Washington, DC: NASW Press.

Declassification. (1991). *Social work speaks* (2nd ed., p. 202). Silver Spring, MD: National Association of Social Workers.

DSM-IV revises psychosocial axis. (1994, January). *NASW News*, p. 14.

Enacting the "contract." (1995, January 5). *Washington Post*, p. A1.

Ewalt, P. L. (1994). Visions of ourselves. *Social Work, 39*, 5–7.

Falck, H. S. (1988). *Social work: The membership perspective*. New York: Springer.

Family and Medical Leave Act of 1993, P.L. 103-3, 107 Stat. 6.

Family-leave regs revision adds clinicians. (1995, February). *NASW News*, p. 1.

Fisher, I. (1995, April 5). Pataki will lift some regulations for health care. *New York Times*, pp. A1, B4.

Flexner, A. (1915). Is social work a profession? In *Proceedings of the National Conference of Charities and Correction* (pp. 576–590). Chicago: Hildman Printing Co.

Getzel, G. S. (1983). Speculations on the crisis in social work recruitment: Some modest proposals. *Social Work, 28*, 235–237.

Gibelman, M. (1983). Social work education and public agency practice: Reassessing the partnership. *Journal of Social Work Education, 19*(3), 21–28.

Gibelman, M., & Schervish, P. (1993). *Who we are: The social work labor force as reflected in the NASW membership*. Washington, DC: NASW Press.

Ginsberg, L. (1988). Social workers and politics: Lessons from practice. *Social Work, 33*, 245–247.

Goleman, D. (1985, April 30). Social workers vault into a leading role in psychotherapy. *New York Times*, p. C1.

Gun group's crime ads shot down. (1994, October). *NASW News*, pp. 1, 12.

HHS, NASW commend federal social workers. (1987, April). *NASW News*, pp. 1, 12.

Hiratsuka, J. (1989, May). "Get tough" crime stand hinders rehab. *NASW News*, pp. 3, 13.

Hiratsuka, J. (1990, February). Managed care: A sea of change in health. *NASW News*, p. 3.

Hiratsuka, J. (1992, July). NASW health-reform bill is introduced. *NASW News*, pp. 1, 8.

Hopps, J. G., & Collins, P. M. (1995). Social work profession overview. In R. L. Edwards (Ed.-in-Chief), *Encyclopedia of social work* (19th ed., Vol. 3, pp. 2266–2282). Washington, DC: NASW Press.

Hopps, J. G., & Pinderhughes, E. B. (1987). Profession of social work: Contemporary characteristics. In A. Minahan (Ed.-in-Chief), *Encyclopedia of social work* (18th ed., Vol. 2, pp. 351–366). Silver Spring, MD: National Association of Social Workers.

Image-building plan under way. (1988, November). *NASW News*, p. 8.

Jayaratne, S., Davis-Sacks, M. L., & Chess, W. (1991). Private practice may be good for your health. *Social Work, 36*, 224–232.

Jones, C., & Novak, T. (1993, June). Social work today. *British Journal of Social Work, 23*, 195–212.

Kahn, E. M. (1984). The voluntary sector can remain alive—and well. In F. D. Perlmutter (Ed.), *Human services at risk* (pp. 57–74). Lexington, MA: Lexington Books.

Minahan, A. (1982). "It was the best of times, it was the worst of times." *Social Work, 27*, 291.

Moss, M. S. (1994, September). Association returns fire as crime-bill foes take shots at profession. *NASW News*, pp. 1, 10.

National Association of Social Workers. (1973). *Standards for social service manpower*. Washington, DC: Author.

National Association of Social Workers. (1981). *Standards for the classification of social work practice*. Washington, DC: Author.

National Association of Social Workers. (1994). *NASW code of ethics*. Washington, DC: Author.

Oil price plunge forces cuts in services. (1986, October). *NASW News*, p. 3.

Omnibus Budget Reconciliation Act of 1989, P.L. 101-239, 103 Stat. 2106.

Pecora, P. J., & Austin, M. J. (1983). Declassification of social service jobs: Issues and strategies. *Social Work, 28*, 421–426.

Profession gets higher profile in media. (1987, January). *NASW News*, p. 7.

Richmond, M. (1917). *Social diagnosis*. New York: Russell Sage Foundation.

Rosenfeld, J. M. (1983). The domain and expertise of social work: A conceptualization. *Social Work, 28*, 186–191.

Saxton, P. M. (1988). Vendorship for social work: Observations on the maturation of the profession. *Social Work, 33,* 197–201.

Schneiderman, L. (1983). *The future context of social work practice.* Unpublished manuscript, Council on Social Work Education, New York.

Schorr, A. L. (1988). Other times, other strategies. *Social Work, 33,* 249–250.

Shepherd, D. K. (1995, April). Will I feel any pain? The human toll of state and city budget cuts. *Currents,* pp. 1, 8–10.

Social work deans: A commentary on profound change and its meaning for the profession. (1995, January). *Currents,* pp. 1, 5.

Specht, H., & Courtney, M. (1994). *Unfaithful angels: How social work has abandoned its mission.* New York: Free Press.

Stewart B. McKinney Homeless Assistance Act of 1987, P.L. 100-77, 101 Stat. 482.

Stewart, R. (1984a, March). From the president. *NASW News,* p. 2.

Stewart, R. (1984b, November). From the president. *NASW News,* p. 2.

Stewart, R. (1985, March). From the president. *NASW News,* p. 2.

Taubman, S. (1985). Doing less with less. *Social Work, 30,* 180–182.

Turem, J. S., & Born, C. E. (1983). Doing more with less. *Social Work, 28,* 206–210.

Violent Crime Control and Law Enforcement Act of 1994, P.L. 103-322, 108 Stat. 1796.

Weatherley, R. (1984). Approaches to cutback management. In F. D. Perlmutter (Ed.), *Human services at risk* (pp. 39–56). Lexington, MA: Lexington Books.

Walz, T., & Groze, V. (1991). The mission of social work revisited: An agenda for the 1990s. *Social Work, 36,* 500–504.

White, B. W. (1993, February). Possible dreams hold key to change. *NASW News,* p. 2.

Whiting, L. (1995). Vendorship. In R. L. Edwards (Ed.-in-Chief), *Encyclopedia of social work* (19th ed., Vol. 3, pp. 2427–2431). Washington, DC: NASW Press.

mental
health

introduction
to part I

Social workers in mental health focus on meeting the needs of mentally ill people, both those with major mental illnesses or those with less devastating emotional problems, and those vulnerable to mental illness. Although adults are usually perceived as the population prone to mental illness, there are as many children and adolescents with treatable mental conditions, many of which are not properly diagnosed. According to the National Institute of Mental Health (NIMH), more than 7 million children and adolescents in the United States have mental disorders; depression, obsessive–compulsive disorder, phobias, and substance abuse frequently occur in people under 20 years of age ("Mental Illness Not Uncommon," 1991). Although social workers in mental health also occupy supervisory and managerial positions, most provide services directly to individuals and families.

The largest proportion of NASW members identify their primary practice areas as mental health. In 1991, 32.7 percent of respondents indicated that mental health was their primary practice area, up slightly from 31.3 percent in 1988 (Gibelman & Schervish, 1993). Proportionately more MSWs and DSW/PhDs have a primary practice of mental health as compared to BSWs. Those in mental health also tend to have more years of experience than NASW members in other primary practice areas. Men are proportionately overrepresented in mental health practice compared to their numbers in the overall NASW membership, and a higher proportion of white members work in mental health compared to other ethnic groups (Gibelman & Schervish, 1993).

Some estimates show that social workers are the dominant providers of mental health services in this country; in approximately 1,000 counties, one-third of the counties in the country, social workers are the only licensed providers of mental health services (Goldstein, 1994). As much as 65 percent of all psychotherapy and mental health services are provided by social workers (Goldstein, 1993a). The role of social work in the mental health system is likely to grow as other professions stand still or lose ground. In 1993, only 500 medical school graduates selected a residency in psychiatry, and universities awarded fewer than 3,500 doctorates in psychology; in the same time period, schools of social work graduated 9,000 MSWs (Goldstein, 1994). A 1985 *New York Times* science section headline claimed that "Social Workers Vault Into a Leading Role in Psychotherapy" ("*Times*: Profession Leads," 1985). In 1975, the numbers of practicing psychiatrists and clinical social workers were virtually identical (26,000 and 25,000, respectively). At the same time, there were 15,000 clinical psychologists and 6,000 marriage and family therapists. By 1985, there were 60,000 clinical social workers, compared to 38,000 psychiatrists, 28,000 counselors, and 33,000 psychologists.

Defining Clinical Social Work

Casework traditionally has been the predominant method of social work practice. But in 1980, editors of *Social Work* noted that the term "clinical social work" had emerged in the profession's vocabulary in the 1970s, replacing "social casework," "treatment-oriented social group work," "social treatment," "psychiatric social work," and "direct practice" (Minahan, 1980).

Social workers perform mental health services in community mental health centers, state and county mental hospitals, private psychiatric hospitals, psychiatric units in general hospitals, veterans organizations, and outpatient facilities (Lin, 1995). Across the settings, social workers in mental health share a common focus. After several years of developmental work, NASW (1984) adopted the following definition of *clinical social work*:

> Clinical social work shares with all social work practice the goal of enhancement and maintenance of psychosocial functioning of individuals, families and small groups. Clinical social work practice is the professional application of social work theory and methods to the treatment and prevention of psychosocial dysfunction, disability, or impairment, including emotional and mental disorders. It is based on knowledge of one or more theories of human development within a psychosocial context. (p. 4)

Clinical social work draws from many theoretical frameworks, with some practitioners using a single perspective and others using several (Swenson, 1995). The person-in-situation perspective is central to clinical social work practice, which includes interventions directed to interpersonal interactions, intrapsychic dynamics, life support, and management issues. Services include assessment, diagnosis, treatment, client-centered advocacy, consultation, and evaluation. Clinical social work is undertaken within the objectives of social work and the principles and values set forth in the *NASW Code of Ethics* ("Vendorship Push," 1984).

In 1984, the NASW Board of Directors first approved *Standards for the Practice of Clinical Social Work*, which have the following goals:

- to maintain and improve the quality of services provided by clinical social workers

- to establish professional expectations so that social workers can monitor and evaluate their own clinical practice

- to provide a framework for clinical social workers to assess responsible professional behavior

- to inform consumers, government regulatory bodies, and others, such as insurance carriers, about the profession's standards for clinical social work practice. (NASW, 1984, p. 5)

Clinical social work has evolved with new theories, intervention strategies, and a more sophisticated client population. For example, the complexity of working with children when there is a suspicion of child sexual abuse has led to a recommendation that social workers play a more active role in the assessment process to aid the family court to protect children and lay the groundwork for effective intervention and treatment (Strand, 1994). Pozatek (1994) argued that the profession and its practitioners need to adopt a position of uncertainty to challenge the notion of objectivity that has characterized practice to date.

Settings of Mental Health Practice

Traditional settings in which social workers deliver mental health services include

- community mental health centers

- family and child service agencies

- inpatient psychiatric facilities

- industry-based employee assistance programs

- private clinical social work practice with individuals or groups

- Veterans Administration hospitals

- inpatient and outpatient psychiatric units of public and private hospitals.

Social workers in all of these settings work in both rural and urban areas.

Frequently, mental health social workers work as part of a team composed of professionals and ancillary personnel from several disciplines who work collaboratively to provide a wide range of services with and for clients who have a mental disorder and their families (Barker, 1995). Typically, these teams are composed of a psychiatrist, social worker, psychologist, and nurse. Interdisciplinary cooperation was the keynote of a 1990 panel discussion led by NASW. The panel urged mental health professionals to collaborate in order to provide the most effective service delivery system and to play a more active role in mental health legislation and policy making ("Mental Health Providers' Cooperation," 1990).

Mental health is somewhat a "catch-all" category. Although social workers in other service areas also identify themselves as "clinical social workers," the term is primarily used to describe those who provide mental health services.

The Future

Mental health practice in the future will be substantially affected by the nature and content of health care reform legislation. Although initial reform initiatives failed in the 101st Congress, there is every indication that the debate is just now beginning and that some type of health care reform will be enacted soon. A key question for social workers is whether and to what extent mental health will be part of the package and whether social workers will be recognized as care providers. As Goldstein (1993b) stated, "given mental health care's chronic underdog status in the hierarchy of health care benefits, these concerns are justified" (p. 2).

NASW has taken an active role in arguing for health care reform that includes mental health and substance abuse benefits and recognizes social workers as qualified (and reimbursable) providers of these services (Hiratsuka, 1994). Other mental health disciplines also have been lobbying for health care reform that will protect, if not expand, mental health benefits. The American Psychological Association, for example, has adamantly opposed managed care as the route to universal health coverage (Zimet, 1994). But managed care has already become a central philosophy and organizing theme for the delivery of health care services.

The escalating costs of health care have prompted insurance companies to raise costs while decreasing the scope of coverage. Employers have responded by asking employees to carry a heavier burden of the costs or by changing to some type of managed care plan, leaving behind indemnity plans that gave employees a choice in providers. Coverages perceived as unessential, such as mental health, are being cut back or eliminated (Shallcross, 1991).

Concerns in the professional literature in regard to the health care reform movement have been threefold: (1) social work's commitment to enactment of legislation that provides universal, comprehensive, affordable, and equitable coverage (Mizrahi, 1993); (2) the impact of the trend toward a managed care environment on the availability and quality of mental health services for specific populations (Wetle, 1993); and (3) the impact of managed care on the practice of mental health social work (Alperin, 1994; Brown, 1994).

Public sentiment concerning mental health coverage remains mixed, with costs figuring prominently. But a 1993 poll showed that 80 percent of respondents supported coverage of mental health services in a reformed health system (Goldstein, 1993b). In addition, the Clinton administration has backed mental health coverage.

Cooperation among the mental health professions (social work, psychology, psychiatry, and nursing) in service provision and in policy-making has been identified as an essential strategy to protect access to and quality of services ("Mental Health Providers' Cooperation," 1990). Although collaboration has been hampered at times by professional proprietorship and competition, the professions generally have worked together in the interest of clients and the mental health field.

Important issues confront our nation and our profession in the evolution of a managed health care system. Certain types of expensive, specialized care are already being rationed and the demands for controls on health care expenses, including mental health, will continue to dominate the provision of services. But it is not just a self-serving matter of reimbursement rates for social work services or length of allowable treatment by insurance companies. The heart of the health care debate concerns the escalation of costs of maintaining a system that has failed many Americans who receive no care, inadequate care, or inappropriate care (Edwards, 1990). Edwards saw an important role for social workers within this managed care environment:

> Social workers are in a unique position to play a pivotal role in managed care systems. We possess specialized skills as well as knowledge of alternative service-delivery methods. And we have extensive experience in providing quality service to clients in an environment of fiscal constraint. (p. 2)

To ensure that the social work profession is able to participate fully in decisions about the health care system of the future, Edwards (1990) advised social workers to become well versed in the ethical and legal issues involved and be able to specify the appropriate practice roles and skills they are able to assume in the managed care system.

Growing Emphasis on Research

The future of social work practice in mental health will also be affected by a growing body of knowledge about the effectiveness of different types of interventions. In recent years, the quantity and quality of social work research in the area of mental health has expanded considerably. In 1993 NIMH funded two projects to strengthen social work's research capabilities. These awards are part of a strategy to bring the profession's research capabilities up to the level of those of other mental health disciplines and to strengthen the link between research and practice ("NIMH Grants," 1994).

A $2.4 million, five-year grant was awarded to the George Warren Brown School of Social Work at Washington University in St. Louis, Missouri, to establish a Social Work Research Development Center and conduct a study of mental health services for teenagers. NIMH also awarded a three-year $332,600 contract to the Institute for the Advancement of Social Work Research to assist in developing interest in and participation of mental health researchers. This institute was created jointly by NASW and four other social work organizations to increase social work's research capabilities through technical assistance, research development workshops, career recruitment, information sharing, and collaboration and cooperation among researchers, practitioners, and agencies ("NIMH Grants," 1994).

Other competitive grants are anticipated that will create research development centers in schools of social work across the country. These grants will be used to build institutional research capabilities and support research projects focused on particular areas of mental health.

Labor Force of Tomorrow

The expressed interests of students currently enrolled in social work education programs provides one index of what the profession will look like in the future. Of the 15,853 master's degree students declaring a field of practice or social problem concentration in November 1993, 4,133 cited mental health or community mental health as their specialty and another 184 cited occupational–industrial social work as their specialty (Lennon, 1994). The dominance of social workers is secured by recent trends in the number of professionals entering psychiatry and psychology (Goldstein, 1993a). Psychiatrists and psychologists are entering the labor market in substantially smaller proportions than are social workers and, concurrently, social workers are able and willing to continue their dominant role as providers of mental health services.

References

Alperin, R. M. (1994). Managed care versus psychoanalytic psychotherapy: Conflicting ideologies. *Clinical Social Work Journal, 22,* 137–148.

Barker, R. L. (1995). *Social work dictionary* (3rd ed.). Washington, DC: NASW Press.

Brown, F. (1994). Resisting the pull of the health insurance tarbaby: An organizational model for surviving managed care. *Clinical Social Work Journal, 22,* 59–71.

Edwards, R. L. (1990, January). Benefits, pitfalls seen in managed care. *NASW News,* p. 2.

Gibelman, M., & Schervish, P. H. (1993). *Who we are: The social work labor force as reflected in the NASW membership.* Washington, DC: NASW Press.

Goldstein, S. R. (1993a, March). Our new challenge: Being "insiders." *NASW News,* p. 2.

Goldstein, S. R. (1993b, May). Reform: Mental health can benefit. *NASW News,* p. 2.

Goldstein, S. R. (1994, July). If past is prologue, future is bright. *NASW News,* p. 2.

Hiratsuka, J. (1994, July). Health reform moving. *NASW News,* pp. 1, 10.

Lennon, T. (1994). *Statistics on social work education in the United States: 1993.* Alexandria, VA: Council on Social Work Education.

Lin, A.M.P. (1995). Mental health overview. In R. L. Edwards (Ed.-in-Chief), *Encyclopedia of social work* (19th ed., Vol. 2, pp. 1705–1711). Washington, DC: NASW Press.

Mental health providers' cooperation seen crucial. (1990, June). *NASW News*, p. 10.

Mental illness not uncommon among youth. (1991, January). *NASW News*, p. 17.

Minahan, A. (1980). What is clinical social work? *Social Work*, *25*, 171.

Mizrahi, T. (1993). Managed care and managed competition: A primer for social work. *Health & Social Work*, *18*, 86–91.

National Association of Social Workers. (1984). *NASW standards for the practice of clinical social work*. Silver Spring, MD: Author.

NIMH grants bolster research efforts. (1994, January). *NASW News*, p. 14.

Pozatek, E. (1994). The problem of certainty: Clinical social work in the postmodern era. *Social Work*, *39*, 396–403.

Shallcross, H. M. (1991). Companies want to know how to buy mental health care. *Personnel*, *68*, 19.

Strand, V. C. (1994). Clinical social work and the family court: A new role in child sexual abuse cases. *Child & Adolescent Social Work Journal*, *11*, 107–122.

Swenson, C. R. (1995). Clinical social work. In R. L. Edwards (Ed.-in-Chief), *Encyclopedia of social work* (19th ed., Vol. 1, pp. 502–513). Washington, DC: NASW Press.

Times: Profession leads in therapy. (1985, June). *NASW News*, p. 10.

Vendorship push, clinical training urged. (1984, April). *NASW News*, p. 3.

Wetle, T. (1993). Mental health and managed care for the elderly: Issues and options. *Generations*, *17*, 69–72.

Zimet, C. N. (1994). Psychology's role in a national health program. *Journal of Clinical Psychology*, *50*, 122–124.

case
management

The increasing emphasis on cost controls and cost-effectiveness in the delivery of health and mental health services has led to shortened inpatient stays and a corresponding reliance on outpatient services. *Case management,* "a procedure to plan, seek, and monitor services from different agencies and staff on behalf of a client" (Barker, 1995, p. 47), is an effective method to help in the transition from hospital to community. In addition, case management has increasingly been recognized as an important tool to provide services to the long-term mentally ill population, thus overcoming the lack of community support, services, and trained personnel that have marred service delivery in the past (Kanter, 1987; Rapp & Chamberlain, 1985).

Standards for the practice of case management have recently been advanced in light of the prevalence of case management functions within health and mental health settings (Brennan & Kaplan, 1993). Case management has also been promoted as a means to produce systems change (Austin, 1993) and as an inherent component of managerial practice (Wolk, Sullivan, & Hartmann, 1994). Although there are variations in the definition of case management, there is general agreement that it is essentially a coordinating process. Effective case management requires continuity of care, emotional support, managerial interventions to address various needs, and enabling of client resourcefulness (Kanter, 1987). The tasks range from assessing clients' needs and planning service to therapeutic intervention (provided directly or delivered through another source) and monitoring and evaluating clients' progress. The case manager is a broker and advocate for the client, as the following vignette suggests (Harris, 1987).

Case Management in a Residential Setting

St. Vincent's Hospital offers a variety of programs for chronically mentally ill people, ranging from a self-contained residential rehabilitation center for seriously impaired clients to outpatient vocational training programs. Southwood, the residential rehabilitation program, represents the newest component of the agency. Social workers at all levels of the hierarchical ladder perform a variety of functions in this setting. Phyllis Anderson, MSW, is one of the case managers.

Phyllis is involved in every aspect of client services. As a case manager, Phyllis interfaces with a variety of people on behalf of Southwood clients. On a typical day, Phyllis may talk to the patient liaison at Aurora State Mental Hospital to facilitate the admission of a new client; the county police to clarify an incident involving Southwood clients at the local shopping center; and a local pharmacist to double-check possible side effects of a client's medication or to determine the protocol for a new client prescription.

Phyllis meets individually at least once a week with clients assigned to her, typically 15 or more of the residents of Southwood. The purpose of these meetings is to discuss their issues and concerns and to review their progress and plans. In addition, every week Phyllis confers with the consulting psychiatrist about her concerns and observations regarding the clients and provides feedback about their progress on medication, participation in Southwood programs, their demeanor, and other issues.

Should a client require rehospitalization, Phyllis communicates with the relevant physicians and the hospital social worker about both the client's condition and the discharge plan. This plan involves either a return to Southwood or an alternative program, depending on the client's suitability for continued community integration. Part of Phyllis's job involves networking with county and hospital officials to determine the most suitable placement for a client.

Case management is a recognized component of social work practice and it has always been a feature of casework practice. It may be the predominant function carried out by a social worker, or one function among many. The work roles and activities of the case manager, however, are not always clear. For example, Werrbach (1994) identified differences in staff perceptions regarding the role of the case manager, the case manager's "ideal" work activities, and barriers to role implementation.

Although the importance of case management services is widely recognized, there is a debate about who should provide such services. Rising costs have made it prohibitively expensive to use highly trained, experienced professionals as case managers.

References

Austin, C. D. (1993). Case management: A systems perspective. *Families in Society: The Journal of Contemporary Human Services, 74,* 451–459.

Barker, R. L. (1995). *Social work dictionary* (3rd ed.). Washington, DC: NASW Press.

Brennan, J. P., & Kaplan, C. (1993). Setting new standards for social work case management. *Hospital & Community Psychiatry, 44,* 219–222.

Harris, D. V. (1987, April). Case management is gaining popularity in the public sector. *NASW News*, p. 2.

Kanter, J. (1987). Mental health case management: A professional domain. *Social Work, 32*, 461–462.

Rapp, C. A., & Chamberlain, R. (1985). Case management services for the chronically mentally ill. *Social Work, 30*, 417–422.

Werrbach, G. B. (1994). Intensive child case management: Work roles and activities. *Child & Adolescent Social Work Journal, 11*, 325–341.

Wolk, J. L., Sullivan, W. P., & Hartmann, D. J. (1994). The managerial nature of case management. *Social Work, 39*, 152–159.

community mental health

The community mental health movement gained momentum after World War II as a recognition of the failings of institutional care. Deinstitutionalization of chronically mentally ill people from hospitals was also facilitated by the development of psychotropic medications, which, with proper monitoring, would allow those with serious mental illness to live in the community.

Community mental health centers, partially financed and regulated by the federal government, are local organizations that provide a range of psychiatric and social services: inpatient and outpatient care; partial hospitalization; emergency and transitional services; screening and follow-up care; and programs oriented specifically toward special populations, such as older people, children, and substance abusers (Barker, 1995). A National Community Mental Health Care Council survey reported that, between 1990 and 1993 the client population of community mental health agencies grew by more than one-third ("Mental Health in Demand," 1995).

Social workers in community-based programs function in a variety of roles, depending on a given client's level of impairment and the approach of the agency involved (Budson, 1981). Within this practice area, social workers provide everything from direct service to agency administration. Case management is an essential component of community-based practice.

Program Management in a Community Mental Health Center

The Nassau Community Mental Health Center is a nonprofit agency that relies heavily on state and county dollars, as well as third-party reimbursement from Medicaid and Medicare. The agency was started in the mid-1970s when it became evident that, in this affluent community, there were a large number of homeless, chronically mentally ill people who were not receiving any services. The center offers a variety of programs, including psychiatric consultations, medication dispensing and monitoring, shelter care, and vocational training programs.

The shelter program was initiated last year when the center applied for and received a first-time grant under the Stewart B. McKinney Homeless Assistance Act. Ellen Turner was hired as the program manager shortly after the center received notification of funding. The shelter program does more than provide a temporary night-time residence; its aim is to help chronically mentally ill people with no fixed address locate a permanent living situation and gain the maximum degree of independent functioning.

As manager of the newly created shelter program, Ellen was responsible for getting the program off the ground. During the first few weeks on the job, Ellen spent a lot of time recruiting and hiring staff. Understaffing is a problem in direct service for mentally ill people, as many professionals prefer to work with populations that have a more positive prognosis for growth and change. But Ellen was able to hire some energetic, enthusiastic people who were truly committed to working with this population. The staff is small; in addition to Ellen, there are two full-time social workers, two student interns from a local school of social work, a housing specialist, a facilities manager, and several part-time employees who perform housekeeping tasks. Center staff are also involved, including the vocational trainers and the psychiatrist who prescribes and monitors medication.

During the first month, Ellen worked with the center's executive director to lease the shelter site, arrange for building modifications, and order furniture and supplies. The goal was to have the shelter operational within the first 10 weeks; with a lot of overtime, Ellen met this deadline.

By the third month, the smell of wet paint still permeated the building and workers were adding the finishing touches, but the shelter was ready to receive referrals from the center staff. All shelter clients are already center clients, some for medication and monitoring and others for consultation following discharge from a psychiatric hospital. Staff at the center were briefed on the types of clients who might be referred to the shelter program, and a referral form was prepared for their use. Criteria include a diagnosis of chronic mental illness, a history of consistent use of medication and follow-through on medical appointments to monitor medication, and a current status of homelessness. In addition, referrals are encouraged for clients who are able and motivated to hold a full- or part-time job.

Ellen hopes to phase in participants over several months. She knows that with any start-up operation there is a need to modify the program and services based on actual experience. During the first few weeks, 15 clients were referred to the program. All clients are screened by a social worker to determine whether they meet the established criteria for participation, and Ellen sits in on several of these screenings to observe the process. She encourages the social workers to ascertain the clients' eligibility for federal benefits, such as Medicaid, Medicare, or Supplemental Security Income. Twelve of the 15 are found to be good candidates for the program and are immediately relocated to the facility. There they receive an orientation by one of the social workers; they are given specific tasks for which they are responsible, such as helping prepare meals; and they are encouraged to participate fully in the day-to-day operations and activities of the facility. Meanwhile, the social workers are able to begin applying for benefits for five of the clients whom they consider eligible; several other clients are already receiving benefits.

During this early phase of the program, Ellen meets twice a week with the staff to get feedback about operations and issues. During these meetings, the staff discusses clinical and administrative issues in a roundtable, egalitarian atmosphere that fosters brainstorming about any and all components of the program. In one of these meetings, staff devise a format to develop individual program plans for clients that involve the clients' active participation and input. The program plan is the major focus of all staff–client interaction and will be used to assess progress. The plans will include medication compliance issues, vocational and employment goals and timetables, tasks assigned within the facility, personal hygiene issues, and any interpersonal relationship problems.

In addition to staff meetings, Ellen conducts weekly supervision meetings individually with all direct service staff. During these sessions, which usually last 45 minutes to one hour, Ellen evaluates the employee's performance, listens to concerns, provides feedback, and entertains specific ideas for program development or implementation.

As the program manager, Ellen interfaces with a variety of people on behalf of center clients. On a typical day, Ellen may talk to the state employment office to check on new job listings for which her clients may be eligible; the public housing office about pending client applications for subsidized housing; or a family member who wants to know about the possibility of an overnight visit.

Ellen is pleased with the progress during the initial months of the program. It is time for her to write her first quarterly report to the U.S. Department of Housing and Urban Development, the funding agency, and she has a lot of solid progress to report. She knows that the future holds many challenges, but the program's solid base makes her optimistic about its future.

As a middle-level manager in a satellite program of a community mental health center, Ellen interacts with administrators, funding agencies, staff, and clients. As the program gets under way, Ellen will have increasing contact with staff of other agencies as she and her staff seek jobs and housing for clients. Program planning and development are paramount functions for Ellen in this start-up operation. Ellen also must handle the logistics of preparing the facility for its residents. And, she must recruit, screen, hire, and train the staff in collaboration with the center's executive director. Staff supervision is another important component of her job.

When the program becomes fully operational, Ellen's functions will extend to interorganizational coordination as she serves as liaison to the funding agency and participates in contract renegotiations. In addition, Ellen will need to design and implement an evaluation plan to show that the program is meeting its intended goals.

References

Barker, R. L. (1995). *Social work dictionary* (3rd ed.). Washington, DC: NASW Press.

Budson, R. D. (1981). Challenging themes in community residential systems. *Issues in Community Residential Care, 11*, 105–114.

Mental health in demand. (1995, January). *NASW News*, p. 14.

disaster relief

Crisis interventions initiated because of natural or other disasters have both health and mental health components. Disaster relief is discussed here under the umbrella of mental health because physical health and safety needs following an earthquake, flood, airline crash, or hurricane are handled by hospital emergency rooms and public health officials, as discussed in part III.

Crisis intervention is a therapeutic process used to help clients in crisis develop effective coping mechanisms. Effective intervention may lead to positive growth and change by acknowledging the problem, recognizing its impact, and learning new or more effective behaviors for coping with similar predictable experiences (Barker, 1995). Precipitating crises can be of an emotional, physical, or environmental nature. Loss of a job, for instance, can precipitate an emotional crisis, as can a serious illness. Furthermore, environmental or natural disasters can be financially, emotionally, and physically devastating to individuals, families, and communities, as the following examples illustrate.

On a fall afternoon in 1994, U.S. Air Flight 427 crashed just before landing in Pittsburgh. All 132 people on board were killed. Local mental health professionals were called to the scene to talk and listen to those responsible for removing the wreckage and the bodies. Talking about what they see helps workers cope with tragedy (Geraghty, 1994). Even for emergency medical workers, who are accustomed to working at disaster scenes, the stress of an airplane crash is especially great. Geraghty quoted one member of a disaster response team who noted that "this type of work is so overwhelming that without immediate support, it could be incapacitating" (p. A7).

In 1989, social workers played similar disaster-relief roles when United Airlines Flight 232 from Denver to Chicago experienced a mid-air engine explosion and had to make an emergency landing in Sioux City, Iowa. Social workers in that city mobilized to gather the names of survivors, provide information to family members, offer support and crisis intervention to families of the survivors and victims, and provide solace and comfort to emergency workers (Hymes, 1989a).

In 1986, following the explosion of the space shuttle *Challenger*, social workers in Houston offered free counseling to the families of the astronauts and to NASA employees ("20 Houston Social Workers," 1986). And in Concord, New Hampshire, home of Christa McAuliffe, the school teacher who was part of the space shuttle's crew, social workers affiliated with her school counseled teachers and students, dealing with reactions that ranged from grief to fear to anger ("Social Workers Aid *Challenger* Mourners," 1986). Social workers also participated in panel discussions for parents concerned about the impact of the tragedy on their children and continued to counsel parents, students, and school personnel.

In the aftermath of Hurricane Hugo in 1989, which caused widespread devastation across the East Coast, social workers joined in relief efforts to provide food, supplies, and people-power. Hymes (1989b) quoted a hospital social work director in South Carolina: "We were mental health counselors, but there was so much going on that our roles varied. We mopped floors, cooked, and distributed food and clothing. It was a different role of helping people" (p. 4).

Social workers similarly mobilized in August 1992 when Hurricane Andrew ripped through Florida and Louisiana. Social workers joined with the American Red Cross to pull together mental health treatment teams from around the country to provide crisis intervention, emotional support, and concrete services to hurricane victims and members of the volunteer relief teams (Moss, 1992). Staff of local agencies such as the Metro Dade County Department of Youth and Family Development sprung into action, even though many of them had been devastated by the hurricane (Hiratsuka, 1992).

When one of the most violent earthquakes in U.S. history hit the San Francisco Bay area on October 17, 1989, social workers rallied to provide crisis and support services and consultation. Social workers of the U.S. Army, Navy, Air Force, and Public Health Service were in San Francisco for a conference when the earthquake struck, and they joined in relief efforts by aiding distraught hotel guests and, later, volunteering to gather medical supplies, helping in the kitchen, establishing phone trees to contact families and friends outside of the area, and providing emotional support (Hymes, 1990). In the days following the quake, social workers from the area provided crisis intervention to residents who had lost their homes, belongings, and, in some cases, loved ones.

In 1993 floods ravaged the Midwest, causing about 50 deaths and $12 billion in damage in a nine-state area and leaving 70,000 people homeless. Social workers took part in all facets of the relief work, many volunteering their time. They sorted supplies, helped clients fill out disaster assistance applications, staffed shelters, recruited and coordinated volunteers, and consoled families who had lost their homes. Social workers also prepared to assist individuals and families with the long-term emotional traumas that were anticipated once the waters receded. Social workers made referrals to the community mental health system for people requiring long-term counseling (Hiratsuka, 1993).

The 1989 Exxon Valdez oil spill and the massive cleanup in its aftermath disrupted communities and called into action social workers in the area.

Katherine Kritze, a social worker in Valdez, cited the increases in domestic violence and drug and alcohol abuse in Valdez following the spill. The town of 2,700 swelled to over 10,000 with the influx of cleanup and rescue crews, creating additional strains on the community (Hiratsuka, 1989b).

Increasingly, crises are precipitated by the actions of human beings. The following vignette recounts one such episode.

Crisis Teams Bring Emotional Support and Concrete Help

On August 20, 1986, a part-time mail carrier, Patrick Henry Sherrill, entered the U.S. Post Office in Edmond, Oklahoma, and shot and killed 14 of his coworkers, wounded six others, and then killed himself. The next day, a team of victim-assistance experts flew to Edmond to help local counselors deal with the emotional aftermath in this close-knit community. Social worker Barbara Kaplan, of Newton, Massachusetts, was one member of the seven-person crisis team organized by the National Organization for Victim Assistance in Washington, DC, at the request of Oklahoma's attorney general. Kaplan had been a shooting victim herself in 1981, when she and two other therapists were shot by a former patient at a mental health center. Kaplan lost an eye; the others died ("Aftermath," 1986).

Upon arrival in Edmond, the crisis team held a planning meeting with officials from the Oklahoma Department of Mental Health and the local mental health center. The team agreed to concentrate their efforts on support and guidance for those personally affected by or witness to the shootings. The team decided that contact with the victims and their families would be left to local practitioners who could offer extensive follow-through. With the assistance of local officials, a meeting was held with post office managers, local clergy, and mental health experts in the community to discuss how to approach an all-staff meeting with post office employees later that day. At the afternoon meeting, everyone was given the opportunity to express their grief, shock, anxiety, and anger. Of the 80 postal workers who attended, nearly half spoke.

In the days that followed, the team divided up to train various service-providing groups that would deal with the aftermath of the tragedy. Part of the training included distinguishing between a more neutral approach typically used in therapeutic situations with the more nurturing and supportive counseling appropriate with victims of crime. The importance of supervision was also stressed, as the service providers needed to talk about their own feelings ("Aftermath," 1986). The team dispersed a week later when the plan was in place and providers were equipped to provide the needed ongoing services.

In this situation, social workers engaged in the functions of assessment, support, and counseling to help those who witnessed the shooting. But equally important was their role in organization, mobilization, and exchange, which made it possible for different agencies in the community to interact and share resources in a time of need. Finally, extensive planning and supervision were needed to avoid duplication of services and to make sure that all needs were met.

Sadly, our world is marked by many tragedies induced by interpersonal and intergroup conflict. Terrorism is no longer an isolated event. The January 1989 shooting deaths of five Southeast Asian school children in Stockton, California, prompted a multifaceted response by social workers. About 25 social workers from the county—along with school psychologists, public health nurses, other health professionals, and interpreters—were brought into the community as part of the crisis response. Social workers worked with traumatized children, parents, teachers, and rescue workers. In-school counseling services were offered to parents and children, school personnel, and those involved in the rescue effort. Social workers visited hospitals to help families whose children were killed or wounded and they also were present in the classroom during the ensuing weeks to help teachers and students deal with the emotional aftermath. In the weeks after the shooting, a group of Southeast Asian social workers from other areas of the state visited Stockton to conduct a needs assessment for immediate and longer-term needs of the community, families, and children. This latter effort took place in recognition of the importance of cultural factors and the need to consult community leaders about how to best provide services (Hiratsuka, 1989a).

On April 19, 1995, a man-made blast ripped through the Alfred P. Murrah Federal Building in Oklahoma City, killing 168 people, including a number of small children. This terrorist bombing sent shock waves throughout the country. Social workers and others quickly mobilized to meet the emotional and concrete needs of the community residents ("Offering Help in Bombing's Aftermath," 1995). At hospitals, schools, churches, mental health centers, and police stations, social workers donated their time to counsel individuals and groups, coordinate a statewide mental health hot line, and link injured victims with their relatives (Smith, 1995). Terrie Fritz (1995), president of NASW's Oklahoma chapter, identified several important lessons from this experience for the profession of social work:

- Support efforts that are proactive and assist communities in planning for effective and efficient disaster responses.

- Engage in and contribute to national policy debate, discussion and development surrounding individual rights versus public well-being and protection.

- Continue our work as professionals and as an organization in the area of violence prevention. This is our best hope that the devastation in Oklahoma will not be repeated. (p. 5)

References

Aftermath of a massacre: Member is tapped for crisis team after post office shooting. (1986, October). *NASW News*, pp. 1, 8.

Barker, R. L. (1995). *Social work dictionary* (3rd ed.). Washington, DC: NASW Press.

Fritz, T. (1995, June). One from the heartland. *NASW News*, p. 5.

Geraghty, M. (1994, September 21). Helping people cope with disaster. *Chronicle of Higher Education*, p. A7.

Hiratsuka, J. (1989a, April). School shooting evokes a crisis response. *NASW News*, p. 3.

Hiratsuka, J. (1989b, July). Needs seen in Exxon spill's aftermath. *NASW News*, p. 1.

Hiratsuka, J. (1992, November). After Andrew.... *NASW News*, pp. 1, 4.

Hiratsuka, J. (1993, October). Facing the aftermath of the flood. *NASW News*, p. 3.

Hymes, T. A. (1989a, October). Crash in Sioux City triggers relief effort. *NASW News*, p. 3.

Hymes, T. A. (1989b, November). In Hugo's wake, professionals reach out. *NASW News*, p. 4.

Hymes, T. A. (1990, January). Social workers aid in quake's aftermath. *NASW News*, p. 4.

Moss, M. S. (1992, October). Andrew's victims aided. *NASW News*, p. 1.

Offering help in bombing's aftermath. (1995, May 4). *Chronicle of Philanthropy*, p. 5.

Smith, R. (1995, June). In the wake of the blast. *NASW News*, pp. 3, 5.

Social workers aid *Challenger* mourners. (1986, March). *NASW News*, pp. 1, 6.

20 Houston social workers offer counseling to NASA. (1986, March). *NASW News*, p. 6.

employee assistance programs

Occupational social work refers to the "provision of professional human services in the workplace" (Barker, 1995, p. 260). Kurzman (1987) defined occupational social work as "programs and services, under the auspices of labor or management, that utilize professional social workers to serve members or employees and the legitimate social welfare needs of the labor or industrial organization" (p. 899).

An *employee assistance program* (EAP) is a set of prepaid services available to workers whose productivity is affected by any number of issues including marital or family problems, financial strains, job stress, dependent care problems, and alcohol and drug abuse. The concept behind EAPs is that workers who struggle with personal concerns are absent and tardy more often and are not as productive as other employees.

EAPs are among the most popular methods of intervention in the workplace ("Occupational Practice," 1985). Large companies often establish their own EAP programs and hire mental health professionals to deliver the services, whereas smaller companies may contract with independent counseling providers.

There are four primary designs for EAP services (Van Den Bergh, 1995):

1. *internal* programs, in which EAP staff are employees of the organization

2. *external* programs, in which services are provided by a contractor, usually off-site

3. *consortium* programs, which allow several employers to combine resources and get "group coverage" (these are most effective in organizations that have a logical connection or affiliation with each other)

4. *association* programs, which serve occupational membership groups such as NASW or the American Medical Association.

EAPs were first introduced to American corporations in the 1980s; by 1991, 45 percent of the full-time workforce was covered by an EAP (Blum, Martin,

& Roman, 1992). EAPs are an effective way to address a specific population within its natural life space. In addition, social workers can assist clients without the usual constraints of eligibility requirements often found in the public sector; employees can receive a full range of social services simply as a result of their employment status (Kurzman, 1987).

With the emergence of EAPs, in 1984 NASW commissioned an Occupational Social Work Task Force to address the relevant standards and practices in the occupational field (Stewart, 1984) and issued a statement on occupational social work, declaring it "a legitimate field of practice with a developing focus and a body of knowledge that calls for a full range of appropriate skills" ("Social Work, Public Policy Stands Okayed," 1994, p. 11).

A 1985 NASW survey of occupational social workers ("Survey Results Released," 1986) revealed that they are usually licensed, practice in a wide variety of settings, and perform functions ranging from delivery of direct services to data analysis and fiscal management. The vast majority (79 percent) held an MSW degree or its equivalent and had an average of 11.2 years of social work experience. Almost 62 percent were employed in the private sector, 32.3 percent of whom worked in for-profit organizations. The problems they addressed included, in order of frequency of response, alcoholism, marital difficulties, mental health problems, drug abuse, and problems related to job stress. Forty percent of respondents provided direct service and 35 percent worked in management.

EAP workers are employed by labor unions, corporations, government agencies, and private organizations; others provide services on a contractual basis (NASW, 1993). Some companies have in-house EAPs, and others have contractual arrangements for EAP services. Smaller companies tend to be more hesitant to get involved with an EAP due to cost and to the belief that the company is small enough to deal with its own employee issues. However, many small companies have entered into a consortium with other small businesses to defray the costs of obtaining EAP benefits ("EAP Growth," 1986).

Regardless of the setting, EAP social workers confront a variety of issues including eating disorders, chemical dependency, domestic violence, financial concerns, physical disabilities, and job stress. In addition, many occupational social workers have expanded their role to include assistance in managing mental health benefits (NASW, 1993).

Social workers have long embraced the concept of person-in-environment and recognized the impact of outside influences on an individual's actions. Similarly, social workers are recognizing that although individual workers come in for assistance, their problems are usually rooted in issues at home, work, or the community (Googins & Davidson, 1993). In fact, a recent study reported by Rensberger (1994) indicated that employees who exhibit cynicism do not necessarily have negative or pessimistic attitudes; rather, they may have normal, positive personality traits and are simply reacting to what they perceive as unsatisfactory conditions at work. Because occupational social workers are trained to understand environmental as well as individual issues, they can intervene on a macro level and address organizational issues that may be at the root of many problems that confront individual workers on a regular basis (Googins & Davidson, 1993).

The roles of social workers employed in EAPs have expanded and changed in recent years, in part as a result of the changing demographics of the American workforce and the restructuring of many American industries. Social workers are now faced with helping employees live with shaky job security, cope with job loss, and mobilize to find new jobs. Some EAP social workers have adopted an organizational focus and have developed programs of dependent care and acquired immune deficiency syndrome (AIDS) education, researched the extent and severity of employee substance abuse problems, and consulted with supervisors about employees who have job performance or behavioral problems (Googins & Davidson, 1993). In this macro view of EAP work, client issues are matched with business issues. Table 6-1 provides examples of macro interventions.

Googins and Davidson (1993) wrote that EAPs should "help employees maximize their ability to handle life events and to help corporations anticipate and adapt to changes brought about by the life events of employees and the community" (p. 480). Life events can be anything from divorce to chemical dependency to caregiving to terminal illnesses. In addition, occupational social workers are uniquely qualified to help physically disabled employees and their employers. Disability cases raise a variety of issues for which social work expertise can be applied, including workplace requirements, individual physical and emotional needs, and public policy (Mudrick, 1991). EAPs are also a

Table 6-1
Examples of Macro Interventions

Client Issues	Business Issues
Dependent care	Absenteeism and lower productivity
Adequate health care and managed care	Competitive benefits, health cost containment, and recovery of employees
Drugs	Security, image, theft, productivity, and liability
Job change and reassignment	Changing technology, skill mix/excess, and employee population
Relocation adjustment and work–family issues	Cost of products, job travel/stress, and workload/deadlines
Aging workforce	Pension plan, health care, succession planning, and skill mix in changing technology

Source: Googins, B., & Davidson, B. N. (1993). The organization as client: Broadening the concept of employee assistance programs. *Social Work, 38,* 481.

bridge between employees and the corporation: They help employees find solutions to their problems while they help corporations understand various life events affecting employees (Googins & Davidson, 1993).

The aging workforce brings with it several issues needing the intervention of occupational social workers. Increased longevity and early retirement trends often mean economic hardship for older workers. The phenomenon of early retirement compounded with a diminishing number of youths entering the labor market results in a shortage of available workers (Mor-Barak & Tynan, 1993). For the many healthy older employees who wish to continue working in their professions, EAPs can help with financial planning, referral services, education, and support groups. In addition, EAPs can help corporations understand the issues of aging and develop programs to assist their older employees so that they can continue working (Mor-Barak & Tynan, 1993).

Just as individuals confront life events, so do organizations. Because of global marketplace competition, corporate "downsizing" and restructuring are no longer isolated or idiosyncratic occurrences. *Downsizing* is a euphemism for the termination of employment because of organizational considerations that are not related to employee performance, such as an unanticipated reduction in agency income or elimination of some programs or services. Every business day since January 1993, an average 2,389 U.S. workers have been informed that they are losing their jobs. In the first nine months of 1993, 449,364 employees were laid off, with estimates that more than 600,000 layoffs would be announced by the end of that year (Swoboda, 1993). The characteristics of those losing their jobs have changed. In recent years, it is older workers and those in service-producing industries and white-collar occupations who are more likely to lose their jobs than their counterparts in the workforce of a decade earlier (Gardner, 1995).

Downsizing and restructuring can have debilitating effects and have been described as a "drawn-out, emotionally messy process that wounds the survivors as well as those who lose their jobs" (Knox, 1992, p. 2). Downsizing produces tremendous anxiety, and EAPs must help individual workers reduce stress, continue a strong job performance, and plan for the future. EAPs must also help corporate executives deal with the intense stress and guilt they often feel during periods of cutbacks.

Social workers practicing in EAPs face some constraints unique to that setting. For example, the reason EAPs were introduced into industry had less to do with concern for employees than with ensuring a productive workforce. Because of legal protections offered to workers who are ill or disabled, firing workers because of their behavior outside the workplace (even if it affects performance inside the workplace) can be risky and costly for a corporation. Part of the cost is in hiring and training new employees, so companies have found it less costly to address their employees' problems and keep them healthy than to terminate their employment (Green, 1994). Social workers in EAPs need to understand the corporate value system—with its emphasis on accountability, productivity, and profitability—while maintaining their focus on the provision of services to individuals ("Viewing Work and Social Work," 1985).

As the field of EAPs continues to develop, several issues could affect future professional growth. Akabas (1995) and Kurzman (1987) noted that confidentiality concerns have consistently plagued EAP workers: Is it possible for a social worker to maintain a client's confidentiality when the social worker is employed by the client's organization? Confidentiality is a critical issue, because a breach of confidentiality could result in the client losing his or her job or being the victim of discrimination and ostracism. Not only must the social worker scrupulously adhere to the *NASW Code of Ethics* (NASW, 1994) in regard to confidentiality, but he or she must also reach an agreement with the manager of the corporation before ever seeing a client.

Another issue that frequently confronts occupational social workers is motivation. In a profession that began helping poor and needy populations, work in a corporate environment is a quite different approach (Akabas, 1995; Kurzman, 1987). Finally, there is an important concern regarding occupational social workers as agents of change. Social work has always focused on serving the individual in the environment. Will occupational social workers continue to help individuals or will they serve corporations that view individuals simply as a means of production (Kurzman, 1987)?

Generally, EAPs provide either direct or indirect services. The primary direct service is that of assessment and referral with some brief counseling and assistance (NASW, 1981). Most EAPs allow as many as three sessions per employee per presenting problem, with the belief that more than three sessions moves from assistance into actual treatment (NASW, 1981; Van Den Bergh, 1995). Indirect EAP services include the social work functions of organizing and planning regular training sessions and educational seminars for employees and supervisors. EAPs generally attempt to provide preventive services before problems arise—such as sexual harassment training and racial and ethnic sensitization seminars (NASW, 1981; Van Den Bergh, 1995).

Occupational social workers confront a wide range of issues in a variety of settings. Because they are in the unique position of serving both individuals and organizations, many different social work functions are required, including assessment, diagnosis, identification, support, counseling, advocacy, referral, organization, mobilization, exchange, program development, coordination, consultation, and evaluation (NASW, 1981). The following vignette indicates one of the many situations an EAP worker may encounter.

Downsizing

It seemed that almost everybody who lived in Chickasha, Oklahoma, worked at the Deers Manufacturing Plant. Tommy Merton had worked there for 28 years and his son had worked there for five. Even his youngest daughter was planning to work there when she graduated from high school in June.

The plant was all Tommy had ever known. His father and his grandfather had worked there. His wife knew all the other wives, and she was happy. Every day, Tommy punched in at 7:30 A.M. and punched out at 5:00 P.M. It was his life, and he loved it.

However, Tommy had been hearing rumors that the company had lost several major customers and was going to have to lay off some workers in order to cut operating costs. Tommy felt bad for the new workers; no doubt they would be the first to go. He thought he was safe—he was almost ready for his 30-year plaque.

On December 12, Tommy was called to the office of the plant's director, Mr. Dorn. He asked Tommy to sit down and then began explaining the plant's financial situation. He thanked Tommy for all of his hard work, but told him he was going to be one of the first 100 people let go. Tommy was speechless. Mr. Dorn then asked Tommy to go down the hall and see Mr. Lee, the EAP staff person. Tommy did what he was told—he didn't know what else to do. As he entered Mr. Lee's office, Tommy began to realize what had happened; he had been fired. After 28 years of hard work and loyalty, he had been fired. He dismissed Mr. Lee with the wave of his hand, stood up, and walked out past the other workers who watched in disbelief and offered words of reassurance that rang hollow.

Mr. Lee sat and stared at the empty chair. He took a deep breath and began assessing the situation before him. He knew that after all 100 employees were dismissed, the problems would not be over— they would just be beginning. Mr. Lee knew that the survivors, those who did not lose their jobs, would face feelings and frustrations similar to those felt by survivors of any major trauma.

In the ensuing weeks, Mr. Lee heard workers talking about their fears of being fired. They wondered why Tommy, the best worker they knew, had been laid off. They expressed a great deal of guilt. How, they wondered, would Tommy and the other laid-off workers be able to celebrate Christmas?

The survivors were angry and frightened as they realized that the company to which they had devoted their lives had returned no loyalty to them. Mr. Lee realized that individual counseling and referrals, although important, were not going to be enough. He decided to begin a "survivor training program" to help workers cope with the loss and continue to work productively. Mr. Lee organized the workers into several groups that met weekly, and he attended and facilitated the meetings. He encouraged the workers to talk openly about their feelings of fear and guilt. He then arranged for Mr. Dorn to come to all the groups to answer questions. Mr. Lee explained to Mr. Dorn that the workers were afraid of losing their jobs and needed to understand why the layoffs had occurred. Mr. Dorn agreed to explain the financial concerns of the plant that led to the layoffs and the future operating plans.

The survivor training appeared to help workers deal with their fears and feelings of guilt, as well as helping them recommit to the organization and their jobs. However, Mr. Lee knew that studies showed companies that downsize once often do it again. He did not want the workers to be caught unaware if another cutback was necessary, so he advised them to take an active role. He wanted them to feel that they had some control over their lives, even if they did get laid off, so he counseled the survivors on the importance of continuing to do quality work. He also suggested they pay close attention to any news about the company's financial status by asking questions and reading the local business paper. Finally, he reinforced the importance of their support for each other.

In addition to working with the employees, Mr. Lee explained to Mr. Dorn the importance of letting workers know the positive effects the cutbacks were having on the plant's financial stability. He told Mr. Dorn that employees may become cynical if they are not aware of positive changes brought about by the painful process of downsizing. Mr. Dorn agreed to work with Mr. Lee to produce a quarterly operations statement for all employees so that they would know about the plant's progress in dealing with the loss of market share and the increased global competition.

As this vignette illustrates, EAP workers must be able to interact effectively with individual employees as well as to understand organizational and systemic functions. Mr. Lee engaged in individual and group counseling and fulfilled the social work functions of assessment, diagnosis, support, counseling, enabling, referral, program development, coordination, and consultation. Although the individual counseling, survivor training program, and quarterly newsletter all had a positive effect, Mr. Lee knows more cutbacks will produce more challenges.

References

Akabas, S. H. (1995). Occupational social work. In R. L. Edwards (Ed.-in-Chief), *Encyclopedia of social work* (19th ed., pp. 1779–1786). Washington, DC: NASW Press.

Barker, R. L. (1995). *Social work dictionary* (3rd ed.). Washington, DC: NASW Press.

Blum, T., Martin, J., & Roman, P. (1992). A research note on EAP prevalence, components, and utilization. *Journal of Employee Assistance Research, 1*, 209–229.

EAP growth lies in small-business area. (1986, November). *NASW News*, p. 5.

Gardner, J. M. (1995, April). Worker displacement: A decade of change. *Monthly Labor Review*, pp. 45–57.

Googins, B., & Davidson, B. N. (1993). The organization as client: Broadening the concept of employee assistance programs. *Social Work, 38*, 477–484.

Green, S. A. (1994, October 2). When it's cheaper not to let people go down the drain. *Washington Post*, p. H6.

Knox, A. (1992, March 15). The downside and dangers of downsizing. *Washington Post*, p. H2.

Kurzman, P. A. (1987). Industrial social work (Occupational social work). In A. Minahan (Ed.-in-Chief), *Encyclopedia of social work* (18th ed., Vol. 1, pp. 899–910). Silver Spring, MD: National Association of Social Workers.

Mor-Barak, M. E., & Tynan, M. (1993). Older workers and the workplace: A new occupational challenge for occupational social work. *Social Work, 38,* 45–55.

Mudrick, N. R. (1991). An underdeveloped role for occupational social work: Facilitating the employment of people with disabilities. *Social Work, 36,* 490–495.

National Association of Social Workers. (1981). *NASW standards for the classification of social work practice.* Silver Spring, MD: Author.

National Association of Social Workers. (1993). *Choices: Careers in social work.* Washington, DC: Author.

National Association of Social Workers. (1994). *NASW Code of Ethics.* Washington, DC: Author.

Occupational practice: Booming business. (1985, April). *NASW News,* p. 11.

Rensberger, B. (1994, December 19). Psychology: Learning cynicism on the job. *Washington Post,* p. A2.

Social work, public policy stands okayed. (1984, October). *NASW News,* p. 11.

Stewart, R. (1984, October). From the president. *NASW News,* p. 2.

Survey results released. (1986, May). *NASW News,* p. 12.

Swoboda, F. (1993, December 9). Xerox to cut 10,000 jobs over the next 2 to 3 years. *Washington Post,* p. B14.

Van Den Bergh, N. (1995). Employee assistance programs. In R. L. Edwards (Ed.-in-Chief), *Encyclopedia of social work* (19th ed., Vol. 1, pp. 842–849). Washington, DC: NASW Press.

Viewing work and social work. (1985, July). *NASW News,* pp. 10–11.

military social programs

The U.S. Armed Forces have employed active duty professional social workers for more than 50 years. Social workers serve in every branch of the military, both as commissioned officers and as civilian employees. The military society is almost like a microcosm of the entire social work field of practice, and military social workers provide interventions in diverse areas such as military family policy, child welfare, health care, substance abuse, mental health, hostage repatriation, and humanitarian relief. Most of the people served by military social workers are active duty personnel and their families, veterans and their eligible family members, or civilians who are eligible for special military assistance (Garber & McNelis, 1995).

In providing this wide range of services, social workers in the military practice on both micro and macro levels. Micro interventions include direct service counseling, advice, assistance, and referral in cases such as child neglect or substance abuse. Macro skills are developed as a result of military training in leadership, administration, and management (Garber & McNelis, 1995), and military social workers may find themselves using these skills to develop special programs such as child care for active duty members or to shape defense policy for families of the military reserve.

Whitworth (1984) noted that military families are unique in at least eight ways: (1) mobility, (2) separation, (3) periodic absence of parents, (4) adjustment of children, (5) overseas living, (6) high-stress and high-risk jobs, (7) conflicts between the needs of the family and the needs of the military system, and (8) authoritarian management environment. These eight factors have a tremendous impact on the mental and emotional health of an individual and his or her family. Therefore, many health and social services programs have been created to address the unique needs of this population.

Although social work in a military setting can be rewarding, there are some drawbacks. A typical military career usually includes multiple assignments that are often decided by organizational need rather than by personal or professional choice. Social workers in this arena must be flexible, although civilian social workers are generally less mobile than those who are on active duty (Garber & McNelis, 1995).

A second factor to consider is that at some point in a military career, almost every military social worker will serve in an isolated or overseas tour of duty. Social workers in the military system must also deal with the often overwhelming influence of the larger command on individual service members and their families (Garber & McNelis, 1995).

In addition to actual employment with the military, social workers may serve this population through a limited number of private organizations. For example, the American Red Cross is guided by the mission of serving the men and women of the Armed Forces and their families. The goals of the Armed Forces Emergency Services Division of the American Red Cross are to provide members of the military and their families with timely and reliable emergency communications and case management services, 24 hours a day, worldwide. Specifically, the Red Cross has developed an emergency communications division (EMERCOMM) that is equipped with the latest technology and a round-the-clock staff to send emergency messages to American military personnel stationed around the world (American Red Cross, 1995).

In addition to emergency communications, the Red Cross provides casework services such as financial assistance for emergency travel when a family member needs to go to the bedside of a seriously ill loved one in the military. The Red Cross also provides information and referral services when Red Cross services do not address specific needs (American Red Cross, 1995).

Although the Red Cross frequently employs paraprofessionals, social workers also function as caseworkers and program directors. For example, a social worker may be in charge of a chapter's emergency services division, which encompasses services to the armed forces. In this role, the social worker would exercise the functions of organizing, exchange with other community service agencies, administration, program development and evaluation, and supervision.

In addition to the American Red Cross, TAPS is an organization that serves family members, friends, and colleagues of active duty military personnel who have been killed. In this type of organization, a social worker may provide more direct service such as counseling, assistance, and referral.

The end of the Cold War has brought many changes to the U.S. Armed Forces. Major cuts in military budgets have had a pronounced effect on military communities and their social services programs. In addition, the restructuring of the nation's health care system may further affect military services in the future; if universal coverage is approved, health care for military members and their families within the United States may be virtually eliminated. As a result of these concerns, military social work is experiencing a time of uncertainty (Garber & McNelis, 1995).

Social workers play many roles in the armed services. For example, they have helped ease the transition of political hostages from captivity to freedom. Lt. Col. Calvin Neptune, a social worker and former member of the European

Command Seventh Medical Command Stress Management Team, was one of those responding to the emotional trauma experienced by hostages and victims of terrorist attacks (Hiratsuka, 1989). Stress management team members responded to the hijackings of a TWA jetliner in Athens, Greece, in 1985 and, in the same year, the terrorist attack on the ship *Achille Lauro*. They also responded to the 1986 explosion at the Chernobyl nuclear power plant and the release of captives in Beirut. The team operates on the belief that early intervention can help prevent posttraumatic stress disorder. The stress management team is composed of interdisciplinary mental health professionals who try to meet the immediate needs of hostages and victims by attending to their safety and shelter and by providing crisis intervention and supportive counseling. Team members also provide consultation to agencies involved in processing hostages.

The U.S. involvement in the Persian Gulf Conflict in 1991 also propelled social workers into action. To ease the public's anxieties over the war, social workers, both civilian and military, staffed crisis hot lines; assisted children and families of military personnel; helped families handle separation anxiety and fears; and offered support groups, counseling, and financial and other types of aid (Hiratsuka, 1991b). Daryl O'Brien, a social worker and counseling services supervisor at Navy Family Services in Norfolk, Virginia, ran a hot line that fielded about 1,400 calls a day from those requesting information and needing comfort and support. According to O'Brien, much of the work consisted of "helping people understand that theirs are normal reactions to a very abnormal situation" (Hiratsuka, 1991b, p. 3).

Social workers in schools and agencies throughout the country responded to the needs of children and parents who were distressed by the powerful impact of the televised images of the war. Katie Cooney-Scholzen, a school social worker in Racine, Wisconsin, conducted a workshop to equip school administrators and support staff to help teachers respond to the war-related concerns of children (Hiratsuka, 1991b). And social workers, along with other mental health professionals, staffed a USA *Today* "Kids and War" hot line to field questions and respond to fears and concerns about the war (Hiratsuka, 1991a). As the troops returned, social workers worked hand in hand with Red Cross chapters to conduct "reunion" workshops to help soldiers and their families return to their family routine (Moss, 1991).

Social workers have also helped U.S. troops to adjust to extraordinary assignments. A case in point is Somalia, a nation wracked by famine, disease, and civil war. In 1993, 21,000 U.S. troops were sent to Somalia and, although their mission was to secure food deliveries, they were fired upon and engaged Somalis in several military actions.

Before troops left for Somalia, social workers briefed soldiers on what to expect in regard to the ravages of famine and how to respond, practically and emotionally. They were counseled about preventive medicine, family separation, and other issues of concern. Predeployment briefings with their families focused on the stress of separation and the supports available. Some Army social workers accompanied the troops to provide ongoing assistance in daily health procedures, counseling, drug awareness and prevention, and help dealing with crises. On-site services operate on the premise that counseling is most effective when provided as close as possible to the scene of action (Hiratsuka, 1993).

References

American Red Cross. (1995). *Armed forces emergency services handbook*. Washington, DC: Author.

Garber, D. L., & McNelis, P. J. (1995). Military social work. In R. L. Edwards (Ed.-in-Chief), *Encyclopedia of social work* (19th ed., Vol. 2, pp. 1726–1736). Washington, DC: NASW Press.

Hiratsuka, J. (1989, January). Easing the trauma for released hostages. *NASW News*, p. 5.

Hiratsuka, J. (1991a, March). Hotline volunteers respond to kids' anxiety over war. *NASW News*, p. 3.

Hiratsuka, J. (1991b, March). Social workers lessen Gulf War's trauma. *NASW News*, pp. 3–4.

Hiratsuka, J. (1993, February). Somalia force aided to face painful scene. *NASW News*, pp. 1, 12.

Moss, M. S. (1991, April). Returning troops aided. *NASW News*, p. 1.

Whitworth, S. (1984). *Testimony on military families*. Hearings of the Select Committee on Children, Youth and Families, U.S. House of Representatives, 2d Session. Washington, DC: U.S. Government Printing Office.

private
practice

One of the most profound and far-reaching changes in the social work profession has been the movement of social workers into independent practice. The private practice of social work has been defined as "the process in which the values, knowledge, and skills of social work, acquired through sufficient education and experience, are used to deliver social work services autonomously to clients in exchange for mutually agreed payment" (Barker, 1995b, p. 294). In private or proprietary practice, the social worker is employed directly by the client and is paid by the client either directly or through a vendorship arrangement. Private practitioners usually provide for their own offices, personnel benefits, staff support, record keeping, and so on (Barker, 1995a).

Barker (1992) delineated 10 criteria to identify a social worker in private practice. The private practitioner

1. has the client as the primary obligation

2. determines who the client will be

3. determines the techniques to be used in service to this client

4. determines practice professionally, not bureaucratically

5. receives a fee for service directly from or on behalf of the client

6. is educated as a social worker

7. is a sufficiently experienced social worker

8. adheres to social work values, standards, and ethics

9. is licensed, certified, and registered, where applicable, to engage in private practice

10. is professionally responsible. (p. 16)

Private practice is predominantly focused on the direct delivery of clinical social work services. The circumstances under which private practice is carried out are influenced by the policies of the states regulating it, the standards of professional associations, and the insurance companies that determine reimbursement rates (Karger & Stoesz, 1994).

Some have asserted that the significant movement within the profession toward private practice has been explained and justified as the result of the need to expand the profession's mission to reflect the realities of economic and social change (Jayaratne, Davis-Sacks, & Chess, 1991; Saxton, 1988). In reality, the interest in private practice converged with licensing and vendorship—external variables—to shape the course of the profession. Social work licensing laws, granting formal government authorization to practice, are now in effect in all 50 states. *Vendorship* is "the practice of providing goods and services for specific fees that are charged either to the consumer or to a third party" (Barker, 1995b, p. 400), such as a health insurance company, government agency, or business organization. The social worker in private practice is a vendor, one who sells a product or service.

Many social workers pursue careers in private practice to escape the bureaucratic constraints of many public service jobs. Some want a higher income with more freedom to determine their own schedules and clientele. In addition, many social workers have found that private practice is the only way they can remain in direct practice, because if they stay at a service agency they will be promoted to an administrative or supervisory role (Barker, 1995a). Furthermore, cutbacks in funding for social services agencies have greatly reduced the number of available positions, thereby forcing some social workers into private practice simply to remain in their chosen profession (Barker, 1995a).

Along with the many positive aspects of private practice are some difficulties. For example, the expense of establishing and maintaining a private practice can be large and the income is often unpredictable. Typically, less than half of the money social workers collect from clients is spendable: Most of the income goes for overhead expenses such as taxes, health and other insurance, education, and retirement (Barker, 1995a).

In addition, many private practitioners experience burnout from overworking themselves in an attempt to make the practice successful. They must devote a tremendous amount of time to activities such as business records, insurance forms, and educational activities. Furthermore, the isolation of the private practitioner often facilitates burnout because there is no immediate social and professional support from colleagues. Finally, social workers in private practice often face legal problems, with malpractice litigation a constant threat (Barker, 1995a).

Federal and state legislation has boosted private practice. In 1986, Congress enacted the Federal Employee Health Benefits Program (FEHBP), which allows workers to seek mental health services from social workers and be reimbursed for the services received. The law requires FEHBP insurance carriers that offer mental health benefits to cover the services of qualified (state licensed or certified) clinical social workers. Insurers are prohibited from requiring supervision of the services by other health care professionals ("FEHBP Enacted," 1986).

In 1961 NASW formally endorsed a definition of private practice (NASW, 1974):

> A private practitioner is a social worker who, wholly or in part, practices his profession outside the aegis of a governmental or duly incorporated voluntary agency, who has responsibility for his own practice and sets up his own conditions of exchange with his clients and identifies himself as a social work practitioner in offering his services. (p. 40)

In 1962 NASW established minimum standards for private practice, including a master's degree from an accredited school of social work; professional certification by the Academy of Certified Social Workers (ACSW), the only certification available at that time; and five years of acceptable, full-time supervised agency employment (Barker, 1992). These standards have been modified slightly over the years and, in recognition of the growing number of social workers in private practice, NASW (1991) published NASW Guidelines on the Private Practice of Clinical Social Work.

Most services provided by social workers in private practice are in the "soft services" category. Psychotherapy, for example, is "the specialized, formal interaction between a social worker or other mental health professional and a client (an individual, couple, family, or group) in which a therapeutic relationship is established to help resolve symptoms of mental disorder, psychological stress, relationship problems, and difficulties in coping in the social environment" (Barker, 1995b, p. 305). Psychotherapy is an umbrella term that covers several modalities, including family therapy, supportive treatment, behavioral therapy, transactional analysis, and group psychotherapy. More than 200 distinct types of intervention and theoretical schools have been identified in mental health (Barker, 1995b).

A Social Worker in Private Practice

Wendy, a 46-year-old private clinician in Chicago, describes herself as a psychotherapist and clinical social worker. She works in a downtown office, which she shares with three other licensed social workers, and sees only individual clients ranging in age from 18 to 65. Her practice involves long-term, open-ended psychotherapy. Approximately 75 percent of her clients qualify for some type of insurance reimbursement, with the remaining 25 percent covering the cost themselves. Her fee is $85 for a 50-minute session and she spends between 30 and 35 hours per week seeing clients.

By choice, her office hours are from 7:30 A.M. to 3:30 P.M. Her downtown office provides easy access for most of her clients, who are either within walking distance or a short subway ride. Wendy believes that location has been critical to the success of her practice. Referrals from clients and from other clinicians are her major source of clients, and in her 14 years of practice she has managed to maintain a full schedule. She sees most of her clients once or twice a week. In the first few sessions, she evaluates the client and determines the parameters of the therapy, including whether to refer the client to a psychiatrist for medication, the frequency of visits, the specific problems to be addressed, the fee arrangement, and other issues.

To fine-tune her skills as a private practice clinician, Wendy has participated in post-graduate training at an analytic institute and attends professional conferences on a regular basis. She has also served as a supervisor for social workers in training.

Wendy has concerns about the future of her practice, particularly in light of the managed care movement. She believes that clients' choice of providers is becoming too limited. Several of her clients have had to terminate therapy because of insurance company limitations on the number of visits allowed. Her fear is that attempts at cost containment will result in a very altered picture for her practice and others.

The private practice of social work is a controversial topic within the profession. The arguments against private practice have focused on value conflicts with professional ethos, including discrimination against less affluent people and failure to provide services to those who cannot afford them (Barker, 1992; Karger, 1989; Merle, 1962). Other arguments note the potential depletion of social workers in agencies and the importance of agency norms and standards for practice (Barker, 1992). Private practitioners, on the other hand, argue that clearly defined roles and activities can exist in private practice and, in fact, the need to provide potential consumers with information about their services makes role clarification and delineation essential (Barker, 1992). The counterarguments also refute the discrimination claim with the assertion that agencies also select the clients they wish to serve on the basis of ability to pay or some type of means test, religion or ethnicity, or type of disability or other personal characteristic, such as gender. Less frequently refuted are claims that private practice usually excludes poor people because of geographic, social, or financial barriers (Barker, 1992). Concerns about depleting the agency-based labor force have not been borne out (Williams & Hopps, 1990).

The issue of fee-for-service in the private sector has been the subject of substantial debate among social workers. Barker's 1983 article "Private Practice Primer for Social Work" drew an unusually large number of letters debating the question of sliding fee scales, appropriate fee-setting, and third-party reimbursement (Cook, 1984; Elbaum, 1984; Phillips, 1984; Wikler, 1984). The debate continues. Specht and Courtney (1994) unequivocally viewed the movement toward private practice as negative when they wrote: "'We believe that social work has abandoned its mission to help the poor and oppressed and to build communality" (p. 4). In their view, community problems are increasing while social work as a profession is devoting itself more and more to "the psychotherapeutic enterprise," and the profession now seeks overridingly to "perfect the individual" rather than acting on a belief in the "'perfectibility of society."

These concerns about social work's mission were stated in a letter to the editor of the NASW News ("Letters," 1993):

I have been a member of NASW for more than 25 years, and in that time I have seen the profession move away from its primary purpose to a private-enterprise model. By normative definition, social work should be socially based and socially accountable. As my colleagues move more and more rapidly to private practice . . . I see a systematic move away from the social problems plaguing our cities and our nation, toward a short-cut route to psychotherapy. . . . As a profession, we accepted the role to be spokespersons and the advocates for those who were on the fringe of society. We had the responsibility to struggle with the powers that would ignore, exploit, discriminate. We were called idealists and we were proud; we were called liberal or even radical and we were proud; we were expected to take up causes to be visible in the never-ending struggle for social justice. Look where we are now! (p. 14)

Some have questioned whether private practice is a legitimate setting for social work ("Marketing," 1987). For-profit organizations increasingly are settings for social work practice, and some professionals have expressed concern about the effect this has on the norms of practice and about its implications for professional standards and values (Beckerman & Fontana, 1993).

Despite critics from within and outside the profession, private practice continues to be a popular choice. The enthusiasm for private practice has been attributed to several factors, including the prestige and income that private practitioners enjoy compared to their salaried and agency-based counterparts. The salary potential for private practitioners is generally higher than for agency-based social workers in direct practice (Gibelman & Schervish, 1993). Private practice also offers a degree of autonomy not available in traditional agencies, including a level of specialization that is individually determined (Karger & Stoesz, 1994).

Private Practice: Not Just Psychotherapy

Neil, a 36-year-old white college graduate, is an engineer with a stable employment history. He is described by his social worker, Melinda, as physically unattractive and as having poor personal hygiene habits. Neil is a Vietnam veteran, but says this is not an issue for him. His tour of duty did not include combat.

Neil met Melinda when, as part of her community outreach activities, she conducted a lecture about relationships at Neil's place of employment. Neil attended the lecture and then called Melinda for an appointment.

Neil's presenting problem is depression and social isolation. He has been on only a few dates and has never had sex. Although he talks about crushes on women, he has not followed through with them or, on the rare occasion where he has shown interest in a woman, he has been rebuffed. He talks of feeling despondent and hopeless.

Neil has been in therapy before but refuses to let Melinda send for his records. He has not stayed with any treatment over time. Based on this history, Melinda explains that therapy is not a magic or instantaneous cure and that what he gets out of treatment depends, in large part, on his investment in it.

During the first two sessions, Melinda took a detailed psychosocial history through which she learned that Neil's father is an intellectual who has always been very critical of his son. Neil perceives his mother as nonnurturing. Neil received little affection from either of his parents, who divorced when he was 10. He has one brother who is married and has three children, but there is little communication between the siblings. He has difficulty describing his family—what they are like, how they interrelate. His health history is basically good. At age 10 he suffered a head injury as the result of a fall. There is no evidence of neurological involvement, but Neil feels that all of his problems stem from this accident, although he admits that even before his fall other kids teased and made fun of him. There appears to have been little laughter in his early life, although a strong achievement orientation apparently was present. Melinda noted certain compulsive features: Neil keeps his apartment very clean and dusts each day; he ascribes to a high moral code, self-imposed, and he does not believe in sex before marriage; his thought patterns are black and white with no shades of gray; and he is also a perfectionist who is easily disappointed by the fallibility of others.

Neil has health insurance that covers his therapy visits, but during the first two months he broke several appointments, with advance notice. He said it is hard to get himself together to go to therapy because he feels bad and depressed most of the time. Getting to work each day is a major accomplishment.

On the basis of the psychosocial assessment, Melinda gave a tentative diagnosis of obsessive–compulsive disorder with major depression. The first goal was to get Neil stabilized on medication, which required a referral to a psychiatrist. In fact, Neil went to three different psychiatrists for an evaluation; he didn't like the first two because he felt they didn't care enough about him. He was satisfied with the third psychiatrist, who put Neil on an antidepressant. Neil also is narcoleptic and takes Dexedrine for this condition. Neil experiences emotional peaks and valleys, which he attributes to the Dexedrine. Melinda asked him to document his highs and lows to help determine if they are biological or emotional. His sleep disorder prevents Neil from sleeping well at night.

Neil is unwilling to commit to a service plan. Melinda sees the major treatment task as engaging him in a relationship, with therapy focusing on emotional support and relationship-building. Neil has no role models for healthy relationships. The focus of discussions is on how Neil feels, how medication is working for him, and how he is making it through each day. The approach is psychodynamic, and Melinda is hopeful that Neil will develop greater insight into his family relations and identify traits learned from his parents that no longer work for him. Melinda suspects that he learned his rigidity from his parents. After several months in treatment, Neil agreed to attend a therapy group run by Melinda. After about a year he dropped out, saying only that he had had enough and wasn't getting anything from it. A few weeks later, in an individual session, Neil reported that he had found another group led by a male therapist that is focused on improving relationships. Melinda suspects that Neil has stayed with this group because he has developed a crush on a woman in the group. Although he has hinted about this crush, he has not been willing to verbalize his feelings directly. He has also resisted Melinda's suggestion that he attend a singles social group.

After two years in treatment, Neil became more amenable to following through on referrals. Melinda referred Neil to a sleep disorder clinic. Neil was not willing to release a copy of the clinic's findings to Melinda, but reported that the clinic confirmed a diagnosis of narcolepsy. He is being maintained on Dexedrine for narcolepsy and Prozac for depression. In time, Neil occasionally reports that he is "doing okay," a new acknowledgment that there could be bright days. Neil's depression still concerns Melinda and the consulting psychiatrist; despite medication, there are times when Neil is considered a suicide risk. For example, after his home was burglarized he became despondent for weeks.

The focus of treatment remains on maintenance. Melinda suspects that Neil will be in treatment for a long time; the security of the therapeutic relationship has provided a center of stability for him. Ultimately, Melinda hopes that he will be able to form a relationship with someone who will provide this stability within a loving relationship.

Although Melinda exhibits the skills of referral and coordination, the primary functions enacted are assessment, diagnosis, identification, support, and counseling. The goal of each of these functions is to enhance Neil's problem-solving, coping, and developmental capacities. Melinda practiced active listening skills and empathetic responses in communicating with Neil to explore his current situation and coping techniques.

There are some less obvious skills evidenced in this vignette. Melinda's pro bono workshop for company employees was actually part of a systematic marketing plan. Melinda budgets a portion of her time to marketing and promotion. Related strategies include providing brochures; making person-to-person contacts with other health and mental health providers; and visiting referral sources, including churches, community centers, and businesses. Visibility is extremely important to bringing in business ("Marketing," 1987).

Private practitioners also treat people in groups. The following vignette describes a private practitioner's group approach for people who are afraid to travel in an airplane. The group intervention described below illustrates that a behavioral approach, combined with the support of group members in similar circumstances, can be an effective tool.

Group Therapy and Fear of Flying

Marsha's job requires that she travel out of town at least once a month, sometimes to distant cities. Marsha has never liked to fly. She grew up near LaGuardia Airport in New York City. One day when she was 10 years old she was walking home from a birthday party with several friends. All of a sudden the sky lit up, as if fireworks were going off, and then she heard a horrible noise. When Marsha got home she learned that an airliner taking off from LaGuardia had exploded over Jamaica Bay, killing all passengers.

Twenty years later, Marsha has flown all over the world, never happily. Takeoffs are moments of acute anxiety for her. She jokes that she is responsible for holding up the plane with her knees. By the time she reaches her destination she is exhausted. Going straight from the airport to a business meeting is difficult; she really needs 24 solid hours of sleep. Marsha has tried all types of things to deal with her fears—tranquilizers, alcohol, even hypnosis, without success.

Nancy Marks, a social worker who has established a for-profit Behavior Therapy Center, specializes in working with phobic disorders. Following the crash of an airliner outside of Pittsburgh, she got so many calls that she decided to form a short-term group for people with a fear of flying. This problem is not new for the social workers at the center, but interventions have generally been on a one-to-one basis.

In the group, Nancy encourages people to talk about their specific fears, their experiences flying, and what was happening in their lives when they first became aware of their phobia. Then Nancy helps the group members plan a plane trip for the last session of the group—kind of a "graduation" send-off. Members discuss where they will go, how they will purchase the tickets, how much time they will need to get to the airport, and other logistics. In subsequent sessions, Nancy guides the group in psychodrama— playing out the flying experience using imagery and relaxation techniques. These techniques include exercises for group members to challenge negative thinking, control obsessive thinking, and become more comfortable in their environment ("Counseling," 1985).

At the fourth of seven sessions, Nancy takes the group to the city's major airport. With the cooperation of a major airline, arrangements are made for the group to board an aircraft, talk to the pilot and crew, and learn as much as possible about the mechanics of flying. At the next session, the group thoroughly "debriefs" about this experience.

Finally, it is the seventh and last session. Marsha and the other six group members show up as scheduled for their graduation flight. The tickets are provided free of charge by the airline; they will take off, fly at cruising altitude for an hour, and then land back at the airport. They all go together, sit in seats they had selected for themselves on the earlier airport visit, and listen to Nancy's final instructions. All goes well; the group members are able to use the techniques they have learned for a successful flight.

The fear of flying for many people is an outgrowth of the shock they feel when they hear about plane crashes—so many deaths occurring at one time in a manner that is outside of anyone's control. Other factors include a lack of understanding about how planes operate and fear of the unknown ("Counseling," 1985). The fear may be about crashing, but it may also center on claustrophobia, the fear of confined spaces. Some people feel a slight apprehension about flying, whereas others will not board a plane under any circumstances. To varying degrees, this phobia can be disabling. It is estimated that 25 million Americans will not fly ("Counseling," 1985). The kind of group just described has shown high success rates.

This example illustrates several different professional functions. First, Nancy used assessment, identification, support, and counseling when working with the group members. She then listened carefully to what they were saying about themselves and how they responded to each other. She also used organization and coordination skills as she worked with airlines to arrange a practice flight. Finally, Nancy used her skills to enable the group members to help themselves and, ultimately, to overcome their fear of flying.

At any point in time, practitioner interests are both shaped by and help to shape the future of the profession. The growth of social work in private practice was made possible by a permissive and enabling economic and political climate. An increasing number of consumers wanted the service and either could afford to pay for it themselves or had insurance that would cover all or part of the expense (Barker, 1992).

As with other social work practice areas, the socioeconomic and political context of American society will affect the future of social work in private practice. The demand for private practitioner services in social work and allied professions may diminish because of changing demographics, values and priorities, and cost factors. Barker (1992) noted that "the value and efficacy of therapy and social services in private practice have still not been clearly demonstrated to the public or to the third parties who help pay the bills" (p. 139).

The advent of managed health care poses special challenges for the independent practice of social work, particularly in regard to real and potential income and the limitations on the choice of preferred intervention modalities. *Managed care* refers "to a service delivery system in which treatment decisions are monitored in order to conserve clinical and fiscal resources" (Edwards, 1990, p. 2). The overall objective of this system is to ensure that clients receive the care they need in the most cost-effective manner. Clearly, the private practice of social work will be one of the service areas most directly and dramatically affected by health care reform (Strom, 1992).

Health care cost containment is a primary goal of government and insurance providers, as evident in the growing popularity of health maintenance organizations (HMOs), preferred provider organizations (PPOs), independent (or individual) practice associations (IPAs), and a number of hybrid prepaid health plans. Employers are opting to self-insure or use lower-cost alternative service systems for their enrolled employees ("Staying Afloat," 1986). Government cost-capping trends have grown steadily over the past decade, with renewed impetus to cut Medicaid and other entitlement programs following the 1994 elections. It is estimated that by the year 2000, at least half of the U.S. population will receive health and mental health care through some form of managed care arrangement ("Staying Afloat," 1986).

The concern about the cost of health care, including mental health care, has some legitimacy. Although many insurance companies limit mental health coverage available to their employees, the cost of employees' mental health services rose 57 percent over a five-year period and in 1993 stood at $22 billion (Landers, 1994a).

The implication for social workers, particularly those in solo or small group private practice, is clear: Treatment effectiveness and cost containment must go hand in hand. The model of short-term, problem-focused therapy fits best with these dual operating principles. The flow of client referrals is also likely to be stemmed. Demonstrating the effectiveness of treatment and achievement of planned outcomes will be increasingly stressed as managed care companies look for hard data to determine who can best treat what types of problems

(Landers, 1993, 1994a). These companies examine client relapse and recidivism rates and study treatment reports to determine the fit between diagnosis, treatment, and client outcomes and satisfaction (Landers, 1994a).

Other effects of managed care that are already in evidence are increased competition among practitioners for access to the few available slots on provider panels and the intrusion of managed care providers or employers into the selection of providers and treatment decisions. Social workers who work with a number of managed care companies may also find that they must alter their service approach to meet the dictates of each (Landers, 1992a). Questions about whether the social worker or an agent of the managed care firm should determine a client's treatment involve both practical and ethical considerations for the profession (Landers, 1992b).

The emphasis on cost containment means that a referral to an individual private practitioner outside the prepaid system is rare. Instead, HMOs award competitive contracts to organized practitioner groups that offer the services HMOs cannot provide; the contracts are for specific services at low overall cost ("Staying Afloat," 1986). Private practice social workers in some areas of the country have already experienced a drop in the number of fee-for-service cases in favor of "full-risk capitation" arrangements, by which the managed care company negotiates a flat fee that covers the therapy clients are authorized to receive over a set period of time (Landers, 1993). This arrangement requires that practitioners specify in advance the course of therapy.

The future of the private practice of social work is thus tied to the course of health care reform. Some predict the demise of solo private practice, projecting that these practitioners will either need to affiliate with groups that accept third-party payers or forgo clients with insurance in favor of those who can afford to pay for treatment (Landers, 1993).

In spite of these trends, interest in private practice remains strong among those entering the profession. Clearly, the profession needs to monitor the impact of managed care on private social work practice over time. Meanwhile, social workers must be able to promote themselves within the managed care system and show their capability as independent contractors. In addition to using their skills in grant writing and contract negotiating, social workers must organize themselves, band together, and develop a service model and package of services that is acceptable to and congruent with managed care providers ("Staying Afloat," 1986).

References

Barker, R. (1983, October). Private practice primer for social work. *NASW News*, p. 13.

Barker, R. L. (1992). *Social work in private practice* (2nd ed.). Washington, DC: NASW Press.

Barker, R. L. (1995a). Private practice. In R. L. Edwards (Ed.-in-Chief), *Encyclopedia of social work,* (19th ed., Vol. 3, pp. 1905–1910). Washington, DC: NASW Press.

Barker, R. L. (1995b). *Social work dictionary* (3rd ed.). Washington, DC: NASW Press.

Beckerman, A., & Fontana, L. (1993). Fieldwork in proprietary agencies and private practice settings: The perceptions of fieldwork coordinators in graduate social work programs. *Journal of Teaching in Social Work, 7,* 113–128.

Cook, D. (1984, January). [Letter to the editor]. *NASW News,* p. 25.

Counseling tames travelers' flying fears. (1985, November). *NASW News,* p. 11.

Edwards, R. L. (1990, January). Benefits, pitfalls seen in managed care. *NASW News,* p. 2.

Elbaum, P. L. (1984, January). [Letter to the editor]. *NASW News,* p. 25.

FEHBP enacted. (1986, April). *NASW News,* p. 1.

Gibelman, M., & Schervish, P. H. (1993). *Who we are: The social work labor force as reflected in the NASW membership.* Washington, DC: NASW Press.

Jayaratne, S., Davis-Sacks, M. L., & Chess, W. (1991). Private practice may be good for your health. *Social Work, 36,* 224–232.

Karger, H. J. (1989). Private practice: The fast track to the shingle. *Social Work, 34,* 566–567.

Karger, H. J., & Stoesz, D. (1994). *American social welfare policy: A pluralistic approach.* New York: Longman.

Landers, S. (1992a, June). Managed care: New accent on quality. *NASW News,* p. 3.

Landers, S. (1992b, November). Managed care: Who decides treatment? *NASW News,* p. 3.

Landers, S. (1993, July). Providers ponder a managed-care future. *NASW News,* p. 3.

Landers, S. (1994a, September). Managed care's challenge: "Show me!" *NASW News,* p. 3.

Landers, S. (1994b, November). Supergroups: A "big pond" survival tactic. *NASW News*, p. 3.

Letters to the editor. (1993, November). *NASW News*, p. 14.

Marketing: A lifeline for private practice. (1987, October). *NASW News*, p. 5.

Merle, S. (1962). Some arguments against private practice. *Social Work, 7,* 12–17.

National Association of Social Workers. (1974). *Handbook on the private practice of social work.* Washington, DC: Author.

National Association of Social Workers. (1991). *NASW guidelines on the private practice of clinical social work.* Silver Spring, MD: Author.

Phillips, D. G. (1984, January). [Letter to the editor]. *NASW News*, p. 25.

Saxton, P. M. (1988). Vendorship for social work: Observations on the maturation of the profession. *Social Work, 33,* 197–201.

Specht, H., & Courtney, M. (1994). *Unfaithful angels: How social work has abandoned its mission.* New York: Free Press.

Staying afloat on health care's new wave. (1986, June). *NASW News*, pp. 3, 8.

Strom, K. (1992). Reimbursement demands and treatment decisions: A growing dilemma for social workers. *Social Work, 37,* 398–403.

Wikler, M. (1984, April). [Letter to the editor]. *NASW News*, p. 18.

Williams, L. F., & Hopps, J. G. (1990). The social work labor force: Current perspectives and future trends. In L. Ginsberg et al. (Eds.), *Encyclopedia of social work* (18th ed., 1990 suppl., pp. 289–306). Silver Spring, MD: NASW Press.

rural social work

The problems experienced by rural Americans often go unrecognized, but they are real and have worsened in recent years (Edwards, 1989). Rural Americans account for almost 25 percent of the total U.S. population and include about a third of the nation's elderly, over half of whom live in poverty. Overall poverty rates in rural areas are higher than those in urban areas. Rural Americans also suffer disproportionately higher rates of maternal and infant mortality; chronic illness and disability; and morbidity related to cancer, diabetes, high blood pressure, stroke, heart disease, and lung disease (Edwards, 1989). Homelessness, often thought of as an urban problem, is increasing in rural areas.

The past decade has been one of crisis and change for rural populations. Many farmers, for example, have found that they can no longer afford to operate. Farm auctions and foreclosures have become commonplace, accompanied by huge amounts of debt and a high emotional toll ("Farm Communities Dig In," 1987; "Social Workers Aid Harried Farm Families," 1985). In addition, rural manufacturing has steadily declined, resulting in widespread unemployment (Edwards, 1989). The resulting stress on rural communities is reflected in the rising rates of child abuse and neglect, divorce, and suicide and an increased demand for mental health services. Rural Americans often lack access to the range of services they need.

The protracted nature of the economic problems in rural communities has led some social workers to call for a hard look at farm policies and ways to revive rural economies ("Farm Communities Dig In," 1987). Rural social workers are working as advocates, both on the local level to help communities help themselves and on the national level to support legislation that authorizes mental health services to rural communities. In concert with this advocacy, social workers have realized that the economics of rural life must be addressed if the problems facing this population are to be solved (Edwards, 1989).

Because of a lack of sufficient mental health facilities and in some cases any mental health facilities at all, rural social workers often find themselves as the only line of defense against a mounting array of social ills (Hiratsuka, 1990).

For rural social workers, family and community involvement is a necessity. In one midwestern rural area, social workers organized and trained a group of "peer listeners," individuals trained to intervene with their neighbors to help with problems of depression and suicidal behavior ("Social Workers Aid Harried Farm Families," 1985). Outreach and education are also an essential part of the social worker's role.

Programs throughout the Midwest have been developed to include rural community outreach, peer-listening training, crisis hot lines, and stress-relief retreats (subsidized weekend trips to a church camp for farm families to help alleviate family stress). Support groups organized by social workers provide help for an array of problems, including drug addiction and domestic violence. In the words of one rural social worker, "We have to take the self-reliance exhibited by the farm community and use it as a strength. Because we are so few in number, we must train rural residents to help themselves" ("Farm Communities Dig In," 1987, p. 4).

In many rural communities, social workers have helped to recruit and train volunteers and to involve neighbors, families, clergy, and other natural support networks. The Rural Response Program of the Northwest Iowa Mental Health Center initiated support groups and a mediation service to work with farmers and their creditors ("Farm Communities Dig In," 1987). Other efforts include helping churches and agencies better respond to the needs of farmers, organizing farmers for political action, offering crisis hot lines, and conducting community meetings to provide information on available services and encourage support networks. The self-reliance of many farmers and the stigma often associated with mental health services require social workers to go into the community to provide services ("Farm Communities Dig In," 1987).

Rural social workers are often employed by public-sector agencies such as public welfare, child welfare, and mental health. They tend to work out of relatively small, isolated offices and confront a wide range of problems. Many social workers who are accustomed to urban diversity often enter a rural environment expecting to work with a more homogenous population. But rural communities are diverse, in terms of both population characteristics and presenting problems (Davenport & Davenport, 1995).

A typical mental health social worker in a rural environment may use the functions of assessment and counseling when working with survivors of sexual assault or domestic violence, and the functions of organizing and coordinating to develop a support group, organize a task force, or implement an emergency food pantry. In addition, a rural social worker may advocate and lobby legislators for increased funding and services (Davenport & Davenport, 1995).

The generalist practice model, with its focus on the social worker's ability to assess problem situations and identify when and where intervention is needed, is usually the best method for rural social work. Rural social workers must also be able to develop relationships with other local service providers and with state and local organizations. Social workers in this area of practice must be flexible and able to adapt to their surroundings and the needs of their clients (Davenport & Davenport, 1995).

Mental Health Needs in a Rural Area

Rina Williams is a 32-year-old mother of five whose husband, Dale, runs their 500-acre corn and soybean farm in northeast Iowa. For each of the past two years, a drought has ruined a large proportion of their annual harvest, overhead costs have increased, and crop prices have dropped. The bank is threatening foreclosure. Dale has been drinking heavily and the marriage is falling apart—communication lines have broken down.

Jim Walker, a social worker employed at a mental health center serving six Iowa counties, has recently seen several women for first-time appointments with complaints of depression, marital problems, and family dysfunction. Recognizing the impact of the farm crisis on these and other rural families, Jim tries a community intervention approach. He knows that farmers can be tough customers; because of long-standing resistance to mental health services in the community, particularly among the men, there is little chance of involving some of these men in family or individual therapy. Therefore, Jim takes a two-pronged approach: First, he organizes a support group to help the wives cope, then he organizes the first of what he hopes will be an ongoing series of community meetings to discuss the farm situation and its impact on the community. To gain the participation of the men in the community, Jim invites several of them to serve on a planning committee to identify topics for discussion, hoping that this will help create a sense of ownership and give them a stake in the success of the program.

To reduce the stigma associated with the mental health center, the first community meeting is held in a local school. The topic selected by the planning committee is helping children cope with the financial, social, and emotional impact of the farm crisis. Members of the planning committee and residents in attendance agree that an increasing number of children suffer from depression or acting-out behavior. The residents then turn to Jim for help in solving the problem, but Jim simply tells them it is their meeting and asks them what they want to do. By responding this way, Jim hopes to empower the residents and allow them to solve their own problems.

After several minutes of silence, a woman begins to talk about her son: He has nothing to do after school, and the school cannot afford an athletic program. Other parents begin to echo her experiences. The kids seem to be bored and, as a result, some are depressed and act out. Turning to the youths at the meeting, Jim asks them what they think of the situation. The youths are excited to be asked to express their opinions, and many of them offer suggestions.

After several hours of discussion, a tentative plan is developed for the youths to operate their own "country store." Some of the youths offer to make carpentry items such as wooden stools, shelves, and benches. Others are interested in making jewelry from dried flowers and stone. Still others are interested in learning the business end of running the store—everything from ordering stock to arranging shelves. After several more meetings, the community decides to work together to build the store, and the youths will work there after school. Special positions such as store manager and accountant will rotate among them every month.

In addition to guiding and facilitating local meetings, Jim uses his contacts in the town to get a small loan from the bank for supplies and to secure agreements from local merchants to display and sell some of the store's goods.

In this case, Jim uses the social work function of assessment to identify the social problem confronting the residents of the community. He also engages in enabling as he assists the residents to develop their own self-help skills. Jim uses the functions of organizing, mobilization, and coordination to start the support group for wives and to develop the planning committee for the community meetings. Finally, Jim engages in negotiation and exchange to access local resources.

References

Davenport, J. A., & Davenport, J., III. (1995). Rural social work overview. In R. L. Edwards (Ed.-in-Chief), *Encyclopedia of social work* (19th ed., Vol. 3, pp. 2076–2085). Washington, DC: NASW Press.

Edwards, R. L. (1989, October). Social work's vital role in rural areas. *NASW News*, p. 2.

Farm communities dig in for the long haul. (1987, February). *NASW News*, p. 4.

Hiratsuka, J. (1990, September). Study sees rural care shortage. *NASW News*, pp. 1, 14.

Social workers aid harried farm families. (1985, May). *NASW News*, p. 3.

veterans services

More than 41 million men and women have served in the military during wartime since the American Revolution; the largest proportion are men and women who served in World War II and who are now 65 years of age or older (Becerra & Damron-Rodriguez, 1995; Rothman & Becerra, 1987).

The Department of Veterans Affairs (VA), established in 1930, is the largest single system of health care for veterans (Rothman & Becerra, 1987). Its major programs include health care delivery, pension and compensation benefits, educational benefits, housing assistance, life insurance, vocational rehabilitation and counseling, and administration of cemeteries and memorials (Rothman & Becerra, 1987). In addition, the VA also offers domiciliaries, nursing home care, hospital-based home care programs, adult day health care centers, respite care, hospice care, and geriatric evaluations (Foster, 1989). VA benefits are administered by three units: (1) the Veterans Health Administration (VHA) provides health and mental health care services; (2) the Department of Veterans Benefits (DVB) provides pension and compensation benefits, including educational, housing, and vocational assistance; and (3) the Department of Memorial Affairs (DMA) administers burial benefits (Becerra & Damron-Rodriguez, 1995).

VA medical centers and ambulatory care clinics throughout the country provide services to veterans with honorable discharges. Because of space limitations, eligibility requirements are based on a priority system. Veterans who were exposed to Agent Orange, former prisoners of war, and World War I veterans are given highest priority; non–service connected veterans with other VA pensions or those who meet established income criteria are given lower priority (Foster, 1989).

Veterans deal with issues ranging from mild stress reactions to chronic mental illness and homelessness. VHA operates one of the most comprehensive mental health services in the nation and provides special programs for veterans confronting chemical dependency, dual diagnosis, and posttraumatic stress disorder (Becerra & Damron-Rodriguez, 1995).

Social workers generally work as members of interdisciplinary teams and provide a wide range of services including direct clinical care, development of outreach services, development of new methods of treatment, discharge planning, evaluation, and crisis intervention. In an outreach or counseling center for veterans, social workers play an important role in making referrals to the VA for inpatient care and in coordinating community resources, a critical link to providing cost-effective, high-quality care (Rothman & Becerra, 1987).

The Legacy of a War on One Man

In February 1991, Army serviceman Dave Burton was serving in the Persian Gulf Conflict when he stepped on a land mine. Both of his legs had to be amputated below the knee. He returned home with an honorable discharge and some serious psychological issues to confront. Dave began drinking heavily and was constantly morose and depressed. His wife, Debbie, was concerned about him and convinced him to go to the San Diego Veterans Administration Medical Center, where he met with Jake Adams, a social worker.

Jake had done a great deal of research on delayed stress response, a common symptom among Vietnam veterans, and the effect of stressful life events. Jake interviewed Dave and made a brief assessment of Dave's psychosocial situation. He met with Dave several more times before suggesting that Dave participate in the Readjustment Counseling Service provided by a community outreach center of the San Diego VA. The Readjustment Counseling Service was based on a model that blends group process, self-help principles, and psychotherapy. Dave agreed to join an eight-member veterans' "rap group" that Jake facilitated.

Dave attended the rap groups every week and met with Jake individually every other week. Dave also attended Alcoholics Anonymous meetings regularly. In addition, Jake helped Dave obtain training provided by the VA in computer science. Dave was then able to get a job with a local accounting firm as a computer programmer. Change did not occur quickly, but it did occur, and Dave slowly accepted and adapted to his new lifestyle.

In this case, Jake provided direct mental health services. Jake first conducted several interviews to assess and diagnose Dave's psychosocial situation. He then provided counseling, support, and advice in his biweekly sessions with Dave. He also provided referral services by getting Jake involved in Alcoholics Anonymous and the Readjustment Counseling Service and used his coordination skills to help Dave access other VA programs such as the computer training and job search services.

Homeless Veterans

A 1988 VA study indicated that 80 percent of homeless veterans have general psychiatric or substance abuse problems (Hymes, 1990). One of the most common psychiatric problems among veterans is *posttraumatic stress disorder* (PTSD), a psychological reaction resulting from the experience of an event that is outside the range of usual human experience, such as an accident, military combat, assault, rape, or natural disaster (Barker, 1995). A veteran with PTSD may relive war scenes or act out in explosively violent or extremely depressed behavior (Hymes, 1990). Many of these veterans end up homeless.

The Homeless Chronically Mentally Ill Program offered under the auspices of the VA Medical Center in Atlanta serves veterans who have been homeless for at least 30 days; do not have a dishonorable discharge; and have chronic mental illness, alcoholism, or drug addiction. Social workers and other professionals work with the veterans in rehabilitation programs lasting one to six months. The focus of intervention is on addiction treatment, employment, and self-sufficiency. The program in Atlanta began in 1987, and there are 42 similar programs in 26 states (Hymes, 1990).

References

Barker, R. L. (1995). *Social work dictionary* (3rd ed.). Washington, DC: NASW Press.

Becerra, R. M., & Damron-Rodriguez, J. (1995). Veterans and veterans services. In R. L. Edwards (Ed.-in-Chief), *Encyclopedia of social work* (19th ed., Vol. 3, pp. 2431–2439). Washington, DC: NASW Press.

Foster, Z. (1989). Mutual help groups for emphysema patients: Veterans Administration Medical Center. In T. S. Kerson & Associates, *Social work in health settings: Practice in context* (pp. 177–193). New York: Haworth.

Hymes, T. A. (1990, January). Homeless veterans embark on new life. *NASW News*, p. 2.

Rothman, G., & Becerra, R. M. (1987). Veterans and veterans' services. In A. Minahan (Ed.-in-Chief), *Encyclopedia of social work* (18th ed., Vol. 2, pp. 809–817). Silver Spring, MD: National Association of Social Workers.

career
opportunities

The following sample job listings illustrate the range of employment opportunities for social workers in mental health. Although these listings are based on actual classified advertisements, they do not represent current job listings.

Clinic Administrator

Child guidance center is seeking an experienced MSW mental health administrator with strong clinical, organizational, and community relations skills. Must have previous administrative/supervisory experience in mental health setting and thorough knowledge of child development, individual, family, and group therapy modalities and Asian outreach activities. Must be a well organized, detail-oriented leader with a multicultural orientation. Minimum of eight years' post-MSW experience.

Clinical/Administration

Readjustment Counseling Service of U.S. government agency has positions available nationwide in a highly innovative and successful system of over 200 community-based multiservice centers. These clinical/administrative positions are for social workers with experience or skill in working with Vietnam veterans as well as more recent veterans of combat. Social workers with recent military mental health experience or significant experience treating posttraumatic stress disorder are encouraged to apply.

Community Mental Health Services Supervisor

Mental health services agency is seeking a community mental health services supervisor for the agency's adult outpatient program. Duties include supervision of a team of seven master's and/or bachelor-level case managers. Candidates must possess three years of professional experience in the fields of mental health, rehabilitation, social services, or substance abuse, of which at least one year must have involved professional clinical experience serving people with mental illness, and possession of a master's degree from an accredited college or university with specialization in nursing, psychology, social work, counseling, education, adjunctive therapy, or related area.

Counseling, Stress Management

Master's degree in psychology, counseling, or related field to work on an "as needed" basis on major declared disasters for the Federal Emergency Management Agency. You will provide stress management services to the people who help disaster victims. You will receive full training in disaster stress management, but experience and skills in this field, and especially in proactive counseling, are strong assets. Spanish bilingual skills are also needed.

Director of Adolescent Residential Treatment

Highly recognized, multiservice agency is seeking a knowledgeable, clinically oriented professional. Responsible for a 74-bed residential treatment program for emotionally disturbed youths, male and female. Position requires MSW or equivalent degree, clinical experience, and knowledge in providing therapeutic milieu.

Director of Evaluation Team

Inpatient mental health treatment center for adolescents and adults is seeking an experienced clinician to direct an assessment and referral team. Person should have clinical experience and skills in assessment and intervention as well as knowledge of mental health continuum. RN, LCSW, or MA required. Previous supervisory experience desired.

Director of Rehabilitation Services

Seeking a mental health professional to direct psychiatric rehabilitation services for the seriously mentally ill on-site and in community settings. Supervise professional staff, monitor program budgets, and coordinate with state and county agencies. Experience in psychosocial rehabilitation and management is a plus. Master's degree in social work and LCSW or related human services field or a doctorate in psychology required in addition to at least four years' relevant experience, two of which should have been in an administrative and/or supervisory capacity.

EAP Case Manager

A leading provider of network-based managed mental health, substance abuse, and employee assistance programs is seeking an experienced licensed mental health case manager. Applicant must have at least five years' post-master's clinical experience in the area of mental health/substance abuse. Candidate must be a registered nurse or hold a master's degree in social work. Preferred candidates will have a minimum of two years' experience working in an internal or external EAP to a client company, or equivalent experience utilizing community resources. Experience with management consultations/referrals and critical incident debriefings preferred. Excellent communication, organizational, and customer service skills a must. Working knowledge of computers desired.

EAP Counselors

A managed care company specializing in psychiatric and chemical dependency is seeking several EAP counselors to support their 24-hour EAP program. The successful candidates will have a master's degree, preferably in social work, and a minimum of three years of experience in the managed care industry with an emphasis on mental health. LCSW highly preferred.

Executive Director

A faith-based counseling agency of an ecumenical nature seeks an executive director. Demonstrated skills in counseling, administration, and eligibility for state licensure or certification as a mental health professional/counselor required. Membership in the American Association of Pastoral Counseling and ordination desired. Candidates must have skills and knowledge regarding the integration of psychology and theology in the therapeutic process. Doctoral degree preferred.

Executive Director

A well-established comprehensive community mental health center with a $3 million budget serving a four-county area seeks a chief executive officer. Minimum requirements include a master's degree in public–business administration or related area and five years' administrative and/or supervisory experience or equivalent experience/education. Preference will be given to candidates with mental health or health administration experience.

Manager, Housing Options

MSW, license-eligible social worker sought. As the manager of the Housing Options program, you will be responsible for the supervision and management of group homes, transitional apartments, regional housing, and independent living skills programs for adults who have severe and prolonged mental illness. Responsibilities include compliance with policies and procedures designed to promote quality services and the attainment of program goals and objectives. Other tasks include clinical and administrative supervision of the programs and responsibility for performance standards to assure the provision of efficient and cost-effective service delivery. Administrative/supervisory experience, especially in residential services, strongly preferred. Must have track record as a strong team player.

Psychiatric Social Worker

MSW required. An accredited 1,000-bed, forensic psychiatric hospital is accepting applications. Social workers function as part of interdisciplinary teams responsible for assessment, treatment, and court evaluations. Duties include treatment, documentation, court reports, and activities that involve family and community liaison. California license is a prerequisite, although social workers with recent MSWs or from out of state are eligible and have one to four years to obtain licensure with supervision provided.

Psychiatric Social Worker
Full-time position to perform skilled and intensive clinical social work with adults and their families. The selected applicant will have three years' experience providing psychiatric social work services, including diagnostic evaluations, crisis intervention, case management, and home visits; MSW degree from an accredited school of social work with field training in a psychiatric or clinical setting; bilingual (English/Spanish) skills; licensure or eligibility for licensure within one year of appointment; and a valid driver's license. Prefer experience providing family therapy and outreach services to emotionally disturbed youths and their families.

Social Work Supervisor III
Position provides administrative and clinical supervision to crisis intervention and time-limited treatment programs. The position is attached to the adult mental health services unit of a comprehensive mental health center. Program is looking for an individual who wishes to participate in our TQM efforts as well as work to develop a positive response to the changes in the health care industry. Master's degree from an accredited school of social work or counseling experience; or a bachelor's degree from an accredited school of social work and three years of social work or counseling experience; or a four-year degree in a human services field or related curriculum including at least 15 semester hours in courses related to social work or counseling and four years of social work or counseling experience. Special conditions: Prefer licensed or certified MSW with experience in a community mental health setting and/or training/experience in Beck's Cognitive Therapy.

Social Workers
Social work positions exist in medical centers, outpatient clinics, nursing home care units, and Veterans Outreach Centers. Specialized programs such as outreach to the homeless and treatment of posttraumatic stress disorder are an ongoing part of federal government's commitment to provide the best care to our nation's veterans. Professional career opportunities exist nationwide for individuals possessing an MSW.

Therapist Consultants
A nationally recognized community-based mental health center is looking for professionals to join our growing team. Opportunities available to work as a therapist–supervisor, substance abuse program, and therapist–supervisor, crisis stabilization program. Center has a team approach to treatment, quality clinical supervision, and supportive work environment. Candidates must have a master's degree in social work or PhD in clinical psychology with a minimum of three years of clinical experience and be license eligible.

Therapists

Per diem positions for experienced therapists at nonprofit psychotherapy center serving the lesbian, gay, and bisexual community. Free supervision hour provided. Black and Hispanic applicants especially encouraged. Supervisors and group therapists also needed.

Training/Systems Coordinator

Emergency services operation has an immediate full-time opportunity for a qualified individual to identify training needs of paid and volunteer staff for disaster services. Perform needs assessment and help the public become more aware of and prepare for potential disasters. Work requires a professional knowledge of human services—normally acquired through a bachelor's degree in social services, education, psychology, or a closely related field. Job requires professional level of disaster and emergency services experience—normally acquired through one or two years of paid or volunteer experience in emergency services.

Triage Intake Coordinator

Leader in national managed health care is seeking a triage coordinator to support its newest venture, a psychiatric and chemical dependency managed care company. Responsibilities include handling confidential client member calls, recording information, and counselor referrals. Assign appropriate case managers to calls that come in, handle follow-up calls, check eligibility of members when necessary. Assess emergencies and respond effectively to the urgency of these situations. Requirements include a bachelor's degree, preferably in the human services, and an interest in the mental health care field.

children and families

introduction
to part II

Social services agencies across the United States continue to battle the most severe psychosocial problems afflicting individuals and families. The extent, complexity, and seriousness of today's social problems are well known and documented daily on the front page of major newspapers across the country. The incidence and severity of poverty, infant mortality, unemployment, child abuse and neglect, drug and alcohol addiction, human immunodeficiency virus (HIV) and acquired immune deficiency syndrome (AIDS), crime, homelessness, and neighborhood violence, among other social ills, are escalating.

The problems families and children experience result from and are intertwined with housing, employment, income, health, and mental health. What makes families and children a distinct area of social work service is its focus on the family. Thus, for example, mental health is viewed less as an individual problem than in terms of its probable effect on the family unit.

The profound changes families have experienced over the past 50 years are evident in the disparity between the "ideal" family type—a husband, wife, and two or more children at home, with the husband as the sole breadwinner—and reality. Most U.S. families represent exceptions to the "ideal." In 1994, half of American children were living in a setting other than a "traditional nuclear family" (Vobejda, 1994).

Family today may mean a number of things: single-parent households; multigenerational families sharing a household; two-earner families; unmarried cohabitating partners, some with children, some without; "blended" families with remarried spouses; and others (Macarov, 1991). This variety of family forms suggests the broad range of services families may need to survive and thrive. Current trends are likely to continue, and new trends that will affect family dynamics and require new types of supports and services from social services agencies and social workers will emerge. Methods of intervention must adapt to meet changing needs and circumstances (Macarov, 1991).

In addition to the change in the family structure, there has been a change in the median household income, which decreased by 1.7 percent between

1989 and 1990, during which time there was a simultaneous increase in the number of people living in poverty (Johnson & Wahl, 1995). One possible factor in the rising family poverty rates may be an increasing number of premarital births combined with a high divorce rate. As a result, the proportion of children living with just one parent rose from 9 percent in 1960 to 25 percent in 1990 (Johnson & Wahl, 1995).

Dramatic increases in child poverty, homelessness, substance abuse, and violence exacerbate the strains on families. As a result, service needs are expanding. Burton-Nelson (1989) quoted Judy Hall, former NASW associate executive director, testifying before a House subcommittee:

> Some of the problems we see today—such as boarder babies with AIDS, or the prevalence of child abuse cases involving drug abuse by parents—were not typical in earlier decades. Many of the problems associated with today's child welfare cases will not be resolved simply by requiring parents to go to counseling or to get parenting education. In many instances, families need jobs, housing and income supports to stay together. (pp. 1, 7)

Changes in lifestyles and values have also affected the types of problems clients experience. For example—

- Gay and lesbian adolescents have been identified as a negatively stigmatized group that requires social support and intervention at the family and societal level (Morrow, 1993).

- With developments in modern technology and a more accepting social climate, surrogate parenting is now a more accepted form of family creation for infertile and involuntary childless couples. How surrogacy affects the family unit and the welfare of children has been identified as an area for social work intervention (Blyth, 1993).

- Because of increased life expectancy, more generations are likely to exist in family or kinship networks that may include spouses and former spouses, in-laws, children, and step-children (Johnson & Wahl, 1995).

NASW classifies children and families as distinct areas of practice. In 1993, child services ranked second among primary practice areas (following mental health), with 16.3 percent of members citing this as their major practice area; family services ranked fourth at 11.4 percent (Gibelman & Schervish, 1993).

Child and family services is an extremely broad area of social work practice, reflecting the breadth and depth of problems encountered by families and children today. Social workers may specialize according to type of problem, population, or service area. Specializations include adoption, child protective services, runaway and homeless youths, homeless families, foster care, home finding, day care, domestic violence, rape crisis service, resettlement and immigration, child prostitution and pornography, teen pregnancy, teen suicide, family life education, juvenile justice, and gay and lesbian adolescents. Of course, the problems encountered by families often cross-cut other areas of practice. For example, teenagers may have alcohol or substance abuse problems, and families may require mental health counseling.

Child welfare as an area of practice dates back to the origins of social welfare in this country and to the birth of the social work profession. It refers to "that part of human services and social welfare programs and ideologies oriented toward the protection, care and healthy development of children" (Barker, 1995, p. 57). As this service area has evolved, its boundaries have extended to meet changing human needs and social conditions. The earliest child welfare services centered on child protective services and foster care. Today child welfare encompasses, among other areas, family preservation, services to homeless families and runaway youths, and early intervention. Federal and state legislation has periodically been revamped to address burgeoning needs in this area. For example, the Adoption Assistance and Child Welfare Act of 1980 (P.L. 96-272) signified a new thrust in child welfare. A new emphasis on home-based programs to prevent out-of-home placement of children led to a rapid expansion of family preservation programs and services. This mandated shift in how child welfare services are conceptualized and delivered has left agencies scrambling to hire staff with the knowledge, values, and skills of family preservation (Hodges, Morgan, & Johnston, 1993).

Services to families and children are often provided in a volatile climate in which public opinion is loudly and persistently voiced. Stories about brutalities inflicted on children often end with indictments against child welfare systems and their social work personnel. Television news magazines seize on stories concerning the well-being of children because of the intrinsic public interest in them. The unfortunate conclusion to many of these tragic stories is that the family and children have long been known to the child welfare system. Media outrage fuels public outrage and the result is a cry that "something must be done."

The Future

Social workers in the field of child welfare services are cognizant of the changing demographics of their clientele: The population is increasingly multicultural and children who are members of racial and ethnic groups are disproportionately represented in the child welfare system (Liederman, 1995). In addition, the drug abuse epidemic that has ravaged the country in recent years has had a tremendous impact on the child welfare system. Familiar safety nets are no longer adequate to handle cases where substance abuse and addiction are involved. However, drug and alcohol abuse by both adults and children is not the only problem facing child welfare workers. HIV and AIDS have increasingly affected children, adolescents, and their families (Liederman, 1995). In 1993 the U.S. Department of Health and Human Services reported that if current trends continue, AIDS will soon rank in the top five causes of death for women, children, and adolescents (Liederman, 1995).

Social workers in the area of child welfare services will inevitably need to examine the issue of welfare reform and how it will affect the children and families who need services. Child welfare advocates, including social workers, have been advocating primarily for programs that promote parenting, encourage self-sufficiency, include quality child care, emphasize the prevention of adolescent pregnancy, and provide access to health care and affordable and safe housing (Liederman, 1995).

Given the diversity of problems, populations, and services within child and family services, it is not surprising that the settings in which social workers practice are similarly broad. Public agencies, however, often are given statutory responsibility for service provision, such as in the investigation of child abuse. As public social services agencies come under increasing public scrutiny and attack, contracting with voluntary agencies has become a popular alternative. The vast national network of nonprofit agencies providing services to families and children includes both sectarian and nonsectarian organizations.

References

Adoption Assistance and Child Welfare Act of 1980, P.L. 96-272, 94 Stat. 500.

Barker, R. L. (1995). *Social work dictionary* (3rd ed.). Washington, DC: NASW Press.

Blyth, E. (1993). Children's welfare, surrogacy and social work. *British Journal of Social Work, 23*, 259–275.

Burton-Nelson, M. (1989, July). Congress told of strains on child welfare. *NASW News*, pp. 1, 7.

Gibelman, M., & Schervish, P. H. (1993). *Who we are: The social work labor force as reflected in the NASW membership*. Washington, DC: NASW Press.

Hodges, V. G., Morgan, L. J., & Johnston, B. (1993). Educating for excellence in child welfare practice: A model for graduate training in intensive family preservation. *Journal of Teaching in Social Work, 7*, 31–48.

Johnson, G. B., & Wahl, M. (1995). Families: Demographic shifts. In R. L. Edwards (Ed.-in-Chief), *Encyclopedia of social work* (19th ed., Vol. 2, pp. 936–941). Washington, DC: NASW Press.

Liederman, D. S. (1995). Child welfare overview. In R. L. Edwards (Ed.-in-Chief), *Encyclopedia of social work* (19th ed., Vol. 1, pp. 424–433). Washington, DC: NASW Press.

Macarov, D. (1991). *Certain change: Social work practice in the future*. Silver Spring, MD: NASW Press.

Morrow, D. F. (1993). Social work with gay and lesbian adolescents. *Social Work, 38,* 655–660.

Vobejda, B. (1994, August 30). Study alters image of "typical" family. *Washington Post,* p. A3.

adoption

Adoption is both a legal and child welfare function and process in which a person, usually an infant or child, is taken permanently into one's home and, with the legal transfer of the individual from the birth parents to the adopting parents, is treated as though born into the adoptive family, with all rights and privileges therein (Barker, 1995). In recent years, many U.S. families have chosen to adopt children born in foreign countries, including Russia, Romania, Korea, and Vietnam.

Although adoptions occur through a variety of means, Barth (1995) identified four general adoption categories:

1. *Stepparent* adoptions refer to the adoption of a child by the spouse of a parent.

2. *Independent* adoptions occur when parents place children directly with adoptive families of their choice without an agency as an intermediary.

3. *Agency* (or relinquishment) adoptions are overseen by public or private agencies and occur when there is a voluntary or involuntary legal termination of parental rights to the child.

4. *Intercountry* adoptions involve adoption of foreign-born children by adoptive families.

In addition to these four categories, Barth (1995) discussed special-needs adoptions. These involve children who have a specific factor or condition (for example, ethnic background, age, membership in a minority or sibling group, or the presence of physical or emotional handicaps) that makes it difficult to place the child with adoptive parents without providing financial or medical assistance.

The Adoption Assistance and Child Welfare Act of 1980 (P.L. 96-272) provided the impetus for states to ensure that children were not left to linger in the foster care system. The legislation took a dual approach: (1) Provide family preservation services to strengthen families so that removal of the children is unnecessary or that children are returned to their biological parents as quickly as possible, and (2) when the goal of returning home cannot be achieved, free children for adoption. Embodied in this approach is the concept of *permanency planning,* "a systematic effort to provide long-term continuity in dependent children's care as an alternative to temporary foster placements" (Barker, 1995, p. 278).

Most social workers in the area of adoption provide direct services to all parties. Social workers offer nondirective counseling services to pregnant women on their options: abortion, retention, or placement of the child. Social workers also link pregnant women with needed medical, educational, housing, or financial services.

In addition, social workers conduct home studies of potential adoptive parents to evaluate the family and the physical and emotional environment for the child who is to be placed. As part of the assessment process, the social worker explores with the applicant family such issues as infertility, openness to adoption, willingness to accept a special-needs child, willingness to prepare for their new responsibilities, and the need to deal with adoption issues throughout the child's life.

If the home study results in approval, the process proceeds to matching a child with the prospective parents. When the match is made, the social worker helps prepare the child and adoptive parents for their initial and follow-up meetings. Information about the child is provided to the parents, who may be encouraged to join a parent support group.

Adoption has been described as a lifelong experience that may require a range of support services (Landers, 1993). A key role for social workers is to prepare adoptive parents to help children deal with their unique struggles. Postadoption services are a growing component of adoption practice as older adoptees deal with identity, loss, and self-esteem issues; medical or educational problems that may have a genetic or hereditary basis; and contact with birth parents.

Historically, adoption services have ceased once the child was placed in the adoptive home and the adoption was finalized. Even today, postadoption services are not always available. But social workers increasingly recognize the need for such services, especially with the growing number of families who are adopting older or special-needs children. Similarly, the increasing number of international adoptions has created a need for families to understand different cultures and backgrounds (Landers, 1993). Social workers in adoption and family service agencies have responded to these needs by establishing support groups for adoptive families and offering individual counseling. In addition, some agencies have established outreach programs for postadoption families, and social workers often visit adoptive homes to see how well the adoption process has worked for the family (Landers, 1993).

Love at First Sight

Anne Casey, a 32-year-old computer analyst, had recently been laid off from her job. With time on her hands, she decided to volunteer at a local residential child care facility for infants and very young children who have no place else to go. Many of these children were "boarder babies," children who were abandoned at birth. One of the infants Anne worked with was three-month-old Terrence, who was born HIV-positive.

After several weeks of volunteering, Anne realized that she had developed a strong attachment to Terrence. She thought about him all the time and wanted to make him a permanent part of her life. She talked with staff at the child care facility about adoption. Social workers there were honest with her about Terrence's questionable long-term prognosis. Although the immune systems of some babies born HIV-positive are able to self-correct, other babies develop full-blown AIDS. It was too early to tell with Terrence but the risks were certainly there.

Anne was not deterred. One of the social workers at the facility referred her to the county department of social services to begin the adoption application process. The department would need to conduct a home study for this single-parent adoption.

Madelyn Smith, the public child welfare agency's social worker assigned to this case by the Adoption Resource Branch, referred Terrence for a determination of eligibility for subsidized adoption, based on his at-risk (or special-needs) status. Subsidies are available to families that adopt special-needs children (including older children and children with disabilities) without a means test, although their financial situation is taken into account. The subsidy agreement specifies the amount of the assistance payment, the types of services or other assistance to be provided, and the duration of the agreement (Pecora, Whittaker, Maluccio, Barth, & Plotnick, 1992).

In this case Madelyn met with Anne several times to conduct the home study and to prepare the subsidy application. She also obtained financial information from Anne to determine if Anne was financially stable, in view of the fact that she had recently lost her job. Fortunately, Anne had accepted a full-time, salaried position at another company. Anne also agreed to attend weekly adoption courses for parents of children with special needs as well as monthly information sessions on HIV and its progression. Madelyn was impressed with Anne and her willingness to put the necessary energy into providing a quality home environment for Terrence. After consulting with her supervisor and the medical professionals on the multidisciplinary team at the residential facility, Madelyn determined that Anne would be allowed to adopt Terrence and receive a subsidy to help in the care of his illness.

In this case scenario, Madelyn carried out the social work function of assessment as she attempted to determine Anne's emotional and financial stability to parent an infant with HIV. Madelyn also identified future problems and used referral and organizational skills to ensure that proper resources and supports were in place to help Anne meet these challenges, such as the weekly adoption classes, the HIV information sessions, and the subsidy. In addition, Madelyn offered Anne support and counseling in making this major decision. Finally, Madelyn engaged in consultation both with her supervisor as well as the other members of the multidisciplinary team to get their feedback and suggestions.

References

Adoption Assistance and Child Welfare Act of 1980, P.L. 96-272, 94 Stat. 500.

Barker, R. L. (1995). *Social work dictionary* (3rd ed.). Washington, DC: NASW Press.

Barth, R. P. (1995). Adoption. In R. L. Edwards (Ed.-in-Chief), *Encyclopedia of social work* (19th ed., Vol. 1, pp. 48–59). Washington, DC: NASW Press.

Landers, S. (1993, May). After adoption: Aid ends, needs don't. *NASW News*, p. 3.

Pecora, P. J., Whittaker, J. K., Maluccio, A. N., Barth, R. P., & Plotnick, R. D. (1992). *The child welfare challenge: Policy, practice and research*. New York: Aldine de Gruyter.

child
abuse

In 1993, state child protective services agencies received and referred for investigation an estimated 2 million reports of alleged child abuse and neglect. The number of children reported annually to state child protective services agencies has more than tripled over the past 17 years for which data have been collected and maintained. More than 1 million children were substantiated as victims of child abuse and neglect in 1993. Of these, approximately 48 percent of cases were neglect, 24 percent were physical abuse, 14 percent were sexual abuse, and 15 percent were other forms of maltreatment (U.S. Department of Health and Human Services, 1995).

Child maltreatment is one of the primary reasons that parents and children are referred or reported to child welfare agencies. Although there is no universal definition for child maltreatment in the United States, Pecora, Whittaker, Maluccio, Barth, and Plotnick (1992) identified five major categories consistently used to codify such cases: physical abuse, sexual abuse, physical neglect, educational neglect, and psychological maltreatment. They also determined that although reporting rates for child abuse vary according to many different factors, low-income and ethnic-minority parents are disproportionately represented in the reporting statistics.

Public child welfare agencies carry the burden of managing the increase in the number of reported and substantiated child maltreatment cases without an equal increase in staff and resources. This challenge is especially great in cases of serious physical abuse or chronic physical neglect (Pecora et al., 1992).

Child protective services have recently been defined as human services "provided to children whose caregiver is not providing for their needs" (Barker, 1995, p. 56). Child protective services also refer to a range of interventions provided by social workers and other professionals on behalf of children who may be in danger of harm from others. Social workers in this area usually are employed by a public agency. They may also work for the courts or law enforcement agencies. Their primary job is to investigate situations in which a child may be at risk.

The goal is to ameliorate the situation, minimize further risk, and arrange for alternative placement and resources for the child at risk (Barker, 1995).

Although there has been improvement in recognizing and reporting cases of child abuse and neglect, social workers continue to face numerous obstacles in providing services. For example, parental substance abuse is highly correlated with child maltreatment and death, and poverty also appears to play a major role in abuse and neglect cases (Brissett-Chapman, 1995). Social workers are then faced not only with the child abuse issue but also with issues of substance abuse and a lack of familial and community resources.

A social worker in child protective services must be able to understand the importance of psychosocial interventions. Although various indicators of abuse have been identified, there is no definitive pattern and no universally accepted treatment; therefore, social workers must be able to interact with a multidisciplinary, multiagency team to monitor and ensure an effective plan of care that includes identification, planning, treatment, and follow-up (Brissett-Chapman, 1995).

Social workers in this area engage in a variety of social work functions, drawing on many different skills. For example, during the initial interview the social worker will use assessment and diagnosis skills to determine whether the child is at risk of further abuse and to arrive at an appropriate treatment for both the child and the family (Brissett-Chapman, 1995). The primary goal in cases of abuse and neglect is to protect the child by helping the parents to recognize and change behavior that is harmful to their children. In doing this the social worker will often carry out the social work functions of advice and counseling, enabling, referral, and support.

After providing the initial services the social worker must then determine if the detrimental conditions have been corrected. If the situation has not improved, the agency may initiate action, either with parental cooperation or by a petition to the court to mandate appropriate services or substitute care for the child (Brissett-Chapman, 1995).

Macrolevel interventions are also important in this area. Social workers must carry out the functions of identification and advocacy to call for public policy changes that improve services to abused and neglected children and their families (Brissett-Chapman, 1995).

Because the decision to remove a child is ultimately a legal one, social workers in child protective services routinely provide testimony to the court in its decisions about the disposition of such cases. Although the NASW Code of Ethics (NASW, 1994) is the guiding light for social workers, it is no longer a sufficient safeguard against malpractice suits (NASW Insurance Trust, 1990). Therefore, social workers must be prepared and professional when presenting case information.

A Day in Court

Joanie Clay is a social worker for the Spring Valley Department of Social Services (DSS) outside of Chicago. This is her first social work job since receiving her MSW eight months ago. She works in child protective services and carries a caseload of almost 60 children. One of her more troublesome cases has been seven-year-old Joshua. His mother has a serious problem with alcohol and drug abuse. His father works the night maintenance shift at the Spring Valley Hospital and spends his days asleep or at the local bar. Joshua's next door neighbor frequently feeds him and she reported the situation to child protective services.

During the past month, Joanie has been trying to work with the family to take better care of Joshua. However, on a recent icy day, Joanie visited the house and found no heat. Joshua was huddled on his bed in his underwear, and he had not eaten since the day before when the neighbor fed him a sandwich. He did not know where his mother or father were.

Joanie found clothes in the house and helped Joshua dress. However, she could not locate his coat and improvised by wrapping him in a blanket. She then drove Joshua to the DSS office, stopping first at the luncheonette outside the office to purchase a container of milk, a hamburger, and a cookie for him.

There are several supervised playrooms in the DSS office and Joanie left Joshua in the care of the volunteer then in charge. First, however, she showed Joshua where her desk was and assured him that she would be back to get him in a short while.

Joanie then sought out her supervisor to determine an immediate course of action. Together, they decided that the appropriate plan would be to get a court order to legally remove Joshua from the home and place him in foster care until a full investigation could be completed. Without voluntary parental consent, Joanie knew she would have to testify in court about her observations and actions in the case.

Joanie's supervisor worked with her about her forthcoming court appearance and explained the importance of being prepared, precise, and informed. Joanie also knew the importance of maintaining a professional demeanor in both her appearance and her testimony. She had observed other social workers testifying as expert witnesses during her training with the department, but this was her first time on the witness stand. As an expert witness, Joanie can answer hypothetical questions posed by lawyers and offer her own opinions.

By the time of the hearing, Joanie had visited the courtroom alone to get a feel for it. She also prepared index cards documenting her own educational and professional experience to refer to in the witness box. Joanie then reviewed the case thoroughly before the hearing and put it in chronological order.

On the day of the hearing, Joanie felt relaxed and confident. She knew that she would have to use precise and descriptive words and body language to help the judge see and hear what she had witnessed. Joanie's supervisor warned her about the cross-examination process, which can put social workers on the defensive. For example, she told Joanie not to answer more than the question asked, to be prepared for negative questions about herself and any previous decisions she had made, and to answer all questions truthfully and with confidence.

The time spent in preparation was worthwhile. Joanie was able to respond with confidence and authority to the questions posed to her. During cross-examination, she realized that the attorney was trying to identify inconsistencies in her statements. She was able to clarify and confirm her observations and findings to the apparent satisfaction of all concerned. In fact, the judge thanked her for her succinct and professional testimony.

As an expert witness, the social worker must tell the whole truth with objectivity and clarity (NASW Insurance Trust, 1990). As an expert witness, Joanie engaged in the functions of consultation and advocacy to improve the plight of the child at risk.

In this instance, Joanie represented child protective services in the agency's capacity to offer advice and counsel to the court to assist in judicial decision making. There are times, however, when a social worker may be called on to testify and the confidentiality of the social worker–client relationship becomes an issue. The granting of client privilege is decided on a case-by-case basis, although privileged communication clauses may be included in state licensing laws. Social workers often are not granted privileged communication status. An exception is a 1988 New York State Supreme Court ruling that statements made to a certified social worker in confidence could not be introduced in a criminal trial. The court upheld the application of the social worker–client privilege during the trial of a man accused of sexually abusing his nine-year-old daughter. The court held, in part, that changes in the use of privilege had to come from the legislature, not the courts, and that requiring social workers to disclose confidences in child abuse cases is for "the protection of the child and not . . . the punishment of the offender" ("New York Court Upholds Confidentiality," 1988, p. 14). Earlier, New York's privileged communication statute was upheld in the 1978 case of *Community Service Society (CSS) v. Welfare Inspector General* ("Communication Privilege," 1978).

References

Barker, R. L. (1995). *Social work dictionary* (3rd ed.). Washington, DC: NASW Press.

Brissett-Chapman, S. (1995). Child abuse and neglect: Direct practice. In R. L. Edwards (Ed.-in-Chief), *Encyclopedia of social work* (19th ed., Vol. 1, pp. 353–366). Washington, DC: NASW Press.

Communication privilege at stake in New York. (1978, November). *NASW News*, p. 7.

National Association of Social Workers. (1994). *NASW code of ethics*. Washington, DC: Author.

National Association of Social Workers Insurance Trust. (1990). *The professional as witness: Testifying with authority* [Video presentation]. Silver Spring, MD: Author.

New York court upholds confidentiality. (1988, October). *NASW News*, p. 14.

Pecora, P. J., Whittaker, J. K., Maluccio, A. N., Barth, R. P., & Plotnick, R. D. (1992). *The child welfare challenge: Policy, practice and research*. New York: Aldine de Gruyter.

U.S. Department of Health and Human Services. (1995). *Child maltreatment 1993: Report from the states to the National Center on Child Abuse and Neglect*. Washington, DC: U.S. Government Printing Office.

child welfare practice in public settings

The enormous task of preventing or ameliorating poverty and its manifestations has been delegated to the public social services systems. A public agency may provide services directly or purchase selected services from other public, voluntary, or proprietary agencies (Demone & Gibelman, 1989). There is a strong historical tie between the development of public social services and that of the social work profession (Specht & Courtney, 1994). The expansion of the social work profession, in fact, has paralleled periods of public social services expansion, most notably in the 1930s and 1960s.

When public social service agencies have been asked to do more, they have often confronted a host of barriers to their effectiveness, including large caseload size, insufficient personnel and financial resources, high staff turnover, and lack of community awareness and support (Horejsi, Walz, & Connolly, 1977; Pecora, Whittaker, Maluccio, Barth, & Plotnick, 1992; Rycraft, 1994). Problems of professional status, recruitment, retention, and burnout have long been identified with the public social services and attempts to correct these conditions have been hampered by the resulting negative reputation afforded this area of practice (Gibelman, 1983; Jayaratne, Chess, & Kunkel, 1986; Pecora et al., 1992; Zischka, 1981). Continuing problems include vacant or frozen staff positions resulting from budget cutbacks; caseload sizes ranging from 60 to 200 children per worker; and too little time and too few staff allotted to freeing children for adoption and recruiting adoptive families ("System Overload," 1991; Thompson, 1991a). Too often, lack of staff hinder the ability of public agencies to emphasize prevention services for troubled families. In Washington, DC, the court found that staffing shortages had contributed to the city's failure to provide adequate protection for the foster children in its care (Thompson, 1991a, 1991b).

High caseloads, low salaries, and lack of training opportunities continue to threaten the capability of child welfare agencies to prevent and ameliorate child abuse and neglect ("Feds Told About Child Welfare Morass," 1990). In fact, studies have shown that children are being harmed not only by their parents but by the public welfare system established to ensure their protection ("System-Overload," 1991). NASW past president Dorothy Harris, testifying before a House subcommittee, noted that "making our child welfare agencies fully functional, positive forces in the lives of children and families requires immediate efforts to recruit, retain and train large numbers of qualified staff" (as cited in "Staff Called Key," 1993, p. 6).

During the 1970s, many states eliminated training requirements for social workers, a movement known as "declassification." Results of a nationwide study of child welfare agencies showed that of 25 states responding, none required entry-level workers to have a BSW or MSW degree ("Study Shows Minimal Standards," 1987). However, some jurisdictions have begun to reclassify social work jobs. In the District of Columbia, for example, an MSW is required for people occupying positions titled "social work."

Nationwide, public social services agencies continue to report difficulties hiring and retaining public child welfare caseworkers, despite the ever-growing need for professionals within this sector and ongoing efforts to attract more social workers to this area of practice ("Child Welfare Panel," 1987; "Public Child Welfare's Crisis," 1986; Rycraft, 1994). Specifically, there have been problems maintaining an adequately large and culturally diverse workforce that reflects the diversity of the clientele (Liederman, 1995). The work is demanding and the conditions are often less than optimal, but there is the need and opportunity for social workers in public child welfare services (Harris, 1986).

In February 1990, the NASW Family and Primary Associations Commission formed an interorganizational task force on child welfare staffing issues. Members included representatives from the Child Welfare League of America, the American Public Welfare Association, and the National Center for Social Policy and Practice. The task force reaffirmed the need for staffing, hiring, and retention measures to ensure service provision by qualified child welfare professionals. The task force further concluded that efforts to improve child welfare systems should focus on the needs of urban and rural areas, differences in public- and private-sector pay levels, child welfare workers' safety and supports, training of supervisors, and collaboration between schools and agencies ("Group Presses Ahead," 1990).

Efforts to improve the service delivery capacity of public child welfare agencies are illustrated in the following discussion of the work of Clarice Walker, former Commissioner of the D.C. Commission on Social Services.

A Social Worker Heads Up a City Agency

[Note: The information for this case study is drawn from Mencimer, S. (1994, April 17). Reluctant bureaucrat. *Washington Post Magazine*, pp. 15–18, 28–30.]

In 1991, Professor Clarice D. Walker, a social worker who taught at Howard University and conducted research on foster care in five cities, testified as an expert witness against Washington, DC, in the case known as *LaShawn v. Kelly*. For social workers employed by the city's child welfare agency, this was a time of intense frustration. These social workers joined with child welfare advocates in accusing the city of not only failing to help vulnerable children but doing children great harm through grossly ineffective and often dangerous child foster care services.

As a result of the *LaShawn* case, the city was ordered to overhaul the foster care system. In order to do this, however, a new social services commissioner was needed for one of the most beleaguered agencies in the city government. The D.C. Commission on Social Services has a budget of $420 million and 2,800 employees. The commission is responsible for foster care, the juvenile justice and detention systems, welfare and food stamps, day care, early childhood development, paternity and child support, crime victim assistance, and all the city's programs for the homeless and the mentally and physically disabled.

Eight people had previously held the position of commissioner over the preceding five years and, in their search for a new leader, city officials turned to a person who was both an unlikely and an inevitable candidate. Although Clarice Walker was well known in academia and exhibited great expertise in her testimony, she had practically no bureaucratic experience. Walker accepted the job after being pressured by city officials to do so and began work in February 1992.

Although the D.C. Commission on Social Services is one of the largest, most unwieldy bureaucracies, the issues that Walker confronted are issues that social workers at any level of public administration may face. For example, despite the vast volume of cases handled, Walker faced tremendous difficulties modernizing the agency's infrastructure and computer systems as well as upgrading the qualifications and experience level of staff hired. Walker also learned that her job involved an unimaginable number of meetings, during many of which she tried to secure more money and resources. A typical day for Walker included meetings with staff, the city administrator, officials of Freddie Mac Home Loan Mortgage Corporation, and contractors who want to begin a program to prevent teenage pregnancies. Walker also made public appearances at conferences, ceremonies, and fundraisers.

Just these tasks are enough to fill a full day, but there is more. Walker was also responsible for managing the agency's budget, procurement, policy-making, and personnel. To develop a more efficient commission, Walker enlisted the aid of various consultants to examine how city money is spent in child care programs and to determine how the city can obtain federal money currently unavailable because the city has failed to meet federal standards.

In assuming her position, Walker developed priorities for the allocation of her time and attention. She explained that one of her major priorities was family services: "I am concerned about ensuring that in our delivery of social services, we are family centered—child focused but family centered—so that wherever we can touch a child's life, we also recognize that there is a family there" (p. 17).

Despite her intentions and strong will, Walker also had difficulty with the obstacles that confront all social workers, such as the escalation in substance abuse and its relationship to worsening social conditions. "The safety net you used to provide just isn't enough anymore," explained Walker. "Those programs in place are being challenged like never before" (p. 18). She also had to do battle with extremely time-consuming bureaucratic requirements to make even the smallest change in operating procedures or personnel.

Although Walker came to the job with great knowledge of child welfare and a desire to improve the system, it is difficult to assess her success simply because of the vastness of the problems she confronted. One of her major accomplishments was the improvement of the agency's tracking system, which, for the first time, was able to provide reasonably accurate information about the number of children being served and where they are located. However, Walker came to rejoice in the small victories, realizing that major changes are difficult and do not happen overnight.

Walker's efforts have been both praised and criticized. But unlike many administrators and direct services workers, Walker did not become cynical: "I don't feel like I have worn out yet. I have been energized by the challenge. I think if you can take a few chunks and tackle those problems, you can get some satisfaction." (p. 30)

Clarice Walker, who left the commissioner's job at the end of 1994 to return to her academic post, took on problems that would challenge the most seasoned administrator. She used her social work skills both in administering the agency and in working with and maintaining her staff. The social work functions she performed are numerous and include management, supervision, coordination, staff development, planning, and policy development. In addition, social work administrators are required to conduct needs assessments and program analyses and identify, develop, implement, and evaluate strategies to meet demands for accountability, efficiency, and effectiveness (Gowdy & Freeman, 1993).

One of the most important contributions of public social services agency managers is a willingness to examine new ways of operating. A fresh approach is extremely important in public social services agencies, which often become inflexible and resistant to change because they need to conform to state law and because there is relative permanence of employed staff (Ginsberg, 1995). As Clarice Walker quickly discovered, public social services managers must be knowledgeable not only about social work but also about accounting, law, and computer technology (Ginsberg, 1995).

Social workers in family and child services perform a number of roles in diverse practice settings, addressing a broad range of societal problems. In providing direct services, social workers assess the presenting situation, offer counseling and assistance, and coordinate the family's access to services in the community. In addition, social workers may participate in legal proceedings related to the determination of child abuse and neglect. Social workers may also use their supervisory skills to develop and administer programs, departments, or entire agencies. Social workers in the child welfare area also bring their advocacy skills to the surrounding community and help local groups organize to improve social institutions, systems, and practices (Liederman, 1995).

Reisch (1995) classified the three basic functions that social workers perform in public social services settings:

1. The *linkage* function helps clients access necessary programs and services. Examples include information and referral networks, legal services, support groups, and crisis hot lines.

2. The *therapeutic and control* function occurs through a variety of government-funded services, such as probation and adult protective services.

3. The *enhancement* function focuses primarily on the growth and development of the individual client or family. Such services are frequently referred to as "quality-of-life" services and include senior citizen centers and homemaker services.

These and other programs are designed to help individuals or families achieve enhanced self-support, to prevent abuse and neglect, to prevent inappropriate institutionalization, to link people with necessary services, and to help maintain family stability (Reisch, 1995).

References

Child welfare panel seeks to attract social workers. (1987, January). *NASW News*, p. 8.

Demone, H. W., & Gibelman, M. (Eds.). (1989). *Services for sale: Purchasing health and human services*. New Brunswick, NJ: Rutgers University Press.

Feds told about child welfare morass. (1990, May). *NASW News*, p. 13.

Gibelman, M. (1983). Social work education and public agency practice: Reassessing the partnership. *Journal of Social Work Education, 19*, 21–28.

Ginsberg, L. (1995). Public services management. In R. L. Edwards (Ed.-in-Chief), *Encyclopedia of social work* (19th ed., Vol. 3, pp. 1974–1981). Washington, DC: NASW Press.

Gowdy, E. A., & Freeman, E. M. (1993). Program supervision: Facilitating staff participation in program analysis, planning, and change. *Administration in Social Work, 17*, 59–79.

Group presses ahead on need to raise child welfare staff. (1990, April). *NASW News*, p. 14.

Harris, D. V. (1986, July). "Small miracles" can add up to big gains in child welfare. *NASW News*, p. 2.

Horejsi, J. E., Walz, T., & Connolly, P. R. (1977). *Working in welfare: Survival through positive action*. Iowa City: University of Iowa School of Social Work.

Jayaratne, S., Chess, W. A., & Kunkel, D. (1986). Burnout: Its impact on child welfare workers and spouses. *Social Work, 31*, 53–59.

Liederman, D. S. (1995). Child welfare overview. In R. L. Edwards (Ed.-in-Chief), *Encyclopedia of social work* (19th ed., Vol. 1, pp. 424–433). Washington, DC: NASW Press.

Mencimer, S. (1994, April 17). Reluctant bureaucrat. *Washington Post Magazine,* pp. 15–18, 28–30.

Pecora, P. J., Whittaker, J. K., Maluccio, A. N., Barth, R. P., & Plotnick, R. D. (1992). *The child welfare challenge: Policy, practice and research.* New York: Aldine de Gruyter.

Public child welfare's crisis under scrutiny. (1986, May). *NASW News,* pp. 1, 30.

Reisch, M. (1995). Public social services. In R. L. Edwards (Ed.-in-Chief), *Encyclopedia of social work* (19th ed., Vol. 3, pp. 1982–1992). Washington, DC: NASW Press.

Rycraft, J. R. (1994). The party isn't over: The agency role in the retention of public child welfare caseworkers. *Social Work, 39*, 75–80.

Specht, H., & Courtney, M. (1994). *Unfaithful angels: How social work has abandoned its mission.* New York: Free Press.

Staff called key to child welfare reform. (1993, June). *NASW News,* p. 6.

Study shows minimal standards for child welfare agency jobs. (1987, June). *NASW News,* pp. 1, 17.

System overload endangers kids, study says. (1991, March). *NASW News,* p. 16.

Thompson, T. (1991a, February 11). Trial reveals foster care's dead end in D.C. *Washington Post,* p. D1.

Thompson, T. (1991b, February 12). D.C. foster care workers tell of horrors, pressures. *Washington Post,* p. A1.

Zischka, P. C. (1981). The effect of burnout on permanency planning and management supervision in child welfare agencies. *Child Welfare, 60*, 611–616.

domestic violence

Television and radio can focus society's attention on social problems in a way that is immediate, dramatic, and lasting. For years, social workers have been working with the victims of domestic violence in courts, shelters, and hospital emergency rooms. But in 1994 the public's awareness of this long-standing problem reached an all-time high with the arrest of O.J. Simpson for the murder of his ex-wife and her friend. In the onslaught of publicity that followed, most of the country heard a tape recording of a 911 call made by Nicole Brown Simpson in which she begged for assistance against the intrusion of her ex-husband. Further reports revealed that the police had been called to the Simpson home at least eight times because of marital violence (Vobejda, 1994).

Four million women are beaten by their boyfriends or husbands each year; an average of 1,500 women died each year during the 1980s as a result of domestic violence (Vobejda, 1994). Domestic violence occurs across all socioeconomic groups.

It often seems incomprehensible that battered spouses remain in abusive relationships. Davis (1995) explained that women are often held captive by their own sense of powerlessness and that many women are socialized to accept sole responsibility for their marriage and their children. The fear that if they leave they will have to care for themselves and their children without assistance shackles many women with a sense of hopelessness and despair. In addition to regaining a sense of power, battered women's survival also depends on society's progression in recognizing the right for women to obtain employment and adequate financial compensation, as well as safe and affordable housing (Davis, 1995).

Assistance to battered women must take the form of a continuum of services to improve their economic and psychological independence. Shelters offer temporary protection in a safe environment where women can learn that the abuse they have suffered was not caused by their own failures. Shelters also help women develop confidence in their ability to live on their own, away from the abuser (Davis, 1995). In terms of economic support, women may turn to Aid to Families with Dependent Children (AFDC) for temporary assistance; however, they often need education and training to help them obtain permanent employment (Davis, 1995). Finally, battered women may need affordable housing and legal assistance to help them in the often long and contentious process of separation, divorce, and child custody arrangements (Davis, 1995).

During the past 20 years, a network of services has developed under public and private auspices across the country to address the problem of domestic violence. Grassroots coalitions have played an important role in service provision; these coalitions have also been instrumental in prodding public agencies to make use of available public funds to expand programs and services (Davis, Hagen, & Early, 1994). Social workers in this area work in family agencies, mental health clinics, shelters, public child welfare agencies, and hospitals or other medical facilities.

A Battered Woman Finds a Safe Haven

Becky is a 30-year-old mother of two young boys, ages three and five. She has been married for seven years and for four of those years, she has been beaten by her husband. It started when her husband lost his job at the railroad company. He collected unemployment and started drinking heavily. He then got a job driving a cab and would come home at all hours of the night, usually after having several drinks. The children were usually asleep when he got home, but Becky waited up even though she knew what would probably happen. She tried to make everything perfect so that he would not get angry, but there was always something.

Two nights ago, Becky's husband got home at midnight and was furious that she had left the light on at the end of the driveway. He yelled at her that she was wasteful and ungrateful, and he began pushing and hitting her. When the five-year-old ran downstairs and tried to stop the beating, his father pushed him into the wall, stormed out, and drove off into the night. Becky was horrified that he had pushed their son, so she gathered up the two boys, packed a small bag, and drove to Safe Haven.

Safe Haven is a small shelter for battered women and their children. Becky learned about it when she visited the department of social services last month. Estelle, the social worker at the shelter, welcomed Becky and her children. She gave them one of two empty rooms and a key to a locker where they could put their belongings. For the next two days, Estelle let Becky and the boys just relax and be together in safety. She met with Becky for an hour every day and with each of the boys for 30 minutes. Estelle then arranged for transportation to get the boys to and from school, and she alerted their teachers and the school principal that the boys were not to go with their father if he tried to pick them up.

Estelle then began working with Becky, who had a high school education but very little other training. Residents are generally allowed to stay at the shelter for six months, so Estelle worked with Becky to develop goals and life skills to maintain her own employment and residence and care for her two boys after she had to leave the shelter. Estelle helped Becky apply for AFDC for temporary support and signed Becky up for local computer training courses at the library, where Safe Haven had developed a working relationship.

Safe Haven had sent many previous residents to subsidized apartments in another town; although the boys would probably have to change schools, both Becky and Estelle thought the move might be for the best. Estelle and Becky liked the apartment and, since Estelle was with Safe Haven, the management agreed to hold it for six months or until Becky had the first month's rent.

In addition to her computer courses, Becky participated twice a week in a support group at Safe Haven. Becky learned that it was not her fault that her husband was abusive, that it was his problem rather than hers. Her sons participated in a support group for children that helped them understand the situation and to learn that violence is not an appropriate way to deal with frustration and anger.

After five months of training and counseling, as well as the job she had as a secretary at the telephone company, Becky had saved up enough money to make the first rent payment. Before Becky moved, Estelle helped her contact a lawyer who worked with Safe Haven and specialized in abuse cases. The lawyer agreed to counsel Becky for a minimal fee. In their new home, Becky and her sons finally felt free.

In this case Estelle exhibited the functions of assessment, identification, support, and counseling as she interacted with Becky and her sons. She also showed excellent coordination and organization skills as she had already developed relationships with many agencies such as the local library and the subsidized housing complex. Furthermore, by helping Becky get proper training, employment, AFDC benefits, and legal assistance, Estelle used the social work functions of referral, case management, and advocacy. Although all social work functions are important, advocacy is one area where social workers must get involved, especially in the realm of domestic violence. With their special training and focus on person-in-environment, social workers are able to "frame the problem of woman abuse within the larger social context and to advocate at a national level for policies that truly empower all women" (Davis, 1995, p. 787).

In a marriage between family and children's services and forensic social work falls the practice area dealing with abused and battered spouses in which social workers must deal with both the one abused and the abuser. It is in the intervention with those who abuse that the courts can become involved. Often an individual convicted of spousal abuse will be mandated to complete a program for abusers. Usually, it is social workers who begin and run these ongoing programs (Vobejda, 1994).

Breaking the Cycle of Violence

[Note: The information in this case study is drawn from "Program Helps Batterers Break Cycle." (1990, February). NASW News, p. 17.]

In Ann Arbor, Michigan, three social workers began a program to address the problem of spousal abuse. Alternatives to Domestic Aggression is sponsored by Catholic Social Services and is designed for men who batter their wives. Its nine-month, 36-session format addresses two problems in tandem, battering and substance abuse, because more than half of the men enrolled in the program suffer from some kind of substance abuse problem. The focus of the program is to educate the men about the "cycle of violence"—the mounting tensions, violent response, contrition, and reconciliation—and to teach them new methods of coping with conflict in a relationship.

According to David Garvin, one of the social workers involved in the program, many of the batterers were themselves abused as children. For these men, battering is a perpetuation of a multigenerational cycle and the only method they know for dealing with human conflict. To quote Garvin, "Battering is a learned behavior. Lots of abusers were battered as children or had witnessed their mothers or siblings being hit" (p. 17). Garvin's job is to re-educate his clients about how to operate in intimate relationships.

Another key issue for these social workers is the intervention of the state in domestic violence cases. According to Garvin, it should not be left to the victim of abuse to press charges because these victims can be easily intimidated or cajoled into dropping the charges. Sometimes timely intervention in spousal abuse cases can prevent these situations from getting worse or escalating to homicide.

The program suffers from a high dropout rate. Frequently men go into treatment to get their partners back and once this goal is accomplished, their motivation wanes. It is also a relatively long program with strict requirements. However, of those who have completed the program, none has relapsed.

When working with batterers, it is important that social workers be able to assess the situation and provide counseling without passing judgment. Social workers in this area must also enable battering spouses to recognize their ability to change their behavior. Social workers often use the functions of referral and coordination to help clients access other resources such as support groups.

References

Davis, L. V. (1995). Domestic violence. In R. L. Edwards (Ed.-in-Chief), *Encyclopedia of social work* (19th ed., Vol. 1, pp. 780–795). Washington, DC: NASW Press.

Davis, L. V., Hagen, J. L., & Early, T. J. (1994). Social services for battered women: Are they adequate, accessible, and appropriate? *Social Work, 39,* 695–704.

Program helps batterers break cycle. (1990, February). *NASW News,* p. 17.

Vobejda, B. (1994, June 19). Allegations focus national attention on society's response to spouse abuse. *Washington Post,* p. A18.

family
preservation
services

Intensive family preservation services (IFPS) have emerged as one of the most widely used models in family-based services to prevent out-of-home placement of children and preserve and strengthen the family unit (Bath & Haapala, 1993). IFPS focuses on the delivery of intensive and varied services in the home. Different programs have different foci but most are family centered, intensive, and relatively short-term (for three weeks to three months); available 24 hours a day; composed of clinical and concrete services; flexible; focused on limited objectives, such as stabilizing families in crisis; and delivered by social workers who carry small caseloads (Landers, 1994).

Family preservation services are intended to stabilize the family at risk, alleviate dangerous conditions, strengthen the family's ability to function in the community, and improve the family's problem-solving and coping skills (Compher, 1983). Many families who are referred for preservation services have multiple and complex problems involving child abuse or neglect, sexual abuse, alcohol and other drug abuse, and delinquency (Tracy, 1995).

Strengthening a Family's Functioning

Denise, a recent MSW graduate, works in the Family Preservation Unit at Northern Virginia Family Services. She usually carries a caseload of three families at a time and primarily engages in short-term crisis intervention. She recently closed a case and was assigned a new family, the Santiagos. Ms. Santiago is a divorced single mother with three boys, ages eight, five, and three. The boys' father still resides in El Salvador and provides no child support.

The family was referred by the five-year-old's teacher, who suspected child abuse and neglect. The boy is often dirty and she recently noticed a large bruise on his right leg and another one on his right arm. Denise calls Ms. Santiago and explains that the agency has been contacted because of concern for the family and that she would like to visit with them. Since Ms. Santiago speaks little English, Denise switches to Spanish. Ms. Santiago is initially wary of arranging an appointment and claims that everything is fine. However, Denise explains that once the agency receives a complaint, it is her responsibility to follow through. With reluctance, Ms. Santiago agrees to the home visit, which is scheduled for the next day.

Upon arrival at the Santiago home, Denise notices that the home is sparsely furnished but that it is neat and clean. The children are all home. Denise notices bruises on the arm of the five-year-old, but does not immediately question the mother about them. Instead, her initial goal is to make Ms. Santiago feel at ease and to establish a relationship with her. Denise talks with Ms. Santiago and the children to get an idea of their living situation. She finds out that Ms. Santiago works two full-time jobs to support her family. Therefore, she is rarely home and often leaves her children to care for themselves, with the eight-year-old in charge.

Denise recognizes the hurdles Ms. Santiago has faced to provide a decent home for her family, and suggests that perhaps the agency might be of some help. At that point, Denise mentions the bruises on the child's arm. Ms. Santiago responds that the child bruises easily and must have bumped into something. Denise arranges to come back the next day. Although she is concerned about the bruises, the children do not seem to be at immediate risk.

During the next session, Denise asks Ms. Santiago about leaving the children at home with an eight-year-old. Ms. Santiago appears confused and explains that in El Salvador an eight-year-old is generally considered old enough to care for younger siblings. Denise pursues the subject of the Salvadoran culture and how it differs from American culture. In subsequent sessions, Denise talks with Ms. Santiago about her general methods of discipline, and Ms. Santiago finally admits that the bruise on her son's arm happened when she grabbed him to break up a fight between him and his older brother.

From her talks with Ms. Santiago and the children, Denise determines that this is not a typical child abuse case. Ms. Santiago is struggling to make a living in this country and she is simply using the child care methods acceptable in El Salvador. Ms. Santiago explains that she would like to spend more time with her children, but that she cannot afford to work only one job. She is adamantly against receiving public support despite Denise's encouragement to apply for it. However, she does tell Denise that her sister lives in the area and gives Denise her phone number. Denise arranges to meet with the sister, who indicates her desire to help and agrees to come over in the afternoons and evenings to take care of the children after school.

Denise then talks with the mission director of Ms. Santiago's church, who agrees that the Santiago family is qualified for the adopt-a-family program sponsored by the church. This program matches financially stable families with families who are struggling to make ends meet. Assistance is provided in the form of weekly meals, help with child care, and even some financial donations.

Finally, with Ms. Santiago's consent, Denise arranges for her to attend a weekly support group for working mothers at the local library. A supervised play group for children under the age of six is provided there, and children ages six and over participate in their own facilitated group to deal with their feelings about their mothers' absence from the home and to learn ways to help make the situation easier.

In this case, Denise engaged in short-term crisis intervention. Through personal interviews with the client family, she performed the function of assessment and identification of any environmental problems. She also was sensitive to the cultural differences that affect childrearing practices. The interventions Denise used are based on a strengths perspective method of counseling in which the focus is on the client family's personal strengths and resources. In addition to providing concrete assistance, Denise links Ms. Santiago and her children to available services, such as the support groups and the adopt-a-family program at the church. In pursuing these creative sources of support, Denise carried out the social work functions of referral and coordination.

In addition to crisis intervention, social workers in family preservation usually draw on family systems, life space intervention, ecological, and cognitive–behavioral theories (Hartman, 1993). Depending on the presenting problem, services may be therapeutically oriented or they may be more focused on coordinating services or court supervision (Compher, 1983).

Tracy (1995) listed five primary goals of family preservation services:

1. to allow children to remain safely in their own homes

2. to maintain and strengthen family relationships

3. to stabilize the crisis situation that precipitated the need for placement

4. to increase the family's coping skills and competencies

5. to facilitate the family's use of appropriate resources.

Family preservation services are based on the assumption that many children could remain at home rather than enter the foster care system if services were provided earlier and more intensively (Tracy, 1995). Although this ideology is not new to the social work field, widespread implementation of family preservation programs did not occur until passage of the Adoption Assistance and Child Welfare Act of 1980 (P.L. 96-272). This act calls for "reasonable efforts" to prevent family disruption, reunite those families that have been separated, and place children in permanent rather than temporary settings if they cannot be reunited with their families (Tracy, 1995).

Family preservation services are for only those families at imminent risk of placing a child in the foster care system. Generally, these families have many problems and are involuntary clients in that they have not sought services and may be resistant to them because they perceive them as interference. Therefore, social workers must work to engage the client in a trusting relationship. Social workers in this field must use active listening skills and empathic communication during assessment to establish a nonjudgmental tone. After the assessment and diagnosis stage, the social worker uses support, advice, counseling, and referral functions to help the family overcome their sense of failure, hopelessness, and hostility (Tracy, 1995).

As with child protective services and foster care services, social workers providing family preservation services are employed by both public and voluntary agencies. The involvement of voluntary agencies in this area has resulted largely from the increased use of purchase-of-service arrangements. Small caseload size remains a critical factor in ensuring the delivery of intensive services.

Perhaps one of the strongest contributions of this approach is that of *empowerment*—recognizing and using the resources and personal strengths of the family members (Tracy, 1995). However, the primary goal of family preservation is the child's well-being, and there are times when the child is simply not safe in the home and must be placed in a safe, nurturing, and permanent environment. For this reason, family preservation services should be viewed within a continuum of child welfare services that includes both preventive work before a crisis evolves as well as long-term, supportive services, a range of temporary out-of-home placements, family reunification services, and adoption and postadoption services (Hartman, 1993).

References

Adoption Assistance and Child Welfare Act of 1980, P.L. 96-272, 94 Stat. 500.

Bath, H. I., & Haapala, D. A. (1993). Intensive family preservation services with abused and neglected children: An examination of group differences. *Child Abuse & Neglect, 17*, 213–225.

Compher, J. V. (1983). Home services to families to prevent child placement. *Social Work, 28*, 360–364.

Hartman, A. (1993). Family preservation under attack. *Social Work, 38*, 509–512.

Landers, S. (1994, July). Preserving families: A balancing act. *NASW News*, p. 3.

Tracy, E. M. (1995). Family preservation and home-based services. In R. L. Edwards, (Ed.-in-Chief), *Encyclopedia of social work* (19th ed., Vol. 2, pp. 973–983). Washington, DC: NASW Press.

foster care

A child is placed in foster care when it is determined that the parent or care-taker is unwilling or unable to care for the child (Fontana & Moolman, 1991). Foster care takes place in single-family homes, group homes, and residential settings (Pecora, Whittaker, Maluccio, Barth, & Plotnick, 1992). The intent is a temporary placement while a permanent plan is made and implemented. In reality, however, "temporary" too often turns into "permanent," and many chil-dren have lingered in foster care or been switched from one foster home to another. The number of children in foster care continues to rise. Between 1986 and 1991, the number grew by 53 percent, from 280,000 in 1986 to 429,000 in 1991 (Landers, 1994).

Foster care services generally are provided by nonprofit agencies financed by public agencies, which are legally charged with responsibility for the child through purchase-of-service arrangements. There are variations in foster care service provision among the states, but there are more similarities than differ-ences due to the mandates of the Adoption Assistance and Child Welfare Act of 1980 (P.L. 96-272). Although the effectiveness of the foster care system has been questioned in the past, a recent study examined highly traumatized chil-dren over an 18-year period and revealed that 60 percent of them were sus-tained by foster care and went on to lead well-adjusted lives ("Study: Foster Care Can Work," 1991).

Social workers in foster care evaluate children and their families to help determine the need for placement; evaluate potential foster homes, through a home study process, as to appropriateness for placement; monitor the foster home during placement; and help legal authorities and the family determine when it is appropriate to return the child to the natural family (Barker, 1995).

Ryan Needs a Home

Ryan, a five-year-old African American, was abandoned by his mother in a train station. Police found Ryan curled up in a corner, dirty and hungry. They called the department of human services intake division, and a social worker, Sue Williams, came to get Ryan.

First, Sue took Ryan to the local hospital for an examination; their next stop was a fast-food restaurant.

Ryan was withdrawn and frightened. He would shake his head in response to questions but would not talk. Sue took Ryan back to the office, where her supervisor had already begun the search for an immediate foster care placement for Ryan until his family could be located or other more permanent plans could be made for him. Both Sue and her supervisor knew that the foster parents selected for Ryan must be able to offer him the emotional support he desperately needed following his abandonment. Fortunately, they found such foster parents in the McKinleys.

Sue called the McKinleys and told them everything she knew about Ryan and his situation while Ryan busied himself with a coloring book in the agency's playroom. The McKinleys already had one adopted child and two foster children living in their home, but agreed to take Ryan too. Sue attended to the paperwork necessary to obtain a clothing voucher, and she and Ryan stopped at a local store to buy him a change of clothes, pajamas, and toiletries. Then they went to the McKinleys.

Sue stayed with Ryan and the McKinley foster family for 90 minutes, easing Ryan's transition into yet another unfamiliar place and updating the McKinleys about his situation. Sue promised Ryan that she would return the next day to check on him, and then scheduled several more visits in the days following Ryan's placement. Sue discussed with the foster parents the need to enroll Ryan immediately in the local public school, where he would enter kindergarten. Ryan's possible adjustment reactions to a new school were also reviewed.

Back at the office, Sue processed requisitions to obtain an emergency clothing allowance for Ryan, applied for Medicaid on his behalf, and referred him to a child psychiatrist for a complete psychiatric evaluation. She then tried to phone Ryan's family, but the number had been disconnected. She mailed a certified letter asking them to contact her as soon as possible, but she was not optimistic about hearing from them.

Because children coming into the foster care system have experienced or are at risk of physical, sexual, or emotional abuse, the social worker's initial focus is on crisis intervention—ensuring a safe and secure environment for the child for as long as necessary. The actual determination of abuse and neglect occurs either in other divisions of the agency or in the courts. It is essential that the foster care worker coordinate with the child protective services social worker so that long-term plans can be made for the child.

Should there be a legal determination that the child has in fact been abused, the foster care worker becomes the primary provider of services to the entire family. A plan for the family as well as the child is prepared, detailing all of the recommendations of the court regarding conditions and requirements for reunification. For example, if a judge ordered Ryan's mother to receive detoxification and then after-care substance abuse services, these services would become part of the service plan.

Implementing the service plan involves the foster care worker in the functions of information and referral and case management. Parent education, substance abuse counseling, individual and family therapy, psychiatric evaluations for the parents and the child, job training, and other services that may be recommended to promote the reunification of the family are provided by an array of community agencies. Barker (1995) defined the social work function of *referral* as

> The social work process of directing a client to an agency, resources, or a professional known to be able to provide a needed service. This process may include knowing what the available resources are, knowing what the client's needs are, facilitating the client's opportunity to partake of the service, and following up to be certain that the contact was fulfilled. (p. 318)

The foster care worker must see that referrals are made to appropriate agencies, that there is follow-up to ensure that the services are in place and being used, and that the services provided to the child and the family are coordinated. The social worker also arranges family visits, as per court orders, and makes periodic and scheduled appearances in court to report to the judge about case progress.

Social workers in foster care must engage in an array of professional functions, including assessment, identification, support, counseling, enabling, and referral. In the preceding example, Sue's interventions with and on behalf of Ryan illustrated the concrete and practical tasks involved in foster care work. Emergencies are the norm in this field of practice and the unexpected must be anticipated.

Some children from troubled families have severe emotional problems that affect the success of foster care placements. In the following example, alternatives to foster care are considered.

An Unsuccessful Placement and the Search for Options

Joanne Medley is a social worker in the out-of-home placement unit of Family and Child Services in Chicago. Under contract with the Cook County Department of Social Services, Family and Child Services, a nonprofit agency, provides intensive services to children in out-of-home placement.

On Monday morning, Joanne receives a call from Mrs. Elkin, the foster mother of nine-year-old Joseph Smith, asking that he be removed from the home immediately. The previous evening, Joseph had a violent outburst. He was verbally abusive to the foster mother and then hit a younger foster sibling over the head with a baseball bat. The younger child had to be taken to the emergency room, where he received 10 stitches in his forehead.

Joanne immediately requests the use of an agency car to visit the foster home. While she awaits approval, she reviews the case record.

Background

Joseph came into foster care a little over a year ago. He and his three siblings were left alone in their home for several hours and a neighbor found the two youngest children locked in a room with the door tied shut. The children had attended school only sporadically. The home was in filthy disarray and crack cocaine was found on the premises.

Following the removal of the children from the home, the mother disappeared and has not been located. The identity of Joseph's father has not been revealed. The only known relative is the maternal grandmother, who is recuperating from a stroke and is unable to care for Joseph or his siblings. A termination of parental rights hearing is scheduled in two months; pending the outcome of that hearing, Joseph may be legally free for adoption.

Joseph has serious emotional, social, and academic problems. He often uses profane and sexually explicit language and exhibits aggressive behavior toward his peers and open defiance toward most authority figures. Before he was placed in the Elkin home two months ago, Joseph had lived in five different foster homes in one year and had exhibited adjustment problems in all of them. One foster parent had, in her words, "gone beyond the breaking point" and had whipped Joseph with a belt. Consequently, Joseph was removed from that home and then experienced three more unsuccessful placements. The several changes in foster homes also meant changes in schools; Joseph is far behind in school and has already been left back one grade. He was scheduled to begin weekly therapy sessions but refused to go.

Immediate Intervention

The issue is clear: Mrs. Elkin has exhausted her personal resources and patience and another placement must be found for Joseph today. Joanne calls the Home for Boys, a residential care facility in Chicago, to see if they will take Joseph on an emergency basis. Mary, the social worker there, says that she will need to speak with the director and will call back that afternoon. Joanne then drives out to the Elkin home.

When Joanne arrives, Mrs. Elkin informs her that Joseph has taken off on his bicycle and she has no idea where he has gone. She had told him to go to his room to await Joanne's arrival, but instead he blurted profanity and left abruptly. On a hunch, Joanne calls Mrs. Cheddar, the foster parent of two of Joseph's siblings. Yes, Mrs. Cheddar responds, Joseph is there with his sisters. Mrs. Cheddar had tried to reach Joanne at the agency just a short time ago.

Joanne talks with Mrs. Elkin to see if there is any possibility that she would continue to keep Joseph. Joanne is not surprised that the answer is no. Mrs. Elkin explains that she cannot risk the potential danger to the other children. She is afraid that something even more serious will happen next time. It is clear that Mrs. Elkin is emotionally distraught about the events of the previous evening and that her assessment of the potential danger is realistic. Joanne talks with Mrs. Elkin for several minutes to reassure her about her decision and to thank her for her efforts to work with Joseph. She then asks Mrs. Elkin to pack up Joseph's things.

Joanne then drives over to the home of Mrs. Cheddar. Joanne and Joseph have a good relationship, stemming from the several outings they have taken together, including a recent trip to the zoo. Joanne asks to speak with Joseph alone, and they go to the kitchen to talk. Joanne asks Joseph about the events of the previous evening. As is his pattern, Joseph externalizes all responsibility and blames the younger child for initiating the fight; he feels that his actions were justified. Joanne then calmly but firmly reminds Joseph of their past discussions about the use of profanity and violence and the consequences of this behavior. She explains that Mrs. Elkin is so fearful of more harm to the other children that she cannot let Joseph return.

Joseph's response is surprising. Instead of playing his usual tough-guy role, he quietly sheds a few tears and allows Joanne to hug him. Joanne then explains that she will take Joseph back to the office and they will find a place for him to stay while she investigates longer-term possibilities.

When they arrive back at the office, there is a phone message from Mary at the Home for Boys. The facility can accept Joseph, but only for 30 days. Joanne is relieved but knows that it will take a lot of work to find an appropriate long-term placement for Joseph. Beginning tomorrow, psychological tests will be scheduled, along with a full evaluation at the local psychiatric hospital. Joanne has already spoken with her supervisor about the possibility of placing Joseph in a residential treatment center.

Joanne takes Joseph to lunch so that she can tell him about the Home for Boys and what will happen next. Joseph has again adopted his tough-guy stance and shows no emotion at the news of yet another placement. Joanne again brings up the subject of therapy and asks him to think about it some more.

The Plan

Joanne arranges for an aide to pick up Joseph's things from the Elkin home and take them to the Home for Boys. She then drives Joseph to the home and introduces him to Mary. Before she leaves, Joanne talks with Joseph about immediate plans: Joseph will attend school on the premises, a visit with his brother and sisters will be arranged for the weekend, and appointments to see some special doctors will be scheduled. Joseph does not ask about these doctors, which is out of character, but he is clearly distracted by his new surroundings and is eager to break away.

Back in the office, Joanne makes a list of the arrangements that must be made for Joseph. These include referrals for psychological and psychiatric testing and initiating the process of finding a residential treatment facility that will be able to take Joseph within the next 30 days. Joanne schedules a conference with her supervisor to discuss this case and to seek direction on possible residential placements. She then turns to the stack of phone messages awaiting her attention.

In this case, Joanne worked with both Joseph and the foster parents. She used the functions of assessment and identification to determine the nature and extent of the presenting problem, and then offered support and counseling to both clients. Information and referral are also important skills as evidenced by her use of psychological and psychiatric referrals. Crisis intervention is again a necessary mode of intervention. Finally, Joanne engaged in coordination and negotiation to access other community services that are necessary for Joseph.

References

Adoption Assistance and Child Welfare Act of 1980, P.L. 96-272, 94 Stat. 500.

Barker, R. L. (1995). *Social work dictionary* (3rd ed.). Washington, DC: NASW Press.

Fontana, V. J., & Moolman, V. (1991). *Save the family, save the child: What we can do to help children at risk*. New York: E. P. Dutton.

Landers, S. (1994, July). Preserving families a balancing act. *NASW News*, p. 3.

Pecora, P. J., Whittaker, J. K., Maluccio, A. N., Barth, R. P., & Plotnick, R. D. (1992). *The child welfare challenge: Policy, practice and research*. New York: Aldine de Gruyter.

Study: Foster care can work, despite odds. (1991, April). *NASW News*, p. 16.

homeless families

For a growing number of families for whom the ravages of poverty, lack of affordable housing, and unemployment have diminished life's options, home may be a shelter, welfare hotel, or the streets. In fact, families are the fastest growing segment of the homeless population ("Families Swelling Ranks of the Homeless," 1988). A "typical" homeless family is made up of a single parent and two or three (often preschool) children. Most homeless parents are not substance abusers or mentally ill; they have simply fallen through society's safety net. In the following vignette, corporate downsizing has taken its toll.

A Family on the Streets

Greg was 22 years old when he married Jenny, who was 20 years old and five months pregnant. Greg was a construction worker for Burlington Works and he was helping to build the new Central Bank building for $12 an hour. Greg and Jenny had a small, sub-standard efficiency apartment, but at least it was a roof over their heads.

Two months after Greg and Jenny's marriage, Burlington Works cut Greg's pay to the minimum wage of $4.25 an hour. Jenny began to skip her obstetrician appointments to save money. Two weeks later Greg was fired. The construction foreman explained that the bank job was almost complete and no more new construction was anticipated until next year at the earliest. Greg and Jenny were scared; they could not afford to pay their rent. There were no family resources to call upon; Jenny's mother was deceased and her father was an alcoholic with whom she had purposely lost contact several years ago, and Greg had not spoken to his parents since he moved out when he was 15 years old. They had no other relatives and few friends in the area, so they moved into their old, rusted station wagon.

When Jenny went into labor, she and Greg went to the emergency room of the county hospital. There Jenny gave birth to a healthy, although slightly underweight, baby girl they named Alicia. Greg told the social worker at the hospital that they had no home and had been living in their car. The social worker talked to

Greg and Jenny about their options and then referred them to the Streetwork Project in Burlington, which provides year-round assistance to homeless families.

When Jenny, Greg, and Alicia arrived at Streetwork, they were assigned a social worker, Carol Marks. In an initial meeting with Jenny and Greg, Carol learned that Greg had a high school education and some experience in construction and auto repair and that Jenny needed one more year to earn her high school diploma. Carol was aware that the young family needed immediate shelter, and fortunately, there was an available room in the emergency shelter at Streetwork. Because they also needed long-term assistance, she arranged to meet with them daily to help Greg find employment and to help Jenny get her General Equivalency Diploma. Carol also arranged for Alicia to receive immunizations and a complete health assessment.

As Carol counseled Jenny and Greg she became aware of their troubled lives, and she urged them both to go to self-help groups. She suggested Adult Children of Alcoholics for Jenny and a fathering group for Greg. Carol believed that these opportunities would allow them to develop their socialization skills and form a support network of peers. She also advised them on the importance of family planning and arranged for them to meet with a Planned Parenthood counselor who came to Streetwork every two weeks.

Carol enjoyed working with Jenny and Greg. They were young and had fallen into the trap of homelessness and poverty, but they were motivated to change their circumstances. Some of Carol's clients had been homeless so long they had given up hope, but Jenny and Greg actively participated in counseling sessions with her and attended the group meetings she suggested. Shortly after their arrival, Greg began an auto repair job with the county. Carol helped them open a banking account and with guidance and support, they were on their way to self-sufficiency.

In addition to direct services, Carol used her referral skills when she arranged for Greg and Jenny to meet with the Planned Parenthood counselor and attend group support meetings. She also engaged in the function of enabling by helping them maximize their self-help skills to find employment and finish high school.

The high mobility of the homeless population makes it impossible to arrive at a precise number of homeless people in the United States. The traditional stereotype of a homeless person is a white, alcoholic male. But in fact homelessness affects men, women, and children of all races and ages (Bloom, 1990; Connell, 1987). A recent study of homelessness in 26 cities revealed that the number of homeless families is now equal to the number of homeless single men ("In Brief," 1994a). One reason homeless families are not visible is that they often live in cars or makeshift accommodations away from busy downtown areas.

Another issue that has complicated measurement of the homeless population is the lack of consensus in defining homelessness. Although most people agree that "homeless" refers to people who do not have a place to live that is either owned or rented, there is less agreement about whether it also refers to people who live with others for long periods of time or who reside in single-room-occupancy hotels (First, Rife, & Toomey, 1995). Definitions of homeless families are also unclear. People are usually counted as part of a homeless family only if they have dependent children who are homeless with them; if their children are staying with someone else, the parents are classified as single adults, a practice that ignores the devastating effect of homelessness on the family (First, Rife, & Toomey, 1995).

Almost every study or report presents a different statistic; however, one fact remains consistent: The number is steadily increasing. Why are so many people homeless? Several generally accepted explanations for homelessness have been offered: deinstitutionalization, lack of adequate housing, lack of community resources, poverty, and a decrease in federal support programs (Bloom, 1990; Hall, 1990). Unemployed people or those earning low wages usually are not able to purchase medical insurance, and their illnesses can force them into extreme poverty. Their homelessness in turn denies them the network of supportive relationships that is essential to mental health. As a result, every effort is made to reunite homeless mentally ill people with their families.

The homeless mentally ill population faces a wide range of problems for which comprehensive services are rare. Often they are excluded from programs for homeless people because they are mentally ill, and they are excluded from services for mental illness because they are homeless ("Hearing Focuses," 1991). Organizations such as the National Alliance for the Mentally Ill work to support families with mentally ill members and to increase support for the treatment of and research into severe and chronic mental illnesses (Hall, 1990).

For families with children, the cost of housing has been a major contributor to homelessness. Housing policy experts say that the real estate boom of the 1980s resulted in increased housing costs and fewer affordable rental options (Thompson, 1993). Urban renewal efforts that have swept through many areas of the country have replaced older, low-cost, inner-city dwellings with downtown shopping malls and other developments (Bloom, 1990). In addition to the urban housing crunch, an increasing number of rural farmers have lost their homes to foreclosures resulting from falling crop prices and rising operating costs (Bloom, 1990; Connell, 1987).

Homelessness and poverty are inextricably linked as both continue to increase throughout the United States (Hall, 1990). Unfortunately, because of a low minimum wage and constantly rising costs, employment is no guarantee against homelessness. In fact, nearly 25 percent of homeless people are employed (Hall, 1990; "In Brief," 1994b). In addition, many workers and their families have migrated to "boom towns" in remote areas that offer many low-paying jobs but few opportunities for low-cost housing. As a result, many families in these areas live in homeless shelters, bunkhouses, cars, campgrounds, and abandoned buildings ("In Brief," 1994b).

Homeless families often move from inexpensive, substandard housing to overcrowded settings with extended family or friends, and finally into shelters, if there is room (Hall, 1990). Although homeless families already lack stability in their lives, family members are often separated if there is not enough space to house them together (Thompson, 1993). In 1991, shelters in Maryland turned away 38,246 homeless people, half of whom were families and children (Thompson, 1993). And a study by the National Coalition for the Homeless showed a dramatic 49 percent increase in families in emergency shelters in the District of Columbia between 1990 and 1991. For families turned away from shelters in Washington, DC, there is a waiting list for public housing; in June 1993, 12,000 names were on the list (Thompson, 1993).

Children in homeless families, as well as homeless youths who have been separated from their parents and siblings, often face a number of psychological and physical problems. Statistics confirm that children are the fastest growing group of the homeless population in the United States (Hiratsuka, 1989). The estimated 700,000 homeless children in the United States are twice as likely as other children to develop chronic illness. They are also more likely to fail in school and to experience mental health problems ("Campaign for Homeless," 1989). They are forced to live with no sense of privacy or ownership. They are often scared and alone and, because they have had to grow up too fast, they are often pessimistic and cynical. Social workers who work with runaway and homeless youths must be able to practice the following social work functions (Bass, 1995):

- Outreach—Social workers need to be able to work with youths in areas where the youths are most comfortable.

- Intake and assessment—Social workers must be able to assess the child's situation adequately. For example, there may be a need for a referral to a treatment program or the child may be in a potentially abusive situation.

- Case management and coordination with other service providers—It is essential that social workers coordinate with other service providers in order to provide the most complete array of services.

- Information and referral—Information and referral to appropriate agencies are essential social work functions when dealing with this population group.

- Aftercare—Social workers must help the youths they encounter develop comprehensive plans for their own care.

- Advocacy—Social workers who work with youths are in the best position to identify community needs and advocate for necessary service development.

A recent study of homeless students in Madison, Wisconsin, revealed that more than two-thirds performed below their grade level and between one-third and one-half exhibited behaviors indicative of a need for further psychiatric assessment (Ziesemer, Marcoux, & Marwell, 1994). As the authors of the study explained, "Homelessness indicates a potential risk to a child's ability to succeed in school and community environments—the risk is substantial for a majority of children" (Ziesemer et al., 1994, p. 665).

In 1987 Congress responded to the growing national crisis of homelessness and enacted the Stewart B. McKinney Homeless Assistance Act (P.L. 100-77).

This act specifically addressed the problem of educating homeless children and awarded federal grants to states for the education of homeless children and the removal of barriers to school attendance for this population. However, the federal grants did not provide any money to states for direct services, and although the intent of the legislation is praiseworthy, the lack of adequate funding has resulted in little, if any, change in most states (Hiratsuka, 1989).

A demonstration project conducted by the National Health Care for the Homeless Program and funded by the Robert Wood Johnson Foundation and Pew Memorial Trust sent teams of physicians, social workers, nurse practitioners or physicians assistants, and medical–clerical assistants to 19 cities to provide health care screening, assessment, treatment, and referral in shelters and other facilities for homeless people. Statistics on the health problems of the 18,000 homeless participants showed that the largest percentages of clients were afflicted with mental disorders, emotional disturbances, and active alcoholism ("Project Reports 18,000 Homeless Treated," 1986). Social workers provided a range of services, including care and referral services, advocacy for clients who needed entitlement benefits, case management in coordinating services, and skill development services.

Social workers work with homeless people in both public and private settings, sectarian and nonsectarian. The nonprofit sector operates most of the homeless shelters in the United States. In direct service, social workers counsel and advise clients on ways to decrease stress and alleviate crises, and they provide referral services when necessary.

Social workers can also get involved in program planning and community organization to benefit and empower homeless people. For example, many more shelters are needed for short-term, immediate emergency needs and there is a longer-term need for low-cost housing options. Social workers are already very involved in coordinating a new emphasis on home ownership as private nonprofit organizations purchase housing units, renovate them, and then sell them at low interest for local tax benefits (Bloom, 1990).

Ziesemer et al. (1994) outlined the key tasks of social workers involved in the area of homelessness. Social workers must help those who are already homeless, and they must also work to change conditions and prevent an increase in the numbers of poor and homeless people in the future. To do this social workers take on advocacy roles and work to help homeless families deal with the multiple stressors in their lives. Some changes that may help improve the plight of homeless people are keeping shelters open all day, providing day care and preschool programs to homeless children, allowing homeless families to stay together, and providing support services during a shelter stay as well as follow-up services after departure.

Furthermore, in order to make real and lasting change, social workers must exercise the function of coordination. They must work with other primary service providers in health care and education as well as secondary service providers such as transportation and parks employees (Hall, 1990). Such a multidisciplinary approach is essential in order to provide a comprehensive service network to the homeless population.

References

Bass, D. (1995). Runaways and homeless youths. In R. L. Edwards (Ed.-in-Chief), *Encyclopedia of social work* (19th ed., Vol. 3, pp. 2060–2068). Washington, DC: NASW Press.

Bloom, M. (1990). *The drama of social work.* Itasca, IL: F. E. Peacock.

Campaign for homeless hits high gear. (1989, February). *NASW News*, p. 3.

Connell, S. (1987). Homelessness. In A. Minahan (Ed.-in-Chief), *Encyclopedia of social work* (18th ed., Vol. 1, pp. 789–795). Silver Spring, MD: National Association of Social Workers.

Families swelling ranks of the homeless. (1988, March). *NASW News*, p. 4.

First, R. J., Rife, J. C., & Toomey, B. G. (1995). Homeless families. In R. L. Edwards (Ed.-in-Chief), *Encyclopedia of social work* (19th ed., Vol. 2, pp. 1330–1346). Washington, DC: NASW Press.

Hall, J. A. (1990). Homelessness in the United States. In L. Ginsberg et al. (Eds.), *Encyclopedia of social work* (18th ed., 1990 suppl., pp. 159–174). Silver Spring, MD: NASW Press.

Hearing focuses on severe mental illnesses. (1991, November). *NASW News*, p. 17.

Hiratsuka, J. (1989, March). Homeless kids face barrier to schooling. *NASW News*, p. 3.

In brief. (1994a, April). *NASW News*, p. 7.

In brief (1994b, September). *NASW News*, p. 10.

Project reports 18,000 homeless treated. (1986, July). *NASW News*, p. 5

Stewart B. McKinney Homeless Assistance Act of 1987, P.L. 100-77, 101 Stat. 482.

Thompson, T. (1993, June 27). D.C. has scant help to offer families with nowhere to go. *Washington Post*, p. A1.

Ziesemer, C., Marcoux, L., & Marwell, B. E. (1994). Homeless children: Are they different from other low-income children? *Social Work, 39,* 658–668.

parent education

Parent education is a service that may be recommended for parents who have abused or neglected their children, teenage parents who lack knowledge of child development and childrearing, or parents about to adopt a special-needs child. Social workers assess the need for this service, recommend and refer clients to parent education programs, and often run the groups. The following example, which describes an actual program, highlights how these groups function.

Teaching Parenting Skills

[Note: The information in this case study is adapted from Brown, D. L. (1994, June 27). Helping mothers to get a handle on parenthood. *Washington Post*, p. B1.]

The Parent Empowerment Program teaches specific, concrete parenting skills to African American parents in an inner-city community. Social workers run group seminars geared to young African American mothers who face both early parenthood and poverty. These seminars give the young mothers, ranging in age from 14 to 38, a chance to share their burdens and experiences and to learn new, more effective methods of coping with the problems small children present, particularly small children in poverty.

The social workers ask specific questions of the group members, such as, "What do you do when your child disobeys you?" For the most part, the mothers immediately seek a solution in physical punishment, regardless of the age of the child or the circumstances of the situation. It is the responsibility of the social worker as facilitator of the group to present alternative methods of disciplining children while not sounding judgmental or critical of the mothers' present methods and conditions. Latitia, one of the social workers involved in these meetings, has learned that the group process can be a major part of the learning process for these mothers. Many times, the older, more experienced mothers can present new views and new ideas for coping with disciplining children without sounding overbearing or critical. As a group facilitator, Latitia has learned to bring all of the mothers into the interactive process.

Another focus of the group is a kind of mourning process for the women who had children before they had the chance to finish school or to grow up themselves. Latitia has found that these women need the opportunity to air these feelings of loss and hopelessness if this cycle is to be broken. Many of them speak of the regret they feel over never having finished school and how this lack of education has hurt their ability to care for their offspring. Many of them seek to counsel other teenagers about the dangers and pitfalls of teenage sex and the need to take precautions for protection against pregnancy and the transmission of disease.

As an adjunct to the parenting skills program, social workers explain to their clients how to sign up for the Summer Youth Employment Program, teach interviewing skills, and provide transportation to job interviews. Employment is a key piece of the puzzle if these women are to become self-sufficient and able to leave the welfare roles, an almost universal goal among the clients.

Latitia has also sought to teach her clients how to be advocates for their children. Specifically, these women banded together and sought greater coverage and protection from the local police as a result of reports of a man dressed as a clown who had been luring children with candy and balloons on the streets of their neighborhood. Latitia knows that the more control the women exercise over their lives, the more empowered they feel and the greater the likelihood that they will assume responsibility for themselves and their children.

One of the clients sums up the feelings of most of the others when she says, "My dream for my child is I want her to be able to say, 'My mommy is somebody.' I want her to say, 'I am somebody.' I want her to dream and don't stop dreaming. I want her to be all she can be."

In this example, Latitia engaged in detection and identification to determine the barriers facing these young mothers. She used her skills in counseling and support to help the young women prepare to parent their children. Finally, she engaged in enabling and advocacy to help these mothers recognize and use their own strengths and abilities to bring about positive change for them and for their children.

Teenage Fathers, the Forgotten Parents

Efforts to address the epidemic of teenage pregnancy in the United States have not always included teenage fathers. Julie Greene, a social worker in the Family Service Agency of San Diego, decided to create a program that would involve teenage fathers and help overcome the barriers to their greater participation in their children's lives.

Julie set up an initial meeting with the social worker in the San Diego Unified School District and the social workers at two local community health centers. They all agreed that a group approach is an effective strategy to keep new teenage fathers involved and avoid abandonment. Past early intervention projects with teenage fathers have shown positive results.

They decided that the group would start on a pilot basis and the focus would be twofold: (1) to provide emotional support to the teenage fathers and encourage their effective participation in the lives of their children and (2) to provide practical education and guidance to fathers as they assume a parenting role.

The immediate issue was recruitment: how to locate participants for the program and how to interest them in participating. The social workers decided to find the teenage fathers through the expectant mothers. Pregnant teenagers at local health clinics and Planned Parenthood facilities were informed about the group that was forming for parents and were encouraged to bring along their partners.

In the initial sessions, it was clear that the eight teenage fathers in attendance faced depression and a feeling of hopelessness about their future. They spoke of being perceived as the "heavies" by parents and grandparents; they were blamed and seen as "bad" by people whose views they valued. Julie helped the fathers to verbalize their reactions and feelings and how they have responded to these accusations and perceptions. Group support gives these young men a feeling of connection and helps keep them from becoming completely alienated and thus more likely to abandon the mother and the child. Male social workers conducted separate groups to provide specific, concrete advice to these young men. The focus of the groups and the program is encouraging these teenagers to remain in school and to stay involved in the lives of their offspring.

Julie encouraged the fathers to maintain frequent contact with the mother and child and to provide help with child care as well as providing financial resources. She knows from experience with other groups that peer pressure and peer accountability are important forces in altering teenagers' behavior.

Reference

Brown, D. L. (1994, June 27). Helping mothers to get a handle on parenthood. *Washington Post*, pp. B1, B4.

career
opportunities

There is a broad range of career opportunities in the field of family and children services, examples of which are listed below. However, the new conservative thrust in government has threatened massive restrictions and elimination of many family and child programs. It is essential for social workers in this area to bring their skills, knowledge, and experience to the debate and to be actively involved in the formulation of public policy.

Clinical Manager

Innovative, dynamic family preservation organization is seeking a team-oriented clinical manager who will oversee the operations of an intensive wraparound service delivery model. Candidate will have a minimum of five to 10 years of supervisory experience and comprehensive knowledge of program design and implementation, community-based services, annual goals and objectives, and budget expertise. Team model orientation based on an empowerment of families and children mission statement. Interactive skills a plus. LCSW an absolute requirement.

Clinical Social Worker

Department of social work seeks a skilled and enthusiastic social worker to provide clinical social work services to patients and families served by the neurobehavior unit. This university-affiliated program provides diagnosis, evaluation, and treatment to children, adolescents, and young adults with developmental disabilities using an interdisciplinary model of service provision. The qualified candidate for the neurobehavior unit must have an LCSW-C or be LCSW-C eligible. Experience working with individuals with developmental disabilities or hospital pediatrics is preferred. Applicants must be knowledgeable about and sensitive to social and cultural issues of significance to the African American community in order to meet the needs of our diverse population.

Director, Child Abuse Program

A nationally known child abuse program is seeking a senior-level professional with excellent clinical, program development, grant-writing, administrative, and supervisory skills. Candidate must be innovative and entrepreneurial and have a proven track record in the child welfare/child abuse field. Research, program evaluation, and computer skills highly desirable. Candidates should have an advanced degree in one of the social sciences or related fields and 10 years of progressive experience in child welfare/abuse.

Director, Head Start

Nonprofit agency is seeking a qualified individual for the position of Head Start director. The selected individual will be responsible for the day-to-day operations of the Head Start Program with a $1 million budget. To qualify, applicant must have a bachelor's degree in early childhood education, social work, psychology, management, or related field. An advanced degree in related field is preferred. The applicant must have five years of responsible supervisory experience, program and budget planning, a minimum of two years of experience working with young children, excellent public relations and communication skills, and knowledge of federal and county social services regulations.

Executive Director

Public agency employing 700 professional and support staff, with an annual budget of $70 million, seeks CEO. Agency serves 25,000 children and their families a year through an array of contemporary child welfare programs. Program and financial management, community planning, policy development, legislative, and community affairs experience required. Demonstrated leadership abilities, along with a master's degree in relevant field and upper-level management experience, required.

Executive Director

Responsibilities include program development and administration, fundraising and grant writing, financial management, staff supervision. Requirements include administrative experience in the area of human services or related field with demonstrated ability to manage programs. Master's degree preferred and experience required.

Executive Director

Nonprofit organization serving families of children with disabilities seeks leader with proven training, management, and grant-writing skills; knowledge of effective strategies for promoting family and professional partnerships; ability to promote collaboration at the local/state levels; and excellent public speaking and interpersonal skills. Requires knowledge of special education/disability issues.

Executive Director

Special-needs adoption/foster agency seeks experienced administrator and supervisor for local agency and national program. Responsible for overall functioning of agency including board relations, budgeting, fundraising, implementing policies, and directing adoption program.

Family Service Program, Support Manager

State agency seeks an individual with a minimum of a bachelor's degree and experience in program development, quality assurance reviews, dispute resolution, and management evaluations on multiple programs related to child and family services. MSW/LCSW preferred.

Foster Care Coordinator

An energetic, innovative, and self-disciplined person is sought to direct a growing therapeutic foster care program under the auspices of a residential treatment program. Responsibilities include administrative supervision/coordination of program, clinical supervision of direct care team, monitoring of foster parent licensing process, training of foster parents, and foster child/foster family matching and placement. Person must possess an MSW and have foster care experience. Supervisory experience also strongly desired.

Program Administrator

A 100-year-old nationally recognized child welfare agency seeks hard-working, creative individual to assist executive director in developing new community-based, aftercare alternatives for youngsters completing residential treatment program. Responsibilities also include selected administrative duties and work with public and private funding sources. Candidates must have a master's degree plus five years of progressively responsible supervisory and program development experience. Some experience with Medicaid funding a plus.

Social Service

Domestic violence program seeks case manager. Licensed MSW/BSW with two years' case management experience in fields of homelessness, addiction, pregnancy, or domestic violence. Bilingual candidates strongly encouraged.

Social Services Director

Private nonprofit/county cooperative program involving social services, health, and mental health. Supervise shelter operations, including budget, personnel, food services, and facility. Education or experience equivalent to master's degree in human services administration or related field. Experience in supervision of residential program important.

Social Worker

A nonprofit social services agency is actively seeking MSWs for its Family Preservation Program to provide services to prevent the need for out-of-home placement of family members through crisis intervention and skills-based treatment. Requirements: state license; available to client families 24 hours, seven days a week; bilingual preferred. Must have working knowledge of cognitive behavior skills and crisis intervention. Experience in working with troubled families preferred.

Social Worker

Seeking a qualified licensed social worker to direct case management, placement, and family preservation services for abandoned, abused, and neglected infants residing in our transitional home. Should be creative and willing to shape and execute new social programs. Direct experience in child welfare, foster care, and adoptions a must. A small caseload and exceptional executive support allow a very special opportunity for a very special person to make a real difference in the lives of children.

Social Worker (Adoption)

A nonprofit international adoption and child welfare agency is recruiting for an adoption social worker for its headquarters. Primary responsibility is caseload management of adoptive families in China. MSW required; Mandarin speaking skills preferred and/or experience with Chinese communities. Some overseas travel required.

Therapeutic Foster Care Homes Coordinator/
Wrap Around Specialist

Full-time position available for licensed social worker to develop and coordinate a therapeutic foster family program. Experience necessary to provide training and ongoing services. A major part of the position will be in-home work with the adolescents and their families. Responsibilities include ensuring that appropriate therapy is being provided to the adolescents and seeing that foster families have the appropriate support and training. Excellent opportunity for individual with good managerial skills who likes to work independently.

Therapeutic Foster Care Program Director

Opening for a mental health professional to direct an established therapeutic foster care program for seriously emotionally disturbed adolescents. Master's degree in social work or related field required, with supervisory, clinical, and management skills.

Therapist, Juvenile Sex Offender Treatment Program

Work on a multidisciplinary team serving 20 kids ages 13 to 15. Requires experience working with juvenile sex offenders and a master's degree. We are a nonsecure residential treatment center serving 94 juveniles in four district units. We have a well-developed program for treating sex offenders using a differential model.

health care

introduction
to part III

A large proportion of the social work labor force works in health settings or deals with problems that are health related. NASW's 1984 statement on "Social Work Practice in the Health Care Field" stated, in part, that

> The social worker is the strategist in prevention and health care. The unique role of the social worker is in helping people to understand and use their strengths, their relationships and their social environment to maintain and enhance their social roles and optimum functioning capacity. . . . Existing and future health care programs must include social work services. ("Social Work, Public Policy," 1984, p. 11)

Health as an area of social work practice has a long history. Ida M. Cannon started the first hospital social work department in 1905 at Massachusetts General Hospital (MGH) for the primary purpose of helping patients make a smooth transition from the hospital to the community. Richard Cabot, the physician who directed MGH in 1905, recognized the importance of psychosocial care in comprehensive treatment and the importance of continuity of care and therefore included social workers as home visitors in his clinic at MGH. These goals continue to guide present-day hospital social workers as they strive to ensure that progress made in the acute medical care arena is maintained when the patient returns to the community (Oktay, 1995; Rossen, 1987).

Two historic events had a tremendous impact on hospital social work. The first was the passage of Medicare legislation in 1966, which mandated that if social work services were provided by participating agencies, such services must be directed by a professional with a master's degree in social work. As Medicare caseloads increased, so did the number of hospital social workers. The typical client was an elderly patient over 65 years of age and his or her family. These patients generally suffer from one or more chronic illnesses that require adjustment to lifestyle changes. Although elderly people continue to be a large portion of patients, the role of hospital social workers has expanded and includes many different types of clients and settings (Rossen, 1987).

The second historic event also occurred in 1966 when the American Hospital Association established the Society for Hospital Social Work Directors. This organization strengthened the credibility of hospital social workers by facilitating the participation of social workers in the hospital industry and by establishing professional accountability standards (Rossen, 1987).

Social workers in the area of health are employed in a variety of settings, including hospitals, hospices, medical clinics, health maintenance organizations (HMOs), nursing homes, and health organizations. This latter category includes national organizations and their state and local affiliates concerned with specific diseases, such as the Multiple Sclerosis Association, American Cancer Society, Lupus Foundation of America, Asthma and Allergy Foundation, American Lung Association, and the March of Dimes Birth Defects Association.

These settings of practice fall under public, nonprofit, and for-profit auspices. Nursing homes are seldom under public auspices; typically, they have been nonprofit but increasingly, they are for-profit. Hospitals and medical clinics may be under public, nonprofit, or for-profit auspices. Hospices tend to be under nonprofit auspices, whereas HMOs are for-profit. Health organizations typically are nonprofit. Under these different auspices social workers work in various program areas including child immunization programs, family planning, maternal and child health, genetics counseling, hospital discharge planning, emergency room care, hospice, AIDS clinics, and support groups related to specific diseases.

A common theme throughout this book is the overlapping boundaries of the areas of service occupied by social workers. Although there are distinct settings of health practice, such as hospitals, the problems of patients in these settings are by no means confined to the physiological. Their needs range from aftercare services to grief counseling following the death of a child. Social workers often work with the families and friends of people with health problems. For example, social workers in a hospice setting may work primarily with elderly or younger terminally ill people (such as people with AIDS), but they also offer services to the families and friends of terminally ill patients. Teen pregnancy is a health issue, but also is a family and child services concern and so is frequently the focus of social workers practicing in school settings.

Social workers in non–health settings also need to be attuned to the interplay between physiological and emotional problems, such as the effects of medication, the impact of chronic illness on the patient and the family, and the psychosocial and economic consequences of debilitating disease. Thus, social workers in all areas of service are concerned with the health of their clients.

Medical clinics were identified as the primary practice area of 12.2 percent of the NASW membership in 1991 (Gibelman & Schervish, 1993), ranking third among all practice areas. In the NASW classification of practice areas used at the time, the medical clinic was the only one of 16 categories specific to the health field. In regard to practice setting, hospitals were ranked second among all settings, with 20 percent of the members citing hospitals as their primary setting. Medical clinics (ranked third among all settings of practice) followed close behind, with 16.2 percent citing medical clinics as their primary setting. As noted above, the practice of social work in health is not necessarily carried out in a traditional health care setting and, conversely, a health setting does not mean that practice is exclusively health focused. The setting indicates where one works, and the practice area indicates the focus of practice.

The Future

Social workers who are thinking about entering the field of health care should be cognizant of the expected trends. For example, the present form of managed care will probably give way to more selective contracting and networks of providers. In addition, there will most likely be an increase in fiscal management of care rather than clinical management (Edinburg & Cottler, 1995). In the new health care arena, clinical social workers will still be called on to provide inpatient and outpatient services in medical, rehabilitation, and psychiatric settings. In all settings, social workers will have to deal with the insurance company's case managers in care issues such as discharge planning and type of service (Edinburg & Cottler, 1995).

However, in all likelihood the social work role in managed care companies will grow. Social workers are increasingly working as administrators, supervisors, clinical directors, and case managers. Social workers will also advocate for patients in the managed care system to help them understand their benefits and how to access services. In addition, social workers must be major players in shaping health care policy to ensure adequate and affordable coverage for all citizens (Edinburg & Cottler, 1995).

References

Edinburg, G. M., & Cottler, J. M. (1995). Managed care. In R. L. Edwards (Ed.-in-Chief), *Encyclopedia of social work* (19th ed., Vol. 2, pp. 1635–1642). Washington, DC: NASW Press.

Gibelman, M., & Schervish, P. H. (1993). *Who we are: The social work labor force as reflected in the NASW membership*. Washington, DC: NASW Press.

Oktay, J. S. (1995). Primary health care. In R. L. Edwards (Ed.-in-Chief), *Encyclopedia of social work* (19th ed., Vol. 3, pp. 1887–1894). Washington, DC: NASW Press.

Rossen, S. (1987). Hospital social work. In A. Minahan (Ed.-in-Chief), *Encyclopedia of social work* (18th ed., Vol. 1, pp. 816–821). Silver Spring, MD: National Association of Social Workers.

Social work, public policy stands okayed. (1984, October). *NASW News*, p. 11.

eating disorders

The interplay between physical and emotional illness is particularly apparent in the range of problems that fall under the category of eating disorders, a group of mental disturbances that are usually first evident in childhood or adolescence and involve maladaptive or unhealthy patterns of eating and ingestion (Barker, 1995). There are several types, including anorexia nervosa and bulimia nervosa.

Anorexia Nervosa

Anorexia nervosa is an eating disorder most often encountered in girls and young women. Those suffering from this disorder refuse to eat over extended periods of time; as a result they experience severe weight loss, malnutrition, and cessation of menstruation. Barker (1995) noted that "the usual medical criteria for this diagnosis include the loss of 15 percent or more of one's body weight. This life-threatening condition is related to a disturbed body image and an exaggerated fear of becoming obese" (p. 21). The *Diagnostic and Statistical Manual of Mental Disorders, 4th edition* (DSM-IV) (American Psychiatric Association [APA], 1994) defines *anorexia nervosa* as a psychopathogenic condition that is characterized by spontaneous or induced vomiting, extreme emaciation, amenorrhea, and other biological changes.

In diagnosing a person with anorexia nervosa, the amount of weight lost is an important factor. In general, a person with the condition must weigh less than 99 pounds. In calculating body weight, two methods are most frequently used. The weight–height formula that is used by insurance companies indicates anorexia nervosa if an individual has lost at least 25 percent of his or her average body weight. The other measurement tool, the average body weight table of women ages 15 to 69, indicates anorexia nervosa when a person weighs less than 75 percent of his or her average body weight (Logan, 1995). The DSM-IV (APA, 1994) lists several essential features of this syndrome that should be investigated when working with a client who may have anorexia nervosa (quoted in Logan, 1995):

- intense fear of becoming obese, even when underweight
- disturbed perception of one's own body weight, size, or shape
- refusal to maintain body weight above the minimal normal weight for one's age and height
- in females, the absence of at least three consecutive menstrual cycles. (p. 805)

Bulimia Nervosa

Bulimia nervosa is an eating disorder in which a "pathologically excessive appetite with episodic eating binges is sometimes followed by purging. The purging may occur through such means as self-induced vomiting or the abuse of laxatives, diet pills, or diuretics" (Barker, 1995, p. 43). The disorder is also characterized by a compulsive preoccupation with food and a compulsive need to keep the behavior secret (Yudkovitz, 1983). Although bulimics are similar to anorexics in that they are concerned with body weight and are overly concerned with gaining weight, they tend to maintain a more normal body weight and some may even be obese (Logan, 1995) because many of them go on extremely long binges, ingesting huge amounts of high-calorie foods that are impossible to completely purge.

The binge–purge cycle of bulimia is as dangerous as, if not more dangerous, than the starvation practices of anorexics. Binging and purging can upset the body's balance of electrolytes, which can cause fatigue, seizures, muscle cramps, irregular heartbeat, and decreased bone strength and density (Logan, 1995). Furthermore, the repeated vomiting can damage the esophagus and stomach and cause glands to swell, gums to recede, and tooth enamel to erode (Logan, 1995). According to the DSM-IV (APA, 1994), the major characteristics of bulimia nervosa are

- recurrent episodes of binge eating, averaging two episodes per week for at least three months, with lack of control over eating behavior
- regular self-induced vomiting, use of laxatives, or rigorous dieting and fasting to counteract binge eating.

Compulsive Overeating

In addition to anorexia and bulimia, compulsive overeating is another food-related addiction. Although bulimics may compulsively overeat, they tend to purge afterwards. On the other hand, *compulsive overeating* is uncontrollable binge eating that is not accompanied by starvation or purging methods (Logan, 1995). Binge-eating disorder (BED) is characterized by frequent episodes of uncontrolled binge eating. Even when they are not hungry, people with BED often overeat and feel a loss of control about their food intake. The disorder affects 2 percent of the general population and 30 percent of people in medically supervised weight control programs ("Binge-Eating Disorder," 1994).

Eating Disorders as a Target of Social Work Intervention

Most eating disorders and compulsive behaviors begin in adolescence, and both anorexia and bulimia are more common in females (Logan, 1995). Most patients with anorexia and bulimia are white. Recent studies have indicated that this fact reflects socioeconomic factors and help-seeking patterns rather than an ethnically based incidence pattern (Logan, 1995).

A number of different theories and models have been used to explain the etiology of various eating disorders. There is no one correct model; therefore, social workers must attempt to assess, identify, and diagnose the core psychopathology of the disorders (Logan, 1995). In dealing with this complicated condition, social workers must be concerned with assessing the common secondary pathologies of eating disorders as well. For example, there may be family and interpersonal problems, personality disorders, substance abuse, or depression (Logan, 1995).

Social workers in this field who practice in hospitals and other institutional settings generally handle a number of clients who are noncompliant and involuntary. Often the patient refuses to acknowledge his or her eating problem (Logan, 1995). The trend in treating eating disorders has been toward a multidisciplinary approach including social workers, physicians, and nutritionists (Logan, 1995). Usually, clients with eating disorders are treated first for physical symptoms to ensure their medical stability before progressing to psychosocial and supportive issues (Logan, 1995). Social workers in this area may work with individuals, families, or groups; they not only use the functions of assessment and diagnosis, they frequently use referral and coordination in a multidisciplinary approach (Logan, 1995). Social workers are encouraged to advocate for societal changes that will cast aside the worship of thinness and focus on self-acceptance in the socialization of young women.

Mary Anne Cohen, a clinical social worker and director of the New York Center for Eating Disorders, began a weekly radio program in 1990 called "French Toast for Breakfast: Declaring Peace with Emotional Eating." The program aired in the tristate area of New York, New Jersey, and Connecticut and emphasized a need to make peace with eating problems with action techniques and strategies ("People in the News," 1990). The goal was to inform people about alternative behaviors and how to cultivate them. Other social workers engage in direct practice with youths and adults who suffer from eating disorders, as the following vignette illustrates.

Cassie's Story

Cassie is an 18-year-old college freshman at the College of William and Mary. She is from Wilmington, Vermont, and her parents and brother still live there. Cassie was an all-around athlete in high school where she won numerous state and regional athletic honors in soccer, volleyball, and basketball. However, Cassie decided not to pursue her athletic career in college because she told her mother she "wanted to be a normal girl without big muscles and with lots of dates."

When she arrived at William and Mary, Cassie went on a diet. She wanted to be prettier and thinner than all the other girls. She began running five miles every morning and would have only an apple for breakfast. After her first two classes, she would go swimming. She often skipped lunch or she would eat only a rice cake with a piece of fat-free cheese. She went to an aerobics class every afternoon for an hour and ran again for an hour after that.

Cassie began to lose weight quickly. By Christmas she had lost 15 pounds. By March she had lost 45 pounds and her 5'7", 90-pound frame was nearly a skeleton.

She was forced to leave school for medical reasons and she returned home to Vermont. Her mother was worried about her and her father was extremely angry. "Why don't you just eat?" he would yell. Finally, Cassie entered the local hospital as an inpatient. Her weight had dropped to 85 pounds and the doctor said her body would soon begin to use the heart muscle for fuel. Cassie began to meet with Barbara, a social worker at the hospital, who specialized in eating disorders.

Barbara worked with Cassie every week. They would talk about everything from Cassie's family, to sports, to boys, to school. Barbara also referred Cassie to a support group that met at the hospital once a week. At these meetings Cassie was able to see people like herself who had lost so much weight they were now in the hospital being fed through tubes in their arms. Cassie was shocked at how sick they looked, and she slowly realized that she looked just like them. She also saw people who had fought their anorexia or bulimia and won. They looked so happy and free. Cassie wanted to feel that way; she did not want to have to worry about everything she ate or obsess about exercising after every meal. She began to realize that being ultra thin did not bring her love and happiness. When Cassie told this to the social worker, Barbara secretly breathed a sigh of relief. Cassie had taken the first step—she had recognized and admitted the problem. And she had decided to fight back.

In this vignette, Barbara engaged in assessment and diagnosis to determine the best way to treat Cassie and communicate with her. She also coordinated with the doctors and participated as part of the interdisciplinary hospital team. Finally, she used referral skills by helping Cassie to attend the group meetings where she could see and talk with others with similar problems. In this way, Barbara was able to help Cassie escape her self-imposed isolation and recognize that there was hope.

References

American Psychiatric Association. (1994). *Diagnostic and statistical manual of mental disorders* (4th ed.). Washington, DC: Author.

Barker, R. L. (1995). *Social work dictionary* (3rd ed.). Washington, DC: NASW Press.

Binge-eating disorder can signal other illness. (1994, November). *NASW News*, p. 13.

Logan, S. L. (1995). Eating disorders and other compulsive behaviors. In R. L. Edwards (Ed.-in-Chief), *Encyclopedia of social work* (19th ed., Vol. 1, pp. 805–815). Washington, DC: NASW Press.

Yudkovitz, E. (1983). Bulimia: Growing awareness of an eating disorder. *Social Work, 28*, 472–478.

family planning

A Program for Teenage Fathers

Becky Mills is the school social worker at Brackton South, a public high school in San Francisco. She is busy with several different cases, ranging from a ninth-grade boy whose parents are divorcing to an 11th-grade girl who is anorexic. Martha Crow, a social worker with the Ford Foundation in New York, calls Becky to let her know that the Foundation has joined with other organizations to fund programs in major cities targeting teenage pregnancy. She explains that they are already sponsoring several programs for teenage mothers and are interested in programs for teenage fathers. She wants to know if Becky's school would be interested in serving as a demonstration site for this project.

"Teenage fathers?" Becky asks. Martha explains that, contrary to the common stereotypes, many of the young men want to contribute and be a part of their child's life, but they often lack resources and need a great deal of assistance. Becky tells Martha that she will talk to her colleagues and the school principal and call back within the week.

Becky sits at her desk and considers the proposal. She knows that Brackton South is an urban school with a large population of low-income students. She also knows she has worked with six pregnant teenage girls in the last year. Of the six, three of the fathers dropped out of school to earn money for child support.

In the next week Becky does a great deal of research, talks with her colleagues, and explains the opportunity to the school principal. They all agree that teenage pregnancy is a school and a community problem. But the principal asks Becky why they should spend time working with the teenage fathers. If the pregnancy has already occurred, why not dedicate resources to the mother? Becky presents her research findings and explains that often the young father may want to help but he may not know how, so he may drop out of school to support the child or he may go to the other extreme and offer no assistance at all. After Becky's presentation, the group decides that support for teenage fathers is needed. Becky agrees to work full-time to develop a program, and the other workers agree to take Becky's share of new cases. The decision to proceed is made and Becky calls Martha with the news.

Becky begins to review case files on past work with pregnant teenagers. She finds many cases in which the teenage father dropped out of school to provide financial support. Although this indicates responsible intentions, Becky knows that the program will need to help fathers find ways to contribute financially and stay in school so that they can eventually improve their employability and earning potential. Becky's plan is to have school social workers counsel teenage fathers who plan to drop out. The social worker would discuss the consequences of a future of minimum-wage jobs, assess the teenage father's situation and, if possible, help him get a part-time job so he could stay in school. The social worker may also help the teenager reduce his class load or receive tutoring if necessary.

Many of the cases Becky reviewed showed teenage fathers who are depressed and who have no hope for their future. They are often condemned by their own family as well as the family of the teenage mother. In her program, Becky plans to have social workers facilitate communication between the teenagers and their parents to ease the tension in an already stressful situation.

In the file Becky also finds a paper presented at NASW's 1985 professional symposium. The author interviewed 20 unmarried teenage mothers six months to a year after they gave birth. The study confirmed that many of the maternal grandmothers displayed negative opinions of the teenage fathers. However, the study also showed that eight of the 20 young men had regular daily contact with the mother and the child, gave emotional and financial support, and helped with child care arrangements. The study also indicated that four of the other 12 fathers had more distant relationships with the mother, but they still contributed financially and saw the child three to four times a week. The remaining eight fathers had no contact and offered no support to the mother or the child.

Because 60 percent of the fathers in the study exhibited a desire to support and be a part of their child's life, Becky decides that her program will address the situation early, with social workers encouraging expectant mothers to bring expectant fathers to meetings and counseling sessions. In addition, the same social worker will work with the teenage parents throughout the pregnancy, delivery, and postpartum stage. Becky believes that this continuous service will eliminate a gap when the young parents may feel alone and confused and lose the momentum of the growth they achieved.

Becky also plans to offer services that include child care, health and sex education, individual and group counseling, parental training, career assistance, childbirth preparation, paternity establishment assistance, and a healthy meal program. Becky decides that she will be pleased with the program if it has the following results:

- reduces repeat births to the same teenage parents

- increases school retention among both teenage mothers and fathers

- raises infant birthweight.

With her proposal complete, Becky arranges a meeting to review her ideas with her colleagues and the school principal before sending the plan to Martha at the Ford Foundation.

Although social workers involved in family planning work with clients of all ages, the rate of teenage pregnancy in the United States is reaching near epidemic proportions and warrants special attention ("Male Teenagers Confront Paternal Roles," 1986). Becoming a parent as a teenager is associated with many other social problems: school dropout, poor employment prospects, and poverty (National Commission on Children, 1993). The National Commission on Children reported that one in 10 girls under age 20 (a total of more than one million) becomes pregnant each year, and approximately 50 percent of pregnant teenagers give birth. Both the number and rate of births increased sharply between 1986 and 1991. More recently however, the statistics show a downward trend. The birthrate of teenagers ages 15 to 19 fell 2 percent between 1991 and 1992 ("Teenage Pregnancies," 1995).

Most family planning services in the United States are provided by state and local health departments, neighborhood health clinics, school-based clinics, and Planned Parenthood (Conner, 1987). Planned Parenthood is a private, nonprofit agency with affiliates throughout the country that provides reproductive health services ranging from birth control counseling to abortion, sterilization, and infertility services. The organization also offers a variety of education and training programs, including sex education, family planning, and services for people with disabilities. The public affairs program of Planned Parenthood publicizes important issues such as prenatal education and reproductive health (Kerson & Peachey, 1989).

Family planning traditionally has been a controversial topic. In the past, sexuality was not discussed and there was a great lack of knowledge regarding human reproduction, particularly among adolescents. The medical profession contributed to the public's ignorance by considering birth control a social rather than medical issue. It was not until 1965 that the federal government recognized the importance of family planning services by providing financial resources. Title X of the Public Health Service Act of 1944 is administered by the U.S. Department of Health and Human Services and is the only federal program specifically directed toward family planning services (Kerson & Peachey, 1989).

As the social and political acceptance of family planning services increased, so did the technology. Currently there are many different types of birth control including an oral contraceptive, or the "birth control pill"; intrauterine devices (IUDs); sterilization; Norplant (a surgically implanted birth control device); condoms; diaphragms; and vasectomy. Unfortunately, most contraceptives are not 100 percent reliable. Some have detrimental side effects and a degree of risk. Therefore, one of the primary functions of a social worker in family planning is to help clients understand the pros and cons of different contraceptive methods and decide on the most suitable method for each individual's circumstances (Kerson & Peachey, 1989).

Social workers in family planning must perform the basic social work functions of assessing the client's current life situation, identifying any individual physical or mental limitation, supporting the client, counseling the client and others involved, enabling the client to access appropriate resources, and providing referrals when necessary. In the case described earlier, Becky Mills exhibited the social work functions of mobilization, exchange, program development, and coordination. After her program goes into effect, Becky will also need to perform program evaluation to monitor service delivery and determine if the original goals are being accomplished.

Social workers in family planning often encounter teenagers who understand the need for contraception but do not know what kind to use or how to obtain it. Of those who use contraceptives, some do so only casually and ineffectively (National Commission on Children, 1993). As researchers continue to study the problems encountered by pregnant teenagers, questions remain in regard to epidemiology and effective intervention techniques. It is clear, however, that adolescent pregnancy carries significant risks to the health of both the mother and the child. Lack of prenatal care is a common problem among pregnant teenagers, leading to low-birthweight babies, pregnancy complications, and infant mortality (Combs-Orme, 1993).

Although family planning has been widely accepted in the society at large, a controversy currently blazes regarding contraceptive counseling and prescription in school-based health clinics. Such clinics have multiplied in the last several years, and many are in low-income, urban areas with inadequate health care and transportation services ("Birth Control Flap," 1987). These clinics generally operate in junior and senior high schools and are funded by government or private agencies.

Only about one-fifth of student visits to these clinics are for birth control. Former secretary of Education William J. Bennett publicly opposed the distribution of contraceptives by school-based clinics saying they are "abdicating moral authority by making contraceptives available" ("Birth Control Flap," 1987). On the other hand, the former U.S. Surgeon General Joycelyn Elders did not hide her strong belief that such contraceptive distribution was appropriate and necessary.

Social workers in the field are not unified in their opinions on this subject. Some believe that family planning, sex education, and health services must complement the distribution of contraceptives to decrease teenage pregnancy. However, others believe that such education will not affect the pregnancy rate because teenagers get pregnant for other reasons, such as low self-esteem, sexual identity, peer pressure, loneliness, and other internal needs. Those holding this view see the solution as lying in a more comprehensive strategy than family planning alone.

In addition to the functions previously described, social workers who deal with teenage pregnancy and family planning must also be able to communicate and counsel teenagers in a nonjudgmental way. A social worker's ability to gain teenagers' trust and respect may increase self-esteem and help them resist sexual peer pressure ("Birth Control Flap," 1987).

Social workers in family planning also work in health clinics where they review patient charts and interview clients to identify high-risk patients, such as those who are unmarried or who have a physical or mental limitation. Using the social work functions of assessment and counseling, the social worker must attempt to determine the client's current knowledge base and ability to make rational decisions regarding contraceptives and family planning. Factors to be considered are the client's ability to care for herself appropriately, the availability of an adequate support system, and the knowledge of available resources. After assessing the client's base of information, the social worker, who must be knowledgeable in prenatal and perinatal issues, counsels the client on health education, contraception, and family planning. However, if the new information is to be useful to the client, the social worker must use his or her skills to communicate clearly in a manner that the client understands.

Social workers in family planning engage in a variety of functions, from clinical counseling and assessment to research to program design and evaluation. They may work with teenage, young adult, or middle-aged clients in a health department, neighborhood clinic, school-based clinic, or Planned Parenthood organization. They may deal with the acute needs of an unwed, pregnant teenager or they may help a young woman decide on the most appropriate form of contraception. In family planning, the skills unique to social workers are desperately needed.

The inclusion of abortion as a family planning service of some agencies and clinics means that social workers may find themselves in the center of controversy. Abortion is one of the most controversial and long-standing conflicts in the United States. Social workers reflect the diversity of viewpoints on the issue of abortion. However, social workers are trained not to impose their own values on their clients. According to Figueira-McDonough (1995), "Regardless of individual preferences, what is important for social workers is how they can facilitate women's self-determination with regard to reproductive decisions and to what extent they can ensure their clients' access to resources to support their clients' choices" (p. 11).

References

Birth control flap hounds school clinics. (1987, February). *NASW News*, p. 3.

Combs-Orme, T. (1993). Health effects of adolescent pregnancy: Implications for social workers. *Families in Society: Journal of Contemporary Human Services, 74*, 344–354.

Conner, G. L. (1987). Family and population planning. In A. Minahan (Ed.-in-Chief), *Encyclopedia of social work* (18th ed., Vol. 1, pp. 561–571). Silver Spring, MD: National Association of Social Workers.

Figueira-McDonough, J. (1995). Abortion. In R. L. Edwards (Ed.-in-Chief), *Encyclopedia of social work* (19th ed., Vol. 1, pp. 7–15). Washington, DC: NASW Press.

Kerson, T. S., & Peachey, H. (1989). Family planning agency: An unsuccessful contraceptor. In T. S. Kerson & Associates, *Social work in health settings: Practice in context* (pp. 231–245). New York: Haworth.

Male teenagers confront paternal roles. (1986, June). *NASW News,* p. 7.

National Commission on Children. (1993). *Just the facts: A summary of recent information on America's children and their families.* Washington, DC: Author.

Teenage pregnancies. (1995, January 17). *Washington Post* (Health section), p. 5.

genetics

Recent technological developments have allowed physicians to identify genetic disorders and, in some cases, treat the symptoms. There are 3,000 known genetic disorders and there are vast ethical, psychological, and physiological issues involved in the occurrence or risk of a genetic disorder in a family ("Genetic Disorders," 1985). Psychosocial services for families with genetic disorders and birth defects are now recognized as vital components of the interdisciplinary team approach to treatment. Genetic testing and improved medical technology have led to new populations of clients, complicated choices for those clients, and unprecedented psychosocial issues (Rauch & Black, 1995). As a result, social work involvement with people needing genetic services is likely to increase (Rauch, 1988).

One characteristic of genetic disorders is that they are permanent. Entire families are involved in the diagnosis of these disorders and the resulting child-bearing issues. Some genetic disorders, such as Huntington's chorea and Tay-Sachs disease, are degenerative and eventually fatal.

Social workers work directly with families, taking detailed family histories and offering information and referral, supportive counseling, and concrete information (Rauch & Black, 1995). Social workers also participate as part of study teams. For example, as part of a team studying Huntington's disease in one family, a social worker helped locate family members, a process that involved extensive phone work and hours of research in courthouses and libraries locating birth, death, and marriage certificates ("Genetic Disorders," 1985). Once family members were located, it was also the social worker's job to explain the study to them and gain their participation in a blood comparison test of affected and unaffected people.

When working with clients who express genetic concerns, socials workers must practice empathic communication, provide accurate information, and offer quality referrals when necessary (Rauch & Black, 1995). People who have a genetic disorder must deal with a variety of life-affecting tasks: They may need to learn more about the disease, modify their plans to have children, or alter their lifestyle to adhere to medical recommendations. Such adjustments are not easy, and social workers must use the functions of assistance, advice, and enabling to help clients cope with the inevitable changes (Rauch & Black, 1995).

Social workers generally use crisis intervention services in the various stages of diagnosis, illness and hospitalization, and dying and bereavement. Important social work skills in this area include familiarity with specific disorders and the burdens that accompany them, an understanding of psychological and familial effects, and competent assessment skills (Rauch, 1988). Referral and case management are also used (Rauch, 1988; Rauch & Black, 1995).

As it is in many other areas of social work, advocacy is an important aspect of genetic social work. There is evidence that, in addition to genetic disorders, environmental agents are also related to birth defects, so social workers in this field should advocate for programs that prevent maternal drug and alcohol abuse during pregnancy and that promote protection from damaging chemicals or radiation (Rauch & Black, 1995).

Recent biomedical advances have led to the development of a test for Huntington's chorea, which can occur at midlife and cause early death. Those who are tested will know whether they will develop the disease. However, the advances of genetic testing are accompanied by unimagined dilemmas. Social workers must use their skills and resources to make sure the new medical advances are used responsibly and beneficially (Rauch & Black, 1995). The emotional and ethical issues surrounding the decision to be tested are illustrated in the following vignette.

Do I Want to Know?

Judy Epstein was 11 years old when her father died. She only vaguely remembers when he first became ill, but she remembers all too well how quickly he went from being a vibrant, healthy man to a bedridden shell of a man wracked with convulsions and pain. It was the kind of slow death she thought must be the vengeance of a hateful God. At the house after her father's funeral, Judy remembers her relatives whispering about who might be next.

Judy is now 26 years old and has met a man she plans to marry. Steve wants a large family; children, he says, are "what it's all about." Judy knew that Steve felt this way almost the moment they met. And now she must consider the consequences of not having told him that her father died of Huntington's chorea. She is unable to sleep or eat; Steve is eager to set a wedding date.

Recently Judy learned about a new test that can determine whether she carries the gene that would cause her to develop the disease. Does she want to know? Could she deal with it? And if she doesn't find out, how can she proceed with her plans to marry and have children?

Judy calls the Huntington's Society national office in New York to obtain a referral to a therapist who specializes in working with families faced with chronic illness. Anne Milner, a social worker on staff, is available to meet with her. After scheduling an appointment with Judy, Anne reflects on the impact of the new genetic testing. Until now, most of Anne's cases have been people with depression, either the person with the disease or a spouse or other family member. Occasionally, Anne worked with people who had expressed suicidal ideation. However, recently she had begun to see more and more people who are struggling with the issue of whether to have a genetics test.

Anne understands the difficult decision that faces these clients, and her primary mode of intervention is empathic listening and communication. Anne usually meets with the individual client for two to three sessions, during which she gathers history and information regarding the current social support structure. Anne generally assesses the situation, makes an initial diagnosis, identifies areas of need, and offers support and counseling. Anne never makes the decision for a client. She strongly believes in self-determination and the importance of letting the client decide whether to have the test.

Anne invites other family members to subsequent sessions for support or assistance. Anne also frequently refers clients and family members to support groups in the area composed of people who are facing or have faced decisions about genetic testing for themselves or their loved ones. Anne does not provide long-term counseling, considered to be more than eight sessions. The Huntington's Society's large client base requires it to provide short-term, crisis intervention counseling and to offer referrals if further help is needed.

After meeting with Anne twice, Judy decides that she must tell Steve about her father's death and the implications that it holds for their future together. Judy and Steve both come to counseling sessions for the next two weeks and share their concerns and anxiety about having the test performed. In addition to offering support and assistance, Anne refers them to a local support group for people who are struggling with similar issues. After meeting with Anne and attending the support group, Steve and Judy decide that Judy will have the test. Anne wishes them luck and tells them to contact the organization if they need help in the future.

In this case, most of Anne's work is focused on the provision of direct services. She performs assessment and diagnosis in her initial contact with both Judy and Steve. She also identifies areas of need and offers support and counseling to both of them. Anne also carries out the social work function of referral when she helps Judy and Steve get involved in a local support group. Finally, she provides information about the disease and the testing procedures and encourages and enables Judy and Steve to make their own, well-informed decision.

Although Anne primarily carries out direct practice functions, social workers in similar organizations often engage in macro activities such as planning, administration, and supervision. One of the most important social work functions in these areas is that of program development and evaluation. An essential component of social work practice is identifying needs in a specific population or a community and effectively developing and administering a program or service to meet that need.

Anne engages in direct practice in a nontraditional social work setting. The primary mission of the Huntington's Society is not related to the provision of social work services. National voluntary health agencies like this one typically have one purpose: to combat a particular disease, disability, or group of disabilities or to improve the health of a particular group of people. Many organizations have local affiliates to provide community or individually oriented educational and support services and to raise money; many of these local efforts are self-help in nature. In general, national voluntary health agencies provide five types of services: public education, patient services, professional education, research, and community services such as health screening and promoting improved health practices (Gibelman, 1990). However, recently a number of local affiliates and even some national organizations have begun to hire social workers in recognition of the psychosocial and emotional needs of people affected by the disease or disability (Gibelman, 1990).

References

Genetic disorders shadow generations. (1985, July). *NASW News*, p. 3.

Gibelman, M. (1990). National voluntary health agencies in an era of change: Experiences and adaptations. *Administration in Social Work, 14,* 17–32.

Rauch, J. B. (1988). Social work and the genetics revolution: Genetic services. *Social Work, 33,* 389–395.

Rauch, J. B., & Black, R. B. (1995). Genetics. In R. L. Edwards (Ed.-in-Chief), *Encyclopedia of social work* (19th ed., Vol. 2, pp. 1108–1117). Washington, DC: NASW Press.

hiv/aids

In less than a decade, acquired immune deficiency syndrome (AIDS) went from being a virtually unknown disease to the most serious public health issue in the United States and the world (Getzel, 1989). AIDS is an infectious, chronic, and deadly disease caused by the human immunodeficiency virus (HIV), which attacks and destroys the immune system, making the infected person vulnerable to a variety of cancers, nervous system degeneration, and opportunistic infections caused by other viruses or bacteria (Lloyd, 1990). Although opportunistic infections are not ordinarily life threatening in a healthy individual, they can be deadly to a person with AIDS whose immune system has been weakened by HIV (Lloyd, 1990, 1995).

HIV is transmitted by unprotected sexual intercourse with a person infected with HIV; by exposure to infected blood through transfusions, blood-contaminated needles, infected donated body organs, or infected semen; and from an infected mother to the fetus or infant either before, during, or a short time after birth (Lloyd, 1995). Despite the high-technology medical care that prevails in modern society, AIDS has eluded effective treatment and cure.

Statistics provide a compelling picture of the AIDS epidemic, and projections for the future are grim (Frisino, 1994). Unlike many chronic diseases that affect either very young or very old people, HIV attacks young adults during their most productive years. The Centers for Disease Control (CDC) reported that approximately 78 percent of the 401,749 cumulative AIDS cases through June 1994 were men and women between the ages of 20 and 39 (as cited in Lloyd, 1995). The National Commission on AIDS (1993) estimated that more than 1 million other Americans are infected with HIV and that at least until the year 2000, the annual number of new AIDS diagnoses will remain relatively high, between 40,000 and 80,000 per year.

African Americans and Hispanics make up almost half of all AIDS cases, although they represent only 21 percent of the population; three-quarters of women diagnosed with AIDS are African American or Hispanic, as are 85 percent of infants born with HIV infection (Frisino, 1994). AIDS is now the leading killer of African Americans between the ages of 25 and 44, surpassing homicide (Russell, 1994).

The statistics suggest that the AIDS-affected population is expanding in numbers and characteristics. At the beginning of the AIDS epidemic in the United States, the disease largely affected gay and bisexual men, who still account for 65 percent of all diagnosed cases since 1981; the second largest risk group are drug abusers, who make up 17 percent of all cases; and heterosexual men and women who are sexually active and not in long-standing monogamous relationships with uninfected partners, the third largest risk category, represent 4 percent of the cases and are the largest potential population at risk (Getzel, 1989; Rensberger, 1993). The number of American women who contracted AIDS in 1992 grew four times as fast as the number of men. Although the infection rate among men has slowed significantly, high-risk behavior continues in a number of populations, including intravenous drug users, younger gay men, and young heterosexual men (Leigh, Temple, & Trocki, 1993; National Commission on AIDS, 1993). As of July 1992, 872 youths ages 13 through 19 had been diagnosed with AIDS. However, because not all states are required to report cases of HIV infection, national estimates of the number of adolescents who may be infected with HIV are not considered reliable (National Commission on Children, 1993).

Social workers help people with AIDS and their families, lovers, spouses, friends, and colleagues in many different settings. They work in hospitals, state and county social services departments, community health clinics, and nonprofit organizations specifically serving the AIDS population.

Social workers who work with this group face many challenges and must use their psychosocial perspective to understand the influences of both internal and external factors. From the beginning of the epidemic, social workers have played a significant role, both in pushing for appropriate government responses to the crisis and in caring for people with AIDS and educating those at risk of infection (Frisino, 1994). As Leukefeld and Fimbres (1987) noted,

> The AIDS challenge for social work is obvious. Clearly, the lack of pharmacological, immunological, and medical interventions emphasizes the need for psychosocial and behavioral interventions—the traditional focus of social workers. (p. ix)

Shernoff (1990) recounted how one social worker pioneered AIDS prevention and outreach by going into "shooting galleries" in New York City to show intravenous drug users how to clean their needles with bleach and use condoms. Social workers continue to play a vital role in community-based AIDS organizations providing case management, information and referral, service coordination, financial management, education, and advocacy and support services, among others (Frisino, 1994). These social services agencies are often the single most important element in a community's response to the disease (Alperin & Richie, 1989; Frisino, 1994).

NASW News ("Worker's Effort," 1989) reported the story of social worker Ryan James, coordinator of social services at Memorial Medical Center in

Modesto, California. James is responsible for counseling AIDS patients, providing support to them, and accompanying them on visits to doctors. He has also helped AIDS patients obtain AZT, the costly antiviral drug that slows the progress of HIV. James learned that one of his patients had waited weeks to fill his AZT prescription because he could not afford to pay for it. Although most insurance companies will cover a percentage of the cost of AZT, patients must pay the entire amount and then wait to be reimbursed, which can take several weeks. Knowing the importance of this medication for his patient's survival, James began to search for ways to provide him with the medication, and he was able to negotiate with a local hospital to bill the patient's insurance company for the drug. James sees educating the hospital staff, insurance companies, and others involved directly or indirectly in treatment as an important part of his job of helping people with AIDS. When he learned that insurance companies can be billed by local hospitals, he sought to make every AIDS-related group in California aware of this alternative.

The professional values of social workers, which reflect the inherent worth of individuals and their right to self-determination, represent an important counterbalance to the often prejudiced and discriminatory judgments against AIDS patients. Social workers are actively involved as advocates, facilitators, and enablers in hospitals, mental health clinics, and outpatient AIDS programs where they serve patients and their families (Leukefeld & Fimbres, 1987). Social workers advocate for clients in the legal system by assisting them in discrimination cases through legal referrals and ongoing support and acting as case managers to direct people to concrete services. Social workers also work in hospices to ensure the provision of comfort to patients with end-stage AIDS (Tider, 1995). Shernoff (1990) wrote:

> This profession can be justly proud of the often pioneering work done by social workers from the onset of the AIDS health crisis. . . . Even before the significance of HIV was known and complete knowledge of the modes of transmission was verified, social workers began to make important contributions to all profession's understanding of AIDS. (p. 5)

Although HIV/AIDS is similar to other terminal illnesses, this disease is unique in several ways. First, a positive HIV diagnosis often results in society's ostracism and exclusion of the client. Second, this diagnosis often forces the client to disclose a secret that he or she had been keeping from family or friends (for example, homosexuality or intravenous drug use). The client then must deal not only with the medical component of the disease but also with the stress of maintaining important relationships.

Finally, people infected with the HIV virus are often young; most have not begun to accept death as a part of life. This factor is extremely difficult for family members because it reverses the expected life cycle when a child dies before his or her parents (Lloyd, 1990).

The Gay Men's Health Crisis (GMHC), a nonprofit organization, was formed in the early 1980s by gay professionals who felt that the medical and social services available at that time were not responding to the crisis of the AIDS epidemic. As the caseload grew and became increasingly complex, social workers and other professionals joined the organization (Getzel, 1989). Other nonprofit AIDS organizations have used the services of social workers, and social workers now play an integral role in this area of service, as exemplified in the following vignette.

Jason's Story

Jason Jackson was a 30-year-old midtown reporter for a New York newspaper. He did volunteer work at a nursing home and he liked to jog, write poetry, travel, and play basketball. And he had AIDS.

Jackson had gone to the doctor because he was tired and had the flu for almost two weeks. He also had a sore throat and diarrhea. His physician prescribed some antibiotics and then asked if Jason had any reason to believe he may have contracted the HIV virus. Jason responded that he was gay and had had unprotected sex in the past, but now he was in a monogamous relationship. The doctor said he would have to do some tests to find out if Jason had HIV, but before doing so he referred Jason to GMHC to get counseling about the HIV testing procedure.

Jason went to GMHC where he met with Janet Deer, a social worker who had worked at GMHC for nearly six years. Jason explained his concerns to her and told her about his need for an HIV test, and Janet took a detailed personal and sexual history. She tried to assess Jason's previous experience handling crises and then helped Jason determine his degree of risk.

Jason had the test done and found out that he was HIV-positive. He did not believe it at first, but there was no mistake. Jason called his lover, who then admitted that he had had an affair earlier that year. Jason was furious. He hated his lover and he hated himself. He was angry and frightened.

Jason's father is a retired Navy captain and had no idea Jason was gay. Jason believed that neither of his parents would ever accept his homosexuality. His older brother was in Germany serving with the Army. Jason felt completely alone. With nowhere else to turn, he made an appointment to see Janet at GMHC.

Janet's psychosocial perspective was essential in helping Jason come to terms with his diagnosis as well as the relationship issues he would inevitably face when he informed his parents of his illness. She knew that Jason would undergo intense stress and probably some degree of social isolation. As Jason began to develop physical symptoms, his isolation would increase. Janet also knew that at first Jason would be in denial and may isolate himself, a response that may be necessary at first but that can become dangerous when denial contributes to depression, dependency, and despondency. Assessment of the role of denial is a critical task for social workers in this practice area. As the virus began to weaken Jason's body, necessary lifestyle changes would cause resentment. Janet knew that people with HIV/AIDS may experience depression, delirium, and dementia that can alter impulse control, thus putting a person at risk to self and others.

As an initial intervention, Janet counseled Jason independently on the issues he would face, such as coping with and expressing the anger he felt toward his lover and his parents. She helped Jason "come out of the closet" to his parents and prepared him for the consequences. She also referred Jason for group therapy for people with AIDS. The group gave Jason a chance to see how others with AIDS dealt with their personal relationships as well as their medical treatments.

Jason continued to see Janet regularly for several months. He was one of the unlucky ones: He developed full-blown AIDS within months of his initial diagnosis. As Jason's physical condition deteriorated and death became imminent, Janet suggested that he have a GMHC volunteer crisis worker visit him at home every day; she knew that Jason did not want to die in the hospital. This volunteer worker concentrated on being with Jason during times of stress and helped Jason prepare for death. After Jason died, Janet worked with the volunteer and Jason's family and friends to plan a memorial service.

In this example, Janet Deer carried out the basic social work functions of assessment, support, counseling, enabling, referral, and coordinating. In addition, social workers who serve people with AIDS must have special knowledge of the epidemiology of the disease, prevention techniques, and obstacles to behavior change (Lloyd, 1990). They must also be aware of cultural reactions to HIV and AIDS, homophobia, stereotypes of drug users, and social attitudes about people infected with HIV (Lloyd, 1990).

In working with people with AIDS, social workers must focus on changing risk behavior. However, the social worker must also be prepared for instability and recidivism. The basic social work intervention focuses on helping the infected person remain active and productive and as fully integrated as possible, both socially and emotionally. To achieve this goal social workers must be knowledgeable about medical resources, self-help and other support groups, case management services, home health care organizations, and inpatient treatment facilities (Lloyd, 1990).

Social workers in this field must intervene often with family members; significant others; service agencies; social security and public assistance programs; and health care, home care, and hospice services. Social workers must be skilled in direct practice, group work, case management, and resource utilization (Lloyd, 1990). In addition, because there is no cure for AIDS, social workers must focus on disseminating educational information, promoting prevention techniques, and informing the community about the often-misunderstood facts of HIV and AIDS (Taylor-Brown, 1995).

The previous case example took place in a specialized HIV/AIDS service setting; however there is an ongoing debate over the best place to administer medical and social services to this population. Many social workers promote treatment through primary care centers, on the basis that medical and psychosocial needs are more conveniently located so that holistic services can be provided. However, other social workers promote specialized HIV service settings on the basis that all health care workers with this population must have specialized knowledge and training beyond that of staff members at primary health care facilities (Lloyd, 1995).

In addition to the debate about the location of services, this area faces constant pressure to secure adequate funding support. Although resources are currently provided to cities and states through the Ryan White Comprehensive AIDS Resources Emergency (CARE) Act of 1990 (P.L. 101-381), there is no national policy on HIV prevention or treatment services. Therefore, if the Ryan White CARE Act is ever discontinued or if the funding levels decrease, most HIV/AIDS services would be dismantled, leaving clients devastated (Lloyd, 1995).

The issues that have been discussed apply to social work with AIDS and HIV patients regardless of age, sex, race, or color. However, there is one population that warrants special attention: children with AIDS.

A Dying Child

My name is Chris and I am a social worker at the Presbyterian Hospital in New York City. I specialize in pediatric AIDS. I love my work, and I hate my work. When I see the children come in, I feel completely powerless. I know they will die before they have even had a chance to live. I also know that there is probably more than one member in the child's family who has HIV/AIDS. Many of the families are poor and belong to racial and ethnic groups, so they have problems of finances and discrimination in addition to the positive HIV diagnosis. These children are dying alone. They are stigmatized and excluded. The fear, misunderstanding, and ambivalent feelings toward children with HIV/AIDS are exemplified by teachers, playmates, medical personnel, and even morticians.

Most of the children I work with contracted the disease from their mothers at birth. Some are severely ill and are in the hospital; others live at home or in foster care. I don't just work with the children—I can't. The whole family needs help coping with their denial, sorrow, and guilt at having passed on the disease. The family needs to be helped in their grief and then mobilized to support and care for the child. Often, the mother is also dying so I try to help the parents make appropriate custody arrangements. I also try to change high-risk behavior in the parents, and to obtain income support, medical care, and housing assistance when necessary.

In my work, I am forced to constantly reevaluate my own attitudes and bias toward my clients. I must try to understand their culture and the beliefs, values, and life circumstances that have contributed to their situation. I constantly strive to provide education and prevention information, to do whatever I can to reduce the number of children born with AIDS. People ask me how I can work every day with clients who will die. Sometimes I wonder the same thing. But every day, these children humble me by their own strength and vulnerability, and I know that if I am not there for them, who will be?

Social workers were among the first professionals to offer services to children and families affected by the HIV virus (Wiener, Fair, & Garcia, 1995). Social workers who work with children with AIDS may experience feelings of powerlessness because of the dire prognosis, and they must address a range of problems affecting the child and the family. Social workers are called on to help affected families meet their most basic needs for housing, food, and transportation. In addition, social workers often act as case managers by facilitating access to services and coordinating hospital, home, and community care (Wiener et al., 1995). Unless the child's case resulted from a blood transfusion, it is likely that the mother is either HIV-positive or has AIDS ("Specter of AIDS," 1987). Social workers must use the range of social work interventions, from counseling to advocacy, and they often will need to provide mental health services, such as support and advice, to the client and the family (Wiener et al., 1995).

Tapping family support is particularly crucial because the family often faces stigma and condemnation, resulting in a lack of extended family and community support. The hysteria that can accompany community knowledge that a child has AIDS was made obvious in the case of Ryan White, a 15-year-old hemophilia patient who contracted AIDS from a blood transfusion. The family was harassed and Ryan was expelled from school and readmitted only after legal intervention ("Specter of AIDS," 1987). Although improved blood testing has reduced the number of pediatric AIDs cases caused by transfusions of HIV-contaminated blood, the reported number of cases of children born to HIV-infected mothers is on the rise (Hymes, 1990).

Social work involvement in areas of public health such as infectious diseases like HIV and AIDS has increased tremendously. State trends point toward growth in programs in areas of chronic diseases, such as heart disease and cancer; infectious diseases, such as AIDS; and behavioral diseases, such as drug and alcohol abuse (Moroney, 1995). As indicated in the previous vignette, social workers carry out many different functions in this arena:

Social Work Function	Example
Assessment and counseling	Recognizing and understanding the family's denial, sorrow, and guilt and helping them to cope with their emotions
Consultation and coordination	Making appropriate custody arrangements when necessary
Advocacy, research, and program development	Constantly striving to promote education and prevention information and programs

Social workers in the field of pediatric AIDS find that emphasizing the concept of living with AIDS, as opposed to dying from it, is a useful approach in working with children and families. This emphasis on living also helps the social workers cope with the difficulties that their clients face day to day (Hymes, 1990). Lori Wiener, coordinator of the Pediatric HIV Psychosocial Support Program at the National Institutes of Health, observed that

> Persons infected with HIV must bear the burden of societal hostility at a time when they are most lacking psychological and social support. The fears of being rejected, harassed or facing discrimination,

losing insurance and being locked out of schools are major societal stresses. And no one is better equipped to deal with these stresses than social workers. (quoted in Hymes, 1990, p. 4)

Wiener also noted that although there are a variety of foster care programs to meet the needs of HIV-infected children, there is a dearth of programs for uninfected siblings (as cited in Landers, 1993). These children experience the pains of loss, often manifest in poor school performance, acting-out behavior, loss of friends, and isolation.

In addition to actively working with affected families and children, social workers must be involved in community education and prevention services. An example of the power of community organization and advocacy is the development of the New York State Standby Guardian Law, which was developed in response to the growing number of children who were being orphaned by parents who had AIDS. In an effort to prevent a huge influx of children into the foster care system, social workers were essential players in planning The Orphan Project, a research study designed to explore policy options to meet the needs of HIV-affected and HIV-infected children. Social workers also used skills of coordination and organization to bring together public and private organizations, such as Mothers of Children with AIDS, Lincoln Hospital, St. Vincent's Hospital, the New York City Department of Health, the Rose F. Kennedy Center, and many others, to pool their knowledge and local influence in assuring the bill's passage. The result was the formation of a policy with the specific objective of facilitating the appointment of "standby guardians," thus reducing the number of children placed in the foster care system (Letteney, 1995; Vobejda, 1994).

We are seeing a growing number of children who are orphaned as a result of the AIDS epidemic. It is estimated that by the end of 1995, maternal deaths caused by AIDS will leave 24,600 children and 21,000 adolescents orphaned, and unless there is a reversal of current mortality trends, by the year 2000 the total number of children orphaned as a result of AIDS will exceed 80,000 and may reach 125,000 (Landers, 1993). These children bear mental and emotional scars and require services such as advocacy in schools and in the courts, and support groups and counseling for the children and their guardians. Mothers with AIDS also need help actively planning for their children's future, including developing a custody plan.

Whether working with adults or children with AIDS or their families and significant others, social workers in this field of practice have a difficult but essential job. In the words of Caitlin Ryan (1988), a social worker and AIDS activist,

> From the onset until now, working with AIDS has been like fighting a war. The enemy is a disease that has so far thwarted our most sophisticated technology. Beyond its physical toll, AIDS exacts an emotional toll as well. Service providers and survivors alike suffer a form of post-traumatic stress syndrome—from the loss, the fear, the incredible suffering and indignities that the disease and discrimination call forth. (p. 3)

An informal Social Workers' AIDS Network (SWAN) began in New York in 1982 for social workers in the field of AIDS to provide mutual support, discuss cases, and share ideas and experiences. Similar groups have formed in other parts of the country. Participants have found that colleague involvement is energizing and supportive ("Network Helps AIDS Caregivers," 1988).

References

Alperin, D., & Richie, N. (1989). Community-based AIDS organizations. *Health & Social Work, 14,* 165–173.

Frisino, J. M. (1994). *AIDS, testing and confidentiality.* Unpublished manuscript, Yeshiva University, Wurzweiler School of Social Work, New York.

Getzel, G. S. (1989). Responding effectively to the crisis of a gay man with AIDS. In T. S. Kerson & Associates, *Social work in health settings: Practice in context* (pp. 247–266). New York: Haworth.

Hymes, T. A. (1990, July). Workers in pediatric AIDS give, get hope. *NASW News,* p. 4.

Landers, S. (1993, June). AIDS orphans: The unseen casualties. *NASW News,* p. 3.

Leigh, B., Temple, M., & Trocki, K. (1993). The sexual behavior of U.S. adults: Results from a national survey. *American Journal of Public Health, 83*(10), 1400–1408.

Letteney, S. (1995). *Policies affecting women and children in a time of AIDS: New York State's Standby Guardian Law.* Unpublished manuscript, Yeshiva University, Wurzweiler School of Social Work, New York.

Leukefeld, C., & Fimbres, M. (Eds.). (1987). *Responding to AIDS: Psychosocial initiatives.* Silver Spring, MD: National Association of Social Workers.

Lloyd, G. A. (1990). AIDS and HIV: The syndrome and the virus. In L. Ginsberg et al. (Eds.), *Encyclopedia of social work* (18th ed., 1990 suppl., pp. 12–50). Silver Spring, MD: NASW Press.

Lloyd, G. A. (1995). HIV/AIDS overview. In R. L. Edwards (Ed.-in-Chief), *Encyclopedia of social work* (19th ed., Vol. 2, pp. 1257–1290). Washington, DC: NASW Press.

Moroney, R. M. (1995). Public health services. In R. L. Edwards (Ed.-in-Chief), *Encyclopedia of social work* (19th ed., Vol. 3, pp. 1967–1973). Washington, DC: NASW Press.

National Commission on AIDS. (1993). *AIDS: An expanding tragedy: The final report of the National Commission on AIDS*. Washington, DC: Author.

National Commission on Children. (1993). *Just the facts: A summary of recent information on America's children and their families*. Washington, DC: Author.

Network helps AIDS caregivers to cope. (1988, May). *NASW News*, p. 3.

Rensberger, B. (1993, July 31). Evidence of women's increased risk of AIDS pushes search for protection. *Washington Post*, p. A3.

Russell, C. (1994, June 28). AIDS is leading killer of blacks 25 to 44. *Washington Post* (Health section), p. 7.

Ryan, C. (1988, March). A day on the front lines fighting AIDS. *NASW News*, pp. 3–4.

Ryan White Comprehensive AIDS Resources Emergency Act of 1990, P.L. 101-381, 104 Stat. 576.

Shernoff, M. (1990). Why every social worker should be challenged by AIDS. *Social Work, 35*, 5–8.

Specter of AIDS is no respecter of age. (1987, September). *NASW News*, p. 3.

Taylor-Brown, S. (1995). HIV/AIDS: Direct practice. In R. L. Edwards (Ed.-in-Chief), *Encyclopedia of social work* (19th ed., Vol. 2, pp. 1291–1305). Washington, DC: NASW Press.

Tider, T. (1995). *AIDS*. Unpublished manuscript, Yeshiva University, Wurzweiler School of Social Work, New York.

Vobejda, B. (1994, March 29). A legacy of AIDS: Orphans. *Washington Post*, p. A3.

Wiener, L., Fair, C. D., & Garcia, A. (1995). HIV/AIDS: Pediatric. In R. L. Edwards (Ed.-in-Chief), *Encyclopedia of social work* (19th ed., Vol. 2, pp. 1314–1324). Washington, DC: NASW Press.

Worker's effort puts AZT drug in client's grasp. (1989, November). *NASW News*, p. 21.

hospital social work

Hospital social work is a subset of medical social work, the social work practice oriented to facilitating good health, preventing illness, and helping physically ill patients and their families address and resolve the social, financial, and psychological problems related to the illness (Barker, 1995). It is defined as "the provision of social services in hospitals and similar health care centers, most often within a facility's department of social services or social work" (Barker, 1995, p. 171).

The service components of hospital social work include preventive and rehabilitative services, discharge planning, information gathering and providing, assisting patients with the financial and social aspects of their care, and counseling patients and their families. Social work in health care refers both to direct practice, which is based on face-to-face interactions with the client and the family, and indirect practice, which involves interaction with representatives of clients, agencies, and communities.

The functions performed by medical social workers in direct practice vary according to the level of care and the type of health setting. For example, acute care settings require social workers to be involved in high-risk screening, discharge planning, collaboration, and information and referral (Poole, 1995). However, in health care settings that focus on health promotion and prevention, such as a neighborhood clinic, social workers may be involved in needs assessment, education, coordination of services, advocacy, and community and program development (Poole, 1995). Social work functions in the medical field are also guided by national needs and priorities. For example, the defeat of President Clinton's national health care plan and the proposal of the Republican Party's "Contract with America" jeopardize the security of quality health care for all people. All social workers, but especially medical social workers, must practice advocacy, community planning, resource and program development, and policy analysis and development (Poole, 1995).

Social workers in medical settings are frequently assigned to specific units and focus their work on patient needs based on different age groups, gender, diagnosis, or points along the continuum from diagnosis to treatment problems ("Study Gives Profile," 1984). Social workers deal with issues of recovery, progressive disease, and terminal illness.

Hospital social work has become increasingly specialized. Oncology is one such specialization, in which social work roles include counseling for illness-related psychosocial problems and for problems related to rehabilitation and recovery, terminal illness, discharge planning, relaxation and stress-reduction, and grief ("Study Gives Profile," 1984). Other social work roles include helping with tangible resources such as transportation, financial aid, and housing and providing information and referral to self-help groups and community resources. With recent advances in biomedical technology, new specializations emerge, as illustrated in the following vignette.

A Social Worker Helps a Heart Transplant Patient

Gail Mason is the social worker assigned to the heart transplant team at Stanford Medical Center in Palo Alto, California. Mr. Hunt is a 64-year-old man who was admitted to the hospital last night with congestive heart failure. He desperately needs a new heart in order to live.

Mr. Hunt arrived yesterday from Boise, Idaho, with his 63-year-old wife and two daughters, ages 29 and 33. They are all here to participate in the hospital's five-day evaluation period.

First, Gail will try to determine if Mr. Hunt is an appropriate candidate for the extremely delicate and complicated heart transplant procedure. Through interviews with him and his family, she will seek to determine if Mr. Hunt can and will comply with the demanding medical regimen that must be followed after surgery. To make this determination, Gail must learn about Mr. Hunt's past behavior and how his beliefs and behaviors may affect his current health care. For example, she tries to determine his ability to handle stress and his past history of seeking necessary medical care. She also investigates Mr. Hunt's past history of complying with physician instructions. One of the most important indicators the social worker examines is the client's attitude toward taking medication. For example, has Mr. Hunt refused to take medications in the past because they remind him of his illness?

In addition to the issue of medical compliance, Gail attempts to identify patients who have strong support systems and a solid understanding of the complex transplant process. After several meetings with Mr. Hunt and his wife and daughters, Gail recommends him for the procedure, a recommendation approved by his physicians on the basis of the physiological aspects of the case. Gail's role then changes from evaluating to educating the Hunt family and "emotionally immunizing" them in preparation for the upcoming rigorous medical procedures.

After the evaluation period, Mr. Hunt is admitted to the hospital as an inpatient, while his daughters return to their homes in Idaho. Gail must help Mrs. Hunt find local housing and transportation. In addition, the Hunts are extremely nervous about the insurance limitations for financing the surgery. After discussing the issue with them, Gail refers them to the hospital financial department where they receive information on developing a trust fund to collect and manage donations to pay for the surgery.

Now, as Gail has seen so many times, the family enters perhaps the most stressful part of the procedure—the wait. With the current shortage of donors, the wait could last many months, and the stress can bring out family problems that have gone unaddressed for years. Gail meets regularly with the Hunts, individually and together. She also maintains regular contact with the daughters when they visit, answering questions about their father's illness, addressing unresolved family issues, and helping them understand the transplant process.

In addition to helping the family cope with the wait, Gail prepares them for the very real possibility that a replacement heart will not arrive in time or that it will be rejected by Mr. Hunt's body. This is a difficult but essential part of Gail's work with the family.

Finally, a heart becomes available and Mr. Hunt goes to surgery. The procedure is long and difficult, but after eight stressful hours, Mr. Hunt has a new heart and is doing well in recovery. After 10 days of follow-up medical care, he and his wife return to Idaho to face a new lifestyle filled with hope, joy, fear, and a refreshed desire to live life to the fullest.

As medicine becomes increasingly high tech, there is a very real need for social work services. In this scenario, Gail was part of the medical evaluation team involved in the decision whether to accept Mr. Hunt for a transplant. Assessment, however, is only one component of her role. She also helped Mrs. Hunt find local housing and transportation, worked with the family on insurance issues and aftercare requirements, and helped them deal with the stress of the presurgery waiting period. The following specific functions of hospital social work were exemplified in this case:

Social Work Function	Example
Assessment	Determining Mr. Hunt's ability to comply with the medical requirements.
Support	Assisting Mr. Hunt by maximizing his family support network.
Advice and counseling	Counseling Mr. Hunt and his family.
Appropriate referrals	Making referrals to support groups and to needed services such as the hospital financial department.
Coordination	Facilitating communication between Mr. Hunt, his family, and the medical team.

Hospital social workers use many of the same skills and encounter many of the same issues as social workers in other settings, although some aspects unique to hospital social work include the short-term setting, physical and medical components, and collaboration with an interdisciplinary health care team (Rossen, 1987).

In the vignette, Gail Mason specialized in work with transplant patients. Lee Suszycki, a social worker at Columbia Presbyterian Medical Center in New

York City and past president of the National Clinical Network for Social Workers on Heart Transplant Programs, describes the excitement of working "where social work skills are so badly needed to humanize this entire experience and make it real" ("Heart Transplants," 1987, p. 3). In addition to working with transplant patients, there are opportunities for hospital social workers to provide services in almost every area of treatment including medical–surgical, pediatric, psychiatric, obstetric–gynecologic, intensive care, rehabilitation, and emergency services.

Hospital social work is practiced in a variety of public and private, sectarian and nonsectarian settings including general and specialized acute care medical centers; psychiatric hospitals; rehabilitation centers; long-term care facilities, such as nursing homes and adult day care programs; primary care settings, such as health maintenance organizations; ambulatory clinics; and home health programs (Rossen, 1987).

Throughout the years, hospital social workers have exhibited creativity and success in managing their various functions. Ross (1995) noted that "social workers are the only health professionals in hospitals whose responsibilities are closely tied to social health problems, yet disconnected from physical care of patients" (p. 1369). Some serve in clinical roles while others serve as managers for specific programs administered by the hospital in areas such as mental health, aging, and community outreach. Social workers must be able to assess, diagnose, and evaluate the patient's situation and work with the individual and the family to develop a care and evaluation plan (Ross, 1995).

Because hospitalization usually is sudden and requires major personal adjustments, much of hospital social work requires crisis intervention. Unlike social work in any other setting, hospital social workers usually have only five to 10 days to accomplish their goals, and follow-up is often unrealistic because of the steady stream of new patients being admitted every day (Rossen, 1987).

Hospital social work entails clinical counseling, arranging for concrete services after discharge, and intervening with the patient's family. Hospital social work, like other areas of the profession, has both micro and macro dimensions. On the micro level, social workers intervene with individuals and families to alleviate hardship, restore health and mental health, and increase the medical provider's awareness of a particular patient's home environment and personal circumstances. The social worker also plays a crucial role as patients re-enter their homes and communities by helping individuals and families understand the illness, the demands of the treatment, and the potential effects on their lifestyles (Ross, 1995).

On a macro level, social workers facilitate collaboration between health care and community agencies to understand the needs of particular groups of patients. For example, hospital social workers may work with county agencies to provide timely discharge of a child to foster care, which will minimize the time a healthy child spends in an institutional setting, decrease the risk of infection, and free a bed for an unhealthy child (Ross, 1995). Social workers often engage in the functions of planning and evaluating health services and participating in primary prevention campaigns, such as smoking prevention or AIDS education efforts (Oktay, 1995). In addition, several hospital social work departments have contracted with other industries to provide counseling and rehabilitation services, thus providing hospitals with additional sources of revenue (Rossen, 1987).

Current and proposed changes in health care delivery pose major challenges to social workers in this field. Social work in hospitals boomed following the enactment of Medicare and Medicaid in the 1960s because hospitals were able to build social work services into their routine costs and receive reimbursement. As social work departments expanded in hospitals in the 1970s and 1980s, they began to provide services in outpatient programs and emergency rooms (Oktay, 1995). Currently, however, there is widespread acknowledgment that health care expenditures have grown out of control, and the future of hospital social work is being challenged. A 1993 NASW survey of hospital social workers (Landers, 1993b) revealed that closures of hospital social work departments have become more frequent, as have reorganizations of social work departments within hospitals. The move from a traditional social work department to a decentralized model in which social work staff are reassigned to other departments has raised questions about proper supervision and the quality of treatment for patients (Landers, 1993b). In some cases, reorganization has also meant replacing department directors with non–social work personnel.

Many recent developments in the field of health care, such as the introduction of diagnosis-related groups (DRGs, a federally mandated prospective payment mechanism designed to control the costs of medical and hospital care) and managed care, will continue to influence the direction of hospital social work. As reported in Landers (1993b),

> Many hospitals are downsizing their social work departments or eliminating them, leaving psychosocial care to other members of the health care team, or ignoring social aspects of care (outside their own reimbursement) altogether. . . . The resulting inadequate posthospital care and unaddressed psychosocial needs of the patient will inevitably lead to increased utilization and costs. (p. 12)

During this time of uncertainty and change, hospital social workers must redefine the profession's role in the new medical environment and develop accountability standards to ensure the professionalism that is critical for future support and expansion (Rossen, 1987). Clearly there will be continued emphasis on containing costs by controlling the length of hospital stays. Social workers in hospital settings are grappling with questions such as "How will hospital discharge planning be done under managed care?" and "How will managed care affect the survival of social work departments in hospitals and the role of social workers?" Dealing with managed care companies has been described as "labor intensive," sometimes involving several phone calls to determine coverage (Landers, 1993a).

In addition to these challenges, hospital social workers must also address the issues of working in a *host setting*, an organization in which the mission and decision-making practices are dominated by people who are not social workers. Hospitals and schools were two of the first host organizations that began employing social workers. Psychiatric clinics, juvenile courts, prisons, and police departments are other examples (Dane & Simon, 1991).

Dane and Simon (1991) identified the following problems faced by social workers in host settings:

- discrepancies between professional values and those of the organizational leaders

- unusual visibility and high performance expectations that accompany minority status

- devaluing of social work as "women's work" in predominantly male organizations

- role ambiguity and role strain.

As a result of these and other issues, social workers in host settings are often caught in an organizational bind: The hospital administrator emphasizes efficiency and cost containment, whereas social workers focus on patient problems and service needs (Dane & Simon, 1991).

The ability of social workers to make known the cost benefits of their services is essential, especially in a host setting. Harris (1986) noted that

> Not only do professionally trained social workers know best how to accomplish the transition from hospital to community or home-based care, but social work services are crucial to hospitals now as never before for cost-effective care. Early screening, liaison with community agencies, and prompt involvement of patient and family in planning and decision making all promote effective, safe, and timely discharge—essential services when hospitals need to keep costs down. (p. 2)

Despite the pressures of working in a host setting, hospital social workers must share responsibilities without abdicating professional territory. Social workers must always maintain the final review and approval for any shared task so that they may demonstrate their expertise and specialized knowledge in this practice setting (Dane & Simon, 1991).

Discharge Planning

Mary is a 76-year-old widow who has been living by herself in an apartment in Arizona since her husband died three years ago. Her son, who is 50 years old, lives in Los Angeles and visits her twice a year. Yesterday, while Mary was taking her daily walk, she fell and fractured her hip. She had surgery for her hip and will now need physical therapy and six days of hospitalization before she can go home. Once home, she will need continuing help with daily activities and the adjustment to a new lifestyle. Mary's only income is her monthly social security check of $615.

Lying in bed after the surgery, Mary is frightened and unsure of her future. She wishes someone was there to help her.

There is someone to help. Based on her age, health, living status, and income, Mary is designated as a high-risk patient by the hospital intake staff and referred to the hospital social services department. A social worker is then able to assist Mary in many ways.

The basic social work functions of assessment, support, referral, and coordination include the following interventions:

- helping Mary understand what happened to her hip and the medical implications for her future daily activities

- helping Mary work through her fear and frustration at losing some of her independence

- working with Mary to evaluate her eligibility for needed services and ongoing care

- arranging for the appropriate services to assist Mary for a period of time after she leaves the hospital so that she can make a smooth transition to living alone

- helping Mary adjust to her new lifestyle and dependence on others

- facilitating communication among Mary, her son, and members of the hospital team to ensure quality care that includes psychosocial aspects.

Discharge planning is a social service offered in hospitals and other institutions that is designed to help the patient or client make a satisfactory and timely adjustment from a hospital facility to alternative sources of care or to self-care. Functions include helping the client and relevant others understand the nature of the problem and its impact, facilitating the client's adjustment and adaptation to new roles, and helping arrange for postdischarge care (Barker, 1995). Discharge planning responsibilities are a growing aspect of hospital social work.

The Deficit Reduction Act of 1984 (P.L. 98-369) developed a prospective pricing system for Medicare through the creation of DRGs. Under this system, hospitals maximize their profit by decreasing the time the patient spends in the hospital. To help hospitals achieve their goals of shorter stays, one hospital social worker concluded that "much of our attention will have to be focused on more efficient use of patients' stays in the hospital and more timely discharge" (Sheridan, 1984). However, she cautioned that social workers must continue to be cognizant of the nature and heritage of their professional practice. "In our desire to please higher-status professionals, and in our roles as representatives of institutions, let us not forget that we are also advocates for our patients; . . . though social workers may do an increasing amount of discharge planning, we must resist the pressures which would make us nothing more than discharge planners" (p. 27).

The social worker's role also extends to ensuring that needed postdischarge care is in fact provided. A recent study found that discharge plans frequently failed to be carried out in full, with some but not all services delivered (Simon, Showers, Blumenfield, Holden, & Wu, 1995). The role of the hospital social worker must extend beyond the point of patient discharge, to include a discharge follow-up component.

Interdisciplinary Teams

Hospital social workers must also manage the pressures of their membership in an interdisciplinary team. Another social worker, commenting on Sheridan's (1984) remarks, noted that when working as part of an interdisciplinary treatment team in a hospital setting, there is a "desire to please 'higher-status professionals' (i.e., doctors)" and one wears "two hats as we work with the patient and family and also represent the agency" (Goldberg, 1984). In Goldberg's view,

> The task of the social worker is to interpret to the interdisciplinary treatment team that discharge planning is a process of facilitating the return of the patient to the community. This process starts when the patient is admitted and may be relatively easy or very difficult. It involves a psychosocial assessment of the patient in his or her environment, and proceeds in an orderly manner until discharge. The social worker may need to use such techniques as crisis intervention, short-term individual psychotherapy, family therapy, and information and referral to help the patient and family members understand options, work through feelings, and make decisions and take appropriate actions. (p. 14)

The introduction of DRGs and managed care have increased social workers' involvement in discharge planning, often at the expense of other, more interventive, functions. A director of social work in a large urban hospital remarked that the job of the hospital social worker has evolved into "ensuring that the patients leave the hospital as quickly as possible with a smile on their face" (personal communication, November 11, 1994).

References

Barker, R. L. (1995). *Social work dictionary* (3rd ed.). Washington, DC: NASW Press.

Dane, B. O., & Simon, B. L. (1991). Resident guests: Social workers in host settings. *Social Work, 36,* 208–213.

Deficit Reduction Act of 1984, P.L. 98-369, 98 Stat. 494.

Goldberg, A. S. (1984, March). Readers write. *NASW News,* p. 14.

Harris, D. V. (1986, June). From the president: Making the case: Social work & the health care revolution. *NASW News,* p. 2.

Heart transplants: Waiting for new life. (1987, March). *NASW News,* p. 3.

Landers, S. (1993a, July). Providers ponder a managed-care future. *NASW News*, p. 3.

Landers, S. (1993b, September). Social work in hospitals seen in flux. *NASW News*, pp. 1, 12.

Oktay, J. S. (1995). Primary health care. In R. L. Edwards (Ed.-in-Chief), *Encyclopedia of social work* (19th ed., Vol. 3, pp. 1887–1894). Washington, DC: NASW Press.

People in the news. (1990, October). *NASW News*, p. 19.

Poole, D. L. (1995). Health care: Direct practice. In R. L. Edwards (Ed.-in-Chief), *Encyclopedia of social work* (19th ed., Vol. 2, pp. 1156–1167). Washington, DC: NASW Press.

Ross, J. W. (1995). Hospital social work. In R. L. Edwards (Ed.-in-Chief), *Encyclopedia of social work* (19th ed., Vol. 2, pp. 1365–1377). Washington, DC: NASW Press.

Rossen, S. (1987). Hospital social work. In A. Minahan (Ed.-in-Chief), *Encyclopedia of social work* (18th ed., Vol. 1, p. 816–821). Silver Spring, MD: National Association of Social Workers.

Sheridan, M. S. (1984, January). To the editor. *NASW News*, p. 27.

Simon, E. P., Showers, N., Blumenfield, S., Holden, G., & Wu, X. (1995). Delivery of home care services after discharge: What really happens. *Health & Social Work, 20*, 5–14.

Study gives profile on oncology workers. (1984, June). *NASW News*, p. 13.

career
opportunities

A variety of job opportunities are available to social workers in the area of health care. These jobs, a sample of which appear below, range from population-specific (teenage mothers, people with AIDS, people with cancer) to setting-specific (hospital, hospice) in which the social worker works with many different populations. These jobs are based on actual classified ads but are not actual job postings.

Administrative Director, Social Services Department, University Medical Center

A 528-bed regional teaching hospital and tertiary care facility is in search of a talented professional to help maintain high levels of efficiency and responsiveness in our social services department. Managing a staff of approximately 25, you will develop and implement budgets and policies, participate on various hospital committees, and collaborate with administration of patient care groups. Requires an MSW with five years' experience, current state licensure or immediate eligibility, and three years' administrative/supervisory experience.

Deputy Project Director

For national project to prevent HIV and sexually transmitted diseases (STDs) in Hispanic communities. Will assist the project director with the overall implementation of the project, including providing technical assistance and training in HIV/STD prevention and nonprofit management. Master's degree in social work, health education, or related field preferred; at least two years' experience working with a community-based organization; knowledge and experience in the prevention of HIV and STDs in Hispanic communities and in management of nonprofits. Bilingual English/Spanish.

Eating Disorders Program/Behavioral Medicine Program Fellows

Advanced training positions for postdoctoral (or ABD) psychologists, MSWs, or clinical specialists in outpatient Eating Disorders and Behavioral Medicine programs at university-affiliated general hospital. Intensive training in individual cognitive–behavioral and psychodynamic psychotherapies, group, and family treatment.

Executive Director
Medicare-certified agency seeks a full-time executive director who will continue to build on the organization's success in responding to the community need for hospice care for people who are terminally ill. The ideal candidate will have a minimum of a four-year degree in a related field and three to five years of administrative and community relations experience. The candidate will be responsible for day-to-day management of the hospice. Preferred experience with volunteer organizations and a working knowledge of regulations affecting hospice care programs.

HIV Prevention Specialist
This position is responsible for statewide administration and professional activities and will serve as the AIDS Administration's HIV Prevention Specialist for individuals within the state's criminal justice system (Division of Correction, Division of Parole and Probation). Responsibility for all aspects of AIDS health and risk reduction for incarcerated populations, overall design and implementation of community-based projects/activities targeting recently released populations, and monitoring/providing of technical assistance and training to agencies that contract with the AIDS Administration to provide these services. Requires a bachelor's degree in health, human services, education/counseling services, one year of which must be experience providing HIV-related education to individuals within the criminal justice system.

HIV Prevention Specialist Case Manager
Provides case management and counseling to high-risk homeless and runaway youths between the ages of 12 and 23. Experience working with and knowledge of African American youth issues required. Ability to work in multicultural environment and to provide HIV education, prevention, and substance abuse counseling.

HIV/STD Program Associate
Seeking program associate for HIV/STD program. Will develop training activities addressing needs of African American women. Knowledge of women's health issues, HIV/STD, curriculum development, grant writing, training.

Human Services Program Coordinator
Position is responsible for reducing the numbers and rates of child lead poisoning by developing recommendations for legislative change at the state level, recommending effective strategies to further program goals, coordinating and integrating data management systems, designing prevalence surveys and community needs assessments, monitoring grantee performance, developing statewide health

education initiatives, and staffing the statewide task force on lead poisoning. Qualifications include a background in policy development, assessment, technical assistance/consultation, and program management. Competitive applicants will have knowledge of public health and database management.

Manager of Emergency Services

High-visibility nonprofit organization has immediate opportunity for highly motivated individual to manage the emergency services program with responsibility for a consolidated delivery system of casework, services to military families, disaster relief, and an ongoing disaster action plan to assist in meeting local and national relief efforts. Work requires a professional level of knowledge of social work and business administration—normally acquired through a bachelor's degree in social work, business administration, or a closely related field. Requires level of knowledge of program planning, budget administration, supervision of staff and volunteers, application of social work principles, and emergency preparedness such as that acquired through five to six years of progressively responsible experience in a social services agency, two to three years in a supervisory capacity. Requires a high level of analytical ability in order to develop strategies for the disaster action plan and provide services within a complex system of emergency services for disaster victims and military families.

Medical Social Worker

Compassionate care for the terminally ill. Our medical social workers are key members of an interdisciplinary team, with responsibility for diagnostic psychosocial evaluation of the patient/family unit and assistance in counseling and casework. An MSW is required, state license, with two years' experience in health care setting. Experience with terminally ill people and their families preferred.

Oncology Social Work Coordinator

University hospital seeks a clinical social worker whose responsibilities will include assisting oncology patients and families with a variety of psychosocial needs as well as some planning and coordinating of these services within the institution. Candidates must have program development skills and be able to function within a complex interdisciplinary system. Significant oncology background and some management experience required. Must have MSW and be license-eligible.

Program Manager, Rehabilitation Services

A 378-bed acute care facility in an urban area has a full-time opportunity for a program manager to work in a CARF-accredited Rehabilitation Unit. The 30-bed unit features a transitional living apartment and community reintegration activities and treats a variety of patients including CVA, spinal cord, and head injuries. This autonomous position interacts with staff psychiatrists; nurses; and physical, occupational, and speech therapists in coordinating all services for patients. The program manager develops treatment plans, holds progress meetings with patients/families, and does discharge planning. Requires master's degree in social work with three to five years' experience, preferably in a comparable acute care setting. Experience with discharge planning and case management absolutely required.

Senior Research Associate

Senior-level position with responsibility for diverse research and evaluation projects. Private, nonprofit agency involved in health services research, program evaluation, health education, and the provision of health services. The position requires knowledge and experience in research design, methodology, data collection, and statistical analysis. Strong analytic, writing, and interpersonal skills are required. Experience in substance abuse, AIDS, and/or health promotion is particularly desirable.

Senior Social Worker

Major university teaching hospital is currently seeking a senior social worker for a newly created position. This is an excellent opportunity to become a member of our multidisciplinary team assigned to our Bone Marrow Transplant and Cancer Center. Responsibilities include provision of direct social services to oncology and bone marrow patients and their families via psychosocial assessment, counseling, discharge planning, resource development, referral, and group work. MSW, along with ACSW/BCSW or eligibility, required. Minimum of two years' postmaster's experience in an acute care hospital with oncology and bone marrow transplant patients preferred.

Social Worker

Major insurance company has a vacancy for a social worker in its medical review department. Incumbent will interact with subscribers and team members to locate and apply for community resources or alternative funding sources that complement medical case management plans. Requirements for the position are a degree in social work, LCSW/MSW preferred; minimum of three years' clinical social work experience in a hospital, community social service, or government agency; knowledge and experience in assessing community resources and funding for health care; strong organizational/interpersonal/problem solving skills; field work required; data processing experience preferred.

Social Worker/Outreach and Education

Seeking an outreach and education supervisor to oversee personnel and activities related to community outreach events and health education. Qualified applicants must be self-starters with excellent organizational, communication, and supervisory skills.

schools

introduction
to part IV

School social work is a social work specialty "oriented toward helping students make satisfactory school adjustments and coordinating and influencing the efforts of the school, the family, and the community to help achieve this goal" (Barker, 1995, p. 335). Although there are variations in the role of the school social worker because of factors such as the size of the school district, the number of social workers on staff, the role assignment with other helping professions assigned to the schools, and the community context in which the school is located, school social workers typically are called on to help students, families, teachers, and educational administrators deal with a range of problems that affect students, such as truancy, depression, withdrawal, aggressive or violent behavior, rebelliousness, and the effects of physical or emotional problems. Social workers help students overcome barriers to school attendance and academic achievement, promote responsible behavior, and intervene in problem situations to prevent the development of more serious difficulties ("School Social Workers 'Not a Frill,'" 1986).

A manual prepared by the Program on Law and Child Maltreatment of the Boston University School of Law (1986), with funding from the National Center on Child Abuse and Neglect, details the many roles social workers carry out in the schools. The manual notes the growing recognition of the essential services provided by school social workers. "No other school-based professional is prepared by way of training or professional orientation to become involved in the student's home and with such community systems as child protection, mental health and the juvenile court. . . . Moreover, when these linkages are made, we believe that the efforts of other school professionals will be enhanced" ("School Social Workers 'Not a Frill,'" p. 13).

In 1991, 4.7 percent of NASW members indicated that their primary practice area was school social work (Gibelman & Schervish, 1993). The proportion of social workers engaged in school-based practice has increased slightly in recent years; in 1988, 4.3 percent of the NASW membership had indicated that school social work was their primary practice area.

In 1992 NASW established a "school social work specialist" credential to identify social workers who have met rigorous national standards for education and experience in school social work practice (personal correspondence with Isadora Hare, Director of Quality Assurance, NASW, June 16, 1995). Eligibility criteria for this credential include an MSW from an accredited school of social work; at least two years or 3,000 hours of supervised school social work experience (one year of which may come from graduate practicum experience in a school setting); supervisory evaluations and professional references; and successful completion of the School Social Work section of the National Teachers Exam.

In 1994 NASW initiated a school social work section, the organization's first specialty-practice section to serve the diverse interests of the members. Programming directions will be decided by the section itself under its own steering committee. The formation of this section is seen as a way to achieve a stronger national voice for school social workers, including greater opportunity to network, share practice innovations, and promote the use of school social workers (Hiratsuka, 1994).

Diverse Role of School Social Workers

The role of social workers in the schools continues to evolve. Role change has been affected by new and broadened legislation and the increasing emphasis on school-linked services that involve collaboration between schools and community agencies (Hare, 1994). Social workers also have been active in defining their place within the schools and in expanding the boundaries of social work intervention. Table 29-1 lists skills and abilities that are important for social workers practicing in the schools.

Since passage of the Education for All Handicapped Children Act of 1975 (P.L. 94-142), social workers have played an important role in the schools. This legislation and its subsequent amendments mandate the provision of appropriate free educational resources for disabled children (Dane, 1985); the educational system is required to provide services in the "least restrictive environment." P.L. 94-142 and its amendments address issues of equal access, supportive services, and procedural protections for disabled children. Services include special testing, remedial lessons, counseling, and tutoring.

The 1986 amendments to the Education of the Handicapped Act (P.L. 99-457) established a foundation for an early intervention system for infants and toddlers with special needs (DiMichele, 1993). Services may include psychological assessment, parent and family training, counseling, and transition services to preschool programs (Barker, 1995). The Hawkins-Stafford Elementary and Secondary School Improvement Amendments Act of 1988 (P.L. 100-297) also expanded the role of school social workers in its provisions for preventive interventions for high-risk children and youths (Freeman, 1995).

Passage of the Individuals with Disabilities Education Act of 1990 (P.L. 101-476) further improved the original 1975 legislation to ensure the best education for learning disabled and physically disabled students. Improvements aimed to increase access to needed services for students and their families.

Table 29-1

Most Important Knowledge Areas, Skills, Abilities (KSAs) and Job Dimensions for Entry-Level School Social Workers

KSAs in Order of Importance by School Social Workers (N=862)

1. Social work ethics
2. Program development and management skills
3. Social work modalities and procedures
4. Theories of human behavior and development
5. Models of social work practice
6. Multidisciplinary activities
7. Characteristics of pupil populations
8. Public education legislation, case law, and due process

Job Dimensions (Categories of Tasks to Which KSAs Are Applied) in Order of Importance, Frequency, and Task Status

1. Relationship and services to children and families
2. Relationship and services to teachers and school staff
3. Services to other school personnel
4. Administrative and professional tasks
5. Interagency collaboration, prevention, and advocacy

Source: Nelson, C. (1990). *A job analysis of school social workers.* Princeton, NJ: Educational Testing Service.

Social work services have been explicitly added to the definition of early intervention services.

In 1994 President Clinton signed the Improving America's Schools Act (P.L. 103-382), a reauthorization of the Elementary and Secondary Education Act. This new law ensures a greater role for school social workers, among other pupil-services personnel, in helping children succeed in school. School social workers are specifically included in the act's definition of pupil-services personnel. Title I of the act, Compensatory Education, calls for new and expanded roles for social workers in the schools. For example, social workers must be consulted in the development of state plans to help disadvantaged children. Pupil-services personnel, including social workers, are also part of state school-support teams that help schools develop and evaluate programs and identify problems ("Schools Act," 1995).

Another feature of this legislation, the Elementary School Counseling Demonstration Act, provides grants for schools to initiate or expand comprehensive elementary school counseling programs. Programs are required to use school social workers, school counselors, and school psychologists. Under the demonstration act, a school social worker is defined as "an individual who holds a master's degree in social work and is licensed or certified by the state in which services are provided or holds a school social work specialist credential" ("Schools Act," 1995, p. 14).

Approximately 12 percent of school-aged children have disabilities that qualify them for special education resources. These disabilities range from mild to severe (Dane, 1985). Attention-deficit hyperactivity disorder (ADHD), for example, "starts in infancy, childhood, or adolescence and is characterized by impulsive behavior, inattentiveness, and excessive motor activity and short attention span" (Barker, 1995, p. 28). The severity of the behaviors associated with ADHD, however, may fall anywhere along the continuum.

Practice within School Settings

Legislation and its accompanying funds has tended to define the emphasis of school social work practice. For example, the Education for All Handicapped Children Act has encouraged the active involvement of parents in diagnosis and assessment and decision making regarding their children's educational plan. Social workers have altered their practice to incorporate this emphasis by mediating in conflicts about educational decisions; providing information to parents about process, programs, and services; and offering mental health services in the classroom (Alderson, Krishef, & Spencer, 1990; Freeman, 1995).

In some communities, schools have been identified as the logical location for "one-step services," including those oriented to health and mental health. School-based clinics, many of which are located in low-income urban areas, have expanded rapidly in recent years. They provide comprehensive services ranging from mental health counseling, to sports physical examinations, to alcohol and drug abuse counseling, to nutrition and weight reduction information ("Birth-Control Flap," 1987). These clinics are generally located in junior or senior high schools and are operated and funded by government or private agencies rather than by the school systems.

Contraceptive programs for adolescents have been conceptualized as an essential component of school-based services, although not without substantial controversy in some communities ("Birth-Control Flap," 1987; Lagana & Hayes, 1993). In 1994, 50 national organizations, including NASW, issued recommendations to help local, state, and federal policymakers develop integrated service systems that are community-based and school-linked to meet the needs of families and children ("Groups Back School-Linked Service Model," 1994).

School-linked services gained popularity with the rise in child poverty and other social problems such as drug addiction and HIV/AIDS. The concept of service integration in schools has been promoted at different times throughout history, but most recently reemerged in the late 1980s as an attempt to counteract the fragmentation of the social services and the school system and the inability to meet pressing social needs (Hare, 1995).

School social workers have recognized that many outside barriers such as poverty or lack of housing have a tremendous effect on students' educational achievements. School-linked services have gained increasing acceptance as a means to foster collaboration between schools and communities to improve education (Hare, 1995).

The growing service integration movement is based on three major goals:

1. to improve the coordination and efficiency of programs by reducing waste and duplication

2. to improve legal access to comprehensive services by modifying legislative requirements for eligibility through mechanisms such as waivers and pooling separate funding streams

3. to improve the quality and effectiveness of local services by providing comprehensive and well-coordinated services in one easily accessible location (Hare, 1995).

Social workers traditionally have focused on psychotherapeutic clinical work or have become overburdened in the public system and have thus left the development of service integration to other professionals (Hare, 1995). However, social workers must take an active role in the future development of service integration. Their skills in planning, mobilization, coordination, program development, and evaluation are essential in assuring the most effective service delivery system.

Schools have begun to play an active role in initiating coordinated networks of service among agencies delivering a wide range of social services to children and families. Kentucky, for example, under a court-ordered plan for school reform, has established more than 200 family resource and youth services centers to provide education and information to families and to serve as points of entry to all human services agencies. New Jersey also has established a statewide School-Based Youth Services Program to provide a broad range of services to teenagers in recreational settings in or near schools (Landers, 1993). Each site provides health care, mental health and family counseling, substance abuse counseling, job and employment training, recreational services, and information and referral services. Some sites also provide teenage parenthood education, transportation, day care, and family planning (Landers, 1993).

Social workers have been called on to play an active role in increasing educators' understanding of requirements for detecting and reporting child abuse and providing support services in the schools for abused children. Providing consultation and training to school staff, assisting in educational and curriculum planning, serving as community liaisons, developing support systems, and supporting individual and family therapy for abused children have been identified as roles social workers can and should assume in intervening with victims of abuse (Graham, 1993).

School social workers are also involved in helping students and their families cope with issues such as drug and alcohol addiction, HIV/AIDS, and juvenile crime. Social workers are instrumental in developing prevention efforts in these areas (Freeman, 1995).

Most school social workers work in public and private schools. Freeman (1995) cited a study of 862 NASW members who were school social workers. Ninety percent of the respondents worked in public school systems; 4 percent worked in nonpublic school systems; 2 percent worked in social service agencies; and 5 percent worked in other sites such as special preschool programs, residential treatment centers, or children's hospitals. Social workers in the "other" category are classified as school social workers because they are often required to coordinate services with the educational environment.

In current practice, school social workers tend to emphasize services that address educational needs and other issues that may interfere with the student's academic achievement. A 1994 survey of job dimensions and tasks specific to school social work indicated that the entry-level practitioner will need to engage in functions of administration, coordination between home and school, educational counseling, and advocacy to enable families to make use of community resources (Allen-Meares, 1994). In addition, social workers are involved in program development and planning in an effort to promote preventive services, cultural diversity, and community development (Allen-Meares, 1994).

In some jurisdictions, school social workers are beginning to tackle some emerging community problems, such as date rape and youth violence. Pilot programs have focused on attitudes and popular myths that surround dating activity of young people through an experiential learning format (Nightingale & Morrissette, 1993).

In response to the exclusion of Ryan White, a child with AIDS, from a school in Kokomo, Indiana, school social workers prepared to deal with this issue in other school districts. The NASW Commission on Education issued guidelines for school policies on students and employees with AIDS for use by school social workers throughout the country. The guidelines offer steps to protect the identity of AIDS-infected students and workers, suggest case-by-case screening by assessment teams to determine whether affected students and workers should be allowed in regularly scheduled classes, and advise that students not permitted to attend classes be taught by school employees who volunteer for such service ("Commission Issues Policy," 1986).

School social workers have also joined with other pupil-services personnel to devise and implement plans to respond more effectively to the AIDS epidemic. Social workers will increasingly be called on to help students experiencing stress over AIDS-related issues, including HIV testing, loss of family members to the disease, stigmatization, and sexuality in the age of AIDS ("AIDS Elicits New Pupil-Services Role," 1989). Identifying the barriers to service delivery related to AIDS and developing strategies to overcome these barriers are part of the school social worker's job. One outcome of this effort is the publication of a booklet "Guidelines for HIV and AIDS Student Support Services" (National Coalition of Advocates for Students, 1990). This booklet emphasizes prevention education, health-related services, counseling, referral, staff training, policy-making, and service coordination. In addition, it advocates a team approach in helping students understand the HIV epidemic and its impact on them ("Team Seen Key," 1991).

Homelessness is another problem that confronts school social workers on a regular basis. A study by the National Coalition for the Homeless indicated that more than 40 percent of homeless children do not attend school (Hiratsuka, 1989). Furthermore, shelter workers explain that homeless youth who do attend public school are often shunned and ridiculed by other students (Hall, 1990).

To address these issues, school social workers have taken initiatives to develop and implement innovative techniques to help homeless children attend school. For example, school social workers are working with school administrators to develop flexible criteria for the transfer of records and proof of residency, to develop an appropriate transportation system, to organize free breakfast and lunch programs, to provide free or discounted school supplies, and to provide a safe place for the student to keep his or her belongings ("Campaign for Homeless," 1989). Furthermore, school social workers help homeless youths by developing "buddy" programs and helping students develop social supports (Ziesemer, Marcoux, & Marwell, 1994). Social workers are also active in developing school and community awareness programs that help eliminate myths and stereotypes about homelessness ("Campaign for Homeless," 1989).

Another population that often needs the services of school social workers is gay and lesbian youths, who face social, emotional, and cognitive isolation and ostracism from peers. Gay and lesbian youths have higher rates of suicide, alcohol and drug abuse, and HIV infection than "straight" students, not because of their sexual orientation but because of their feelings of worthlessness and isolation caused by the reactions of others to their homosexuality (Hiratsuka, 1993). Social workers work with teachers to infuse information about homosexuality into the curriculum and help parents accept gay and lesbian children. Social workers refer gay and lesbian youths to programs such as the Sexual Minority Youth Assistance League (SMYAL) in Washington, DC, where they can discuss their concerns, meet peers and adults who can serve as role models, and learn how to cope and thrive as gay people in a straight society (Hiratsuka, 1993). Schools in Portland, Oregon, now mandate services to lesbian and gay youths, and school social workers in other school systems throughout the country are seeking to expand programs and information and referral to this population.

Host Setting

An important attribute of social work practice in schools is that it is carried out in *host settings,* arenas that are defined and dominated by people who are not social workers (Dane & Simon, 1991). The inevitable value conflicts and role ambiguity often place social workers in a difficult professional position. For example, school administrators may focus on student absenteeism and, therefore, may reorganize school services and replace social workers with field workers who fulfill the school's mission of simply filling desks rather than following the social work mission of treating and empowering students and their families (Dane & Simon, 1991).

School-based social work practice is also characterized by an emphasis on interdisciplinary practice. Pupil-services personnel sometimes must compete with each other when school districts, strapped for funds, make personnel cuts. But interdisciplinary collaboration and cooperation is more common than competition. The need for and commitment to teamwork and cooperation among the pupil-services disciplines was codified, in 1990, with the issuance of a joint statement: *Pupil Services Essential to Education* (American Association for

Counseling and Development, American School Counselor Association, National Association of School Psychologists, & NASW, 1990). The statement is a product of a task force composed of representatives of American Association for Counseling and Development, American School Counselor Association, National Association of School Psychologists, and NASW. It recognizes the need to keep all these mental health disciplines in the schools as each offers a unique perspective and service required to meet the needs of children in a comprehensive way. The purpose of the task force is

> to support the efforts of counselors, psychologists, social workers and other pupil service professionals in providing a coordinated delivery system designed to serve this country's school-aged youth. The complex needs of students demand the comprehensiveness implied by uniting the skills of trained professionals. Through teamwork, school psychologists, school social workers, school counselors and other pupil-services providers work together to provide coordinated services for students and their families. ("Groups Support Team Approach," 1990, p. 13)

The Future

Schools continue to be an important service for social workers, but in the past several years there have been challenges to school social work because of state fiscal cutbacks. Social workers have come into competition with school counselors and school psychologists. Some states have sought to cut social work positions in budget-cutting moves, sometimes retaining school psychologists and making the choice between the two professions ("Portland to Cut School Social Workers," 1993). In other states, prompt action on the part of social workers has saved jobs. An example is the decision by the Colorado Springs Board of Education in late 1989 to eliminate 14 of the 27 school social workers in the city's largest school district and replace them with counselors who were thought to be less costly. Social workers countered this move by presenting the school board with information about the nature of their services and their cost-effectiveness. Letters of support were also solicited from local and state agencies. Several weeks after announcing its decision, the school board reversed it ("Social Work Jobs Spared," 1990).

Contracting out school-based mental health services has also been a strategy recently employed to keep the cost of services down (Gibelman, 1993). The result has been a growing emphasis on evaluating children to determine their eligibility for federally funded programs and a decrease in direct and ongoing intervention.

The practice of school social work is further hindered by factors such as large caseloads, multibuilding assignments, and the unreasonable expectations of other professionals (Allen-Meares, 1994). Many of the problems experienced by school social workers result from the fact that schools are host settings.

As exemplified by the vignettes presented in this chapter, school social workers use both micro and macro functions. They may provide direct counseling and supportive services to students, parents, and faculty and they may be involved in program planning, development, and evaluation. Regardless of their job description, social workers in this area must become more involved in leadership and policy-making to clearly define the profession's role in the educational system (Allen-Meares, 1994).

References

AIDS elicits new pupil-services role. (1989, January). *NASW News*, p. 18.

Alderson, J., Krishef, C., & Spencer, B. (1990). School social workers' role in implementation of the Education for All Handicapped Children Act. *Social Work in Education, 12*, 221–236.

Allen-Meares, P. (1994). Social work services in schools: A national study of entry-level tasks. *Social Work, 39*, 560–565.

American Association for Counseling and Development, American School Counselor Association, National Association of School Psychologists, & National Association of Social Workers. (1990). *Pupil services essential to education*. Silver Spring, MD: Authors.

Barker, R. L. (1995). *Social work dictionary* (3rd ed.). Washington, DC: NASW Press.

Birth-control flap hounds school clinics. (1987, February). *NASW News*, p. 3.

Boston University School of Law, Program on Law and Child Maltreatment. (1986). *Child abuse, chronic acting out students and public school interventions: A manual for educators*. Boston: Author.

Campaign for homeless hits high gear. (1989, February). *NASW News*, p. 3.

Commission issues policy on AIDS. (1986, May). *NASW News*, p. 12.

Dane, B. O., & Simon, B. L. (1991). Resident guests: Social workers in host settings. *Social Work, 36*, 208–213.

Dane, E. (1985). Professional and lay advocacy in the education of handicapped children. *Social Work, 30*, 505–510.

DiMichele, L. (1993). The role of the school social worker in early childhood special education. *School Social Work Journal, 18*, 9–16.

Education for All Handicapped Children Act of 1975, P.L. 94-142, 89 Stat. 773.

Education of the Handicapped Act of 1986, P.L. 99-457, 100 Stat. 1145 to 1177.

Freeman, E. M. (1995). School social work overview. In R. L. Edwards (Ed.-in-Chief), *Encyclopedia of social work* (19th ed., Vol. 3, pp. 2087–2099). Washington, DC: NASW Press.

Gibelman, M. (1993). School social workers, counselors, and psychologists in collaboration: A shared agenda. *Social Work in Education, 15*, 45–53.

Gibelman, M., & Schervish, P. H. (1993). *Who we are: The social work labor force as reflected in the NASW membership.* Washington, DC: NASW Press.

Graham, T. L. (1993). Beyond detection: Education and the abused student. *Social Work in Education, 15*, 197–206.

Groups back school-linked service model. (1994, June). *NASW News*, p. 7.

Groups support team approach in pupil service. (1990, September). *NASW News*, p. 13.

Hall, J. A. (1990). Homelessness in the United States. In L. Ginsberg et al. (Eds.), *Encyclopedia of social work* (18th ed., 1990 suppl., pp. 159–174). Silver Spring, MD: NASW Press.

Hare, I. (1994). School social work in transition. *Social Work in Education, 16*, 64–68.

Hare, I. (1995). School-linked services. In R. L. Edwards (Ed.-in-Chief), *Encyclopedia of social work* (19th ed., Vol. 3, pp. 2100–2109). Washington, DC: NASW Press.

Hawkins-Stafford Elementary and Secondary School Improvement Amendments Act of 1988, P.L. 100-297, 102 Stat. 140.

Hiratsuka, J. (1989, March). Homeless kids face barrier to schooling. *NASW News*, p. 3.

Hiratsuka, J. (1993, April). Outsiders: Gay teens, straight world. *NASW News*, p. 3.

Hiratsuka, J. (1994, June). First specialty section set to go. *NASW News*, p. 1.

Individuals with Disabilities Education Act of 1990, P.L. 101-476, 104 Stat. 1142.

Lagana, L., & Hayes, D. M. (1993). Contraceptive health programs for adolescents: A critical review. *Adolescence, 28*, 347–359.

Landers, S. (1993, February). Schools vital link in service coordination. *NASW News*, p. 5.

National Coalition of Advocates for Students. (1990). *Guidelines for HIV and AIDS student support services*. Boston: Author

National Foundation for the Improvement of Education. (1986). *A blueprint for success*. Washington, DC: Author.

Nelson, C. (1990). *A job analysis of school social workers*. Princeton, NJ: Educational Testing Service.

Nightingale, H., & Morrissette, P. (1993). Dating violence, attitudes, myths, and preventive programs. *Social Work in Education, 15*, 225–232.

Portland to cut school social workers. (1993, July). *NASW News*, p. 7.

Schools act boosts social workers' role. (1995, January). *NASW News*, pp. 1, 14.

School social workers "not a frill," manual on disruptive students says. (1986, September). *NASW News*, p. 13.

Social work jobs spared. (1990, March). *NASW News*, p. 10.

Team seen key to AIDS-related public services. (1991, February). *NASW News*, p. 11.

Ziesemer, C., Marcoux, L., & Marwell, B. E. (1994). Homeless children: Are they different from other low-income children? *Social Work, 39*, 658–668.

alternative programs

Social workers have taken important leadership roles in identifying alternative educational programs for students in special circumstances. One such example is the Harvey Milk School in New York, an alternative school for gay and lesbian youths. The school is sponsored by the Institute for the Protection of Lesbian and Gay Youth (IPLGY) and is sanctioned by the New York Board of Education.

IPLGY's clinical director, Steve Ashkinazy, a social worker, conceived of the school as a solution for gay and lesbian youths who drop out of school or who are chronically truant. These students, who had not made a secret of their homosexuality, had been ridiculed by teachers and other students, and some had been rejected by their parents. Several had tried to commit suicide, and others had become involved in prostitution and drug abuse ("Troubled Gay Youth," 1985).

The school opened in 1985 in a Greenwich Village church; 20 students initially enrolled. The board of education agreed to pay the cost of an instructor and some class materials; IPLGY paid the remaining costs. The philosophy of IPLGY is that gay and lesbian youths suffer the effects of systematic discrimination and that a learning environment free from harassment might lure them back into school. The premise is to offer students more than an education. Within a supportive environment, they receive nurturing and the chance to observe positive role models, both straight and gay. Students participating in the program receive individual and group therapy after school.

At first, publicity was not favorable. Critical stories ran in the *New York Times* and one tabloid featured a headline: "School for Scandal." The board of education, however, strongly maintained its support. The chancellor of schools Nathan Quinones told reporters: "These are youngsters who, in most instances, [because of their behavioral problems] would never have been allowed to remain in a high school setting previously" ("Troubled Gay Youth, 1985, p. 12).

Restructuring the Schools

In Kentucky, social workers have had an opportunity to participate in a major restructuring of that state's public schools. The Kentucky Education Reform Act of 1990 established a series of mandates, including the requirement that certain schools establish resource or youth centers to meet the needs of students and community residents served by the school. The centers are required to offer preschool and after-school care; parental training for new and expectant parents; summer and part-time job development; employment counseling, training, and placement; drug and alcohol abuse counseling; health services or referrals; and mental health counseling and family crisis services ("Social Work Has Role," 1992). Schools in which 20 percent or more of the students qualify for free school meals are eligible to be resource centers.

The goals for the centers include identifying and overcoming any home or community obstacles that may affect a student's success in school, connecting families with needed community resources, and helping youths recognize and use their strengths. Each resource center is required to provide certain services, but there is flexibility in how these mandates are to be carried out. Centers may be located in the schools or at nearby facilities.

School social workers have been hired to direct or staff the centers. Lyn Lewis, a past president of Kentucky's school social work association, noted that school social workers have been familiarizing school officials and community residents with what they can do and what their potential contributions can be ("Social Work Has Role," 1992).

References

Social work has role in school-revamping. (1992, June). *NASW News*, p. 11.

Troubled gay youth find help in school. (1985, September). *NASW News*, p. 12.

crisis intervention

Two Friends Die

It was a beautiful spring night. Sixteen-year-old Emily Williams and 17-year-old Denise Fowler had been at a party at the home of their friend Bill. Bill's parents were out of town for the weekend and, against his parents' explicit instructions, Bill decided it was time to "party." An older friend of Bill's had been willing to purchase a keg of beer, and Emily and Denise were among those who had had a considerable amount to drink.

It was after midnight when Emily and Denise left the party. Denise was driving the family car. She knew that she was feeling a little tipsy, but thought that she was in good enough shape to drive home. As they were leaving, Jim, a neighbor who was also at the party, hopped in the car for a ride home.

No one will ever know exactly what happened. The police, on a routine patrol, found the smoldering vehicle with the front end embedded in a tree. The impact was so great that the front end of the car was nothing but melted and jumbled steel. Emily and Denise had been killed instantly. Jim had been thrown from the car and was clinging to life.

The lead story on the morning news told the gruesome tale. Cheryl Williams, the social worker in Sun Valley High School, was listening to the news as she prepared to go to work. As the report about the accident reached her consciousness, Cheryl became dizzy and nauseated. The few minutes of immobilization gave way to a sense of urgency—she needed to get to the school right away.

Cheryl arrived at school a half hour earlier than usual and headed straight to the principal's office. The school psychologist and assistant principal were already there, although no meeting had been called. The principal, Ms. Peterson, asked her administrative assistant to notify the other six members of the special services unit to come to her office as soon as they arrived for work.

The focus of immediate attention was on the development of a crisis plan. The students of Sun Valley High would have either heard the news reports or heard about the accident through the grapevine. By the time the students got to school in an hour, they would be at a high level of upset. Of particular concern were the close friends of Jim (who was in critical condition), Emily, and Denise. However, Cheryl and her colleagues were also concerned about the emotional reaction of all Sun Valley students. Death, especially such sudden and tragic death, was not within the life experience of most of the students.

Within 15 minutes, the rough outline of a plan was in place and Cheryl knew what she had to do. Students would be arriving shortly and there was only a little time to put the plan in place. The first step was implemented when the principal made an announcement over the public address system asking that all teachers immediately report to the auditorium. The principal conveyed all the facts she knew, then turned the meeting over to Cheryl, who correctly anticipated that she must first acknowledge and deal with the feelings of the teachers, allowing them to ask questions and express their own upset. Because of time constraints that morning, Cheryl suggested that the teachers get together at the end of the day to talk further about their own reactions, what transpired during the day, and how they dealt with it. Cheryl then provided the teachers with information about what reactions they might expect from their students, how to encourage them to express their feelings, what responses were appropriate, and how to identify students who need special attention (and referral to the social worker). Cheryl indicated that she would be available in her office throughout the day and that any student who seemed especially upset should be sent to her.

Once the teachers returned to their classrooms, Cheryl and the principal conferred briefly about other issues they anticipated arising during the day: calls from concerned parents and calls and cameras from the media. The principal decided to contact central administration to prepare a statement about the accident; in addition to the tragedy itself, there was the issue of alcohol involvement.

During the day, Cheryl saw eight students, most close friends of Emily and Denise. Cheryl also checked with the hospital about Jim's condition. There was good news: Although his injuries were serious, he would survive.

The following day, the special services team again met with the principal to debrief on the events of the previous day and to continue planning. They decided that the principal would contact the families of Emily and Denise, offer condolences, and obtain details about their funerals. These were difficult calls to make. Ms. Peterson correctly anticipated the overwhelming grief the girls' parents were experiencing. She knew that, in the weeks to come, she would want her special services team to involve the parents in substance abuse program planning for the students in the school.

Both sets of parents decided on a small, closed funeral for family members and close friends. When Ms. Peterson relayed this news back to the special services team, Cheryl suggested that the school hold a memorial service so that the other students could say goodbye and express their grief in an open and accepting atmosphere. Ms. Peterson decided to wait a few days, until after the funerals, to invite the families to participate in the memorial service.

The days passed slowly. Some of the students had responded to the initial news with a kind of numbness that was now wearing off and turning to outward expressions of grief. Cheryl continued to counsel students individually throughout the week. The teachers had responded well to the request to identify and refer students who seemed to be having difficulty. Cheryl also recognized that the teachers continued to react strongly to the deaths of their students, and she spent extra time in the teachers' cafeteria talking informally with them.

Ms. Peterson sent a memo to all staff asking for volunteers to help plan the memorial service. Cheryl suggested that several of Emily and Denise's close friends also be asked to participate. The nondenominational service was scheduled for the following Friday. Both Emily and Denise's parents attended the service and several of the girls' friends spoke about their feelings for Emily and Denise.

Although the service went well, Cheryl recognized the need for long-term intervention in the form of an alcohol and drug prevention program. The following week, she spoke with Emily and Denise's parents, and both families were very interested in helping to plan the prevention program. Cheryl also recruited student and teacher participants. Together the group discussed how they could give something back to Emily and Denise by developing a program to prevent this kind of tragedy in the future.

The teachers, pupil-services personnel, and parents tossed around ideas for a long-term substance abuse prevention campaign. When one of the female students spoke up to say she was scared about the prom next month, the group decided that the prom would be the kick-off for the entire program. Although there was already a rule against alcohol at the prom, many of the kids drank heavily before and after the prom. The students and the teachers decided that, although there was no way to prevent drinking, they could launch a campaign that actively promoted an alcohol-free evening.

Cheryl then worked with the students and the parents to have T-shirts designed and printed for the prom that promoted an alcohol-free evening. Cheryl also arranged an agreement with a local taxicab company to provide free transportation that night for students who had been drinking. The taxicab number was posted throughout the school, and stickers supplied by the cab company were included with the prom tickets. If the prom night was successful, the cab company had expressed an interest in developing a more permanent partnership.

In addition, student training sessions were organized to share information about alcohol and drug use, and peer support groups were arranged once a week after school. Cheryl was also coordinating a visit from a local automobile distributor who had designed a car that simulated driving while intoxicated. Students could directly experience the lack of control and the decreased reaction time that result after just one or two drinks.

The planning committee continued to meet and pursue a coordinated, long-term alcohol and drug prevention program. They hope the program will help prevent another tragedy.

In this vignette, Cheryl used both micro and macro social work functions. Following the accident, she used the social work functions of assessment, support, and counseling to help teachers and students work through their emotions. After the initial period of crisis intervention, Cheryl organized and supervised a planning committee of students, faculty, and parents to develop a prevention program. Cheryl engaged in planning and program development with the help of the group members. She also used the social work skills of coordination and exchange when she accessed the services of the taxicab company and the automobile distributor. Cheryl will also need to develop an evaluation tool to monitor the success of the prevention program so that the results can be shared with other schools and similar service arenas.

Teenage Suicide

A Student Questions Whether Life Is Worth Living

Mark doesn't know what to do. His best friend, Bill, has been acting weird lately. He seems distracted all the time, hasn't been taking care of himself in terms of personal hygiene, and just the other day said that he didn't think life was worth living. All this began about two weeks ago, just after Bill's girlfriend, Beth, told him that she didn't want to date him anymore.

At first, Mark figured that Bill was just experiencing some bad days because of the rejection. But here it is two weeks later, and Bill is sounding more and more despondent. The threat of suicide scares Mark. Mark has tried to be a good friend. He has spent a lot of time with Bill these past two weeks and tries to listen and understand. But it is more than he can handle.

This morning, Bill shows Mark an essay he has prepared for English class about his visions of himself in the future. In it, Bill writes that he doesn't have a future, that there is no point in living because things just get worse and worse. Mark can't think of a response, but he knows that he has to do something.

As Mark walks to class, he passes the office of Ms. Cleary, the school social worker. He stops, looks in, and sees that Ms. Cleary is sitting at her desk. He continues down the hall, turns around again, and then stands in place wrestling with himself about whether he should go in. Ms. Cleary spots Mark standing by the door, smiles, and motions for him to come in.

Ms. Cleary and Mark had talked once before, about a year ago when his grades had dropped briefly. Mark sits down in the chair by Ms. Cleary's desk and she asks how things are going. His response "Okay, I guess," leads Ms. Cleary to prod a bit further. "I guess?" she says. "That sounds like you're not sure." It didn't take much encouragement for Mark to blurt out "I don't know if I should squeal on a friend. I just don't know what to do."

Ms. Cleary and Mark then talk for a while about circumstances under which "squealing" is the sign of a good friend, not a bad one. Mark hesitates for only a few minutes; he has received the permission he needs to unload the heavy burden he feels. Mark tells Ms. Cleary that he has a good friend who has changed a lot lately and has started to say scary things about what he intends to do to himself. Ms. Cleary responds by asking if Mark means suicide. Mark nods his head.

"Look Mark," says Ms. Cleary. "I want to talk to you more—a lot more—about your feelings about squealing. But right now there is something important you need to tell me. When people talk about suicide, we have to take it seriously. I want to help your friend and I need you to tell me if he is a student here." Mark nodded again. He had heard about teens committing suicide; in fact, he remembers that another student at the school had shot himself a year or two ago.

Mark still hesitates. "You won't tell him I told you?" "No," Ms. Cleary assures him. "This is between you and me." Very quietly Mark says "Bill Graybar." "Thank you, Mark," says Ms. Cleary. "I know how difficult it was for you to tell me, but you've done the right thing. You are a good friend to Bill. He needs help. Let me see what I can do. In the meantime, let's you and I talk again tomorrow." With the promise that Mark would stop in tomorrow, he leaves for class.

Ms. Cleary sits at her desk for a few minutes trying to figure out the best approach to use with Bill. She looks up his schedule and decides to walk to his classroom; classes will be changing soon, and she thinks she can catch him. She had met Bill on a few occasions, but had never talked with him at any length.

When Bill walks out of class, the last to do so, he looks downcast and distracted. Ms. Cleary intercepts him at the door and asks if she can speak with him. Bill is surprised, but agrees to accompany Ms. Cleary to her office.

Once in her office, Ms. Cleary tells Bill that she understands his girlfriend has broken up with him. She also tells Bill that she has heard he is upset and has spoken about hurting himself. She asks him if this is true. At first, Bill is furious at Mark. He knows Mark must have talked to Ms. Clearly, because Mark is the only person Bill has spoken to about his feelings. Ms. Cleary was expecting this reaction and she tells Bill that his friends care about him very much and that they simply don't want anything to happen to him.

Bill settles down and shrugs his shoulders. He talks briefly with Ms. Clearly about his depression and desire to end the pain. Ms. Cleary listens intently and offers support. However, she tells Bill that she is going to have to call his parents because all threats of suicide must be taken seriously. Ms. Cleary asks Bill wait in her office with her until his parents arrive. On meeting with Ms. Cleary and Bill, it is clear that Bill's parents had no idea how much he was hurting, and now they are scared. Ms. Cleary gives them a referral to a mental health clinic, and they immediately make an appointment for Bill.

Ms. Cleary calls Bill's parents the next day and asks them to have Bill sign a release of information form from the psychiatrist so that Ms. Cleary can monitor his progress and coordinate appropriate services. Bill returns to school after 10 days and meets regularly with Ms. Cleary for short-term counseling concerning issues such as his return to school and the reactions of the other students. Ms. Cleary also meets with Mark to help him resolve his own feelings of guilt and to encourage his friendship with Bill.

In this case study, Ms. Cleary engages in assessment and diagnosis when she first talks with Mark and Bill. She determines that the threat of suicide is real and must be taken seriously. She then discusses appropriate services with Bill and his parents and carries out the function of referral to the mental health center. Finally, Ms. Cleary offers support and counseling to all those involved: Bill, his parents, and Mark.

Threats of suicide are taken seriously by mental health professionals. Suicide has become the second leading cause of death among young people, behind accidents ("Whys' of Teenage Suicide," 1987). The rate of teenage and adolescent suicide has risen dramatically since 1980, with the sharpest increases among young black males, where the suicide rate quadrupled among those ages 10 to 14; the increase in the suicide rate among white females ages 10 to 14 also experienced a sharp increase (Squires, 1995). According to the Centers for Disease Control and Prevention, between 1980 and 1992, suicide rates rose 28 percent among Americans ages 15 to 19 and 120 percent among those ages 10 to 14 (as cited in Squires, 1995).

Various reasons have been offered for the increasing number of adolescents and teenagers who consider or attempt suicide, including high levels of stress, alcohol and drug abuse, academic failure, and the difficulties of normal development, including the desire for independence and the need for acceptance. "Copycat" suicides have also become more common. For example, when four teenagers committed suicide by carbon monoxide poisoning in Berenfield, New Jersey, at least eight suicide attempts (two in nearby communities and six in other parts of the country) were made by the same method ("'Whys' of Teenage Suicide," 1987). Some believe that media attention provides a "blueprint for action" to some teenagers who are already troubled.

Social workers have recognized the need to reach out to at-risk teenagers actively and to educate teachers, school staff, parents, police, and youths about early warning signs and suicide prevention. Teaching young people about warning signs is particularly important, as teenagers turn to their friends before parents and professionals ("'Whys' of Teenage Suicide," 1987). Strategies to prevent youth suicide include training teachers and school officials to identify those at highest risk for suicidal thoughts and attempts, establishing referral programs and suicide crisis hot lines, and educating young people about suicide prevention (Squires, 1995).

School social workers play an important role in developing suicide prevention programs. For example, in a school where there are several "copycat" attempts after an actual suicide, the social worker may set up an awareness and prevention program designed to train school personnel in prevention strategies, involve parents in the program planning process, and coordinate with other agencies in the community.

Actual prototypes for this type of program exist. In the Solanco School District in Lancaster County, Pennsylvania, social workers helped establish a prevention program, known as Project A.L.I.V.E. The aim of the program is to help school administrators, faculty, and students understand, identify, and help potentially suicidal teenagers ("NASW Backs Bill," 1985). The approach goes beyond the individually troubled teenager to attack adolescent suicide on a wider basis. A major component of the program is educational. On the basis of questions raised by students, a lesson plan is devoted to factors that contribute to suicide, statistics, warning signs, strategies for helping troubled teenagers, coping skills for teenagers, and information about available community resources. The emphasis is on prevention.

References

NASW backs bill on teenage suicide. (1985, October). *NASW News*, pp. 1, 2.

Squires, S. (1995, May 9). Sharp rise reported in youth suicides. *Washington Post*, Health section, p. 5.

"Whys" of teenage suicide still unanswered. (1987, May). *NASW News*, p. 4.

difficulties in school

The school dropout problem has been termed a "national crisis." Recent studies suggest that the cost to the nation for each year's dropout "class" is more than $240 billion in lost earnings and foregone taxes (U.S. General Accounting Office, 1990). In 1986 NASW endorsed *A Blueprint for Success*, a guide for developing successful school dropout prevention programs issued by the National Foundation for the Improvement of Education (NFIE) ("Dropout Prevention," 1986). It is estimated that at least 1 million students drop out or are at risk of dropping out of school each year. Reasons may include academic failure, substance abuse, pregnancy, criminal behavior, unemployment, low self-esteem, alienation, immediate economic need, and boredom. These problems may be exacerbated for students by an unresponsive school system ("Dropout Prevention," 1986).

In endorsing the blueprint, NASW emphasized issues such as effective teamwork among school administrators, teachers, pupil-services staff, parents, volunteers, business leaders, and community agencies. NASW also emphasized "a whole-child perspective" that considers development, family, culture, and social factors in the dropout problem ("Dropout Prevention," 1986).

Successful efforts to prevent dropouts include alternative programs centered in and out of schools, vocational education, alternative schools, special programs within schools, early childhood education programs, and summer work programs. Social work interventions may range from psychosocial assessments to advocacy for broad systems change. Strategies include educating school administrators, teachers, and other school personnel about the characteristics of at-risk youth. School social workers can directly provide crisis intervention, case management, and support services for students in the school setting to link students at risk of dropout to other needed services, including mental health evaluations, screening, and treatment beyond the scope of the school. School social workers can also assist in establishing linkages with community service providers to develop more comprehensive and accessible services in the areas of psychological and social functioning for at-risk youths (Franklin, 1992).

A Group Treatment Approach to Preventing School Dropout

Peter Ownings is the only social worker in a school district of 6,500 students. The district is a bedroom community near Indianapolis and includes a minority population of about 30 percent and neighborhoods ranging from very affluent to very poor. Peter has worked in this school district for 10 years, beginning as an elementary school teacher. His teaching experience made him realize that he wanted to help his students in a different way, so he enrolled in Indiana University's MSW program on an extended basis. After four years of part-time study and with his MSW in hand, Peter applied for and was hired as the district's social worker in 1988.

One of Peter's concerns was the increasing number of students who were leaving school before graduation. For many of these students, Peter realized it was too late—they were so uninterested in school that little could be done. Perhaps, he hoped, they would return to get their General Equivalency Diploma (GED) when they realized the importance of education in directing the course of their lives. Peter concluded that the best approach was to address the dropout problem from a prevention standpoint, believing that kids can be turned around if they are reached at an earlier age.

Peter spent many hours talking with teachers and school administrators, getting their views on why students drop out and how they might be helped. He decided to target middle-school children who had poor academic records, discipline problems, or evidence of general maladjustment to school. Peter reviewed the literature on successful dropout programs and, when he attended an NASW symposium that year, he talked with other school social workers about the approaches they had tried. Then he began to formulate ideas for a prevention program in the form of a support group that focuses on issues that are important in achieving academic success.

With the program model in place, Peter turned his attention to recruiting students. He prepared a brochure for distribution to all sixth-, seventh-, and eight-grade students with information about the program. Students were asked to contact Peter if they were interested in participating; the goal in this first effort was to have students identify themselves as volunteers. A week after the brochures were distributed, 15 students indicated an interest. After talking with each of them and their teachers, all but one was considered appropriate for the support group.

At the first meeting, students were asked to enter into a "contract" in which realistic attendance and behavioral expectations for the school term were laid out on an individual basis. For example, Dean had received four "F" and two "D" grades on his previous report card. Dean's goals were to bring two of those grades up. Another student, Amy, had missed school for 14 days the previous term, and few of these absences were related to illness. Her goal was to reduce absences by one-third.

Group meetings were scheduled twice a week, with the students deciding in advance what would be discussed. Topics included vocational planning, alcohol and drug abuse, teen suicide, and teacher "attitudes." Throughout the 30-minute sessions, Peter kept coming back to one theme: These students can succeed in school.

The students were willing participants. They enjoyed the special attention and interest in them. Their teachers began to comment on the changes they saw. At the end of the school year, more than half of the participating students had fulfilled their contracts, and the other half had made substantial improvement.

With the success of this program, Peter was able to obtain a grant through the National Education Association to expand the number of participants for the following year. His hope was to establish this group for more middle-school children and to start similar support groups for children in the ninth grade. Peter knew that behavior problems tend to increase as a result of poor adjustment to high school and the growing lure of alcohol and drugs.

There are a number of reasons why some students do not do well in school. Low priority of education in the home; lack of role models; learning difficulties, such as attention deficit disorder or poor reading skills and study habits; and low expectations on the part of the school are some of the factors associated with students' disaffiliation from school ("Project Helps School Dropouts," 1986). Studies have shown that the dropout rate is higher in urban areas and among low-income, low-achieving youths in racial and ethnic groups, but the dropout occurrence among white, middle-class, high-achieving youths has been on the increase (Franklin, 1992). Among this latter population, a variety of behavioral (including substance abuse), learning, and family disorders have been found (Franklin, 1992).

Peter's work highlights a number of important social work functions. As the school social worker, Peter identified the dropout rate as a serious problem that must be addressed. He then engaged in the functions of coordination and exchange to conduct an informal needs assessment by gathering information from other professionals and extensively reviewing the literature. After the needs assessment was complete, Peter carried out the social work functions of planning, organizing, and program development to implement a support group to focus on the importance of academic success. Peter also used an evaluation tool that allowed him to measure the outcome of the program so that he could secure additional funding from the National Education Association.

Winston's Problem: Attention-Deficit Hyperactivity Disorder

Winston, an eight-year-old African American child, moved to Indianapolis with his family in late August, just in time to begin the new school year. He was placed in Mr. Davis's 3rd-grade class. Winston's school records had not yet arrived from his previous elementary school in Philadelphia, so there was no information available about his past school performance or any problems.

By the second day of school, Mr. Davis knew he had a difficult situation on his hands. Winston could not sit still for more than a few minutes; he was rough in his contacts with the other kids, and Mr. Davis feared that the one or two pushing incidents could easily turn into something worse.

Mr. Davis referred Winston to the director of special education for an evaluation. Winston's case was then passed on to a school social worker, Anise Hopkins, whose first step was to contact Winston's previous school. The social workers and teachers at that school said that no evaluation had been performed but that Winston had demonstrated many behavioral problems and had very few friends. Anise then took Winston to the school psychologist for comprehensive testing.

While she waited for the results, Anise observed Winston's behavior in the classroom, interviewed Mr. Davis, reviewed past records, talked with his parents, and took a complete social history through interviews with both Winston and his parents. Anise also had Winston's parents complete a behavioral checklist to determine specific areas of difficulty.

After considering all of this information, along with the results of the psychological testing, Winston was diagnosed with attention-deficit hyperactivity disorder (ADHD). Anise referred Winston for a complete physical and neurological exam. She also talked with the physician about Winston's diagnosis and the possibility of medication. A medication was prescribed, and Anise worked extensively with Winston's parents to educate them about the disorder and the effects of the medication. In addition, Anise worked with Winston on a regular basis to establish a self-monitoring behavioral system, which has been shown to change classroom behavior over time. Anise then worked with Mr. Davis to develop and implement a reward system to reinforce Winston's positive behaviors. Anise also began to work with Winston individually for social skills training, for which a behavioral approach is also used.

In this case, Anise engaged in assessment and diagnosis to determine the presenting problems. She then used her coordination and organization skills as she interacted with the professionals at Winston's previous school as well as with Mr. Davis. Anise further engaged in the functions of advice and counseling to Winston's parents as she helped them understand more about the disorder and the medications. Finally, she carried out the function of referral in her work with the psychologist and physician to determine the reasons for Winston's behavior.

Not all children with attention-deficit disorder manifest hyperactive behavior. When hyperactivity is not present, teachers and pupil-services personnel may overlook the condition as an explanation of a child's difficulty in school. Boys are more likely than girls to be assessed as having attention-deficit disorder, even with identical hyperactive behavior (as cited in "Attention Deficits Often Overlooked," 1994).

References

Attention deficits often overlooked. (1994, September). *NASW News*, p. 15.

Dropout prevention "blueprint" is drawn. (1986, September). *NASW News*, p. 15.

Franklin, C. (1992). Family and individual patterns in a group of middle-class dropout youths. *Social Work, 37*, 338–344.

Project helps school dropouts. (1986, February). *NASW News*, p. 6.

U.S. General Accounting Office (1990, July). *Home visiting: A promising early intervention strategy for at-risk families* (Report # GAO/HRD-90-83). Washington, DC: Author.

violence

School social workers have assumed an important role in promoting freedom from violence and substance abuse in the schools. With the surge of violence and substance abuse among young people, school social workers are using their skills to recognize possible causal factors and create comprehensive prevention programs. Several themes are being pursued, including gun control, creation of more after-school programs, and classes in parenting and conflict resolution (Loose & Thomas, 1994).

For example, in Urbana, Illinois, conflict resolution is a common strategy. According to school social worker Fred Schrumpf and assistant director of special education in the Urbana School District Donna Crawford, "a healthy school community will use conflict to teach important life skills that promote peace and fairness" (as cited in Landers, 1992b, p. 4). Schrumpf and parent volunteers authored a program guide and student manual based on a conflict resolution program begun in one of Urbana's secondary schools. The program is based on peer mediation, in which selected students are trained to help their peers settle differences. In three years, this program helped resolve more than 500 disputes, 95 percent of which remained successfully resolved (Landers, 1992b). Any student can request mediation or students can be referred to mediation by teachers, administrators, or parents. Agreement among all parties must be obtained, and disputants must work toward an agreement by identifying their own solutions.

The National Education Association reported that more than 280,000 students are physically attacked in U.S. secondary schools each month (as cited in Landers, 1992a). Schools across the nation are beginning to offer training in conflict resolution to school social workers, teachers, and students. Programs that use student mediators to help resolve disputes among their classmates have been found to be the most successful.

Goal number seven of the eight National Education Goals currently guiding the improvement of the nation's schools calls for safe, disciplined, alcohol- and drug-free schools ("Social Workers Strive for Safe-Schools Goal," 1995).

The following vignette illustrates how social workers can help develop a safer school environment.

An Approach to Violence Prevention

Laura Nelson is one of four social workers in the Howard County school system. She is assigned to two elementary and one intermediate school in this largely working-class suburban community. As an experienced school social worker, Laura has an extensive network of colleagues and friends who work in inner-city, suburban, and rural school districts. At a recent statewide symposium on violence in the schools, Laura learned about violence prevention strategies that were being attempted on an ad hoc basis in numerous school districts. The notion of "prevention" stuck with her as the only approach that made sense. Given the incidence of physical assaults and even the use of weapons in other schools, it seemed only a matter of time before Howard County fell prey to the same epidemic.

When Laura returned home from the conference, she decided to take action. She spoke with the Director of Pupil Personnel Services for the county, Ms. Dickson, who wholeheartedly supported Laura's desire to develop a violence prevention program. Ms. Dickson cautioned, however, that it was probably wise to think in terms of a pilot program in one school, thoroughly evaluate the results, and then determine whether the county or perhaps a private source would fund a countywide effort. The rationale for a pilot approach was that the school system was in a budget crunch, and the board of education was not inclined to support new initiatives that had a price tag. On the other hand, if Laura could show promising results in one school, perhaps enthusiasm could be generated for a larger effort. Ms. Dickson did promise to inform the principals throughout the county, as well as members of the board of education, about the pilot program, as Laura had indicated she might need their input.

From everything that Laura had read and heard about prevention programs, the first step was to thoroughly understand the scope of the problem and how people with a stake in the issue—students, teachers, administrators, parents, the police, community residents, and others—viewed the problem. In conducting a needs assessment, Laura decided to use a nominal group approach, basically a workshop that brings together selected participants from various interested groups. The goal is for participants to share their views about the problem being addressed, offer feedback on possible solutions, and identify barriers that may be encountered (see Siegel, Attkisson, & Carson, 1995).

Laura actively sought interested student leaders, teachers, administrators, parents, police, community residents, and religious leaders. They met once a week for four weeks to discuss the issue of rising youth violence and the need for prevention in the schools. During the last meeting, the group developed a tentative list of goals for a violence prevention program. Laura then solicited input from several principals throughout the county as well as members of the board of education and brought their suggestions back to the group. The final five goals were as follows:

1. Create a change in the institutional environment.

2. Build a better school climate that is based on respect rather than power.

3. Provide student and faculty training in conflict resolution and mediation.

4. Develop a peer mediation and counseling program.

5. Provide training to students and faculty in problem-solving skills.

Having agreed on the goals, the next step was to define objectives for meeting them. Laura could have set objectives by herself, but she wanted to continue to receive input from the community and school participants so that they would "buy in" to the program. Therefore, the group selected one member from each population represented, and these members then joined Laura to form a planning committee. It was decided that they would meet once a week and would be joined by the school principal and representatives of the board of education once a month.

The planning committee outlined their agenda for the upcoming meetings. They would first attempt to develop operational objectives for each of the goals, so that instead of vague ideas and concepts they would have a concrete action plan. Their next step was to prioritize the goals and objectives in the order of importance as related to the goal of violence prevention. In addition, they would develop an evaluation measure to determine the success or failure of the program.

Although there was still a lot of work to be done in developing and implementing a violence prevention program, Laura felt good about the input of the planning committee and the planning process. She was confident that this program would be an important step in preventing violence in the schools.

In this case example, Laura engaged primarily in macro social work functions. Through her interaction with other professionals, she identified the problem of youth violence and recognized its devastating effect. She then consulted with her supervisor about developing a prevention program. When she received approval, Laura engaged in the functions of organizing, coordination, and management to develop a group forum. She then carried out the functions of planning and program development to shape goals and objectives. When the time comes for implementation, Laura will also need to engage in the function of mobilization to encourage and empower students and faculty to carry out the program specifics. Finally, Laura will need to evaluate the program so that its results can be studied and possibly duplicated in other schools.

References

Landers, S. (1992a, October). Resolving conflicts: The school of life. *NASW News*, p. 4.

Landers, S. (1992b, October). Urbana: Genesis of a peer-mediation program. *NASW News*, p. 4.

Loose, C., & Thomas, P. (1994, January 2). "Crisis of violence" becoming menace to childhood. *Washington Post*, pp. A1, A19.

Siegel, C., Attkisson, C., & Carson, L. G. (1995). In J. E. Tropman, J. L. Erlich, & J. Rothman (Eds.), *Tactics and techniques of community intervention* (3rd ed., pp. 10–34). Itasca, IL: F.E. Peacock.

Social workers strive for safe-schools goal. (1995, January). *NASW News*, p. 17.

career
opportunities

Despite the popularity of school social work as a professional specialty area, relatively few classified advertisements in major newspapers or the *NASW News* could be located in comparison to listings for other areas of service. One explanation for this dearth of listings is that school social work positions tend to be listed internally within each school system (personal correspondence with Isadora Hare, Director of Quality Assurance, National Association of Social Workers, June 16, 1995). The listings below highlight position descriptions and qualifications listed in recent years for social work positions in the schools.

Clinical Director
Inner-city junior high school program providing individual family and group counseling therapeutic activities and recreational therapeutic activities is looking for a clinical director. Duties include supervising staff in clinical work as well as assisting program director with administrative duties. Requirements include a social work license at the MSW level with at least three years of direct service and two years of supervisory experience. Also requires a real interest in working with teens in an active environment.

Clinical Social Worker
A master's-level social worker is sought for a school-based program to provide intensive therapy to a group of children and their families throughout the year. A minimum of two years' experience providing mental health services to school-aged children and a license or license eligibility is required.

School Social Work Positions
Currently recruiting enthusiastic and energetic social workers to fill school social worker II positions. We require an MSW degree and prefer candidates with school social work experience. Most of the positions require extensive travel within the school district.

School Social Worker

County public school system is building a social worker applicant pool for future positions. Requirements: Master's degree in social work, eligibility for school social work state license, two years' postgraduate experience working directly with children and families in mental health, social services, or educational setting. Ability to write literate reports and articulate well. Ability to speak Spanish, Asian, or Middle-Eastern language preferred. Position involves social/cultural assessments; counseling with individual students, groups, parents, and staff; organizing workshops and training sessions; and community networking.

School Social Worker

Half-time grant position; contract subject to yearly renewal. Master's degree in social work and eligibility for state licensing. Fluent Spanish required; experience with preschool population; experience in providing direct services to families and children; ability to apply professional skills to a wide range of teacher consultations; family counseling; diagnosis and crisis intervention services; ability to write comprehensive reports; ability to serve as a community liaison and to establish effective working relationships with students, parents and school personnel.

Social Worker, School Based

Provide direct therapeutic intervention to a specific caseload of students who have been identified as severely emotionally disturbed and their families. Social work decisions will be made within the context of the students' and families' treatment plan developed by the interdisciplinary school-based team. The nature of the work will require evening hours. All responsibilities will be performed in accordance with the objectives and policies of the school system. Requirements: LCSW-C certified social worker; two years of clinical social work services in treatment setting dealing with children/adolescents and their families.

aging

introduction
to part V

To understand what social workers do when they work with older people, it is essential first to understand the unique characteristics of this population. This chapter includes a brief review of issues affecting older citizens and relevant legislation that defines the approach to social services for this population; a description of the current federal, state, and local framework for providing aging services; and vignettes illustrating the range of social work involvement in this service area.

Social Workers in the Field of Aging

Despite the important roles for social workers in the field of aging, currently a relatively small proportion of social workers are involved in this area. Aging ranks eighth among primary practice areas for NASW members (Gibelman & Schervish, 1993). Data for 1991 reveal that 4.5 percent (3,970) of responding NASW members cited "aged" as their primary practice area, down from 4.7 percent in 1988 when it was ranked sixth among primary practice area.

A larger proportion of BSWs than MSWs work with elderly people. These social workers also tend to be younger and have less experience than members in other primary practice areas. Of NASW members working in the field of aging, women are overrepresented; 84.8 percent are women, compared with 77.3 percent in the overall NASW membership (Gibelman & Schervish, 1993).

A 1988 study by the University of Southern California and the Association for Gerontology in Higher Education projected that jobs serving older people are expected to grow faster than jobs in other areas of practice through the 1990s ("New Jobs Seen in Aging," 1988). Despite efforts to create an awareness of the demand for social workers in the field of gerontology, the number of professionals, at least as measured through the NASW membership, remains small, which suggests that other professional groups are filling the need for gerontological specialists. A report published by the Association for Gerontology in Higher Education, *Social Work and Gerontology: A Status Report*, concluded that social work education is not turning out a sufficient number of practitioners prepared to work with the growing elderly population. A second report, *Strategies for Increasing Gerontology Content in Social Work Education,* urged social work educators to identify and reach consensus on what constitutes a body of knowledge essential to a gerontological social work curriculum; also urged was the infusion of aging-related content throughout the core social work courses ("Too Few Trained for Aging Work," 1991).

In 1993 NASW completed a project, funded by the Department of Health and Human Services, Administration on Aging, to stimulate interest in social work careers with older people and to make available information and training materials to social workers in the field of aging. The project included development of AGENET, a database of the names, addresses, and phone numbers of gerontological social workers throughout the country ("Project on Aging," 1994).

Practice Sites

Social workers work with elderly people in hospitals, nursing homes, hospices, retirement communities, family services agencies, state departments of aging, area agencies on aging, and other related public and private entities. In addition, there has been a rapid expansion in home care services for disabled elderly people because of the rising costs of institutionalization, the desire of most people to "age in place," and the ability of many elderly citizens to remain in their homes if they receive appropriate services (Cox, 1992).

Within these settings, social workers provide services in long-term care, health and mental health, recreation and quality of life, intergenerational issues, death and dying, adult day care, nutrition, housing, and adult foster care. Social workers commonly use functions such as individual and family counseling and support, empowering clients to obtain community resources, and developing programs to strengthen links between formal and informal services (Cox, 1992).

The Population

In 1900, 3 million Americans, or 4.1 percent of the population, were age 65 or older; in 1990, the number had swelled tenfold, to 31.6 million, or 11.3 percent of the total population ("Americans Are Getting Older and Older," 1994). Experts predict that an even more dramatic increase will occur between 2010 and 2030, when the elderly population is expected to increase by 76 percent while the population under age 65 will increase by only 6.5 percent (Taeuber, 1993). The increasing role for social workers in the field of aging is directly related to the absolute and proportional growth of this population.

In addition to the tremendous overall growth in the aging population, the diverse demographics of this population are of special importance to social workers. For example, women generally live longer than men and, therefore, are frequently widowed and are often more economically disadvantaged (Dunkle & Norgard, 1995). Ethnicity is another factor that social workers must consider when working with the aging population. The elderly populations in racial and ethnic groups are increasing at a faster rate than the white elderly population because of higher fertility rates (Dunkle & Norgard, 1995). Finally, poverty rates are also much higher among elderly people of color than their white counterparts. Unfortunately, older people who are poverty stricken are much less likely to be able to move into a better situation and, therefore, their poverty status is much more likely to be long term compared to the general population (Dunkle & Norgard, 1995).

The elongated life expectancy of people has led to the identification of three groups who make up the elderly population: (1) the "young old"—ages 65 to 74; (2) the "aged"—ages 75 to 84; and (3) the "old old"—ages 85 and older (Taeuber, 1993). The term "frail elderly" is used to refer to people age 65 or older who have serious physical or mental health problems, and signifies that not all elderly people have serious health problems (Taeuber, 1993).

A sizable proportion of the older U.S. population experiences a number of problems, including decreased income, physical illness, frailty, altered familial relationships, physical and psychological abuse, alcohol problems, housing problems, and crime victimization (Karger & Stoesz, 1994). In addition, age discrimination—unfair treatment of people on the basis of their age—has affected the ability of older people to obtain and retain employment or be considered for promotions. Ageism, stereotyping, and generalizing about people on the basis of their age also has widespread repercussions for older people. Some of these problems are exacerbated for the elderly members of racial and ethnic groups, with statistics confirming that this group has a much higher incidence of poor education, poverty, substandard housing, ill health, and malnutrition. The delivery of services to minority elderly is often impeded by language and cultural differences, physical isolation, and lower income ("Minority Elderly," 1986). The rapidly growing population of older adults has special needs that must be understood and met in order to allow older Americans to maximize their independence and quality of life (National Association of Area Agencies on Aging [NAAAA], 1993).

Policies and Programs

During the Great Depression of the 1930s, more than half of elderly people were economically dependent on their families, and another 18 percent were economically dependent on welfare programs (Brody & Brody, 1987). To alleviate this predicament, Congress, as part of the Social Security Act of 1935, established programs targeted for older Americans: Old-Age and Survivors and Disability Insurance (OASDI). Over the years, these programs have been expanded to include a large array of benefits and protections. Medicare, Medicaid, and Supplemental Security Income are among the important additions to early legislative provisions for the elderly population (Torres-Gil & Puccinelli, 1995).

Today, OASDI provides the major portion of income for most retirees in the lower- and middle-income levels. Many also receive pensions, income from other assets, or part-time wages (Brody & Brody, 1987). Throughout the years there has been a shift from simply providing a subsistence level of income to actual income replacement. This goal was actuated through Title XVI of the Social Security Act, commonly known as Supplemental Security Income (SSI). SSI is a monthly cash payment to people who are aged, blind, or otherwise disabled and who are living at or below subsistence levels (Brody & Brody, 1987).

SSI benefits have helped many recipients avoid destitution, but only 60 percent of eligible people receive SSI benefits. Furthermore, a reduction in administrative personnel has resulted in significant service delays. The backlog of claims under disability programs is expected to reach 1.1 million by the end of fiscal year 1995, and the average time for processing any disability claim has increased from 87 days in 1990 to 154 days in 1994 (National Council on the Aging [NCOA], 1995).

Another dilemma is the catch-22 of improved medical technology. With dramatic advancements in life-saving interventions, people are living longer but they are often chronically ill and physically or mentally impaired (Taeuber, 1993). Quality of life becomes a tremendously important issue, not only for the patient but also for his or her family and friends. This phenomenon has been referred to as "the failures of success" (Brody & Brody, 1987).

In 1965 Medicare and Medicaid were enacted to ensure medical services without subjecting citizens to the catastrophic costs of acute care. Nonetheless, even with Medicare assistance elderly people continue to spend at least 20 percent of their total income on health care (Brody & Brody, 1987).

Conclusion

Many issues are involved in working with elderly people, and social workers must understand and be sensitive to the aging process in order to be effective. Social workers in this field of practice must seek to increase their own sensitivity by identifying their feelings and attitudes toward elderly people, recognizing how membership in a particular age cohort affects elderly individuals, recognizing the variability among elderly individuals, understanding how gender and ethnic or racial status affect the aging experience, and learning about development in later life (Toseland, 1995). Once the social worker's sensitivity is heightened, he or she can use this knowledge to adapt clinical sessions to better meet the clients' needs. For example, initial contacts with older adults may differ from initial contacts with younger clients. Work with older adults may require that the social worker provide more outreach and more discussion of entitlements to help the clients overcome their reluctance to using needed services and resources (Toseland, 1995).

The vignettes in this chapter highlight some of the issues and situations that confront social workers in this area of service. To provide continuous quality services, social workers must continue to expand and increase their own knowledge of issues related to the aging process (Zuniga, 1995).

Because of their professional training in the ecological perspective, social workers are uniquely qualified to work with elderly people. Social workers in this practice area perform the general functions of assessment, diagnosis, counseling, assistance, advocacy, referral, coordination, program development, supervision, and policy analysis (Bellos & Ruffolo, 1995; Toseland, 1995). Another important social work function in this field is that of empowerment and enabling older citizens and their families to develop a sense of competence (Zuniga, 1995). However, the common thread that runs through all of these functions is that, to be truly effective, social workers must sensitize themselves to the issues of aging and "avoid the stereotypes and negative images that interfere with effective helping" (Toseland, 1995, p. 158).

References

Americans are getting older and older. (1994, October 25). *Washington Post*, Health section, p. 5.

Bellos, N. S., & Ruffolo, M. C. (1995). Aging: Services. In R.L. Edwards (Ed.-in-Chief), *Encyclopedia of social work* (19th ed., Vol. 1, pp. 165–173). Washington, DC: NASW Press.

Brody, E. M., & Brody, S. J. (1987). Aged: Services. In A. Minahan (Ed.-in-Chief), *Encyclopedia of social work* (18th ed., Vol. 1, pp 106–126). Silver Spring, MD: National Association of Social Workers.

Cox, C. (1992). Expanding social work's role in home care: An ecological perspective. *Social Work, 37*, 179–183.

Dunkle, R. E., & Norgard, T. (1995). Aging overview. In R. L. Edwards (Ed.-in-Chief), *Encyclopedia of social work* (19th ed., Vol. 1, pp. 142–153). Washington, DC: NASW Press.

Gibelman, M., & Schervish, P. H. (1993). *Who we are: The Social work labor force as reflected in the NASW membership*. Washington, DC: NASW Press.

Karger, H. J., & Stoesz, D. (1994). *American social welfare policy: A pluralistic approach* (2nd ed.). New York: Longman.

Minority elderly facing special problems. (1986, March). *NASW News*, pp. 3, 14.

National Association of Area Agencies on Aging. (1993). *The national directory for eldercare information and referral*. Washington, DC: Author.

National Council on the Aging. (1995). Public policy agenda. *Perspective on Aging, 24*, 1–32.

New jobs seen in aging. (1988, November). *NASW News*, p. 12.

Project on aging produces a push on careers. (1994, January). *NASW News*, p. 12.

Social Security Act of 1935, IV A U.S.C. §401.

Taeuber, C. (1993, May). Sixty-five plus in America. *Current population reports: Special studies*. Washington, DC: U.S. Government Printing Office.

Too few trained for aging work, reports contend. (1991, February). *NASW News*, p. 10.

Torres-Gil, F. M., & Puccinelli, M. A. (1995). Aging: Public policy issues and trends. In R. L. Edwards (Ed.-in-Chief), *Encyclopedia of social work* (19th ed., Vol. 1, pp. 159–164). Washington, DC: NASW Press.

Toseland, R. W. (1995). Aging: Direct practice. In R. L. Edwards (Ed.-in-Chief), *Encyclopedia of social work* (19th ed., Vol. 1, pp. 153–159). Washington, DC: NASW Press.

Zuniga, M. E. (1995). Aging: Social work practice. In R. L. Edwards (Ed.-in-Chief), *Encyclopedia of social work* (19th ed., Vol. 1, pp. 173–183). Washington, DC: NASW Press.

aging services

The current framework for aging services finds its basis in the Older Americans Act (OAA) of 1965 (P.L. 89-73), which created a national network of federal, state, and local agencies to serve the elderly population. OAA established the Administration on Aging under the auspices of the U.S. Department of Health and Human Services, 57 state offices on aging, and more than 670 area agencies on aging. In addition, the act provides funding to more than 190 tribal organizations in an effort to target the most vulnerable elderly American Indian population (National Association of Area Agencies on Aging, 1993; National Council on the Aging, 1995).

Title III of the Older Americans Act appropriates federal funds to states and territories based on the size of their population over 60 years of age. The states then make grants to local area agencies on aging to administer a wide range of services for older people. Sixty-six percent of these local agencies are public government agencies and 33 percent are private, nonprofit agencies (NAAAA, 1993). Area agencies usually contract with providers rather than providing services directly, although they act as direct service providers if there is no other appropriate program (NAAAA, 1993). Social workers can be involved in aging services on the national, state, local, or direct service levels.

A Social Worker at an Area Agency on Aging

[Note: This vignette describes an actual social worker, Cheryll Schramm, who currently occupies the position under discussion.]

Cheryll Schramm is the director of aging services at the Atlanta Regional Commission (ARC), which has been designated as the Atlanta Area Agency on Aging (AAA). She functions at the macro level of social work practice. In a 1995 interview she described a typical day beginning with a morning meeting of the review panel. Cheryll had worked with the review panel to develop and issue a request for proposals (RFP) to develop a special demonstration project to better serve home-bound elderly people. Many grant applications were received, and today the review panel, composed of community experts from organizations such as the United Way and Grady Memorial Hospital as well as older citizen representatives, would decide which applications to accept.

After the meeting, Cheryll received a call from a representative of the AT&T headquarters office who asked Cheryll if she could help organize a panel discussion for local AT&T offices regarding elder care programs for employees. Elder care counseling has become an important aspect of many business environments. Similar services began years ago with the need to help employees deal with child day care difficulties. However, with the aging of the workforce, employers began to recognize that employees needed elder care support services and counseling for their immediate or extended families who may reside many miles or states away. Cheryll agreed to work with AT&T in developing elder care programs for employees, and her participation exemplifies the expanding role of public–private partnerships in many areas of social services.

Cheryll then went into an afternoon meeting with staff from the Georgia State Department of Labor (DOL). This meeting concerned a contract awarded by DOL to ARC to manage the older workers program of the Job Training Partnership Act. ARC was halfway into the contract, and the meeting was designed to discuss and correct any problems that had developed. To receive this contract, Cheryll worked with her staff to develop a grant proposal and submit it to DOL in response to a request for proposals. This is a function referred to as grantsmanship, and grant-writing skills are critical in all fields of social work to secure program funds. *Grantsmanship* is defined as "the ability to develop proposals for special project funding. The ability includes skills in research design, verbal communication, sales, writing, needs assessment, innovation of new techniques for problem solving, coordination of plans, and political and administrative activity, as well as knowledge about the appropriate sources of project funds" (Barker, 1995, p. 154).

The diversity of roles a social worker carries out at an AAA is seen in the difference between the morning meeting, in which ARC was the funding source, and the second meeting, in which ARC was the funding recipient. In the first meeting, the paramount social work functions were administration, planning, and reviewing. The functions carried out in the second meeting were program development, consultation, coordination, planning, and reviewing.

After the second meeting, Cheryll received a call from the legislative office of the Atlanta Gas Company. The gas company was in the process of pressing for changes in pending legislation and they wanted ARC to help them convince older citizens to contact their legislators in support of the bill. Cheryll responded that ARC has a senior advocacy program with the responsibility to give all the facts to older citizens so that they can make up their own minds. ARC avoids any effort to persuade their constituents to one point of view, firmly believing that once presented with the facts older people are capable of making their own decisions. Cheryll frequently gets calls from organizations with similar requests for legislative support, and she noted that targeting older citizens is a smart tactic. "Older people *will* call. Sometimes legislators will contact us asking us to make them stop calling their offices."

This call highlights another aspect of a social worker's job in this arena, as well as many others—client advocacy. In advocating for a client, social workers may teach the client how to use available services; work to remove obstacles to the client's needs; or argue on behalf of the client's needs.

Finally, there is one last meeting at the end of the day with a woman from Emory Hospital and a man from Wesley Woods Nursing Home. They are applying for a grant from a foundation to carry out a demonstration project aimed at better co-ordination between acute and chronic care systems. Cheryll's participation in this coalition highlights the social work functions of grantsmanship, program development, coordination, evaluation, and planning.

Through consistent, effective outreach and program development, ARC has become a strong foundation in the community. Although this typical day seems quite full, Cheryll explains how she feels about her job, "I love it. It is very rewarding to get together and brainstorm and move from ideas to programs that meet the needs of older citizens" (personal interview, January 27, 1995).

Cheryll's work at ARC exemplifies macro social work at the community level. However, as previously discussed, social workers can also be involved at the direct service or group level of practice. Services to elderly people are typically divided into four categories: access services, community-based services, in-home services, and institutional services (NAAAA, 1993). There are numerous opportunities for social workers in all of these areas.

References

Barker, R. L. (1995). *Social work dictionary* (3rd ed.). Washington, DC: NASW Press.

National Association of Area Agencies on Aging. (1993). *The national directory for eldercare information and referral.* Washington, DC: Author.

National Council on the Aging. (1995). Public policy agenda. *Perspective on Aging, 24,* 1–32.

Older Americans Act of 1965, P.L. 89-73, 79 Stat. 218.

case
management

Access services generally consist of assessment activities in which information is collected concerning the older person's health and financial status as well as other relevant facts. Usually the person's functioning level in terms of activities of daily living is determined and information and an appropriate referral are provided (NAAAA, 1993).

A significant component of access and other services for this population is that of case management. As the baby boom generation moves into middle age, their parents become senior citizens with extended life expectancies and complicated care issues ranging from health care to psychological counseling. Because of a decrease in the average number of children per family, there are fewer familial caregivers for parents as they grow older (Brody, 1986).

Individuals in midlife with significant family and work responsibilities find themselves "sandwiched" between demands to care for their children and demands to care for their parents. The situation is further complicated by the increasing mobility of society, often resulting in long-distance caregiving for older relatives. These situations cause a great deal of stress, both for the caregiving younger adult and the older adult who needs services but does not want to go to an institution.

These factors have led to the emergence of an entirely new practice area. Social workers are becoming private case managers for elderly people whose immediate families are unavailable to provide the necessary care because of geographic distance or other pressing responsibilities (Sloane, 1989). Some private case managers also identify services and service providers in distant communities, using their collegial networks. According to a survey by InterStudy, a health care system research company, MSW-level social workers are the predominant labor force in private case management firms ("MSWs Lead," 1988).

InterStudy identified several trends to account for the emergence of private case management as a distinct field of practice: the growth in elderly population; rising service costs; increasing complexity of the service system for elderly people; inability of public programs to meet all care-coordination needs; and the "entrepreneurial" initiative of human services professionals ("MSWs Lead," 1988). These case management firms tend to be independent and self-managed, to operate on a for-profit basis, and to have small staffs. They charge by the hour but may use sliding-fee scales and other rate-setting methods. The services provided by the social work staff include family and client counseling; housing and nursing home placement; functional, social, and financial assessments; service referrals and monitoring; client evaluation for community-based care or institutional placement; and assistance with eligibility forms and other paperwork associated with human services.

Barker (1995) offered this definition of *case management:*

> A procedure to plan, seek, and monitor services from a variety of agencies and staff on behalf of a client. . . . A case manager. . . coordinates services, advocates for the client, and sometimes controls resources and purchases services for the client. . . . Case management may involve monitoring the progress of a client whose needs require the services of many different professionals, agencies, health care facilities, and human services programs. It typically involves case finding, comprehensive multidimensional assessment, and frequent reassessment. . . . Social workers and nurses are the professional groups most often called on to fulfill this function. Case management is seen as an increasingly important way of limiting problems arising from fragmentation of services, staff turnover, and inadequate coordination between providers. (p. 47)

In 1992, the NASW board of directors approved *Standards for Social Work Case Management* (NASW, 1992). The standards describe case management as "a method of providing services whereby a professional social worker assesses the needs of the client and the client's family, when appropriate, and arranges, coordinates, monitors, evaluates, and advocates for a package of multiple services to meet the specific client's complex needs" (as cited in "Case Manager's Role," 1992, p. 7). The standards, which replace NASW's 1984 *Standards and Guidelines for Social Work Case Management for the Functionally Impaired,* cover 10 specific issues, such as privacy and confidentiality, evaluation and quality assurance in monitoring case management services, caseload size, and educational requirements for social workers (NASW, 1992).

Case managers typically assess the client's needs, locate appropriate services, coordinate and plan for their use, link clients to necessary resources, and monitor the client's progress toward the desired outcome (Garner, 1995). Case managers not only develop individual care plans but also attempt to ensure that the services are delivered in a timely fashion (Rose & Moore, 1995). Social workers in case management play an important role in the decision-making process regarding the use of long-term care for elderly people (Garner, 1995). The five basic social work functions involved in case management include: identification of clients; assessment of needs; service or treatment planning; referral to appropriate services; and monitoring case progression and service delivery (Rose & Moore, 1995).

Case Management Services for Elders

Mary Bartow is 78 years old and had lived in Bismarck, North Dakota, for the last 60 years of her life. Her husband died two years ago and their only child, Matthew, lives in Colorado Springs with his wife, two daughters, and golden retriever. Matthew worries about his mother. She seems depressed and she rarely leaves her house. She refuses to try the local senior center activities and she won't hear of moving to Colorado. She says that she will just stay in Bismarck until she dies, and she doesn't think that will be too much longer.

Matthew didn't know what to do so he went to see the employee assistance social worker at his office. The counselor suggested a case manager for his mother and gave him the name and number of a case management agency in the Bismarck area. Matthew went home and called his mother with the idea. She didn't like it at first, but finally agreed to at least meet with the case manager. Matthew then called the agency and set up an appointment for Dana Carlson, a social worker, to visit his mother.

When Dana first arrived she spent more than an hour talking with Matthew's mother and recognized her depression and loneliness. After meeting with Ms. Bartow a second time, Dana identified three major issues: (1) Ms. Bartow needed to establish contact with other people to reduce her loneliness; (2) she needed to get a complete physical examination and a new prescription for her eyeglasses; and (3) she needed to get at least one nutritionally sound meal a day.

Dana went back to her agency and first contacted Ms. Bartow's doctor to arrange an appointment. She then called the local transportation contractor and arranged for them to take Ms. Bartow to and from the appointment. Dana then contacted a church near Ms. Bartow's home where congregate meals are served every evening to a group of older people. There are often activities after or before the meals sponsored by the local senior center. There was room for another person, so Dana arranged for Ms. Bartow to attend Monday through Friday. She thought this participation would allow Ms. Bartow not only to get a good meal but also to socialize; after she participated in some of the activities offered by the senior center, she might eventually agree to go there during the day. Dana then worked with another transportation company to arrange for daily transportation for Ms. Bartow to and from the evening meals. Of course, before confirming any arrangements, Dana checked everything with Ms. Bartow.

Dana's activities only begin to highlight the coordination between client and services that is essential in effective case management. In this scenario, Dana assessed and identified Ms. Bartow's primary needs. She then offered brief counseling to Ms. Bartow to help her understand the need to go to the doctor and to the church for meals. To get Ms. Bartow to participate, Dana had to have everything organized; if there were difficulties, Ms. Bartow might refuse to continue going. Therefore, Dana used the social work functions of organization, negotiation, and coordination. Finally, it is essential that Dana continually monitor and evaluate the service delivery to ensure that Ms. Bartow is receiving the appropriate care.

References

Barker, R. L. (1995). *Social work dictionary* (3rd ed.). Washington, DC: NASW Press.

Brody, E. M. (1986, March). All generations need the "gift of caring." *NASW News*, p. 9.

Case manager's role clarified by guidelines. (1992, September). *NASW News*, p. 7.

Garner, J. D. (1995). Long-term care. In R. L. Edwards (Ed.-in-Chief), *Encyclopedia of social work* (19th ed., Vol. 2, pp. 1625–1634). Washington, DC: NASW Press.

MSWs lead in private case management. (1988, January). *NASW News*, p. 16.

National Association of Area Agencies on Aging. (1993). *The national directory for eldercare information and referral.* Washington, DC: Author.

National Association of Social Workers. (1992). *Standards for social work case management.* Washington, DC: Author.

Rose, S. M., & Moore, V. L. (1995). Case management. In R. L. Edwards (Ed.-in-Chief), *Encyclopedia of social work* (19th ed., Vol. 1, pp. 335–340). Washington, DC: NASW Press.

Sloane, L. (1989, March 12). Private care managers: One-on-one assistance for the aged. *New York Times*, p. 52.

community-
based
services

As with other age groups, elderly people express a strong preference to remain in their own homes and be cared for by a relative for as long as possible. For every disabled elderly person in a nursing home, one to three equally disabled elderly people reside in the community (Garner, 1995).

Community-based services are generally designed to supplement the work of the primary caregiver. Adult day care is one example of a community-based service. Adult day care provides health, social, and other support services to functionally impaired adults for a prearranged portion of the day, but less than 24 hours (NAAAA, 1993).

Adult senior centers are similar to adult day care, but senior centers are usually for healthier older adults and focus more on social, physical, religious, and recreational activities (NAAAA, 1993). Other examples of community-based services include congregate meals, which ensure a nutritious meal for a group of older people at a group facility; legal assistance programs, which assist elderly people in legal issues ranging from wills to pension problems; and employment services, which help older citizens by providing preretirement counseling as well as training, education, and job placement, if appropriate (NAAAA, 1993).

In addition, elder abuse prevention programs are often considered community services and are generally found in all local departments of social services. These programs are designed to identify and alleviate situations of abuse, neglect, or self-neglect. *Elder abuse* refers to the mistreatment of aged and relatively dependent people by adult children, other relatives, legal custodians, or others who provide for their care (Barker, 1995). Abuse can include physical abuse, psychological abuse, material abuse, and medical abuse (NAAAA, 1993). Unfortunately, elder abuse is all too common.

When such abuse does occur, adult protective services is usually involved in providing assistance. *Adult protective services* is social, medical, legal, residential, and custodial care that is provided for adults who are unable to provide such care for themselves or do not have a family member, friend, or other person who can provide it. Those in need of adult protective services are often incapable of acting judiciously on their own behalf and are consequently vulnerable to being harmed or inflicting harm on others. The courts typically intervene to assign responsibility for care and decisions about care to a social agency or other care facility (Barker, 1995).

As the population ages, social workers have increasingly recognized the need for greater collaboration between professionals and families, both because families have needs of their own and because families often provide much of the care for their aging relatives (Hooyman & Gonyea, 1995). Therefore, many social work interventions include the function of empowering families and helping them to develop and use their own strengths and skills (Hooyman & Gonyea, 1995).

Despite social work assistance, families caring for disabled relatives often confront a confusing and fragmented system of services. Social workers must play a role in planning and coordinating more-extensive services within the community rather than placing the burden of care solely on the shoulders of the family (Hooyman & Gonyea, 1995).

Delivering Adult Protective Services

Mark is a young social worker in the adult services division of the Department of Social Services in Queens, New York. He has a caseload of 25 older adults who are functionally impaired. One case is especially troubling. Ms. Nowles is 68 and is diabetic. She has had two strokes and has gone into a diabetic coma on one occasion. She has numerous gastrointestinal problems and is on six different medications. Ms. Nowles lives with her 45-year-old daughter, Brenda, and her 44-year-old mentally retarded nephew, Robert. Brenda does not work and has a record of drug and alcohol abuse; she is currently on parole for attempting to sell drugs. Robert is unable to hold a job or care for himself.

Mark's primary concern is that Ms. Nowles is often so depressed that she talks of killing herself and ending her misery. Mark worries about the administration of her insulin and the chance of another diabetic coma, which could kill her. Brenda insists that she gives her mother all her medications, but Mark recently found out that Brenda went away for three days and left no one to care for Ms. Nowles. Mark is treating this as an adult protective case, and he knows that he must be able to show true neglect and abuse to remove Ms. Nowles from the home. Complicating the matter further is Ms. Nowles' assertion that she does not want to leave and that her daughter takes care of her as well as anyone else could.

This case exemplifies the dilemmas that social workers face in many abuse cases. Mark must call on a variety of social work skills to handle the case effectively. He must be able to assess the situation and diagnose the presenting problem; give advice and counseling to all family members; support Brenda and help her understand the consequences of neglecting to give her mother the proper medication; constantly evaluate the situation; coordinate services with physicians and other health care professionals; and be ready to take decisive action if the circumstances deteriorate further.

References

Barker, R. L. (1995). *Social work dictionary* (3rd ed.). Washington, DC: NASW Press.

Garner, J. D. (1995). Long-term care. In R. L. Edwards (Ed.-in-Chief), *Encyclopedia of social work* (19th ed., Vol. 2, pp. 1625–1634). Washington, DC: NASW Press.

Hooyman, N. R., & Gonyea, J. G. (1995). Family caregiving. In R. L. Edwards (Ed.-in-Chief), *Encyclopedia of social work* (19th ed., Vol. 2, pp. 951–959). Washington, DC: NASW Press.

National Association of Area Agencies on Aging. (1993). *The national directory for eldercare information and referral.* Washington, DC: Author.

depression

A Social Worker Advocates and Educates about Depression
[Note: The following vignette is drawn from an interview with Dr.
Reynolds on March 8, 1995.]

Dr. Mildred Reynolds is a licensed clinical social worker and a Distinguished Practitioner honored by the National Academy of Practice. But her success has not been painless. In a recent autobiographical article, Dr. Reynolds shared her struggle with clinical depression, which began more than 30 years ago when much less was known about the diagnosis and treatment of depression (Reynolds, 1993). During this time, Dr. Reynolds experienced a loss of appetite, low energy, sleeping difficulties, despair, and hopelessness. Her recurring depression lasted for 24 years before a psychiatrist finally recognized the depression and prescribed the appropriate medication along with supportive psychotherapy.

Since her depression was properly diagnosed and treated, Dr. Reynolds has been enjoying life and looking forward to the future. She is currently working as a private practitioner specializing in loss, grief, and depression. More than half of her clients are age 65 or older. She explained that there is often a great deal of resistance among older clients to admit or talk about their emotions. As a result, the depression often takes the form of physical complaints.

In addition to her practice, Dr. Reynolds volunteers much of her time to educating the public about recognizing and treating depression. She currently serves as a volunteer for the National Public Education Campaign on Clinical Depression, which is sponsored by the National Mental Health Association. The objective of the campaign is to increase public awareness that clinical depression is a treatable medical illness. As a result of the campaign, Dr. Reynolds has made more than 25 presentations. She has also served on a panel to educate writers about the effects of depression on women's health issues. Dr. Reynolds served as the panel expert on depression in elderly people and emphasized that depression is not a normal part of aging and is often masked by grief and physical illness in older people.

Dr. Reynolds furthered her goal of educating the public when she wrote and presented two papers entitled A *Preventive Approach* to Depression in the Widowed Elderly and National Efforts to Combat Clinical Depression at the World Federation for Mental Health Congress in Tokyo in August 1993. At the conference, Dr. Reynolds also chaired a meeting on clinical issues affecting elderly people, including depression.

In addition, Dr. Reynolds has participated in numerous interviews for television, newspapers, and magazines in a courageous effort to tell her story and bring attention to the importance of recognizing and treating clinical depression. Dr. Reynolds's skills as a social worker span the micro and macro arenas of practice. She enjoys her clinical work, but she participates in the macro educational programs to help break down the stigma that surrounds mental illness and depression. "Education is so important because depression often goes unrecognized, undiagnosed, and untreated," Dr. Reynolds explains. "I want people to know that there is help available, and with help, there is hope."

As a clinical social worker, Dr. Reynolds carries out the social work functions of assessment, diagnosis, identification, counseling, and enabling. As she continues to speak out on the issue of depression, she receives numerous calls from older people who are desperate for help and understanding. In working with clients either in person or over the telephone, Dr. Reynolds also uses the social work skill of referral because she often interacts with primary care physicians for medical examinations or psychiatrists for medication evaluations.

In her role as a social worker on a macro level, Dr. Reynolds primarily uses the social work functions of mobilization and policy advocacy. Her persistent efforts to disseminate information about the causes, diagnosis, and treatment of depression bring national attention to an area that is often ignored. Dr. Reynolds has used her social work skills in all of her endeavors and she states, "I am extremely grateful for my MSW. It has probably had more impact on my life than any of my other degrees."

Although most people 65 and older feel satisfied and happy with their lives, there is a relatively high risk of depression among this population. The risk of depression among older citizens is four times greater than in the general population (Henry, 1995). Nearly three out of 100 older people suffer from clinical depression, and most of them do not get the help they need (National Institute of Mental Health [NIMH], 1990). In addition, suicide is a more frequent cause of death in people age 65 and older than any other age group. There are fewer suicide attempts among the elderly population, but more attempts are successful (Hancock, 1990).

To treat depression effectively in the early stages, it is essential to determine the causes (Hancock, 1990). Although these causes may be numerous, there are some primary causes of depression that are particularly important to recognize among older people. First, long-term, sudden, or fatal illnesses can cause or aggravate depression (Hancock, 1990). Poor physical health has also been associated with depression, and this is even more apparent in the older population because as health declines there is an increased need to depend on others (Hancock, 1990). In addition to illness, medications can cause depression (NIMH, 1990).

Another major cause of depression among people 65 and over is loss. People in this age group often experience numerous difficult and life-changing losses such as the loss of a spouse, friends, home, community, employment, income, and status. These losses can contribute to an eroding sense of security and can cause or aggravate depressive symptoms (Hancock, 1990).

In an attempt to facilitate the recognition of clinical depression as opposed to normal mourning, the *Diagnostic and Statistical Manual of Mental Disorders* (APA, 1994) lists criteria for the diagnosis of depression. The presence of depressed mood or loss of interest or pleasure and at least five or more other symptoms over the same two-week period representing a change from previous functioning is required for a diagnosis of a major depressive episode. The other symptoms may include

- depressed mood most of the day, nearly every day

- markedly diminished interest or pleasure in all, or almost all, daily activities

- significant weight loss or weight gain

- insomnia or hypersomnia

- fatigue or loss of energy

- motor retardation or agitation

- feelings of worthlessness or excessive or inappropriate guilt

- diminished ability to think or concentrate

- recurrent thoughts of death or recurrent suicidal ideation (APA, 1994).

The three main modes of treatment include psychotherapy, antidepressant medications, and electroconvulsive shock therapy. These treatments can be used individually or in combination. For severely depressed people who exhibit a risk of suicide, hospitalization is strongly recommended (Hancock, 1990). However, most doctors agree that patients who exhibit symptoms of depression should first undergo a complete physical examination to rule out any physical causes (Henry, 1995).

Social workers in this arena may work as primary therapists or they may be part of a an interdisciplinary team. Most of the social work assistance will be in the form of crisis intervention in an attempt to restore the person to his or her former activity level (Hancock, 1990). The social worker will usually conduct a thorough assessment to gather information pertaining to any past problems and coping mechanisms. The assessment also explores physical health, medication, nutrition, and income level (Hancock, 1990). After the assessment, the social worker may determine that he or she needs to become a friend to the client until other support systems are located or created. Day care centers, which were discussed earlier in this section, are often useful for providing socialization opportunities. The key is not to let depressed people feel alone or unsupported (Hancock, 1990).

The good news is that nearly 80 percent of those with clinical depression can be successfully treated (Henry, 1995). However, the depression must first be recognized and diagnosed. If the symptoms are not recognized and treated early, they will get progressively worse and may lead to severe depression and suicidal tendencies. As the aging population continues to grow, depression in elderly people is a problem that can no longer be ignored. Social workers can play a critical role not only in helping depressed clients but also in advocating for policy change to support programs and services and educating the public.

A Beloved Pet Dies

One Saturday morning, Dr. Ross, a veterinarian, received a phone call from Amy Richards, a 78-year-old widow. Dr. Ross had been aggressively treating Ms. Richards's 14-year-old golden retriever for several weeks, following an episode of severe seizures. Dr. Ross had been honest with Ms. Richards about the prognosis. Jaime was dying, and it was only a matter of days, maybe weeks. Dr. Ross had also told Ms. Richards that a natural death for Jaime might not be pain-free.

Ms. Richards had not had any children, and her husband died 12 years ago. Since that time, Jaime had been Ms. Richards's primary companion; the dog was always with her. Ms. Richards was remarkably fit for a woman of her age, in part because of her exercise program with Jaime and her overall sense of well-being.

When Dr. Ross took the call from Ms. Richards, it was with a sense of foreboding. Since the seizures, he had treated Jaime several times and her condition was rapidly deteriorating. Ms. Richards, in a strained voice, told Dr. Ross that she had decided to "put Jaime to sleep"—that the dog was clearly in pain and she could not stand to see her suffer. An appointment was made for the following day and Dr. Ross said that he would come to the house to get Jaime. He suggested that she think about whether she wanted to be with Jaime when she received the injection and, if so, whether there was a friend she might ask to be with her at the time.

The next morning, Dr. Ross came to the house as planned. Jaime was in the backyard. Because she had somehow managed to get herself up and out that morning without assistance, Ms. Richards wondered about her decision. She asked Dr. Ross directly if he was sure that the time had come. He said yes. She then told Dr. Ross that she wanted to be with Jaime when she was euthanized and that she would come to the animal hospital shortly, but alone. She couldn't think of anyone to ask to be with her.

At the animal hospital, Dr. Ross left Ms. Richards alone with Jaime, who had been mildly sedated, in the examining room. When he re-entered, Ms. Richards was crying softly and talking to the dog. Dr. Ross explained what he would be doing and what Ms. Richards should expect. He then proceeded to administer the injection. During this short time, Ms. Richards caressed Jaime's head and continued to talk to her. As Jaime died, Dr. Ross put his arm around Ms. Richards and talked with her about their happy memories of the dog and the mischief she used to get into as a puppy. He then told her she could stay in the room with Jaime as long as she wanted.

Later that evening, Dr. Ross called Ms. Richards to see how she was doing. He became concerned by her flat voice and lack of affect. It seemed as if the energy had been drained from her. Dr. Ross paused for a moment to consider what he should do. He then asked Ms. Richards if it would be okay if he had an associate of his, Sandy, call on her the next day. He briefly explained that Sandy is a social worker with whom he frequently consults. Ms. Richards agreed.

Over the years, Dr. Ross had observed the crushing psychological impact of the loss of a pet on his clients. About a year ago, he decided to hire a social worker part-time to provide bereavement counseling. He knew this was unusual, although he had heard that a few other vets had brought a social worker onto the clinic staff.

Sandy is an animal lover—she has several cats and dogs of her own. She has also read everything she could about the human–animal bond and has come to believe that the relationship between people and their pets deserves a lot more attention in social work practice. During the past year, Sandy and Dr. Ross had both developed a respect for the important role of social workers in helping people adjust to the loss of a pet. Not all of Sandy's work concerns bereavement; sometimes she helps families decided to give a pet up for adoption or talks with families about the potential impact on children of adopting a pet.

The next day, Dr. Ross asked Sandy to contact Ms. Richards. Sandy immediately phoned Ms. Richards, who answered the phone after seven rings. Right away Sandy noticed the flat affect in her voice. Sandy asked how she was; Ms. Richards said that she was doing fine. But further probing revealed that she had not eaten, had slept poorly, and had resisted the efforts of her friends to offer comfort; clearly, Ms. Richards was suffering from the depression that often is a part of the grieving process. Sandy suggested that she stop by to see Ms. Richards later that day, an offer Ms. Richards accepted with little enthusiasm.

The home visit confirmed Sandy's suspicions about the depth of Ms. Richards's depression. Sandy did not shirk from the subject at hand. She invited Ms. Richards to talk about Jaime, acknowledging in the process how significant the dog had been in her life and the grief that she surely must be feeling. Ms. Richards began to cry as she related a story about the first time she had seen Jaime as a puppy and how they had bonded immediately; Jaime, one of eight puppies, had come right up to her and licked her hands.

In the two weeks following Jaime's death, Sandy paid several visits to Ms. Richards. Sandy encouraged Ms. Richards to grieve openly. Jaime had been cremated; they talked about finding a headstone (perhaps a statue of a dog) that Ms. Richards could place over her buried ashes. Ms. Richards began to shop around at neighborhood stores to find an appropriate statute. At Sandy's urging, she also looked through her many photos of Jaime and selected one to have enlarged and framed. Finally, Sandy learned that Ms. Richards had been an English teacher before retirement and enjoyed writing. She suggested that Ms. Richards commit to paper her feelings about the dog.

Several weeks after Jaime's death, Ms. Richards handed Sandy an ode to Jaime.

Lessons from Jaime
I learned so much from you . . .

How to communicate directly about what you want and need . . .
    In your case, it was barking when you wanted to go out, positioning yourself

where you wanted to be scratched, sitting under the counter by the cookie jar
when it was time for a snack.
Perhaps, thinking of you, it will be easier for me to ask others for what I need.
Not to be ashamed of emotion . . .
You quivered all over when I walked in the door.
Your expression of joy at seeing me made me glad to be home.
In fact, it helped make the house a home.
Love can be unconditional . . .
That the presence and strength of unabashed love elicits the same feelings in turn; it was so easy to love you.
Relationships can be so simple, and yet so profound and meaningful.
You taught me that life's pleasures can be as easy as the throw of a tennis ball; a game of catch could make the day for both of us.
You taught me about loyalty; there could be none greater than you showed me.
You showed me about dignity in aging; you never complained, never showed your pain.
You brought peace and contentment to my life.
You gave total acceptance, devotion, and love.
I hope I gave to you nearly as much and what you needed.
You will always be in my heart and thoughts.
I will miss you and be ever grateful that you were in my life.

Ms. Richards said that it had taken several days to compose the ode and that she had wept through every sentence of it. But now she felt that she had finally said a proper goodbye to her companion and had accepted that Jaime was gone. She now felt that she would be able to manage and perhaps someday she would consider getting another dog.

Sandy plans to continue to visit Ms. Richards periodically and, when the time seems right, will help her make the decision about another pet—not to replace Jaime, for clearly that could never be, but to provide a new companion and faithful friend.

Sandy exemplifies a social worker providing social services in a nontraditional practice setting. Her major role is to provide bereavement counseling concerning the loss of a pet, an event that can precipitate grief and mourning, as well as anxiety, depression, and anger (Sable, 1995). Sandy's interventions are based on a theoretical framework of attachment, in this case specifically focused on the relationship between people and their pets. Theories concerning the affectional bonds between people, such as Bowlby's ethological framework, provide Sandy with insights about the strength and durability of Ms. Richards's bond with Jaime (Sable, 1995). Sandy's review of the pertinent research has led her to the understanding that pet attachment is particularly important among divorced, never-married, or widowed people, and childless couples. One article Sandy recently came across emphasized this point:

Because the substitute attachment of a pet provides closeness, touching, and a chance to feel worthwhile and needed, it may have special value for elderly people, who are apt to experience disruptions in relationships with familiar people, places, and things, as well as declining health, physical incapacity, and limited financial resources. The loss of a pet may compound distress. (Sable, 1995, p. 338)

In recent years, attention to the human–animal bond has increased. Social workers have been among the professionals exploring the meaning and depth of this bond and have been involved in creating and implementing programs that involve pets. Animals have been used as adjuncts to the clinical process to relieve the anxiety of clients. Services have been initiated to bring animals to nursing homes to provide stimulation and companionship for elderly people and, in some instances, animals have become residents of facilities. Animal companionship has been found to minimize loneliness, and tactile stimulation has been shown to have a positive effect on the cardiovascular system (Netting, Wilson, & New, 1987). Any pet owner will confirm that a family dog or cat enriches the quality of life.

Programs involving pets continuing to evolve. Correctional facilities have used companion animals with inmates with positive results. Guide dogs for people who are blind, of course, have provided a level of independence for the owners; recently, "hearing-ear" dogs have been trained to respond to doorbells, alarms, and telephones; and "handi-dogs" help people in wheelchairs (Netting et al., 1987).

In 1978, the Veterinary Hospital of the University of Pennsylvania began a social work service to study the bond between people and their companion animals. The university's Small Animal Hospital has also developed a referral and resource network between clinicians and veterinary students to provide consultation and assistance when pet owners need the interventions of a social worker (Netting et al., 1987). Of the 132 referrals at the hospital in one year, 76 involved the death of pets.

Social workers can contribute their knowledge and skills to help people deal with the loss of a pet through individual counseling, support groups, and consultation with veterinarians. They can also help educate the public about the importance of pets in people's lives (Sable, 1995).

References

American Psychiatric Association. (1994). *Diagnostic and statistical manual of mental disorders* (4th ed.). Washington, DC: Author.

Hancock, B. L. (1990). *Social work with older people* (2nd ed.). Englewood Cliffs, NJ: Prentice Hall.

Henry, S. (1995, February 12). America's hidden disease. *Parade Magazine*, p. 4.

National Institute of Mental Health. (1990). *If you're over 65 and feeling depressed . . . Treatment brings new hope*. Washington, DC: U.S. Department of Health and Human Services.

Netting, F. E., Wilson, C. C., & New, J. C. (1987). The human–animal bond: Implications for practice. *Social Work, 32*, 60–64.

Reynolds, M. (1993). A therapist's struggles with depression. *Focus on Mental Health*, p. 4.

Sable, P. (1995). Pets, attachment, and well-being across the life cycle. *Social Work, 40*, 334–341.

in-home
services

In-home services, such as home-delivered meals and home health care, generally are developed with the goal of delaying institutional care. These services are often carried out by a nurse or physician and include skilled nursing care, health monitoring, and, often, medication distribution. Home health services are covered by Medicare.

A similar service, often called "home attendant service," is not covered by Medicare. Home attendant services generally provide assistance with activities of daily living such as bathing or feeding and do not require skilled nursing care (NAAAA, 1993). Other examples of in-home health services include homemakers, chore services, telephone reassurance, friendly visiting, energy assistance and weatherization, and respite care for caregivers (NAAAA, 1993).

Contrary to popular myths that elderly people are being "dumped" in institutions, American families provide most of care and support for older relatives (NCOA, 1995). However, many of these caregivers have low incomes and cannot afford or locate additional support services (NCOA, 1995). These caregivers are often trying to cope with demands of work or caring for small children in addition to caring for their own parents or older relatives. As a result, caregivers frequently experience burnout that often manifests in self-neglect, internalized anger, and neglect of the patient or the family.

Recognizing the need for caregivers as well as their vulnerability, the U.S. Department of Health and Human Services initiated a Family Caregiver Project to demonstrate the impact of removing barriers or disincentives that inhibit family caregiving. One of the aims of the project was to demonstrate alternative approaches to relieving the stress experienced by caregivers so that they can maintain their own health and their caregiving role ("Project Supports Family Caregivers' Role," 1987).

Respite care is a service that provides temporary care for older adults and allows caregivers to get away and relax. Usually paraprofessionals or skilled nurses, rather than social workers, provide the direct caregiving services. However, social workers can arrange for respite care as case managers or perhaps organize a registry or list of respite caregivers for citizens in need of such services.

Remaining at Home

Carol is 78 years old. She is legally blind in her left eye and partially blind in her right eye. She is paralyzed from the waist down as a result of a stroke and must use a wheelchair. She also has an colostomy bag that must be emptied regularly. However, Carol does not want to go to an institution, and she can remain at home if there is someone to provide care for her by cooking her meals, helping her bathe, and being available in case of emergency.

Carol's sister, Margaret, is a 70-year-old widow who has been living with Carol and taking care of her. Carol and Margaret both enjoy this arrangement. However, Dave Mason, the county social worker who has been involved with the case, has begun to worry about Margaret's health. She frequently appears tired, and she can no longer sleep through the night because Carol has been having severe leg cramps and often calls for her sister. Dave tries to encourage Margaret to take a vacation and visit her son, who lives in Dallas. However, Margaret is afraid to leave Carol.

Dave begins investigating respite care options and finds that Carol and Margaret could afford daytime care only, and most service providers do not offer colostomy service. Carol needs to have someone there at night in case there is an emergency. Fortunately, Dave is able to find several nursing homes that will accept Carol for a week-long stay. Dave then takes Carol to visit the nursing homes so that she can determine which one she likes best.

Carol is initially very unhappy about having to go to a nursing home and Margaret feels quite guilty, but Dave works with them both to explain the necessity of Margaret taking a vacation to rejuvenate herself and restore her own health so that she can continue to care for Carol.

In this case scenario, Dave uses the functions of assessment, diagnosis, and identification to determine the problems that need to be addressed. Dave then uses the functions of enabling, organizing, and coordinating to locate an appropriate provider of respite care. Finally, he uses support and counseling functions to help both Carol and Margaret understand the need for Margaret to take a vacation.

References

National Association of Area Agencies on Aging. (1993). *The national directory for eldercare information and referral*. Washington, DC: Author.

National Council on the Aging. (1995). Public policy agenda. *Perspective on Aging, 24*, 1–32.

Project supports family caregivers' role. (1987, February). *NASW News*, p. 6.

institutional care facilities and housing issues

Myth: Most elderly live in nursing homes. Fact: Four-fifths of the elderly population (over age 65) with long-term-care needs live in the community (NAAAA, 1993).

Myth: Most elderly people do not want to live by themselves. Fact: A 1992 American Association of Retired Persons (AARP) national housing survey indicated an increase in the number of older people who lived alone and preferred to live alone (AARP, 1994).

"Aging in place" has been identified as a primary desire among most older Americans, and 85 percent of the respondents said that they wanted to stay in their own homes and never move (AARP, 1994). However, this preference to live alone appears to indicate a desire to maintain independence rather than a desire to withdraw from society. For example, the most useful services cited by elderly participants were companionship and home visitation. In addition, those in retirement communities responded that the most important aspects of their living arrangements primarily involved social benefits (AARP, 1994).

Unfortunately, the two groups most likely to live alone are those older than 75 and those with incomes less than $12,000, the two groups most likely to suffer serious health deterioration or loss of income that would leave them in a housing crisis (AARP, 1994). Despite the chance of health or income emergencies, more than half of older Americans have done little if any planning for the future. However, as discussed in part VII, there are often few real housing options for those with limited income. Older Americans are not in any way exempt from the burgeoning homeless class.

Housing is a primary need, and social workers must be aware of this critical issue in the aging arena. In addition to using their skills to develop support systems for elderly people who remain in the community, social workers also use the functions of enabling, empowerment, and referral to help older citizens access community services. Finally, social workers must use assessment, coordination, and ongoing case management to help the older client remain in the least restrictive living environment.

Housing is a critical issue for many aging citizens, and it is important to understand the housing options besides nursing homes for the aging population. In addition to family care, there are five other basic categories: (1) assisted living, (2) senior housing, (3) continuing care retirement communities, (4) adult foster care, and (5) nursing homes.

Assisted living arrangements are a midpoint between living individually and living in a nursing home. The older person usually needs daily assistance but not continuous medical care. However, these facilities are not available to all elderly people because they do not generally take Medicare or Medicaid (NAAAA, 1993).

Senior housing services provide a safe and secure residential environment but do not offer the skilled medical care or assistance of nursing homes or assisted living arrangements. Senior housing is usually in the form of rental apartments or group residences. Many such programs offer transportation services, congregate meals, and social and recreational activities (NAAAA, 1993).

One of the newer developments in long-term care is continuing-care retirement communities. These communities offer a long-term contract that basically ensures continuous care as a person ages (NAAAA, 1993). These communities are usually made up of several different types of facilities offering a range of care from simple safety and support to highly skilled nursing services. These communities were designed in an attempt to offer continuous care throughout the aging process. Social workers in these environments provide direct service functions such as assessment, diagnosis, identification, support, and counseling. They are also involved in planning, developing, and evaluating programs for the residents.

Another type of living arrangement for older citizens who cannot live on their own, but who do not have to be institutionalized, is adult foster care— services provided in residential care programs in the private homes of nonrelatives for adults who cannot live independently (Barker, 1995). People who may benefit from adult foster care include those suffering from mental illness or mental retardation or frail elderly people. Social workers employed by such agencies as the Veterans Administration or the Adult Protective Services Division of the state or city Department of Social Services are charged with the responsibility to find foster homes; match them with appropriate adults in need; provide ongoing information and referral, concrete services, and counseling to adult clients; and supervise the foster care arrangement. The foster family, or caregivers, provide room and board and assistance in activities of daily living in exchange for a monthly payment. Adult foster care is often a way to avoid institutionalization for disabled citizens while allowing continued opportunities for social interaction.

Adult Foster Care

Frank is a 69-year-old man with moderate retardation. He had been living with his daughter, but she recently had twins and her husband lost his job. They could no longer afford to care for Frank so the daughter called the Montgomery County Department of Social Services, Adult Services Division.

Mary Ann Savoy is a social worker in the Adult Foster Care Division, where Frank's case was presented at a morning staff meeting. The staff reviewed the intake report from the assessment center and then reviewed the options for foster care. There appeared to be a possibility for a match. When Mary Ann was assigned to take the case, she contacted Frank's daughter and arranged to meet with her, her husband, and Frank.

Mary Ann first attempted to explain the foster care system and the benefits that Frank might be able to get from living in a home rather than an institution. Frank's daughter and son-in-law agreed immediately, but Frank was nervous about meeting a new family. Mary Ann took some time to talk just with Frank. She told him that there would be another person, a 72-year-old man, living with the family also. She told Frank that she would set up a time for him to meet the family and maybe spend a week with them. If he didn't like them, he certainly did not have to stay there. Frank readily agreed to this plan and was somewhat excited about meeting the other man.

Mary Ann then met with the foster family who had been approved by the department. They agreed to take Frank for a trial period of one week. Mary Ann met with Frank and the caregiver two times during the trial period, which concluded with Frank excited about his new surroundings, the caregiver happy with Frank, and Frank's family pleased about his new home.

However, adult foster care does not end with arranging an acceptable placement. Mary Ann now had to begin the task of working with Frank and the foster care family. She helped Frank get a part-time job and set up a savings account. She also worked with the foster family to help them understand Frank's special needs.

After one year in adult foster care with regular monthly visits from Mary Ann, Frank was thriving in his new surroundings. In addition, his foster family and his daughter and son-in-law worked with each other to provide Frank with the best possible living arrangement.

Mary Ann had to assess Frank's situation, diagnosis the situation, and assess the caregiver's lifestyle to determine whether Frank would be a good fit. In addition, Mary Ann performed the social work function of counseling for the caregiver, Frank, and Frank's daughter and son-in-law. She also had to assist Frank to develop skills he needed to live independently and negotiate with him and his family to address any problems.

The last and usually least desirable housing option is a nursing home. Nursing homes tend to vary in size, administration, funding, and level of care. Among the "old old" population (age 85 and older), nearly 25 percent live in nursing homes. Of the remaining 75 percent who are not institutionalized, 45 percent report the need for personal assistance with activities of daily living (Taeuber, 1993).

Generally, nursing homes can be distinguished by the type of care they provide, with the three most common being skilled nursing facilities, intermediate care facilities, and custodial care (Hancock, 1990). All nursing homes must meet specific state guidelines to receive a license, and an increasing number of states are requiring preadmission screening. These screening programs are used to evaluate applicants and ensure that placement is necessary. Furthermore, a preadmission screening is often required before Medicaid will reimburse nursing homes (NAAAA, 1993). The screenings are generally conducted by an interdisciplinary team that includes a social worker. The social worker gathers psychosocial information, assesses the situation, identifies any current or potential problems, and makes a determination about the patient's admissibility to the nursing home (personal communication with C. Schramm, director of aging services, Atlanta Regional Commission, May 24, 1995).

Although most of the nursing home residents are over 65 years of age, there are younger patients who are paralyzed, crippled by arthritis, or impaired by early-onset Alzheimer's or other illnesses (Hancock, 1990). Furthermore, nursing homes are being used as brief treatment rehabilitation facilities in addition to providing long-term care (NAAAA, 1993).

Although some social workers are reluctant to work in a nursing home because of a perceived aura of hopelessness, social workers are much needed and can make a tremendous positive impact (Hancock, 1990). In a nursing home, a social worker must be able to work as part of an interdisciplinary team with other health care professionals; exercise the functions of assessment, diagnosis, and counseling when working with a patient who may be having problems with depression or adjustment to lifestyle; coordinate communication between family members and patients; and encourage and enable the family to take an active role in the patient's care. Social workers in this area can use their creativity in planning, developing, administering, and evaluating programs to better serve the residents.

A Nursing Home Resident

Clara is 95 years old and has been a resident of Northwest Health Care Center, a skilled nursing facility in Topeka, Kansas, for more than 10 years. Her husband and all of her children have died. She has only two granddaughters still living and they are not able to visit her very often. Clara is frequently depressed and lonely. As a result, she concentrates excessively on her own physical ailments and is convinced that her own death is imminent.

Kim Daniels, director of social work at Northwest, has spoken with Clara's social worker, Tom Burns, on several occasions. Tom has told Kim that he is worried about Clara but, with all of his other clients, he cannot spend as much time with her as he would like. He is aware of her loneliness and depression. He believes that she needs to increase her level of social interaction to take her mind off of her own illnesses.

Kim suggests that Tom get Clara involved in floor activities. However, Tom claims that Clara refuses to join the other residents in the day room for any planned activity. Kim considers Clara's situation and recognizes that there are important mental health issues involved. She knows that mental health services for elderly people are inadequate, as reflected in the fact that only 1 percent of nursing home residents can obtain psychological or psychiatric treatment.

Often surrounded by loss and fear, some older citizens look to end their own suffering, which is evident in the disproportionately high suicide rates among the elderly population.

In an effort to address the mental health needs of elderly people, Kim recently spoke with a geriatric counseling firm that offered to provide services to residents at the nursing home. The counselors accept Medicare and Medicaid, so the clients would not have to pay for the services. Kim explains the service to Tom and suggests that he talk to Clara about his concerns and ask her if she would be willing to talk to a counselor.

Clara agrees to meet the counselor once as a trial. Tom then calls Clara's granddaughter and explains the situation to her and invites her to meet the counselor with Clara. Tom believes that if Clara can meet with the counselor just once a week, she will have someone to count on and share her feelings with. Perhaps after she begins to trust the counselor she may feel more comfortable interacting with the other residents.

In this case, Tom carried out the social work functions of assessment, diagnosis, and counseling in his original analysis of Clara's situation. He then facilitated communication with Clara's granddaughter and appropriately coordinated referral services of the geriatric counselor.

In addition to Tom's role in the case, the social work supervisor, Kim, also exhibited several important social work functions. She assessed the situation and identified the client's needs. To have the geriatric counseling service available as an option, Kim had to coordinate, plan, and negotiate with the counseling organization to reach a service agreement. She gave Tom appropriate supervision and guidance in the best way to handle the case.

In addition to nursing home case management and supervision, social workers can also coordinate and plan resident activities. Incorporating knowledge of both physical and emotional factors of aging, social workers can develop and administer programs such as "reminiscence groups," which help older people conduct life reviews to affirm their own existence and resolve any conflicts ("At Life's End," 1985). Using the ecological perspective, their knowledge of human needs, and their skills in planning, organizing, and coordinating, social workers have also been instrumental in understanding the importance of intergenerational programs that allow young children to spend time with older adults. For example, several nursing homes in Georgia and other states have special programs with the Boy Scouts and Girl Scouts in which the children come to the nursing homes to help celebrate residents' birthdays. The adults share their wisdom and experience, and the children bring their liveliness. Interactions such as these allow older residents to once again feel needed and alive (personal communication with C. Schramm, director of aging services, Atlanta Regional Commission, May 24, 1995).

A survey aimed at improving nursing home care indicated that social workers and nursing home administrators agreed about the top psychosocial needs of residents: Of primary importance is "meeting patients' and families' needs for support in making the transition to nursing home care, for help in coping with loss, and for a sense of relatedness and intimacy" ("Nursing Home Study," 1990, p. 15).

The necessary functions of social workers in nursing homes have been outlined in NASW's *Standards for Social Work Practice in Long-Term Care Facilities* (NASW, 1981). The following services should be provided by all social workers in long-term care (Garner, 1995):

- direct social work services to residents, families, and significant others

- assist residents, families, and significant others in the use of services

- strengthen communications among residents, their families, significant others, and staff

- provide a therapeutic environment to promote an optimal quality of life

- promote interaction between the facility and the community.

Unfortunately, there continue to be complaints of nursing home abuse of residents either physically, emotionally, or materially. As a result, all states are required to have ombudsman workers, who are charged with monitoring the implementation of federal, state, and local laws pertaining to nursing home administration as well as investigating and resolving complaints made by or on behalf of individual residents. Typical complaints may involve food service, financial issues, and medical treatment issues (NAAAA, 1993). Obviously, as ombudsmen, social workers must effectively exercise the function of advocacy to ensure that the rights of the patients are upheld.

Demographics indicate that social work in long-term care will increase dramatically in the coming years and that residents of nursing homes are likely to be older and more severely disabled (Garner, 1995). Therefore, social workers in this arena will face great challenges, but they are well-equipped with skills to provide efficient, effective, and caring treatment. In addition, social workers in this area of service must also use the advocacy function to promote policies and programs that benefit and protect the nation's elderly population (Garner, 1995).

References

American Association of Retired Persons. (1994). *Understanding senior housing for the 1990s: AARP survey of consumer preferences, concerns, and needs.* Washington, DC: Author.

At life's end, looking back builds legacy. (1985, September). *NASW News*, p. 3.

Barker, R. L. (1995). *Social work dictionary* (3rd ed.). Washington, DC: NASW Press.

Garner, J. D. (1995). Long-term care. In R. L. Edwards (Ed.-in-Chief), *Encyclopedia of social work* (19th ed., Vol. 2, pp. 1625–1634). Washington, DC: NASW Press.

Hancock, B. L. (1990). *Social work with older people* (2nd ed.). Englewood Cliffs, NJ: Prentice Hall.

National Association of Area Agencies on Aging. (1993). *The national directory for eldercare information and referral.* Washington, DC: Author.

National Association of Social Workers. (1981). *Standards for social work practice in long-term care facilities.* Silver Spring, MD: Author.

Nursing home study: Care is concern. (1990, November). *NASW News*, p. 15.

Taeuber, C. (1993, May). Sixty-five plus in America. In *Current population reports: Special studies.* Washington, DC: U.S. Government Printing Office.

senile dementia, Alzheimer's type

Senile dementia, Alzheimer's type, is the single most prominent irreversible organic brain disease (Hancock, 1990). There is some question among researchers as to whether Alzheimer's disease is a distinguishable, separate disease or a group of several diseases that are similar to each other. Research continues in this area (Hancock, 1990).

It has been estimated that Alzheimer's disease accounts for half of the dementia that appears in older citizens (Hancock, 1990). Although Alzheimer's is marked by memory impairment, there is no set of definite characteristics that indicates the presence of the disease. Rather, Alzheimer's is diagnosed by excluding all other causes of intellectual impairment (Hancock, 1990).

Alzheimer's disease is a progressively deteriorating disease, with three general stages. The first stage is characterized by memory loss and changes in behavior. The second stage includes further memory impairment and loss of other previously acquired skills. The final stage is brief and terminal—the patient will often stop eating and communicating (Hancock, 1990).

There is no cure and no prevention for Alzheimer's disease, and the typical length of survival is five to 10 years (Hancock, 1990). As the disease progresses through the three stages, both the patient and the caregivers confront difficulties that require the skills of a social worker, such as counseling, coordination of services, and case management.

The normal progression of Alzheimer's disease can be further complicated by the presence of depression or paranoia. In these cases, a social worker can concentrate on alleviating the depression or the paranoia, which will lessen the clinical impact of Alzheimer's disease (Cohen, 1986).

A news story (Henry, 1995) described a 77-year-old man, Edwin Hunter, who had Alzheimer's disease as well as severe depression. His wife stated that as his condition worsened, he became increasingly depressed. Finally, Edwin went to see a doctor who prescribed medication, counseling, and exercises to alleviate the depression. The doctor explained, "Since Alzheimer's is generally untreatable, the medical consensus today is that if depression is worsening the

Alzheimer's, then go ahead and treat [the depression] after ruling out any other physical disorders" (p. 67). The patient's wife noted that, after he was treated for depression, her husband, although still plagued by Alzheimer's disease, was calmer and less hostile.

Alzheimer's disease is a tragedy for the entire family. Not only does the afflicted individual suffer serious impairment and eventual death, caregivers must cope with increasing dependence and thus, enormously elevated, personal stress levels. Many Alzheimer's caregivers report high levels of depression and stress, and social workers have come to realize that the caregiver is also in need of intervention from a mental health professional (Cohen, 1986).

In the mid-Atlantic region, social workers have organized an Alzheimer's Caregivers' Respite Program to provide the primary caregiver with temporary relief. Social workers either arrange for alternative care with the community, or, in some cases, provide the care themselves. In other areas of the country, social workers have organized support groups for primary caregivers, allowing these individuals to vent their grief, frustration, sense of loss, and concerns over the deteriorating state of their charge, as well as practical suggestions for coping in an extremely difficult, long-term situation ("Counseling," 1986).

Social workers also help primary caregivers determine when they can no longer provide the necessary care. Once this difficult decision is made, the social worker can help select a nursing home or arrange for an alternative form of care. In many cases, the caregiver also needs grief counseling to deal with the gradual loss of a loved one.

A social worker can also assist the caregiver or family with the economic issues of long-term health care. Medicare and Medicaid regulations are complicated and confusing, especially when they are combined with the already overwhelming responsibility of caring for a person with Alzheimer's disease ("Counseling," 1986).

Alzheimer's Disease: Family Impact

Leigh Hunter has been the social work supervisor of the Alzheimer's wing at Willow Run Nursing Home in Newport News, New Jersey, for almost 10 years. She supervises five other social workers in the wing and provides regular consultation in weekly meetings with each worker. There are 50 patients in the wing at any one time, 10 per social worker.

This morning, Leigh is meeting with one of her most experienced social workers, Annie Winslow. Annie told Leigh she had received a phone call from the son of a patient, 81-year-old Charles, whose wife, Chris, is 78 years old. Charles is in the latter part of the second stage of Alzheimer's disease. He has severe memory impairment and has lost some motor skills. He has also become increasingly agitated and combative. Chris has been caring for her husband at home, but as he gets progressively worse, she and her children are frightened that he will hurt himself or Chris. Finally, Chris's children talked her into admitting Charles to Willow Run so that he could get the care he needs.

Charles is getting the appropriate care, but now Chris is extremely depressed and guilt-ridden. Her son said she rarely leaves the house and is not eating or sleeping properly. He is very concerned about her.

Considering the case, Leigh recognizes that Charles is technically the patient. However, she has always treated the patient and the immediate caregiving family as one unit, believing that the mental health of one greatly affects the mental health of the others. Therefore, she urges Annie to work with Chris's son, suggesting that she try to meet with Chris regularly to counsel her in understanding and coping with her grief. She also suggests that Annie research support groups in the area and help Chris get involved. Finally, Leigh recommends that Chris be made more of an active part of Charles's care plan so that she will not feel as if she abandoned him in his time of need.

In this scenario, Annie is the direct service social worker who must assess the situation and provide assistance, advice, and counseling services to Chris. Furthermore, she performs the function of referral in helping Chris to get involved in a local support group. As a supervisor, Leigh also assessed the situation, then carried out her roles of management, supervision, and consultation in helping Annie determine the best course of action.

References

Cohen, G. D. (1986, February). Alzheimer dysfunctions can be minimized. *NASW News*, p. 11.

Counseling can benefit elderly, caretakers. (1986, January). *NASW News*, p. 3.

Hancock, B. L. (1990). *Social work with older people* (2nd ed.). Englewood Cliffs, NJ: Prentice Hall.

Henry, S. (1995, February 12). America's hidden disease. *Parade Magazine*, p. 4.

illness: hospice care

When people think of hospice care, they often think of a hospital-like facility. But hospice care is a concept rather than a place. The purpose of hospice care is to alleviate the terminal patient's pain and provide psychological, spiritual, and social services to help the patient and the family make the most of life in the final stages of illness (Hancock, 1990).

The hospice concept originated in Ireland in the 1800s and spread to other countries. In the United States, the popularity of hospice programs grew in the middle of this century in response to rapid technological advances in medicine that focused only on physical aspects of an illness while ignoring the patient's psychological and social needs (Proffitt, 1987). In 1990, the National Hospice Organization reported that the number of people served by hospices has more than doubled since 1983, and more than 210,000 individuals and their families are served by more than 1,800 hospice programs in the United States (Richman, 1995).

The concept of hospice care focuses on palliative measures to reduce and alleviate the patient's pain. The emphasis is on care rather than cure. Hospice care attempts to address all of the needs of the patient and the family; therefore, a hospice care team is multidisciplinary and often includes physicians, nurses, social workers, physical therapists, dieticians, speech and hearing therapists, and volunteers (Hancock, 1990).

Barker (1995) defined hospice as "a philosophy of caring and an array of programs, services, and settings for people with terminal illness. Hospice services are usually offered in nonhospital facilities with homelike atmospheres where family, friends, and the significant other can be with the dying person" (p. 171).

In the early 1970s, the American Hospice Movement rose to the forefront as a home-based program that focused on family-provided care with the help of hospice staff (Proffitt, 1987). By the middle of 1984, there were more than 1,000 hospice programs throughout the United States, and most of them were operated by a combination of volunteers and paid staff (Proffitt, 1987). Today, hospice care has grown from being a grassroots movement to becoming an accepted part of the medical establishment (Fish, 1989).

Although hospice care is rooted in home-based care, hospice programs can also be found in hospitals. Some hospice programs are called "scattered bed" programs, in which hospice patients are scattered throughout the hospital in various wards and a hospice team makes daily rounds to visit each patient. Other hospice programs may be on a specific ward or floor of a hospital that is set aside for hospice care (Hancock, 1990).

Nevertheless, most hospice programs are still home-care programs (Fish, 1989; Richman, 1995). Some may be run entirely by volunteers, whereas others are composed of a combination of volunteers and paid staff. Some programs may be supported by private funding, whereas others may have contractual agreements with a Medicare home health agency or be a part of a Medicare-certified home-health agency (Fish, 1989). Despite these different models for hospice programs, the basic concept remains the same: palliative and supportive care for the patient and the family and bereavement care for the family after the patient's death (Fish, 1989).

Hospice care is available 24 hours a day, seven days a week. However, hospice care is available only for terminally ill patients with a life expectancy of three to six months. Generally, hospice care is available to all terminal patients regardless of their ability to pay (Hancock, 1990). In 1982 the Medicare hospice benefit was passed as part of the Tax Equity and Fiscal Responsibility Act (P.L. 97-248). Therefore, Medicare hospital insurance can help pay for hospice care if a doctor certifies the need for it and the care is provided by a Medicare-certified program. In addition, some private insurance companies have begun paying for hospice care (Hancock, 1990).

The medical task in hospice care is to administer analgesics and pain medication at a level that will control pain without reducing awareness. Patients and families often need support and counseling to overcome their fears about using strong medications (Hancock, 1990). The administration of medications in hospice care is quite different from administration in hospitals. In hospice care, the appropriate dosage is given and maintained to avoid patient suffering as medication wears off and it is self-administered or given by a family member rather than by a doctor or nurse (Hancock, 1990).

With such a strong emphasis on alleviating physical pain, what is the role of a social worker on a hospice care team? The social work role is crucial either as a manager or as a direct service worker. A hospice social worker has responsibilities to the patient, the family, the community, and the hospice care team. Social workers in the field of hospice care generally perform functions in five major areas: (1) provision of information and financial assistance; (2) interaction and coordination with the community; (3) administration and management of agencies; (4) performance of clinical work and counseling with individuals and families; and (5) advocacy for the acceptance of the hospice philosophy by patients, the health care system, and society (Richman, 1995).

Social work responsibilities in caring for the patient may include making the initial visit to the patient to assess the patient's and the family's needs. The social worker may conduct a psychosocial interview to develop a plan of care. Hospice social workers also help patients and families identify and take advantage of available community resources. Finally, social workers join with other members of the hospice team to assist the patient in handling unfinished business such as an unresolved quarrel, an unpaid debt, a relationship to be mended, or any legal actions that need to be finalized, such as a will or a power of attorney (Hancock, 1990).

The role of the social worker does not end with the patient's death. One of the social worker's primary responsibilities is counseling family members before and after the patient's death. Hospice care focuses on helping families provide comprehensive nursing and supportive care to patients in their homes. In reaching this goal, social workers play an important role in teaching patients and families that their feelings, concerns, and anxieties are a normal part of the grieving process. Social workers help patients and families deal with their feelings in a constructive way, facilitating communication, and accessing necessary concrete services, such as group bereavement services (Fish, 1989). In addition to helping patients and families, hospice social workers often conduct workshops for fellow colleagues and volunteers to help them understand and deal with their own grief over the repeated losses they experience (Proffitt, 1987).

Hospice care is different from standard home health care, hospital care, and nursing home care in its extensive use of volunteers. Hospice social workers often serve as administrators for the volunteer program and may also supervise volunteers who must handle intense relationships with the families they are serving (Proffitt, 1987).

The most common approaches used by hospice care social workers in assisting the patient and the family are crisis intervention; task-centered casework; and a nondirective, client-centered approach that focuses on listening, supporting, and teaching. In determining what approach to use, the social worker must consider each individual patient's situation, past history, present coping mechanism, and existing supports (Fish, 1989).

Social workers' skills and functions are particularly necessary during the more difficult times, such as when death is imminent. Social workers must use their own knowledge of the complexities of end-of-life planning, including the legal, ethical, and cultural elements of the process. Social workers can also use the functions of empowerment, advocacy, and assistance to help those in the process of dying as well as their families so that they can benefit from community supports in times of need (Kaplan, 1995).

Facing the Death of a Spouse

Will has been my husband for 50 years. Five months ago we celebrated our anniversary. I try to tell myself that a miracle will happen and we will be together for another 50 years, but I know that won't happen. Will is dying of inoperable prostate cancer. The doctor recently said Will had two months to live.

Will is trying to be upbeat. He doesn't want me to be upset. But he is in so much pain. When he doesn't think I am looking, he bites his lip and grimaces in pain. My neighbor is a nurse at our community hospital and she gave me the number of an organization called Oyster Bay Hospice Care. She said they would help Will to live the rest of his life at home without such excruciating pain.

I called the Hospice Care center and made an appointment for a social worker named Marie to come and meet with us. Marie came to our home and talked with us about Will's illness; our family and friends in the area; our involvement in the church; Will's current medication level; and other needs that we have such as transportation, special dietary needs, and so on. Marie was very supportive and she listened to our concerns without telling us what we should do. She explained the hospice care concept and answered all of our questions. I was relieved to hear that I could get assistance in caring for Will at home so that he would not have to die in a hospital. Marie helped me transport Will to the hospital for one day so that the hospice team physicians and therapists could determine the best medical treatment to alleviate Will's pain while still allowing him to be mentally alert.

Since that time I have been caring for Will at home, administering all of his medications. He has been much happier and he is no longer in agonizing pain. In addition, Marie has helped me to get involved in a spousal bereavement group that includes women whose husbands are dying as well as those who are already widows.

Marie has also helped us maintain our religious activities. Our church and Sunday worship sessions have always been very important to us, and since Will has been sick we have had to stop going to church. Marie arranged for the hospice team pastor to visit us weekly to pray with us and guide us in our religious cares and concerns. The pastor's visits have been a wonderful source of inspiration for both of us.

Will is much closer to death now, and I can see him growing weaker every day. However, we are both so grateful that these last few months were a time of treasured enjoyment rather than a time of unending agony. I am still scared. I don't know how I will go on without him, but I am strengthened by the knowledge that Marie and the rest of the hospice care team will be there to support me after Will's death.

In this case, Marie served in the capacity of a direct service worker. In her first several visits with Will and his wife, she conducted a psychosocial assessment to determine the patient's and family's environmental and personal supports. Marie continued to perform the social work function of assessment throughout her work with this family and updated the care plan as necessary. Marie also carried out the function of detection and identification as she identified areas of needed support. She also gave support and assistance to the patient and family with such issues as transportation and dietary needs.

The function of advice and counseling is evidenced in Marie's work with Will's wife as she helped her through the bereavement process. Finally, Marie engaged in the social work function of referral to help Will's wife join the spousal bereavement support group and arrange for regular pastoral visits.

End-of-life decisions have recently been the focus of debate concerning who should make such decisions and how the decisions should be carried out. Social workers, with their empathic understanding of the psychosocial issues involved, should be actively involved in the planning and policy development process that is currently taking place in this arena (Kaplan, 1995). Furthermore, as the medical field is redefined, social workers must also provide empirical evidence of their unique and successful interventions to ensure the importance of social work in this field of practice (Kulys & Davis, 1986).

References

Barker, R. L. (1995). *Social work dictionary* (3rd ed.). Washington, DC: NASW Press.

Fish, N. M. (1989). Hospice: Terminal illness, teamwork, and the quality of life. In T. S. Kerson (Ed.), *Social work in health settings: Practice in context* (pp. 449–469). New York: Haworth Press.

Hancock, B. L. (1990). *Social work with older people* (2nd ed.). Englewood Cliffs, NJ: Prentice Hall.

Kaplan, K. O. (1995). End-of-life decisions. In R. L. Edwards (Ed.-in-Chief), *Encyclopedia of social work* (19th ed., Vol. 1, pp. 856–868). Washington, DC: NASW Press.

Kulys, R., & Davis, S.M.A. (1986). An analysis of social services in hospices. *Social Work, 31*, 448–456.

Proffitt, L. J. (1987). Hospice. In A. Minahan (Ed.-in-Chief), *Encyclopedia of social work* (18th ed., Vol. 1, pp. 812–816). Silver Spring, MD: National Association of Social Workers.

Richman, J. M. (1995). Hospice. In R. L. Edwards (Ed.-in-Chief), *Encyclopedia of social work* (19th ed., Vol. 2, pp. 1358–1364). Washington, DC: NASW Press.

Tax Equity and Fiscal Responsibility Act of 1982, P.L. 97-248, 96 Stat. 324.

career
opportunities

The following sample classified ads suggest the range of opportunities open for social workers in the field of aging but do not constitute actual job listings.

Chief Social Worker

Leading comprehensive health care facility for elderly people seeks LCSW with clinical orientation and experience in long-term care or comparable health-related experience. Key responsibilities include clinical supervision of four MSWs. Caseload and supervisory experience and familiarity with Alzheimer's disease and dementia desirable.

Coordinator of Geriatric Services

Administrative position. Knowledge of community-based services for elderly individuals with psychiatric disabilities. MA degree plus five years' experience.

Director for Adult Day Care

National council seeks a director for adult day care. Will be responsible for developing the funding necessary to support the needs of the adult day care field on a national level and will provide leadership for the activities of the organization. Education and experience in gerontology or related field and experience in generating grants and proposals; an in-depth knowledge of the field of adult day care required.

Director of Geriatric Partial Hospitalization Program

Psychiatric center has an exciting opportunity to direct a multidisciplinary staff in one of its geriatric partial hospitalization programs. As director, you will lead the team of psychiatric services to older adults. Duties will be both clinical and administrative. Qualified candidates will possess an MSW or related professional degree, will be licensed in the state, and will bring clinical experience in treating older adults.

Human Services Program Supervisor

Coordinates licensed adult day care program for memory-impaired and physically disabled elderly. Maintains secure therapeutic environment. Conducts functional assessments. Develops care plans. Conducts family support groups. BA in social work or BS in nursing; two years' experience with elderly/disabled in health related setting and six months' supervisory experience.

Mental Health

Coordinator of geriatric services for county mental health authority. Administrative position. Knowledge of community-based services for elderly individuals with psychiatric disabilities. MA degree plus five years' experience.

Older Adult Specialist

Large, progressive community mental health center is seeking a clinician to provide assessment and treatment for older adults and their families, and aging-related consultation and education. Licensed social worker, registered master's-level psychologist, or licensed psychologist required.

Service Coordinator

Recruiting a service coordinator for the Multi-Senior Service Center. BSW required. Duties include case management, assessment, counseling, documentation, and home visits. Experience working with elderly people and a strong knowledge of community resources required.

Social Worker

Multi-senior services center has an immediate opening for a social worker. BSW required, state license or eligibility for license, and two years of experience in a geriatric long-term-care facility. Strong knowledge of community resources, good problem-solving skills, and ability to communicate with senior citizens. Must have driver's license and own transportation.

Social Worker

Premier provider of hospice services currently has an opening for a social worker to work part-time as needed. This position may develop into a full-time member of the interdisciplinary team providing care for terminally ill patients and their families. Responsibilities include psychosocial assessment, short-term counseling and crisis intervention, discharge planning, and grief support group facilitation. MSW and minimum two years' experience preferred.

Social Worker, Geriatric

University medical center has a part-time career opportunity for an experienced senior psychiatric social worker in its Department of Psychiatry. The ideal candidate should possess an MSW, state license, strong psychiatric experience including diagnostic evaluations, individual, family, and group psychotherapy, a working knowledge of local support services for elderly people, and the ability to work collaboratively in a multidisciplinary, multisite program.

substance abuse

introduction
to part VI

Substance abuse is a major concern in contemporary America, a concern shared by social workers who see the impact of chemical dependency on individuals, families, and children (Magura, 1994). Barker (1995) distinguishes between substance abuse and substance dependence. A person is considered to be a substance abuser when he or she evidences a maladaptive pattern of using certain drugs, alcohol, medications, or toxins despite their negative consequences. However, he or she may not experience withdrawal symptoms.

Substance dependence, according to Barker (1995), involves "continued use; craving; and other cognitive, behavioral, and physiological symptoms that occur through the use of certain drugs, alcohol, medications, and toxins" (p. 370), the discontinuance of which leads to withdrawal symptoms. The signs of substance dependence include preoccupation about the substance; persistent attempts to control its use; reduced occupational or social activities; and continued use despite knowledge of its adverse physical, psychological, or social consequences. Substance abuse and dependence are associated with many other problems, including physical and mental illness, family problems, school failure, unemployment and poverty, and gangs and violence.

Despite the pervasiveness of substance abuse problems, only a relatively small proportion of social workers are involved in this area of service. In 1991, 4.6 percent of responding NASW members indicated that their primary practice area was substance abuse (Gibelman & Schervish, 1993). Magura (1994) urged a greater interest and involvement of social workers in work in chemical dependency treatment, arguing that social workers' commitment and skill are vitally needed.

Social workers involved in the prevention and treatment of substance abuse work in a variety of settings, including health facilities, inpatient and outpatient substance abuse treatment centers, mental health centers, schools, and the workplace (Smyth, 1995). Detoxification units seek to help clients safely withdraw from alcohol and other drugs, generally by gradually reducing the dose of the abused drug. Detoxification programs are usually located in hospitals; however, community-based programs often provide detoxification services. The need for such services is determined by the level of physical dependence on the drug and the medical risk associated with withdrawal, as well as any other physical or psychiatric problems, such as bipolar disorder or heart disease (Smyth, 1995).

Live-in treatment programs fall into two categories: (1) programs that operate within the facility, and (2) programs that provide a supportive and safe living environment to residents who receive treatment services in outside settings. Generally, the first category includes inpatient rehabilitation programs in hospitals or separate facilities, and the second group includes residences, halfway houses, and recovery homes (Smyth, 1995).

Outpatient drug abuse programs focus on helping the clients change their addictive behaviors without the use of methadone maintenance programs or other similar substitute drug products (Smyth, 1995). In addition to these major settings, drug and alcohol screening and treatment can also occur in prisons, courts, welfare agencies, and businesses. Social workers are involved in many aspects of substance abuse treatment, including planning and program development, diagnosis and assessment, information and referral, counseling, and program evaluation (Smyth, 1995).

As the drug epidemic has spread to youths, school social workers have become more active in planning, implementing, and evaluating substance abuse programs. For example, Wisconsin social workers created a drug abuse and dropout prevention program targeted to elementary school children. The state of Wisconsin has funded the Families and Schools Together (FAST) program to serve 40 schools. This program seeks to promote cooperation between schools, mental health facilities, and substance abuse centers ("Schools to Combat Drugs," 1990). Teachers are encouraged to identify children between the ages of six and nine who are considered to be at high risk for school failure, substance abuse, or delinquency. FAST social workers visit the children's homes and offer the family transportation, child care, and free meals to attend weekly program meetings. The entire family is involved and has access to a range of services, including treatment for substance abuse or dependence.

Dimensions

Lifetime prevalence rates of drug abuse in the United States are estimated at 5.8 percent for men and 3.8 percent for women; about 4.5 million women of childbearing age are current drug users and one alcohol- or drug-exposed infant is born every 90 seconds ("Child Abuse Study Faults Drug War," 1992). Nearly half of the women who comprise 30 percent of all illicit drug users are young, between the ages of 15 and 24 ("Women and Addictions," 1995). In their prime childbearing years, these women too frequently give birth to infants who are addicted to drugs and alcohol.

The House Select Committee on Children, Youth and Families found that, in the vast majority of hospitals studied, there was a three- to four-fold increase in births of drug-exposed infants between 1985 and 1989. It is estimated that about 375,000 infants may be damaged by drug exposure each year. Because mothers addicted to crack cocaine may be unwilling or unable to care for their children, use of crack cocaine often results in child abandonment, neglect, or abuse (Hiratsuka, 1989). Indeed, drugs and alcohols have been identified as exacerbating the incidence of child abuse and family violence. A 1992 report by the Child Welfare League of America's North American Commission on Chemical Dependency and Child Welfare concluded that

> Chemical dependency harms children in a number of ways: through prenatal exposure to alcohol or other drugs, through the creation of a postnatal environment that fails to meet their developmental needs, through passive exposure to illicit drugs in their own homes, through the dangers of living in communities ravaged by drug-related violence and crime, through child abuse or neglect associated with parental alcohol or drug abuse. (as cited in "Child Abuse Study Faults Drug War," 1992, p. 7)

A recent U.S. General Accounting Office (GAO) study on the use of illicit drugs and alcohol among adolescents found that (1) although drug and alcohol use among adolescents has declined from its peak in the late 1970s and early 1980s, there is still considerable drinking and illegal drug use among youth; (2) delinquency and early use of alcohol are significantly associated with the use of marijuana and cocaine; (3) the interaction of several risk factors determines the probability of drug use by youths; (4) poverty and place of residence are not significantly related to illicit drug use; and (5) prevention approaches that are comprehensive, community-based, and collaborative are the most effective (GAO, 1994).

Ebie Banks, a social worker employed by a mental health center in Washington, DC, described a client:

> This little boy came in wearing an ultra-suede jacket, a two-piece sweat-suit, and a jewel encrusted Rolex watch. He parked his BMW outside and came in here with his two bodyguards. He said his parents had sent him here because he was having trouble sleeping. He was afraid some people were out to get him. I wouldn't see him in the office because I didn't want the place to get shot up. He offered to pay me—any price. I have talked to him by phone since then. He was 19 years old. (quoted in Hiratsuka, 1989, p. 3)

For adolescents and teenagers, the allure of the drug trade can be irresistible; it provides them with money and the outward signs of success that money can buy.

Social workers work directly with substance abusers in treatment centers and hospitals. They also work with the families of murder victims—youths and adults who have been caught up in drug wars, and with frightened residents of drug-infested neighborhoods (Hiratsuka, 1989). Emily Perry, a social worker in the intensive care unit of DC General Hospital, said:

> We see a lot of repeat gunshot victims. We had a guy 26 years old here for his fourth time. Twice he was shot in the head, one time in the leg, one time in the buttocks. It was drug-related. It's overwhelming. A lot of victims are so young. Their whole value system is different.

They see nothing wrong with dealing drugs. (quoted in Hiratsuka, 1989, p. 3)

Judith Bremner, another social worker in the District of Columbia working with youth, claims that realistic treatment programs are needed. "A lot of times we get parents to the point where they want treatment, but there is a waiting list, or they can only get into a one-week program, which is absurd. It just lets them dry out, not get over their addiction" (quoted in Hiratsuka, 1989, p. 3).

Factors ranging from the deterioration of the family to the glamorization of drug use by various entertainment media have all been charged with partial responsibility for the drug abuse epidemic. Regardless of the specific cause, the problem of drug and alcohol scans all social classes. The costs of pervasive drug abuse are enormous in both law enforcement and social measures ("The Drug Debate," 1985).

Social Work Role

Social workers in all service areas deal with the effects of substance abuse. The resulting problems—emotional scars, physical addiction, fetal alcohol syndrome, school dropout, and violence, among others—are being identified and treated in medical settings, mental health clinics, schools, hospitals, and the courts.

We know that treatment works. A recent statewide California study revealed that $1 spent on drug and alcohol abuse treatment saves that state's taxpayers $7 in punishment costs. Estimates suggest that $1.5 billion in savings were realized from the $209 million spent on treatment in 1992. The study findings indicated the effectiveness of treatment, regardless of differences in types of programs, types of drugs, and race and class of substance abusers ("In Brief," 1994).

Despite the scope of the problem and the efficacy of treatment, the proportion of social workers with a primary area of practice in substance abuse is relatively small. Recognizing the profound need for a skilled labor force in this field, social work educators and practitioners have collaborated to develop curriculum materials on drug and alcohol abuse for use in core undergraduate and graduate social work courses ("Panel Readies 'Core' Content," 1992). These materials include learning modules for existing courses such as research, policy, human behavior and the social environment, and practice in the hope of stimulating greater knowledge among all social workers and greater interest in career opportunities in this field.

In April 1995, the NASW board of directors approved the formation of a specialty section on Alcohol, Tobacco, and Other Drugs to respond to the diverse interests of members. The section is intended to meet the needs of social workers who encounter alcohol- and drug-related issues in their practice, not just those who work in this specific area of service. More than 1,700 NASW members have expressed interest in joining this section ("New Section's Focus," 1995).

All social workers, whether or not they have been trained specifically in treating substance abuse, have the requisite skills in assessment, diagnosis, and counseling. In addition, social workers in this field possess much-needed skills in planning, organizing, program development, and program administration. Finally, as in all social work fields, advocacy and policy development are essential social work functions to ensure proper treatment and effective prevention measures (Smyth, 1995).

References

Barker, R. L. (1995). *Social work dictionary* (3rd ed.). Washington, DC: NASW Press.

Child abuse study faults drug war. (1992, July). *NASW News*, p. 7.

The drug debate: Prosecute or legalize? (1985, October). *NASW News*, p. 3.

Gibelman, M., & Schervish, P. (1993). *Who we are: The social work labor force as reflected in the NASW membership.* Washington, DC: NASW Press.

Hiratsuka, J. (1989, July). Social workers confront drugs, despair. *NASW News*, pp. 3, 5.

In brief. High yield investment. (1994, October). *NASW News*, p. 9.

Magura, S. (1994). Social workers should be more involved in substance abuse treatment. *Health & Social Work, 19*, 3–5.

New section's focus will be alcohol, drugs. (1995, June). *NASW News*, pp. 1, 10.

Panel readies "core" content on drug abuse. (1992, July). *NASW News*, p. 7.

Schools to combat drugs. (1990, April). *NASW News*, p. 16.

Smyth, N. J. (1995). Substance abuse: Direct practice. In R. L. Edwards (Ed.-in-Chief), *Encyclopedia of social work* (19th ed., Vol. 3, pp. 2328–2338). Washington, DC: NASW Press.

U.S. General Accounting Office. (1994). *Drug use among youth: No simple answers to guide prevention* (Report No. HRD-94-24). Washington, DC: Author.

Women and addictions. (1995, January). *NASW News*, p. 7.

alcoholism

Drinking in American culture has long been viewed with ambivalence. On the one hand, Americans view drinking as an acceptable way to escape from the stresses of everyday life; on the other, they view it as a self-indulgent sign of weakness. This ambivalence has colored society's response to alcoholism: Is it a physiological illness or a psychosocial problem?

People who abuse alcohol may experience an array of behaviors that are secondary to their addiction but that inflict extreme pain and hardship on self or others. For example, drunk drivers are blamed for the loss of as many as 25,000 lives in highway crashes each year and hundreds of thousands of severe injuries (Ross, 1992). Other problems related to alcohol abuse include violent crimes, problems with families and friends, financial and job problems, and aggressive behavior. The toll of alcohol abuse is summed up in the following description of the legendary New York Yankee, Mickey Mantle who, at age 63, underwent a liver transplant after a lifetime of drinking had destroyed his liver:

> Mantle was young and strong, but he wasn't dedicated. For all his injuries, which prompted great public lament, Mantle stinted on his rehabilitating exercises, if not skipping them altogether. He took the easier path to a bar with Billy Martin than to a gym or some-place to repair his ailing knees. And this made him feel sorry as years passed, because he knew that despite his legend as No. 7 of the pinstriped Yankees, with 535 home runs in his Hall of Fame career, he wasn't everything he might have been. Even worse, he wasn't the husband he could have been to his ever-devoted wife, the father he should have been to his four sons, because all too often he was doing something else, drinking until it hurt someone, finally himself. (Gildea, 1995, p. A4)

Adult Children of Alcoholics

People who have been raised in the stressful environments created by the alcoholism or substance abuse of their parents have been termed adult children of alcoholics (ACOAs). Many ACOAs have emotional disorders in common, including anxiety, depression, low self-esteem, and anger. In addition they have a predisposition toward alcoholism and substance abuse problems (Barker, 1995). Many ACOAs have sought help through self-help groups or other support groups specifically oriented to their problems.

In His Father's Shadow

Lenny is 27 years old and happily married. He has a good job and good friends, with whom he enjoys going out after work and having a few drinks. However, one drink soon turns into two, which become three or four and sometimes five. His wife, Carol, is worried. However, Lenny gets angry when she brings up the subject of his drinking, and Carol doesn't know what to do.

Lenny's father was an alcoholic. Every night he came home from work and had two stiff drinks before dinner, two with dinner, and two more after dinner. By the end of the night he was angry and irritable and he often lashed out at Lenny and his sister with verbal insults and criticisms. Lenny hated to come home after school and after dinner he tried to get to his room as quickly as possible. He remembers his childhood as a nightmare, never knowing what to expect and never being comfortable at home. No one ever confronted his father about his drinking. When Lenny asked his mother, she just said that he worked hard for the family and she didn't want to upset him more by bringing up the issue. Lenny's father died two years ago from liver disease. His mother is still alive.

Lenny usually doesn't start drinking with the desire to get drunk. He just plans on having one beer and heading home, but it never seems to work that way. Lately, with added pressure from work, he has been drinking more often. And when he comes home, he often is in a bad mood and takes to criticizing Carol and losing his temper over little things. Finally, after one particularly bad scene between them, Carol called Lenny's sister, Marilyn, who had recently quit drinking completely. Marilyn suggested that Lenny go to the local community mental health center which sponsors a group for adult children of alcoholics (ACOA). Carol called the community center and talked with the intake social worker, Judy, who encouraged Carol to urge Lenny firmly and consistently to make an appointment. She also offered to see Carol individually or with Lenny, but Carol decided to wait.

One evening after the office happy hour, Lenny was driving home when he lost control of his car. That incident frightened him; he began to think that perhaps he was turning out like his father. He discussed these feelings with Carol the next morning. She had already mentioned the group to him (which he rejected out of hand), but this time he agreed to make an appointment at the center.

The first step is an intake appointment with the social worker, Judy, which was set for later that week. Lenny was surprised by how easy it was to talk with Judy. He relayed to her his family background and the incident in his car that prompted him to make this appointment. He also acknowledged that he knows how concerned his wife has been about him and that he has not been a good husband lately. Judy, based on her many years of clinical experience, made the connection between Lenny's background and behavior and the alcoholism to which he had been exposed through his growing-up years. Judy asked Lenny if he had ever heard the term "adult children of alcoholics." Lenny recalled reading something about this in a magazine once, but otherwise did not know what it meant. Judy briefly explained the meaning of the term and told him that there are a number of people with adjustment, marriage, and other problems that seem connected in some way to the alcoholism that had permeated their environments growing up. Although not all ACOAs have the same problems, there is an important commonality: the alcoholism of one or both parents.

Judy then told Lenny about the ACOA group at the center and asked if he would like to participate. Lenny was initially eager— perhaps he could begin to get his life back in order. But he was also aware of how difficult it was to get to this first intake appointment. Nevertheless, he agreed to give it a try.

Judy explained that another social worker on staff, Michele, is the group facilitator. The group meets each Thursday evening from 8:00 P.M. to 10:00 P.M., and he could begin next week. First, Michelle needed to discuss with the group that a new member would be joining them and what this meant for them.

The following week, with his wife's urging, Lenny attended the group meeting, but with some trepidation. Was he doing the right thing? Would he see it through? Isn't his problem different than those of the others? When Lenny entered the room, Michelle, who is the group leader, considered greeting him, but decided to wait to see if someone from the group would take the initiative. One of the group members approached Lenny and said, "Welcome, we were expecting a new member tonight. My name is Joe." Lenny felt awkward, but mumbled "Hi, I'm Lenny" and sat down in the group circle.

There was a silence and then Michelle suggested that everyone introduce themselves. Six of the seven previous members were present. Fran began by saying "Hi, I'm Fran, welcome to the group. We're all here tonight except Margot; she had to go to an open school night for her daughter." Jean then said "I'm Jean. I want you to know that we all know how difficult it is to begin in group and we all went through it. You just try to relax and we'll try to make it as comfortable as possible." Each member had a turn. Shirley, another group member, explained that this group takes responsibility for its own process. Some groups, Mary explains, are very structured and others are time limited. This group does not fit either profile. Michelle then introduced herself and complimented the group on their efforts and initiative in welcoming Lenny. She also acknowledged the difficulty in beginnings, both for the new member and the group. She then suggested another go-around, with each person telling Lenny and retelling each other what brought them to the group, how it was going, and what they hoped to get out of it. Michelle also invited Lenny to share what had brought him to the group and what he hoped to get from it.

Lenny realized that his nervousness was gone. As he listened to each group member tell his or her story, he sensed that everyone there was like him. They all had alcoholic parents and, although they had different problems day to day, many of their problems were related to their ACOA status.

At that moment, Lenny committed himself to the group. After several weeks of attending, he also began to see another social worker, Tom, individually and sometimes with his wife. With backing from the group members, Tom helped Lenny talk with his sister and mother about their lives when Lenny's father was drinking too much.

His sister Marilyn also promised to work with Lenny to learn ways to avoid turning to alcohol to solve their problems.

In this case scenario, there were three social workers. Judy was the intake worker, Lenny's first contact with the agency. Her job was to conduct an assessment and, on the basis of an evaluation of the client's situation, offer the support and assistance of the agency. During this initial meeting, Judy also built rapport with Lenny and made him feel that there is help available for his problems. Judy was also the referral agent; she arranged for Lenny to become a member of the ACOA group. Michelle was the social worker who facilitated the ACOA group, and, in this role, she facilitated the group process. She also engaged in the function of enabling, by helping group members develop self-help skills and recognize their own strengths. Advice and counseling were other functions carried out by Michelle, as she helped clarify feelings and interactions and supported group members in experimenting with problem-solving strategies. As an individual therapist, Tom engaged in the direct services functions of assessment, diagnosis, support, and counseling.

References

Barker, R. L. (1995). *Social work dictionary* (3rd ed.). Washington, DC: NASW Press.

Gildea, W. (1995, June 9). At 63, the Mick finally grows up. *Washington Post*, p. A4.

Ross, L. H. (1992). *Confronting drunk driving: Social policy for saving lives.* New Haven, CT: Yale University Press.

new program approaches

Many youths and adults who abuse substances end up in the criminal justice system on felony drug offenses or other crimes associated with the drug epidemic. In the District of Columbia, the Superior Court is trying an alternative to jail. More than 300 men and women who are nonviolent drug offenders have been channeled through the city's new drug court, one of about 30 such courts nationwide. The Clinton administration has advocated for drug courts under the premise that these special courts can force people to get the help they need (Miller, 1995).

The District's drug court is part of a five-year experiment initiated by the DC Superior Court and the DC Pretrial Services Agency with a $5 million federal grant. Defendants are randomly assigned to one of three judges. One judge uses the traditional approach, with plea agreements and the possibility of jail time for the defendant. The second judge offers defendants the chance for intensive treatment. The third judge attempts a behavioral approach, helping defendants stay off drugs by holding them accountable for their behavior and imposing penalties.

The two experimental groups—treatment and sanctions—are based on the assumption that the court's leverage and the skills of the judge will reach addicts at a time when they are prone to listen, just after arrest (Miller, 1995). Participation in the treatment and sanction programs is voluntary and restricted to habitual drug users.

The treatment program is operated through the DC Pretrial Services Agency, which employs many social workers. Once participants are referred for treatment, social workers and other professionals provide counseling, tutoring, group therapy, and drug testing. The program lasts six months, during which time participants' progress is monitored by the court.

Participants in the sanctions program do not receive intensive psychosocial services. However, they are tested for drugs twice a week and if there are infractions, the judge holds them accountable. There are gradations of punishment, the highest level (for multiple infractions) being a week in jail (Miller, 1995).

Federal officials estimate that the treatment program costs about $1,200 per person, whereas it costs about $20,000 to imprison someone for a year (Miller, 1995). The Urban Institute, a Washington, DC, "think tank," will evaluate the results. An interim evaluation showed that participants in the treatment and sanctions group become drug free and remain drug free substantially faster and longer than those handled through the courts in the traditional way.

Reference

Miller, B. (1995, May 8). Addicts get a hand up from D.C.'s drug court. *Washington Post*, pp. B1, B5.

outpatient treatment for drug abuse

Substance Abuse Treatment in an Outpatient Clinic

Max Herrara recently received his MSW and is employed as a social worker in the substance abuse treatment clinic at Middleton Community Health Center in Overland Park, Kansas. Currently Max is involved as a leader for a group of parents who are experiencing various difficulties with their children who either are experimenting with or are addicted to an illegal substance.

One afternoon Max received a call from Jean, a woman in the group. Jean is in her late 40s and has three children. She entered the group because she was having problems with her 18-year-old son, Charlie. Charlie's behavior was out of control. He was not working, was unresponsive to limit setting, and was undergoing personality changes. She suspected he was using drugs or alcohol and he refused to consider treatment for substance abuse despite the urging of his family. The telltale signs included a glazed look in his eyes, an "out of it" demeanor, and behavior she found frightening: He had become loud and rude and seemed to be constantly on the verge of losing his temper to the point of violence. In addition, she had caught him lying several times, something Charlie had not done before.

On this day, Jean called Max in hysterics. She said that Charlie had just tried to assault her and had threatened her with a kitchen knife. She was able to grab her two daughters and run to a neighbor's house. She did not want to call the police, but she wanted Charlie to get help. Max consulted with his supervisor and then arranged to meet Jean at her house so that he could talk with Charlie directly.

When he arrived, Max found Jean standing on the front lawn with her daughters. Charlie was standing in the doorway looking out at them, still holding the knife. However, Charlie appeared to be more confused than angry. Max approached the door and introduced himself to Charlie. He told Charlie that he was a social worker and asked to come inside and talk with him. Charlie agreed, and Max asked him to put the knife away. Charlie complied.

Once they were both inside and seated at the kitchen table, Max commented that the situation appeared to have gotten out of hand and that everyone was frightened. Charlie nodded and dropped his head, although Max noticed tears in Charlie's eyes.

Max continued to try to talk to Charlie, but he was extremely unresponsive. Finally, Max suggested that it might be best for Charlie to be examined at a hospital. At first Charlie appeared angry, but then he shrugged his shoulders and again dropped his head. Max asked if he could call the emergency room at the community hospital to alert them that Charlie would be coming. Finally, Charlie nodded in agreement and Max made the call. He told the hospital personnel about his suspicion of drug involvement as well as possible psychiatric problems. Max then went out and brought Jean back into the house, where she told Charlie that she forgave him and that she would support his efforts to get better.

Max then took Charlie to the hospital and stayed with him while he was interviewed by a psychiatrist. Max was able to provide information on Charlie's family, as Charlie was not particularly responsive during the interview. Max told Charlie that he would visit him if that was okay. Max then returned to Jean's house and told her what had happened. He offered to visit Charlie with her, and told her that he would try to establish a relationship with Charlie in case the Middleton Community Health Center was determined to be an appropriate service provider in Charlie's discharge plan.

In this case, Max engaged in the social work function of assessment to determine the extent of the presenting problem. Max first tried to ensure the personal safety of Jean and her two daughters. After doing this, he then met with Charlie to identify the various problems that needed to be addressed. In his talk with Charlie, Max used his counseling skills and employed active referral techniques in encouraging Max to go to the community hospital. Finally, Max carried out the functions of coordination and exchange in seeking the resources of the community hospital. He also held out the offer of ongoing support and assistance to Charlie and his family.

In addition to their direct services role in preventing and treating substance abuse, social workers also carry out supervisory and administrative roles in this field. The following case indicates some of the administrative issues within an agency and in the agency's relationship with other organizations. This case also highlights some of the ethical dilemmas that can arise in this area of service.

Mediating Interorganizational Issues

Jonathan Singer has been executive director of a nonprofit, community-based outpatient substance abuse treatment center for five years. During this time, the organization has expanded rapidly, including a contract relationship with the county Department of Drug and Alcohol Abuse and a working agreement with the county probation department. Currently, 15 probationers are being seen by the agency for outpatient substance abuse treatment; this treatment is a requirement of their probation. The agreement with the agency specifies that the social workers providing services are to report any "slips" among the parolees, that is, should they be found to be using drugs or alcohol, this would be considered a probation violation and the social workers are expected to report it. Probationers participating in this program specifically and in writing waive their rights to confidentiality in that they give permission for the agency to share any and all information with their probation officer.

In reviewing the monthly progress logs of the social workers, Jonathan notices that there is a surprisingly low number of reports being made to the Department of Probation and Parole about slips. He knows that treatment for substance abuse rarely goes smoothly, that two steps forward are often accompanied by a step backward.

At the weekly staff meeting with the social work staff, eight in all, Jonathan brings up the issue of slips and inquires as to whether the failure to report is a sign of unusually dramatic progress or if there is another explanation. His close working relationship with his staff, built on trust and honesty, allows the social workers to "fess up" to their failure to report. They explain with some indignation that even though the probationers are informed about the limits of confidentiality and the reporting requirement, they feel that to report is to compromise the treatment process. The result might be that the probationer is reincarcerated even though he or she might be making substantial progress.

Jonathan, in fact, agrees with this line of reasoning. He had not been happy about incorporating the reporting clause into the agreement, but had yielded to the pressure of the county because the agreement marked an important beginning for the agency to reach a targeted population. It was his hope that in future agreements, once the agency had proven the effectiveness of its services, the reporting requirement could be eliminated.

But here Jonathan is faced with a dilemma. He is responsible for ensuring contract compliance and he is also responsible for supervising the social work staff and helping them provide the services of the agency. On the other hand, the real or potential compromise to treatment and the social workers' resistance to carrying through on reporting slips are issues that he needs to address. The reporting requirement must be dealt with.

Jonathan discusses the dilemma openly with his staff, noting that he cannot condone their sidestepping the regulations about reporting. In addition to county relationship issues, Jonathan reminds them of their responsibility to support the agency, including its rules. He asks that from now on they come to him with issues before any covert or overt actions are taken. Here, one staff member interrupts and reminds Jonathan that the staff had indeed come to him about this issue. Jonathan patiently clarifies that he had responded to their concerns during that first meeting about the reporting requirement in terms of plans to bring the topic up during negotiations next year; there had been no discussion about circumventing the reporting requirement—this was a step the staff had decided on without discussion or authorization.

Jonathan then broaches the subject of what to do. He acknowledges the strong feelings of the social workers about reporting slips and asks whether the sentiment was so strong that the agency should consider withdrawing from its agreement to serve probationers. The eight social workers are stunned by this possibility and indicate that this would be a great disservice both to the clients and to the agency. One person also voices what many of the others are thinking: Termination of the agreement with the probation department could mean the end of their jobs.

Jonathan sums up the sentiments of the staff: The agency should continue with the agreement. "But what about our obligation to report slips?" he asks. After a lengthy discussion of options, one stands out as the most viable: meet with the contract officers from the Department of Probation and try either to amend the conditions of the agreement or to reach an informal agreement that slips would be handled differently.

Jonathan calls the county contact person, Jeff Daniels (a probation supervisor), and explains the nature of the problem. Jonathan indicates that a useful approach might be to have a joint meeting between himself and his staff and Mr. Daniels and the probation officers who were supervising the agency's clients. After checking with the deputy commissioner, Mr. Daniels calls back to arrange a time and place for the meeting. The meeting is scheduled in conjunction with a regular agency staff meeting to ensure that all workers would be present.

Jonathan begins the meeting with remarks intended to create a climate for open and honest discussion. The social work staff express their concerns that accurate reporting might result in premature violations. They indicate a lack of trust in the probation officers' abilities to recognize when treatment is working in spite of a couple of slips. The probation officers are able to express their concern that social workers tend to "coddle" clients and that clients would be able to "get over on them."

The open yet respectful discussion results in a compromise agreement that no probationer would be charged with a violation for up to two slips without the consent of his or her social worker. This result satisfies the social workers because it gives them an important measure of control over the decision-making process. It also satisfies the probation officers who feel that, ultimately, the decision is in their hands if their probationers continue to slip. Most important, Jonathan feels that the process created a more effective working relationship between the agency and the probation department. Staff of both agencies begin to take back some of the stereotypical feelings they had of each other and replace them with new understanding and respect for differences.

In this case, Jonathan is in an administrative position. However, he still drew on his skills in assessment and identification to determine the extent of the problem, only he applied these skills to a different level of social work intervention. Once the problem was identified, Jonathan exercised organization, negotiation, and coordination skills to arrange a meeting with the contract officers and the social workers. Jonathan also made excellent use of his managerial and supervisory social work skills as he exhibited a supportive yet guiding influence for his staff. Finally, Jonathan was confronted with the inherent ethical dilemmas that can arise in practice, particularly when clients are seen involuntarily or as a condition of probation or parole. Jonathan identified these ethical issues and mediated among clinical, ethical, legal, and agency concerns.

prevention

The importance of addressing substance abuse early is actualized through various types of prevention programs. For example, Chicago's Project Future is designed specifically to lower infant mortality rates. The program is supported primarily by federal grants, and its goal is to improve the family environment through intensive social services, addiction treatment, and medical services. In addition, a neighborhood center offers parents assistance in developing new vocational, lifestyle, and parenting skills ("Schools to Combat Drugs," 1990). Social workers involved in these programs also exhibit their skills of coordination and working and interacting with other professionals as part of a multidisciplinary team (Smyth, 1995). The recognition of the importance of prevention is evident in the increasing number of schools that are instituting curriculum and student training on the dangers of drug and alcohol abuse.

In October 1990 the National Association of State Alcohol and Drug Abuse Directors released the report *Treatment Works: The Tragic Cost of Undervaluing Treatment in the Drug War* ("Addiction-Treatment Savings Claimed," 1990). This report was based on a 15-year study of drug and alcohol abuse, and the findings indicate that treatment for substance abuse is indeed effective in reducing abuse, increasing employment, improving psychological adjustment, and decreasing criminal and other negative behaviors ("Addiction-Treatment Savings Claimed," 1990).

The report also showed that investing in treatment services is economically prudent even though addiction is chronic and may require several episodes of treatment. Current federal expenditures for drug- and alcohol-related law enforcement are three times higher than expenditures for treatment, education, and prevention. The consequences of addiction are further seen in decreased productivity, AIDS, crime, and prison overcrowding. Therefore, it appears that the most effective and economic method of treating substance abuse is to prevent it ("Addiction-Treatment Savings Claimed," 1990).

A Substance Abuse Prevention Program

Thomas is a 15-year-old African American adolescent who lives with his mother and is the oldest of four children. Thomas has had several run-ins with the police, who have found him hanging around with people who use drugs. The police have also caught Thomas in acts of vandalism. One evening Thomas was at the local park hanging out with his friends. The police were notified of suspicious activity in the park and when they arrived, the boys scattered. However, the police found crack cocaine and a pipe, so they rounded the youths up and took them to police headquarters.

This particular precinct works in cooperation with an inner-city multipurpose community-based agency. The agency has received city funds to establish a prevention program in conjunction with local police precincts. The program is composed of an outreach worker at each precinct and two social workers who provide substance abuse counseling. Generally, the clients are youths who are referred to the program in an effort to prevent further abuse or involvement with the criminal justice system.

In this case, the outreach worker contacted Thomas's mother and asked if she could contact the program's social worker so that they could both bring Thomas home and discuss his situation. The mother agreed. The outreach worker then contacted Scott, a recent MSW graduate who is a white man in his early 30s. Scott met the outreach worker and Thomas at Thomas's apartment building. The outreach worker's job of coordinating services was now complete. Scott now had to fulfill the social work functions of assessing the situation, identifying problem areas, and developing a trusting, helping relationship with Thomas.

Scott proceeded with Thomas to Thomas's small apartment in a dirty and unsafe building. Thomas's mother, Jackie, also in her mid-30s, greeted them at the door. The other children were not home so Scott, Jackie, and Thomas sat at the kitchen table to talk. There was a sense of awkwardness as both Thomas and his mother avoided eye contact with Scott. Scott took responsibility for conducting the meeting and began by explaining a little about his agency, the services provided, and the specific prevention program. Scott explained that this program was viewed as an alternative to prosecution through the criminal justice system and that the purpose of his visit was to determine what services Thomas needed and whether the agency could provide them. Throughout Scott's explanation, Thomas and his mother remained unresponsive.

Scott then wanted to get information about Thomas at home and at school. Scott asked Thomas a few questions, but Thomas said there was nothing to tell. He denied any involvement with drugs and said that the police were simply picking on the black kids in the neighborhood. Jackie remained silent. Scott then asked Thomas about his performance in school, to which Thomas responded that he did "fine" and had passed "almost" all of his classes. He declined to show Scott his report card.

Scott asked about previous encounters with the police. Thomas denied that he had ever been arrested before. Scott then turned to Jackie and asked her about Thomas's behavior. Jackie said that Thomas was basically a good boy, although he was occasionally mischievous. She refused to say anything else and claimed that they did not need any services.

Scott recognized the barriers of race, mistrust, and unfamiliarity in providing service to this family and he discussed these barriers with Thomas and Jackie. They seemed surprised at Scott's openness, but they did not verbally respond. Finally Scott explained how counseling worked. He said that Thomas would come to see him once a week so that they could get to know each other better and talk more freely. He also explained the confidentiality of the relationship. Neither Thomas nor his mother seemed convinced, and Jackie asked if Thomas would have to go to court if he did not do the counseling. Scott responded that, counseling or no counseling, a decision about court was up to the police, but that the police took counseling efforts into consideration when determining their course of action.

Jackie turned to Thomas and told him he should see Scott every week. Thomas protested. Scott recognized Thomas's resistance and admitted that Thomas may not need any help but that he would appreciate it if Thomas would simply try the counseling arrangement. Thomas finally agreed. Because Thomas usually plays basketball after school, they arranged to meet after the basketball game on Mondays at 5:30 P.M.

Scott then gave Jackie his card and told her to call him if anything occurred to her that might be useful for him to know or if she ever needed to discuss anything.

This case exemplifies the social worker's role in assessment and problem identification. Scott evaluated the interview with sensitivity to the client's lifestyle and culture, part of the diagnostic process. He also offered preliminary assistance and arranged for a regular counseling relationship through referral to the community agency. On a macro level, the cooperative relationship between the social services agency and the police precinct exemplifies coordination, organization, and exchange so that resources can be used in the most effective manner. This relationship also highlights the creativity that can result from interdisciplinary collaboration.

References

Addiction-treatment savings claimed. (1990, October). NASW News, p. 18.

National Association of State Alcohol and Drug Abuse Directors. (1990). Treatment works: The tragic cost of undervaluing treatment in the drug war. Washington, DC: Author.

Schools to combat drugs. (1990, April). NASW News, p. 16.

Smyth, N. J. (1995). Substance abuse: Direct practice. In R. L. Edwards (Ed.-in-Chief), Encyclopedia of social work (19th ed., Vol. 3, pp. 2328–2338). Washington, DC: NASW Press.

career
opportunities

The field of substance abuse is a difficult yet rewarding arena. Social workers who decide to enter the field of substance abuse can choose from a variety of career paths. The career opportunities listed below serve as examples of the range of social work employment prospects in this service area. For example, social workers can serve as direct practitioners, program directors, or educators. Whether providing direct service or developing and implementing preventive measures, social workers will continue to play an important role.

Chemical Dependency IOP Coordinator
Develop intensive outpatient program from existing small program. Modified medical model. Private practice opportunity. Three to five years' chemical dependency treatment experience. LCSW, LPC, or similar license required; strong marketing background.

Clinical Director
Comprehensive service and research program for women who use cocaine during pregnancy and their children seeks an experienced individual to serve as clinical director. Responsibilities include supervision and management of on-site drug treatment program, home-based family support component, on-site and home-based child development component, involvement with interdisciplinary research efforts, collaboration with other community programs, and report preparation. Requirements: MSW, PhD, or MD, minimum of three years' clinical or research experience, including supervisory experience in child/family psychotherapy or drug treatment.

Clinical Social Work Director
The incumbent will direct a comprehensive substance abuse treatment program encompassing the provision of professional substance abuse treatment services for the substance abuse treatment program at juvenile correction center. Qualified applicants should have knowledge of the principles and practices of

substance abuse treatment and management of services in a clinical setting. Skills in providing a full range of clinical substance abuse services to adolescents including developing and implementing staff development activities are needed. The ability to train and direct employees is needed, along with the ability to develop and interpret agency policies and regulations and operate and maintain an effective treatment program. In addition, familiarization with program accreditation processes is required. Eligibility for certification as a clinical supervisor of substance abuse counselors by the Board of Professional Counselors, state department of health professions, is a condition of employment. Preferred applicants will possess a Certified Clinical Supervisor certificate; a related degree with advanced course work in substance abuse, counseling, or a related field; and experience in program administration and management. This is a restricted position funded for 18 months by a grant to the Department of Youth and Family Services by the Center for Substance Abuse Treatment, U.S. Department of Health and Human Services.

Clinician II/Substance Abuse (Criminal Justice)

Full-time position available to provide substance abuse assessment and services for criminal justice clients. Work closely with jail and probation personnel. Master's degree required. Motor vehicle and criminal history checks required.

Mental Health Crisis Evaluation Therapist

Mental health and chemical dependency facility is seeking a part-time mental health/crisis evaluation therapist to work Saturdays and Sundays from 7:00 P.M. to 3:30 A.M. Position involves crisis intervention for psychiatric/chemical dependency emergencies to include assessments for hospitalization, serving as liaison with hospital emergency room, and interacting with insurance companies.

Overseas Opportunities in Social Work

International corporation that provides counseling services to military adolescents overseas has positions available in Germany, Seoul, and Hawaii. Requirements include a master's in psychology or social work, clinical license/certification, and three years of full-time clinical adolescent substance abuse treatment. Position requires skills in prevention/education, community referral agreements, and outpatient treatment.

Program Coordinator

Health Education/Drug Prevention program seeks program coordinator to work on research, development, promotion, and dissemination of materials and programs related to youth-centered alcohol, tobacco, and other drug prevention programs. Qualifications include three to five years' experience in drug prevention/health education in elementary/secondary school or community youth-serving organization. Proven program supervision and implementation skills. Ability to handle multiple projects simultaneously. Master's degree preferred. Curriculum development and/or grant-writing experience helpful.

Program Manager

Regional alcohol and drug treatment project has an opening for a senior-level professional to manage a federally funded model alcohol and drug treatment services project for the region. The program manager will be responsible for intensive case management services, adherence to budgetary and programmatic requirements, intergovernmental coordination, project performance reporting, and evaluation. Requires a BS and master's degree in social work, social science, public administration, or related field; two to four years of related experience in managing ADD treatment; or equivalent combination of experience and training that provides the position requirements. Ability to administer a "managed care" model ADD treatment project, comprehensive knowledge of ADD services, proficiency in programmatic planning and evaluation, and excellent communication, word processing, and spreadsheet application skills.

Project Manager

There is an opening for a senior-level professional to manage a federally funded model alcohol and drug treatment services project for the region. The project manager will direct the operations of this demonstration project, in coordination with local publicly funded agencies. The successful candidate will oversee the budget and financial allocations of the project; supervise administrative and clinical staff; conduct program planning, data collection, and MIS activities; oversee the development and implementation of direct services to the region; and provide staff support to high-level policy and direct service committees of the program. Candidates should possess a BS degree; master's degree in social work, psychology, social sciences, public administration, or a related field; four years' related work experience or any equivalent combination of experience and training. Knowledge of and experience with AOD programs, research, data collection, analysis, and evaluation is preferred. Familiarity with local government AOD treatment or other related human service programs desirable. Excellent writing, public speaking, word processing, and spreadsheet application skills necessary.

Substance Abuse Coordinator

This supervisory position is responsible for planning, directing, coordinating, and supervising outpatient clinical services offered to a variety of clients in a public substance abuse treatment agency. The agency, of which outpatient services are the largest component, consists of a coordinated system of care and continuum of services, provided either directly or through contractual arrangements. Clients served present with multiple and often complex problems. Most are involved in the criminal justice or social services systems. The coordinator is responsible for prioritizing, assigning, reviewing, and evaluating the clinical work of therapists; developing and evaluating new service components; assisting in the preparation of budget documents and grant applications and reports. Requires master's degree in counseling, social work, or related field plus three years of experience providing direct clinical and diagnostic services to substance abuse clients, of which one year must have included administration, management, and coordination of other therapeutic professionals.

Substance Abuse Counselor

Outpatient treatment program serving Latino population is seeking an experienced substance abuse counselor to provide group and individual counseling for Latino clients. Required: a four-year college or university degree in psychology, social work, or a related field, plus one year of experience in substance abuse counseling. Participation in a substance abuse treatment counseling program can be substituted for the required education on a year-to-year basis. Spanish/English required.

Substance Abuse Treatment Specialist

Progressive mental health center is currently recruiting to fill positions for substance abuse treatment specialist. Duties include providing direct treatment services to alcoholics and their families, developing and offering community education programs, and providing administrative and clinical supervision for substance abuse counselors. Applicants must hold a PhD in clinical psychology or a master's degree in social work in order to meet the license eligibility requirements of the state.

other
areas
of service

introduction
to part VII

There are several areas of social work practice in which relatively few NASW members work, but that are, individually and collectively, important areas of social work concern. Among these are community organizing and planning, corrections, developmental disabilities, housing, international social work, mental retardation, occupational social work, and public welfare. (Because the interventions used in occupational social work are primarily mental health in nature, occupational social work is discussed in part I. Similarly, discussion of community organizing and planning is included in part VIII, Macro Practice).

With a few exceptions, such as mental health or children and families, social workers are spread widely across a large number of practice areas. There is a relatively small social work presence in these other areas of service when taken individually. NASW members who do work in these primary practice areas are disproportionately at the BSW level (Gibelman & Schervish, 1993).

Given the broad range of these other areas of service in which social workers work, the focus in this chapter is on a select few that include the service areas of corrections, developmental disabilities, housing, mental retardation, and public welfare. In many of these areas, practice is carried out in host settings where social workers represent one profession among several and are not the dominant profession in that environment. Dane and Simon (1991) have identified four generic challenges for social workers who practice as guests in host settings:

1. discrepancies between professional mission and values and those of dominant individuals in the employing institution

2. marginality or token status within workplaces employing few social workers

3. devaluing of social work as women's work in settings that are predominantly male in composition

4. role ambiguity and role strain.

To varying degrees these challenges pervade the nature of practice in these other service areas.

References

Dane, B. O., & Simon, B. L. (1991, May). Resident guests: Social workers in host settings. *Social Work, 36,* 208–213.

Gibelman, M., & Schervish, P. H. (1993). *Who we are: The social work labor force as reflected in the NASW membership.* Washington, DC: NASW Press.

criminal justice

In the late 1870s many of those in the social work profession were involved with the criminal justice system and with juvenile detention and reformation facilities (Miller, 1995). Although social work has largely abdicated its role in the field of corrections, a small proportion of social workers still practice in this area of service. It has been argued that the need for social workers in correctional institutions is greater than ever before because of the growing number of incarcerated individuals (Ivanoff, Smyth, & Finnegan, 1993). However, working in corrections is not easy. The pay is often low and the environment can be threatening ("Prison Reform," 1986).

Of 87,265 NASW members providing practice areas in 1991, only 1.2 percent (1,025) cited corrections as their primary practice area. This proportion was down slightly from 1988, when 1.3 percent of the respondents cited corrections as their primary practice area (Gibelman & Schervish, 1993). The largest proportion of social workers in this field hold a BSW as their highest social work degree. And, compared with the overall NASW membership, disproportionately more men than women work in corrections; 40.1 percent of respondents employed in corrections are men, whereas men constitute 22.7 percent of the NASW membership. Compared with other ethnic groups, a higher proportion of African Americans work in corrections.

The three major components of the criminal justice system are law enforcement, the courts, and corrections (Netherland, 1987). Social workers have also been employed by maximum security mental health facilities, such as the McClean/Bridgewater Program at Bridgewater State Hospital in Boston. Here, social workers provide individual, group, and family therapy to patients; they have also been qualified to testify at commitment hearings concerning their patients' mental health ("Social Workers Humanize," 1986). Social workers can play a role in any of these components.

In the area of law enforcement, many social workers work in police departments. Other social workers may work outside police departments in mental health agencies or private practices but they may cooperate professionally with the police. This type of cooperation is beneficial in planning, developing, implementing, and evaluating interprofessional programs (Treger, 1995). For example, the Chicago Police Department employs a social worker to develop and direct individual and family therapeutic programs for police officers and their families. One program provides services to police who experience a traumatic, life-threatening situation, such as a near-fatal shooting. In addition, counselors lead support groups for families of slain officers. The counseling service also provides educational programs on chemical dependency, racial sensitivity, sexual discrimination, stress management, and supervising difficult employees ("Social Workers Humanize," 1986).

Although there are great benefits to working with law enforcement agents, social workers must be cognizant of the problems that can arise in a host setting. There are frequent issues of control, power, and communication that must be discussed and resolved (Treger, 1995).

The field of corrections is typically associated with punishment rather than rehabilitation. However, it has been noted that 10 to 35 percent of inmates in jails and prisons across the nation suffer from serious mental health problems (Severson, 1994). Social workers are being called on to provide clinical services to the almost 2 million people who are incarcerated in this country (Severson, 1994). There are obvious and clear value dilemmas for social workers practicing in this setting. To some extent, these dilemmas are minimized when social workers provide services not as employees of the correctional institution but as independent clinicians.

Statistics show that both the number of individuals incarcerated and the rate of incarceration are at an all-time high in the United States (McNeece, 1995; Netherland, 1987). Statistics also indicate that black and Hispanic people are overrepresented in arrests and convictions. They are also overrepresented as victims (Netherland, 1987).

Alternatives to Incarceration

As the crime rate increases, America continues to build more prisons that do little, if anything, to rehabilitate inmates before release. After serving a sentence, a person is usually released with few of the skills or resources needed to re-enter life outside prison walls. Overcrowded prisons, costs associated with incarceration, and soaring crime rates are causing policymakers to look more closely at alternative sentencing programs, many of which involve social workers (Hiratsuka, 1993). Alternative sentencing takes into account the protection of society; provision of treatment and rehabilitation services; restitution to crime victims; and often some form of punishment, such as restrictions on the offender's freedom or a period of incarceration followed by probation.

Social workers and other professionals involved in alternative sentencing programs are sometimes called "sentencing consultants" or "mitigation specialists" and are responsible for devising practical alternatives to long prison sentences and for influencing judges and juries to accept their recommendations. To devise sentencing proposals, social workers examine the offender's life history and determine what treatment services are needed. They interview the offender and family members, conduct assessments and psychosocial histories, prepare reports including sentencing recommendations, and discuss strategies and options with defense attorneys (Hiratsuka, 1993). Sentencing consultants may be employed independently or they may work for organizations such as the Legal Aid Society or the Public Defender Service. In 1993, the Legal Aid Society of New York City had about 30 social workers on staff.

The Violent Crime Control and Law Enforcement Act of 1994 (P.L. 103-322) provided $9.7 billion for new prisons, boot camps, and alternative facilities that leave traditional prison space for violent criminals (McNeece, 1995). However, this legislation, the largest crime bill in the history of the United States, continues to put more money into punitive than preventive measures (McNeece, 1995). Nevertheless, alternative sentencing programs continue to provide an option to traditional incarceration.

Criminal justice systems draw from various philosophies including retribution, restitution, general deterrence, special deterrence, treatment, incapacitation, and "just deserts" (Netherland, 1987). In addition, a wide variety of programs have been tested and used in the United States as alternatives to incarceration. Some of these programs include probation; parole; fines; and partial confinement, which typically involves work or educational release and special treatment programs for drug and alcohol abuse, mental illness, and sex offenses (Netherland, 1987). Although some of these alternatives have gained in popularity, it is difficult to attract and maintain qualified staff to develop and enhance such programs (Netherland, 1987). Nonetheless, the quickly growing inmate population will eventually cause a crisis of prison and jail capacity. As a result, there has already been a dramatic increase in the use of alternatives to incarceration (McNeece, 1995).

Criminal Court Proceedings

The role of social workers in criminal court proceedings has been rather minimal and is often inappropriately judged as an effort to excuse criminal behavior, whereas social workers have played an active and appreciated role in civil proceedings such as child custody cases (Isenstadt, 1995). The role of social workers in criminal court proceedings is to bring an awareness of the systemic features of the defendant's environment, rather than solely focusing on the person's mental state (Isenstadt, 1995). Social workers, such as Cessie Alfonso, president of Alfonso Associates and of the National Association of Sentencing Advocates, work with battered women who kill their partners. In legal proceedings, Alfonso seeks to illustrate the plight of a battered woman so that the judge and jury can understand why the woman felt she had no alternative except to kill and why she could not leave the abuser (Hiratsuka, 1993).

Social worker Kathleen Williams was called as an expert witness in the sensationalized trial of Lorena Bobbitt, who was accused of maliciously wounding her husband (she severed his penis with a knife as he slept). Ms. Bobbitt maintained that she committed the act after he had raped her. Williams, whose work primarily concerns child and spouse abuse in the military, testified on the impact of abuse on a person's functioning (Landers, 1994).

Social workers may also be involved in the court system as "expert witnesses," a status that is based on significant educational credentials and professional experience. Social workers may act as expert witnesses either during the trial or during the sentencing process (Isenstadt, 1995). In any case, social workers must be clear about their background, knowledge, and experience in the relevant field. They must also remain up-to-date on current research findings in the field, and they should be prepared for confrontational questions that challenge their authority as an expert (Isenstadt, 1995).

Social workers were expert witnesses in several of the most publicized criminal cases in recent memory. For example, Armando T. Morales, professor of psychiatry, social work, and biobehavioral science at the University of California–Los Angeles School of Medicine, testified in the trial of Damian Williams and Henry Keith Watson. These two defendants, both African Americans, were charged in the beating of a white truck driver, Reginald O. Denny, during the 1992 Los Angeles riots (Landers, 1994). Mr. Morales believes that his clinical credentials, his position at a prominent university, and his research experience led to his selection as an expert witness. He testified that the behavior exhibited by the two defendants could be explained by the "group contagion theory," which holds that moods, attitudes, and behaviors are acted out in a thoughtless and impulsive manner in response to a powerful stimulus. In this specific case, the stimulus was the acquittal of white police officers on charges of brutality for beating Rodney King, a black motorist. Defense lawyers credited Morales's testimony as effectively countering prosecution charges that required evidence of criminal intent to commit murder and aggravated mayhem (Landers, 1994).

In addition to the more traditional social work roles in the court system, many social workers earn law degrees and become juvenile judges, prosecutors, or defense attorneys (Ezell, 1995). Although social workers play a role in the court system, many of the profession's most important accomplishments take place outside of the courtroom in advocacy for alternatives to incarceration, education, training, and rehabilitation (Ezell, 1995; Isenstadt, 1995).

Corrections

General social work tasks in corrections include intake, screening, diagnosis, classification, supervision, treatment, and release planning (Netherland, 1987). Several unique social work skills that are essential to correctional work have been identified. First, social workers see clients as part of a total system; therefore, they work with employers, teachers, and family members to identify problem areas and possible solutions. Second, social workers are skilled in case coordination, which is important when working with professionals from other disciplines. Third, social workers effectively identify and use community resources. Fourth, social workers are skilled in individual casework and group work and effectively use techniques such as giving feedback, crisis intervention, setting limits, formulating goals, and predicting behavior (Netherland,

1987). And finally, social workers bring essential advocacy skills to the field of corrections. In this arena, social workers are called on not only to participate in the legal system but to actively advocate for their clients to ensure fair legal proceedings (Lynch & Mitchell, 1995).

In a correctional setting, social workers attempt to establish a meaningful relationship with clients and to help them recognize maladaptive behaviors and make appropriate changes. Social workers also help clients develop learning skills and methods of problem solving that will be necessary in other areas of life. Perhaps most importantly, social workers play an active role in helping clients with release issues such as finding a job, food, housing, clothing, transportation, and relating to others. Social workers often work with the community and coordinate a support system for the client after release from prison (Netherland, 1987).

More current social work efforts in the correctional system have included education and training for inmates on issues such as parental responsibilities, self-esteem, and substance abuse. Social workers also offer counseling services in such areas as health and domestic violence (Gabel & Johnston, 1995). One area of social work service that has gone relatively untouched is that of family reunification services. Social workers are able to support or hinder reunification and strengthening of the family through support of parent–child visitation and appropriate placement, if necessary, of prisoners' children (Gabel & Johnston, 1995).

Advocacy

Advocacy is an important social work function in encouraging adult and juvenile courts to consider alternative and more constructive treatments such as substance abuse counseling or employment preparation (Gabel & Johnston, 1995). By advocating for supportive rather than punitive programs, social workers can help improve the physical and mental health of offenders, their children, and other family members to break intergenerational cycles of reactive behavior, crime, and incarceration (Gabel & Johnston, 1995).

In addition to working with inmates, social workers counsel families in handling psychological, social, and economic issues of the client's incarceration. Frequently, the family also needs help adjusting to the client's return home after release from prison (Netherland, 1987).

Victim Services

One of the newer social work roles in the field of corrections involves work with victims of crimes. *Victimology*, the study of assistance to victims of crime, is a relatively new specialty specifically devoted to providing aid to crime victims ("Crime Victims," 1984). In the 1970s there were very few victim/witness assistance programs; however, this trend began to change with recognition that the criminal justice system was treating the victims worse than the felons. Today there are more than 6,000 such programs (Roberts, 1995). This growth in the number of programs for victims and witnesses of violent crimes is a direct result of funding under the Victims of Crime Act of 1984 (Roberts, 1995). The primary objective of victim and witness assistance programs is to help witnesses cope with their own personal grief and overcome the fear of testifying in court so that they can assist in the prosecution of criminal cases (Roberts, 1995).

Services for victims of crime are not as common as witness programs, and they are usually found in police departments, hospitals, probation departments, or social services agencies (Roberts, 1995). Victims of crime often get overlooked in the criminal justice process at the very time that they need information and help. At this juncture, social workers can help the victim provide the police with the best possible report of the incident. Initially this may involve using techniques to calm the victim. As the case goes through the criminal justice system, the social worker can keep the victim informed about developments in the case and important times, dates, and places in regard to the case. Another function carried out by the social worker is to help the victim apply for victim compensation and advocating in regard to the amount of compensation ("Crime Victims," 1984). In general, victim assistance programs focus on providing crisis intervention within the first 24 hours after victimization. Social workers involved in such programs may provide many services including crisis counseling; assistance with victim compensation applications; emergency financial assistance; food and clothing vouchers; transportation to court, shelters, or hospitals; and referral to mental health centers and social services agencies when long-term counseling and psychotherapy is necessary (Roberts, 1995).

Another area of victim services is the emerging field of victim–offender mediation, which has been growing in popularity and is primarily sponsored by private social services agencies that work in coordination with the courts (Umbreit, 1993). The mediation process is intended to provide an opportunity for crime victims to meet the offender, discuss the offense, and negotiate an agreeable restitution process (Umbreit, 1993). Social workers often serve as mediators for these meetings and discussions (Umbreit, 1993). Social workers in this area of practice provide service throughout the mediation process, which consists of an intake phase, a preparation phase, a mediation phase, and an important follow-up phase (Umbreit, 1993). Using conflict theory as a theoretical base, social workers are active in victim–offender mediation, which requires a commitment to the empowerment of crime victims and offenders to resolve their conflicts and to let go of the painful experience (Parsons, 1991; Umbreit, 1993).

The skills of the social worker are well suited to mediation work. Social workers often engage in enabling and empowerment to assist client systems in resolving conflicts and to learn personal mediation skills that may be used in future conflict situations (Parsons, 1991). Social workers who work with victims of crime may be employed in a battered women's shelter, a hospital, or in the court's social services division, among other settings. Social workers may also be on call to local police departments to assess the needs of victims of violent crime and refer them to community services (Popple & Leighninger, 1993). In addition, as a person acquainted with the circumstances of the case and the impact of the crime on the client, the social worker may be called on to provide testimony when the case goes to trial.

Issues and Opportunities

Certain social work skills have been identified as essential to correctional work. First, social workers see clients as part of a total system; therefore, they work with employers, teachers, and family members to identify problem areas and possible solutions. Second, social workers are skilled in case coordination, which is important when working with professionals from other disciplines. Third, social workers effectively identify and use community resources. Finally, social workers are skilled in individual casework and group work and effectively use techniques such as giving feedback, applying crisis interventions, setting limits, formulating goals, and predicting behavior (Netherland, 1987).

The applicability of social work skills in the field of corrections is evidenced by Michael Samberg, a social worker who became warden of the Virginia State Penitentiary in Richmond in 1986. The penitentiary is a 900-inmate maximum-security prison. The population consists of people with a history of behavior problems or violent crimes, security risks, and repeat offenders. Mr. Samberg holds no illusions about rehabilitating many of the inmates. Instead, the goal is to "reintegrate" the prisoners to change their behavior patterns. He feels that his social work training is an asset "not only in working with inmates, but also administratively, and in dealing with the various agencies, supervisors, and others [he] regularly comes in contact with" ("Prison Reform," 1986, p. 5).

The opportunities for social work practice in the field of corrections are substantial. But there are special issues in this field of practice that help explain why social workers are not more interested in employment in this area of service. First, clients in the correctional system are involuntary; resistance to change is normal and some offenders do not change (Netherland, 1987). Social workers employed in corrections are often viewed by society, by the system, and by the clients as agents of control rather than helpers (DiNitto & McNeece, 1990).

Second, it taxes the professional's ability to suspend personal judgments when working with citizens who have committed heinous crimes, such as rape or murder. In addition, potential turf struggles arise from practice in an interdisciplinary setting. As previously discussed, a social worker in a police department may also lose his or her professional identity as the sole practitioner among so many members of other disciplines ("Social Workers Humanize," 1986).

In correctional settings, two-thirds of all correctional officers are men, and three-fourths are white. The officers generally receive brief on-the-job training that is focused on security issues, weapons, riot control, and so on. There is often a subculture and behavior code among correctional facility staff that emphasizes security and control, keeping a social distance from prisoners, being tough and dominating, and—unfortunately—not listening to social workers (Netherland, 1987).

Another deterrent to entering the field of corrections for many social workers is the fact that most prisons are outdated and overcrowded with fragmented programs and wasted resources. The current prison environment has been characterized as "violent, depressing, regimented, boring, and dehumanizing" (Netherland, 1987, p. 358). Therefore, social workers who decide to enter the field of criminal justice should not only play a role in treating the offender but also get involved in creating public awareness of the problems in the field and initiating changes (Netherland, 1987).

Social workers employed in the criminal justice system are typically public employees in that they work under the auspices of the federal, state, or local government. Many work within an institutional setting such as a prison or jail, although some social workers are employed in probation or parole units that are organizationally based.

Juvenile Justice

The Problems

In 1992, violence took the lives of 2,428 children across the nation; these deaths represented an increase of 67 percent in six years (Loose & Thomas, 1994). Although aggregate crime rates have remained fairly stable, the crime rate among young people has risen dramatically (Fraser, 1995). Furthermore, African American children, youths, and young adults are more affected by violent crime than other groups (Fraser, 1995). However, youths are not only increasingly victims of crime, they are also becoming perpetrators of crime.

Youths are mirroring their adult role models. In 1994, a Times Square billboard in the heart of New York City began to tally two numbers: gun-related deaths and guns in circulation in the United States. On its first day of operation, the digital billboard recorded 220,527,358 guns and 45 gun killings (Stassen-Berger, 1994).

The upswing in juvenile crime became evident in the mid-1980s. Across the nation, juveniles were charged with 112,409 violent crimes in 1992, representing a 47 percent increase in 10 years. Equally disturbing is the fact that the age of juveniles engaged in criminal activity has dropped. In 1992, more than 7,600 children between the ages of 10 and 12 were charged with murder, rape, robbery, or assault, an increase of 71 percent in 10 years; among youths ages 13 and 14, the figure was 25,034, an increase of 74 percent (Loose & Thomas, 1994). School suspensions and expulsions are rising rapidly and weapons are routinely confiscated in schools across the country.

There is a clear relationship between the drug epidemic and youth violence. One teenager reported that he began to sell drugs at the age of 14 and lost several friends to drug deals gone wrong: "If you weren't selling drugs, you weren't nobody. If you sell drugs, you had anything you wanted—any girl, any friend, money, status. If you didn't, you got no girlfriend, no friends, no money. You're a nothing" (quoted in Wilkerson, 1994, p. B12). In addition to drug use and the easy availability of guns, a critical lack of parenting is being blamed for the increase in youth violence. Children who are abused and neglected are considered to be at high risk for delinquency. A family division judge explained that many of the children "have been bounced from family member to family member, without the love and discipline and guidance that children need. They have no anchor or security. They are literally children who are raising themselves" (quoted in Loose & Thomas, 1994, A19).

Duane Weiland, a social worker and Catholic priest in Des Moines, Iowa, runs the Family Assessment Project at a county jail. His work led him to explore the reasons young inmates get into trouble, and he found that most came from families in trouble. His efforts have focused on providing brief therapy with inmates and serving as their link with the community. He, too, sees the need to extend interventions to the families of the young inmates ("Prison Reform," 1986).

Youths who exhibit either delinquent or problematic behavior are often abused, neglected, removed from the home, suspended, expelled, or arrested depending on the nature of the problem and the location (Barton, 1995). The action that is initially taken to deal with the youth is partially determined by the agent of social control involved (for example, psychiatry, family therapy, or social work). Other factors are the resources and motivation of the parents (Barton, 1995). The complexity of delinquency is evidenced by the fact that many of the same families appear in case files of multiple systems. Social workers and other involved professionals recognize this overlap and work to coordinate and integrate services to troubled youth and families (Barton, 1995).

Few areas of the country have remained untouched by the surge of youth crime. A resident of the St. Thomas housing project in New Orleans commented: "It's a shame when the grown people have to hide. . . . That shooting, Lord, it's all around you. You can't rest at night and now there's shots during the day" (Bragg, 1994, p. A28). As a result of such violence, the notion of childhood as a time of innocence is being challenged. The public is demanding that children who perpetuate violent crimes be charged as adults. The Violent Crime Control and Law Enforcement Act of 1994 reflects these views through provisions to try youths in adult courts for certain criminal activities, such as those involving controlled substances or firearms. Although many citizens support stiffer penalties and urge that youths be tried as adults, prevention advocates are pursuing several other programmatic themes, including gun control, creation of more after-school programs, and classes in parenting and conflict resolution (Loose & Thomas, 1994).

Social Work Roles
Social workers may be involved in any aspect of such prevention programs from direct service to planning and development to administration. Programs that have been successful in reducing violence have several basic characteristics. Fraser (1995) asserted that program developers and leaders must be able to

- secure sufficient resources

- obtain support of private and public officials

- involve many population groups in the community, including the youths, in defining the problem, setting goals, evaluating strategies, and implementing a plan of action
- create a set of strategies and activities that focus on immediate, tangible benefits
- hire qualified and committed staff and provide ongoing training
- maintain simple but flexible organizations and budgets
- adhere to original value base in times of adversity.

Social Work Practice with Juvenile Offenders

Betsy Clark is the supervisor of one of the Youth Services Units in Philadelphia. Betsy supervises five other licensed social workers, and she also carries a limited caseload herself. Betsy's Youth Services Unit works with juvenile offenders and their families; however, they do not usually provide therapy. The social workers primarily do case management such as connecting families with the necessary resources by negotiating to purchase services for individuals and families or referring the families to contracted agencies. In addition, the social workers frequently attend court to give the juvenile court judge their recommendations for specific cases.

Most of the cases that come to the Youth Services Unit are in a crisis state. As the supervisor, Betsy frequently meets with the other social workers to discuss necessary action and to predict future problems that may arise. If a youth commits a crime in Betsy's jurisdiction, he or she may be sent to the local maximum security detention center by a judge. If so, one of the five social workers will contact the youth and begin services to the youth and the family, including arranging for an agency to provide counseling or setting up tutoring sessions for the youth. If the youth commits a crime but is not sent to the maximum security detention center, a social worker will work with the youth and the family and may place the child in a community program such as a regular group home, a therapeutic group home that provides limited services, a shelter, or a residential placement.

Although residential placements are a last resort, they are occasionally necessary. If a social worker from Betsy's unit refers a child for residential placement, he or she must be prepared to justify the referral. Betsy often works with and advises the social workers on the best way to present the case.

Recently, Betsy has become frustrated with the lack of community alternatives for juvenile offenders. She believes that the community needs more programs to supplement the basic group homes and residential placements. So she has been actively working with the department of social services, the local detention centers and correctional facilities, and community leaders in the youth services field to develop other alternatives.

In this case scenario, Betsy and the social workers she supervises carried out a variety of social work functions. At the direct services level, functions include assessment, diagnosis, and identification of major problems and issues. Because case management is the primary function of this unit, the social work skills of assistance and referral were frequently used. In supervising the social workers in the unit, Betsy engaged in the administrative functions of supervision, consultation, evaluation, and staff development. Finally, as Betsy participated in activities to improve the juvenile justice arena, she carried out the social work functions of policy analysis, planning, reviewing, and program development.

The goal of the juvenile justice system, like the adult correctional system, is to help prevent and control crime and to adjudicate, incarcerate, and rehabilitate people engaged in illegal behavior. Also as in the adult correctional system, there are many areas of the juvenile justice system that must be examined and restructured to accomplish this goal more effectively. There are indeed various roles in the juvenile justice system for social workers ranging from prevention services to rehabilitation to program planning and development. Unfortunately, social workers, like many other professionals in the criminal justice system, often see themselves as "covert agents of law enforcement" (Miller, 1995, p. 657). To be truly effective social workers must remember their original goal to bring hope, promise, and progress to the criminal justice system and especially to juveniles in trouble. They must use the functions of planning, management, and advocacy to bring about fundamental change in the system (Miller, 1995). Most importantly, "social workers must continue to contribute to and influence the juvenile justice system to ensure that the system remains not only juvenile, but just" (Gothard, 1987, p. 9).

Forensic Social Work

Forensic social work is the practice specialty that focuses on legal matters and educating law and related professionals about social welfare issues and, in turn, educating social workers about legal aspects associated with their work (Barker, 1995).

In the 1960s, people with mental illness generally were cared for by state hospitals; however, in the 1970s legal prosecution began to replace hospitalization (Whitmer, 1983). Today, criminal court judges are faced with the frustrating task of handing down decisions for large numbers of defendants with mental illness. Within the court, there is a sense that the defendant was driven by his or her illness rather than by criminal intent. Therefore, if this illness is left untreated, the person will almost inevitably return to the court at some point (Whitmer, 1983).

In cases of criminal action, the forensic social worker must assess the relationship between the client's mental illness and his or her undesirable actions. The worker then must determine whether a treatment plan could be effective in preventing future criminal activity and must acknowledge to the court that there are certain illnesses that may be clinically untreatable (Whitmer, 1983).

In cases in which a forensic social worker determines that a client can indeed be helped, the social worker develops a case plan. Using the functions of support, counseling, enabling, organization, and referral, the forensic social worker must begin to meet the client's needs immediately upon release from custody (Whitmer, 1983).

The functions of the forensic social worker also include providing expert testimony, or assisting other social workers to provide testimony in courts of law. Such testimony may concern the custody of children, juvenile delinquency, welfare rights, or parental nonsupport.

Qualifying to render expert diagnosis and testimony during a trial is usually decided in case-by-case judicial rulings. One social worker who has qualified on many occasions to provide expert testimony is social worker Hillel Bodek of New York. Bodek, a specialist in forensic work, was qualified in a ruling by a New York county judge as an expert to testify on a defendant's mental competency to stand trial ("Forensic Training," 1985). Mr. Bodek has also been qualified to testify on the issue of criminal responsibility, an issue in regard to the "insanity defense." Judge Stephen G. Crane, a New York State judge, subsequently ruled that "a properly qualified certified social worker may be appointed to act as a 'psychiatric examiner' appointed by the court, the defense, [or] the People…" under New York State law ("Court Ruling," 1985, p. 1). This was the first judicial opinion to rule on a social worker's qualifications to assess a defendant's future placement in either a mental health treatment facility or in the community and to assert the competence of social workers to judge a defendant's mental state at the time of the crime.

References

Barker, R. L. (1995). *Social work dictionary* (3rd ed.). Washington, DC: NASW Press.

Barton, W. H. (1995). Juvenile corrections. In R. L. Edwards (Ed.-in-Chief), *Encyclopedia of social work* (19th ed., Vol. 2, pp. 1563–1577). Washington, DC: NASW Press.

Bragg, R. (1994, December 2). Children strike fear into grown-up hearts. *New York Times*, pp. A1, A28.

Court ruling validates forensic social work. (1985, September). *NASW News*, pp. 1, 6.

Crime victims given increasing attention. (1984, April). *NASW News*, p. 7.

DiNitto, D. M., & McNeece, C. A. (1990). *Social work: Issues and opportunities in a challenging profession*. Englewood Cliffs, NJ: Prentice Hall.

Ezell, M. (1995). Juvenile and family courts. In R. L. Edwards (Ed.-in-Chief), *Encyclopedia of social work* (19th ed., Vol. 2, pp. 1553–1562). Washington, DC: NASW Press.

Forensic training, standards seen as key to "expert" status in court. (1985, April). *NASW News*, p. 14.

Fraser, M. W. (1995). Violence overview. In R. L. Edwards (Ed.-in-Chief), *Encyclopedia of social work* (19th ed., Vol. 3, pp. 2453–2460). Washington, DC: NASW Press.

Gabel, K., & Johnston, D. (1995). Female criminal offenders. In R. L. Edwards (Ed.-in-Chief), *Encyclopedia of social work* (19th ed., Vol. 2, pp. 1013–1027). Washington, DC: NASW Press.

Gibelman, M., & Schervish, P. H. (1993). *Who we are: The social work labor force as reflected in the NASW membership.* Washington, DC: NASW Press.

Gothard, S. (1987). Juvenile justice system. In A. Minahan (Ed.-in-Chief), *Encyclopedia of social work* (18th ed., Vol. 2, pp. 5–9). Silver Spring, MD: National Association of Social Workers.

Hiratsuka, J. (1993, September). Hard times alter views on "hard time." *NASW News,* p. 3.

Isenstadt, P. M. (1995). Adult courts. In R. L. Edwards (Ed.-in-Chief), *Encyclopedia of social work* (19th ed., Vol. 1, pp. 68–74). Washington, DC: NASW Press.

Ivanoff, A., Smyth, N. J., & Finnegan, D. (1993). Social work behind bars: Preparation for fieldwork in correctional institutions. *Journal of Teaching in Social Work, 7,* 137–149.

Landers, S. (1994, April). Crime or punishment: Who's a victim? *NASW News,* p. 3.

Loose, C., & Thomas, P. (1994, January 2). "Crisis of violence" becoming menace to childhood. *Washington Post,* pp. A1, A19.

Lynch, R. S., & Mitchell, J. (1995). Justice system advocacy: A must for NASW and the social work community. *Social Work, 40,* 9–12.

McNeece, C. A. (1995). Adult corrections. In R. L. Edwards (Ed.-in-Chief), *Encyclopedia of social work* (19th ed., Vol. 1, pp. 60–68). Washington, DC: NASW Press.

Miller, J. G. (1995). Criminal justice: Social work roles. In R. L. Edwards (Ed.-in-Chief), *Encyclopedia of social work* (19th ed., Vol. 1, pp. 653–659). Washington, DC: NASW Press.

Netherland, W. (1987). Corrections systems: Adult. In A. Minahan (Ed.-in-Chief), *Encyclopedia of social work* (18th ed., Vol. 1, pp. 351–360). Silver Spring, MD: National Association of Social Workers.

Parsons, R. J. (1991). The mediator role in social work practice. *Social Work, 36*, 483–487.

Popple, P. R., & Leighninger, L. (1993). *Social work, social welfare and American society*. Boston: Allyn and Bacon.

Prison reform: Balancing ideals, realities. (1986, May). *NASW News*, pp. 5, 18.

Roberts, A. R. (1995). Victim services and victim/witness assistance programs. In R. L. Edwards (Ed.-in-Chief), *Encyclopedia of social work* (19th ed., Vol. 3, pp. 2440–2444). Washington, DC: NASW Press.

Severson, M. M. (1994). Adapting social work values to the corrections environment. *Social Work, 39*, 451–456.

Social workers humanize justice system. (1986, March). *NASW News*, p. 7.

Stassen-Berger, R. E. (1994, January 2). Times square billboard tick-tocks a mournful tally of deaths from firearms. *Washington Post*, p. A3.

Treger, H. (1995). Police social work. In R. L. Edwards (Ed.-in-Chief), *Encyclopedia of social work* (19th ed., Vol. 3, pp. 1843–1848). Washington, DC: NASW Press.

Umbreit, M. S. (1993). Crime victims and offenders in mediation: An emerging area of social work practice. *Social Work, 38*, 69–73.

Victims of Crime Act of 1984, P.L. 98-473, 98 Stat. 2170.

Violent Crime Control and Law Enforcement Act of 1994, P.L. 303–322, 108 Stat. 1796.

Whitmer, G. E. (1983). The development of forensic social work. *Social Work, 28*, 217–223.

Wilkerson, I. (1994, December 13). Crack's legacy lives on. *New York Times*, pp. A1, B12.

developmental
disabilities

Developmental disability is "a condition that produces functional impairment as a result of disease, genetic disorder, or impaired growth pattern manifested before adulthood" (Barker, 1995, p. 99). More specifically, developmental disabilities are defined by the Developmental Disabilities Assistance and Bill of Rights Act of 1990 (P.L. 101-496) as severe and chronic conditions that

- are attributable to mental or physical impairments or a combination of both

- are manifested before the person reaches age 22

- are likely to continue indefinitely

- result in substantial limitations in three or more major life activity areas

- require a combination and sequence of special, interdisciplinary, or generic care, treatment, or other services that are of an extended or lifelong duration and are individually planned and coordinated (DeWeaver, 1995).

Conditions classified as developmental disabilities include cerebral palsy, Down's syndrome, epilepsy, mental retardation, and autism. There may also be significant overlap of symptoms among these conditions (DeWeaver, 1995). It is estimated that approximately 3 million people in the United States have developmental disabilities (Freedman, 1995).

Mental retardation is the most common condition among the population of people with developmental disabilities; however, not all people with mental retardation are classified as developmentally disabled because their condition may not be considered severe enough according to the federal definition (Freedman, 1995). The current functional definition focuses on the most severely handicapped population and, therefore, excludes a great many people with mild disabilities, many of whom come from poor families (McDonald-Wikler, 1987). In addition, the condition of poverty is often the root of developmental disabilities because of factors such as malnutrition, tobacco and alcohol use, lack of preventive care, lead poisoning, child abuse, early nutritional deprivation, and lack of interaction (Freedman, 1995; McDonald-Wikler, 1987). Social workers must use their skills in advocacy, coordination, and empowerment to help link poor families to necessary services and resources in their own communities (McDonald-Wikler, 1987).

Although there are many different conditions that may qualify as developmental disabilities, Freedman (1995) listed some general characteristics and needs of this population:

- significant and continuous functional limitations in major daily life activities

- functional limitations related to environmental contexts

- the need for services and supports on an extended or indefinite basis

- the need for multiple, interdisciplinary services in the areas of health care, social services, education, housing, and financial support.

As advances in medical care and biomedical technology continue, people with developmental disabilities are living longer. Therefore, social workers are needed to assist in planning and coordinating long-term services and support for both the affected individual and his or her family (Freedman, 1995).

Social work's ecological perspective is useful in working with people with developmental disabilities. Social workers can be involved at either a micro or a macro level, working with either individuals and families or groups and communities (Freedman, 1995). On a micro level, social workers perform the functions of assessment, diagnosis, advice and counseling, referral, and coordination. On a macro level, social workers are prepared to use their knowledge to identify and mobilize groups and communities to better access available resources. Finally, social workers may also use their skills in planning, advocacy, and empowerment to press for preventive changes in long-term social conditions such as poverty to prevent developmental disabilities or to minimize their negative consequences (Freedman, 1995; McDonald-Wikler, 1987).

Nowhere to Turn

"My baby is dying!" Jay Scranton cried out as he crashed through the emergency department doors of Northtown Hospital in Gainsville, Georgia, carrying his six-year-old daughter who lay limp in his arms. Nurses and doctors rushed to him as he ran down the hall, looking for help. The doctors took his daughter, and a nurse gently guided him back to the waiting area where his wife sat with tears streaming down her face. The nurse then paged Lisa Green, the social worker, who came to talk with the Scrantons.

As they waited to hear the diagnosis, Lisa was able to get a fairly clear understanding of what had happened. Their daughter, Caroline, had fallen asleep on the couch when she suddenly started shaking uncontrollably. Her parents did not know what was happening as they tried to control her thrashing arms and legs. Her jaws were clamped shut and her eyes were rolled back into her head. By the time they arrived at the hospital, Caroline had stopped convulsing and had passed out completely. From the description, Lisa believed that Caroline had had an epileptic seizure, but she waited to talk with the doctors before sharing her beliefs.

It did turn out to be epilepsy, and although the Scranton's were relieved that Caroline was not going to die, they had no idea what epilepsy was or what was involved in caring for it. Lisa briefly educated them about epilepsy, which would be classified as a developmental disability if Caroline continues to be plagued by a serious, disabling form of the disease. However, Lisa knew that the family needed more than her brief description, so she got them involved in the hospital support group for parents of children with developmental disabilities, including epilepsy.

In the meantime, Lisa continued to assist the family as Caroline was being monitored by various doctors who were attempting to determine the best type of medication to control Caroline's seizures without severe side effects. Although these tests were necessary, the Scrantons did not have much money, and what little insurance they had was used almost immediately. However, Lisa was able to help them obtain federal benefits under the Supplemental Security Income program. Lisa also referred the family to the state agency responsible for administering the Developmental Disabilities Assistance and Bill of Rights Act of 1990 to determine the services for which they would be eligible and how they could access them.

After Caroline's medication was stabilized she returned to school. Lisa then coordinated a meeting with Caroline, her teachers, and her parents to discuss the best way to help Caroline take her medication and handle her classmates' questions about her condition. In addition, the teachers agreed to work with Caroline if she had to miss any days of school for medical reasons.

In her work with the Scranton family, Lisa used a crisis intervention framework. The functions of assessment, diagnosis, and identification were carried out to determine the psychosocial issues that needed to be addressed. In addition, Lisa offered support and counseling and she worked with the Scrantons to enable them to access community resources and benefits. Lisa engaged in the social work function of referral when she helped the family access the parental support group. She also engaged in coordination and consultation in her interactions with the interdisciplinary team at the hospital and with Caroline's teachers.

Social workers in the field of developmental disabilities confront various issues depending on the type and etiology of the disability as well as the environmental circumstances of the affected family. Therefore, social work functions ranging from assessment and diagnosis, to referral and coordination, to planning and program development are needed to provide a complete system of service delivery.

References

Barker, R. L. (1995). *Social work dictionary* (3rd ed.). Washington, DC: NASW Press.

Developmental Disabilities Assistance and Bill of Rights Act of 1990, P.L. 101-496, 104 Stat. 1191.

DeWeaver, K. L. (1995). Developmental disabilities: Definitions and policies. In R. L. Edwards (Ed.-in-Chief), *Encyclopedia of social work* (19th ed., Vol. 1, pp. 712–720). Washington, DC: NASW Press.

Freedman, R. I. (1995). Developmental disabilities: Direct practice. In R. L. Edwards (Ed.-in-Chief), *Encyclopedia of social work* (19th ed., Vol. 1, pp. 721–729). Washington, DC: NASW Press.

McDonald-Wikler, L. (1987). Disabilities: Developmental. In A. Minahan (Ed.-in-Chief), *Encyclopedia of social work* (18th ed., Vol. 1, pp. 422–434). Silver Spring, MD: National Association of Social Workers.

housing

Problems and Issues

In the past, home ownership was a safe investment, a tax shelter, and an opportunity to accumulate equity. A home was generally a protected asset and rarely depreciated in value. However, for many people today home ownership is not economically possible. Because of inflation and increasing housing prices coupled with a stagnant or decreasing median family income, many individuals and families simply cannot afford a down payment and regular mortgage payments or obtain necessary financing (Dluhy, 1987).

The Housing Act of 1949 had the lofty goal of providing a decent home and a suitable living environment for every American family (Karger & Stoesz, 1994). The Demonstration Cities and Metropolitan Development (Model Cities) Act of 1966 (P.L. 89-754) promised to "concentrate public and private resources in a comprehensive five-year attack on social, economic, and physical problems of slums and blighted neighborhoods" (quoted in Karger & Stoesz, 1994, p. 357). As housing issues became increasingly complex, a variety of public programs were developed and several studies were performed. These studies indicated that the least costly and most efficient form of assistance was a housing allowance that was paid directly to the low-income resident. This form of assistance would also allow the renter to have freedom of choice about where to live. In addition to direct assistance to occupants, other programs were developed to subsidize landlords and developers who agreed to serve low-income populations (Dluhy, 1987; Mulroy, 1995).

These programs and many others such as mortgage availability, urban renewal, neighborhood development, rent subsidies, neighborhood beautification, and various reinvestment strategies have been attempted throughout the years in an effort to encourage infusion of money into poorer neighborhoods. However, maintaining adequate and affordable housing in a safe and congenial environment remains illusive.

Often the issues raised under the heading of public housing really refer to social problems such as illegal drug trafficking, vandalism, violent crime, truancy, teen pregnancy, and a host of other problems plaguing the residents of urban low-income housing developments. The question becomes one of addressing the totality of these issues, not just revamping the physical facilities. If the array of human needs are not addressed within the neighborhood context, housing will remain unsafe and inadequate.

Linking services to residential neighborhoods has been identified as a realistic approach to overcoming identified barriers in the public housing environment. This is referred to as a neighborhood-based service model, and the structural context is the community. The "one-stop" service center is located in a housing project or multiple housing units as the primary site for the provision of a broad array of social and health services. Residents of that community dominate the planning and governance of such services. (Chaskin, 1992; United Way of America, 1990).

The importance of the neighborhood as the locus of the efforts to address specific social problems, such as the causes and consequences of poverty, has long been identified, but support of neighborhood programs has been sporadic and inconsistent. However, with a significant push from foundations, government has been reformulating how services should be delivered. The inescapable conclusion that people in need are unable to get the necessary services and supports to function independently has led the U.S. Department of Health and Human Services (DHHS) to identify the integration of services to families as a major program management direction. DHHS has also expanded the definition of service integration to encompass the goal of giving families greater choice and control in both identifying the specific social and economic opportunities they wish to pursue and defining the services that will be provided. Gerry and Certo (1992) listed several obstacles to effective services cited by DHHS:

- There is no single point of access at the community level.

- Individual agencies and programs fail to use a unified, interrelated, or holistic approach to meeting family needs.

- Administrative obstacles within programs make it difficult to deliver services effectively.

- There is no single point of accountability in the system.

One-stop service centers are predicated on the identified need for a systems approach to comprehensive programming, reflecting the understanding that the problems and potentials of people, families, and neighborhoods are interdependent and interrelated parts of a whole. In this view, comprehensive programs are "multi-faceted, holistic, integrated—not categorical—efforts" (Eisen, 1992, p. 1). A core element of this approach is that of community partnerships and collaboration; collaboration is the vehicle through which to achieve communitywide solutions.

Populations Served

Social workers who enter the field of housing have the task of helping the disadvantaged populations who need assistance in obtaining quality and affordable housing in the housing market (Dluhy, 1987). The disadvantaged groups most often faced with housing issues are quite diverse. The homeless population is one group that needs assistance because shelters provide temporary housing without long-term solutions (Mulroy, 1995). In addition, people who are mentally ill, developmentally disabled, or physically disabled and criminal offenders also need assistance in finding housing. Group homes are one solution, but many communities resist such homes because of fears of lowered property value and possible violence from the residents. As a result, a social worker may be involved in balancing the needs of the clients to live in the least restrictive setting with the fears and concerns of the community residents (Dluhy, 1987).

Racial and ethnic groups are another population group that often needs assistance. Although all races have made progress toward home ownership since the 1920s, white people are still more likely to own a home than black or Hispanic people. As a result, racial and ethnic groups are overrepresented in public or subsidized housing (Mulroy, 1995).

As the baby boom generation ages, the elderly population living alone faces many housing concerns. Age, impaired health, and isolation all contribute to the older citizen's need for a wide range of services to remain at home rather than in an institution. Services such as home health care, homemaking, chore services, and transportation are often needed (Dluhy, 1987).

In addition to the growth in the elderly population, demographic analyses indicate a tremendous increase in female-headed households and a decrease in the number of households with married couples (Dluhy, 1987). Higher-income married households are much more likely to move from renting to buying a home. Furthermore, never-married, separated, divorced, or widowed households are more likely to move from home ownership to renting (Dluhy, 1987).

Social Work Roles

Social workers in the field of housing have an opportunity to engage in a variety of social work functions and are limited only by their own creativity. Social workers must support public policies that improve the condition of low-income households, especially those populations previously discussed. They must also continue to organize neighborhood residents; provide counseling and relocation assistance; coordinate tenant–landlord relations; plan for social services to assist neighborhood residents; and help neighborhoods, communities, and cities develop realistic housing assistance programs. In addition, social workers need to use their referral skills to provide links with other resources. Finally, social workers must be political advocates for these and other disadvantaged populations (Dluhy, 1987).

Over the years, federal housing developments have retreated and local governments and private foundations have begun to provide housing services to low-income populations. As the emphasis shifts to home ownership rather than rental of public project dwellings, private nonprofit organizations have begun to purchase housing units, renovate them, and then sell them at lower interest rates, with assistance from local governments who provide tax breaks (Bloom,

1990). The following case scenario gives an example of the many opportunities for social workers in such an environment.

Revitalizing a Housing Project

Longwood Apartments is a public housing project in a densely populated city that faces a range of housing and social services issues. A multifaceted strategy is needed to improve conditions at Longwood, and it is just such an approach that the Community Preservation Development Corporation (CPDC) advocates. CPDC is a private nonprofit organization that, in partnership with the U.S. Department of Housing and Urban Development (HUD), CPDC has purchased the Longwood Apartments with the goal of renovating the facility to improve the living environment for the residents. Janelle Baker is a social worker and is director of program development for CPDC. Her role is to determine and pursue the most effective and efficient way to improve the project.

As Janelle begins to research the housing environment, she finds that, according to HUD standardized measures, public housing in this city is considered the worst in the nation. However, for the residents of the Longwood Apartments, like so many other public housing projects, housing represents only a piece of the problem.

Longwood was designed and built in 1966. At that time, the city's housing authority was scheduled to purchase 250 units immediately, and the housing authority could lease about half of the remaining units for rentals as public or assisted housing. The purpose of this plan was to ensure both racial and economic integration. By the early 1970s residents had begun to move in, and the complex was well maintained and safe. However, by 1978, Longwood was a facility in a deteriorating area of the city. Economic stagnation and decline in the surrounding area became a real issue and a source of tension between residents of different economic status. In 1981 two different attempts were made to bring in businesses to the area in an effort to revitalize the community. However, both attempts met with community resistance.

Janelle is aware of the history of the development and past attempts to improve the facility. She decides that her first step should be a needs assessment. Janelle gathers a group of 25 key informants who are local services providers in areas such as schools, retention centers, health clinics, day care facilities, welfare offices, and drug rehabilitation facilities. Using a survey-type questionnaire, Jamie gathers information from these key informants regarding needed services. The identified areas include education, such as tutoring and dropout prevention; substance abuse, such as drug education and prevention and alcohol treatment services; safety issues, such as dark hallways and vandalism; and a need for recreational facilities and opportunities.

In addition to the key informant survey, Janelle also conducts a survey of residents of Longwood Apartments. Like the key informants, residents identify education services, safety needs, substance abuse services, and recreational facilities as needed services in the community. In subsequent meetings with the residents and service providers, Janelle concludes that the concept of "one-stop" services seems particularly suited to this situation. Furthermore, Janelle notes a 1990 United Way study that found that this method of delivering services to a specific population serves to maximize service effectiveness while minimizing the red tape of a disconnected bureaucracy. Because all of the services are coordinated in one physical setting or may even be under one organizational auspice, duplication of services is eliminated. Within this environment, individuals and families receive only those services they need and are not denied any services they seek (United Way of America, 1990).

Janelle decides to develop a grant proposal to seek funding to develop a neighborhood service center in the Longwood community. After obtaining input from the residents, Janelle develops goals and objectives and a rationale for the proposal using the information gathered earlier. She then cites examples of other similar successful projects piloted in other communities. Throughout the proposal, Janelle reiterates the need for resident participation in defining community needs and planning strategies to meet these needs. In addition, Janelle suggests that one-stop services should at least include the following elements: tutoring, employment training and placement, counseling, family planning, pre- and postnatal care, parent education, health services, day care, mentoring, drug and alcohol services, and recreation.

Janelle identifies the high possibility of success for a neighborhood service center in the Longwood community because there are already a number of public and private agencies on the premises. These agencies include an income maintenance satellite office; the Mayor's Empowerment Program Office, which helps residents obtain services; Project Care, which provides health care to area residents; and Mason House, which provides various social services. However, the service providers are currently spread throughout the complex, and many residents are not aware that these services are available to them on-site.

Janelle explains in the grant proposal that an additional resource for Longwood Apartments is that of space within the nearby central plaza area. The unused space would be ideal for locating one-stop service providers. After completing her grant request and discussing some last-minute issues with the resident leadership council, Janelle submits the proposal to the city and awaits word of acceptance.

In this scenario, Janelle engaged in many different social work functions spanning both the micro and the macro arenas. First she engaged in assessment and identification to determine problem areas confronting residents of the Longwood community. She also engaged in enabling and empowering as she helped residents obtain the necessary services and engaged them in the planning and decision-making process. In helping residents access services, Janelle used sound referral practices. Furthermore, she organized and mobilized the residents to identify problem areas that need to be addressed. Janelle then engaged in program development, coordination, and consultation as she surveyed both residents and key informants to complete a needs assessment. Finally, in preparing the grant proposal, Janelle carried out the social work function of planning to determine methods of fulfilling the stated goals and objectives.

Although this case study took place in an urban area where most deteriorating projects are located, housing issues are increasingly plaguing rural areas. An analysis conducted by the Center on Budget and Policy Priorities and the Housing Assistance Council indicated that three out of four rural households pay more for housing than the "maximum affordable amount." HUD has set a standard that housing costs, including rent or mortgage payments plus utilities, are outside the affordable range if they consume more than 30 percent of the household's income ("Study Eyes Housing-Shortage Crisis," 1990). In 1985, the report found that 42 percent of rural poor people spent at least half their income on housing and 26 percent of them spent 70 percent or more of their income on housing ("Study Eyes Housing-Shortage Crisis," 1990). These extreme costs for housing leave these households vulnerable to an economic crisis.

The report also indicated that, as in metropolitan areas, rural black people are more likely than rural white people to live in substandard housing. Furthermore, housing problems appeared to be worse in the South, where more than half of all units showed one or more of the following conditions: evidence of rats, inadequate waste disposal, holes in floors, inadequate heating equipment, cracks in walls, and inadequate water supply. To compound the problem, government assistance through subsidized housing is not available in most rural areas; therefore, major changes in policy and in private sector involvement are needed to improve the rapidly deteriorating rural housing situation ("Study Eyes Housing-Shortage Crisis," 1990).

Social workers entering the field of housing services will be confronted with a range of needs and will need to engage in both direct service and program planning and advocacy functions. Regardless of where they are, whether in an urban or rural environment or in a public or private agency, the need for social workers is great and the opportunities are plentiful.

References

Bloom M. (1990). *Introduction to the drama of social work*. Itasca, IL: F. E. Peacock.

Chaskin, R. J. (1992). *The Ford Foundation's neighborhood and family initiative: Toward a model of comprehensive, neighborhood-based development*. Chicago: Chapin Hill Center for Children, University of Chicago.

Demonstration Cities and Metropolitan Development Act of 1966, P.L. 89-754, 80 Stat. 1255.

Dluhy, M. J. (1987). Housing. In A. Minahan (Ed.-in-Chief), *Encyclopedia of social work* (18th ed., Vol. 1, pp. 821–835). Silver Spring, MD: National Association of Social Workers.

Eisen, A. (1992). *A report on foundations' support for comprehensive neighborhood-based community-empowered initiatives*. New York: New York Community Trust.

Gerry, M. H., & Certo, N. J. (1992). Current activity at the federal level and the need for service integration. In R. E. Behrman (Ed.), *The future of children* (pp. 118–126). Los Altos, CA: Center for the Future of Children, The David and Lucille Packard Foundation.

Karger, H. W., & Stoesz, D. (1994). *American social welfare policy: A pluralistic approach.* New York: Longman.

Mulroy, E. A. (1995). Housing. In R. L. Edwards (Ed.-in-Chief), *Encyclopedia of social work* (19th ed., Vol. 2, pp. 1377–1384). Washington, DC: NASW Press.

Study eyes housing-shortage crisis. (1990, June). *NASW News*, p. 13.

United Way of America. (1990). *"Wrap-around" services for high-risk children and their families: Responding to a national crisis.* Alexandria, VA: Author.

international social work

Who can forget the picture images of the carnage in Bosnia-Herzogovina and the seemingly endless line of Somalian families fleeing their country across the boarder by foot? As we watch these events live on television, we have proof that there are no longer any real geographic boundaries in the world. Isolationism is no longer desirable, even if it were possible (Battle, 1992). Interdependence now describes the social world, and many health and welfare problems know no boundaries. Examples of health and welfare conditions that are international in scope include AIDS and the resettlement of refugees. Cooperation and interaction among countries is essential to address these worldwide problems (Hokenstad, Khinduka, & Midgley, 1992).

International social work focuses on the practice of social work in different parts of the world—the role social workers perform, the practice methods used, and the problems addressed. The term may also apply to the practice of social work in international agencies or programs (Hokenstad, Khinduka, & Midgley, 1992). Social workers in the United States, for example, may be employed by the United Nations and its affiliates, such as the World Health Organization; international voluntary agencies such as the Red Cross; national voluntary agencies that work with or in different countries, such as Catholic Relief Services; or government agencies, such as the Peace Corps, the U.S. International Development Cooperation Agency, and the U.S. Information Agency (Healy, 1995).

Only a small proportion of social workers are employed in jobs that relate to international issues. NASW did not list international social work as a separate primary practice, primary setting, or primary auspice category, so estimates of the number of social workers engaged in this practice area are not readily available. However, in 1991, only 0.2 percent of NASW members indicated a primary practice area of "other," the category that can be assumed to encompass international work (Gibelman & Schervish, 1993). A caveat is that those social workers engaged in international social work may list their practice area as, for example, health or family services.

Some schools of social work have begun to include courses that contain international content, and there is a burgeoning social work literature on international issues and practice (Midgley, 1995). The University of Pennsylvania School of Social Work recently introduced a specialization in international social work, and Columbia University School of Social Work is planning to offer one (Eileen Kelly, Director of International Affairs, personal communicaton, August 30, 1995). International professional associations, notably the International Federation of Social Workers and the International Association of Schools of Social Work, engage in efforts to encourage the involvement of social workers in international practice (Hokenstad, Khinduka, & Midgley, 1992). The leadership of both the U.S. Committee of the International Council on Social Welfare, a worldwide organization of policymakers, and the Interuniversity Consortium on International Social Welfare is largely composed of social workers (Eileen Kelly, Director of International Affairs, personal communication, August 30, 1995).

International social work does not refer to any one type of service or intervention, and social workers involved in this area of service may work in many different settings. For example, social workers may deliver direct services as part of a refugee program, facilitate intercountry adoptions, or carry out disaster relief efforts in countries hit by a natural disaster. Some international work takes place primarily within the United States, such as refugee resettlement; other practice takes place "on-site" in nations around the world working through international agencies, such as the United Nations and its International Children's Emergency Fund, the World Health Organization, or the International Red Cross.

As in other areas of service, social workers in international practice help develop service delivery systems, plan and manage programs, deliver and evaluate direct services, and address the myriad individual and social problems that affect people worldwide. Child custody battles involving parents from different countries and international adoption continue to require social work intervention. Many large corporations operating internationally are hiring social workers to staff their employee assistance programs. The opportunities for international social work practice are expanding.

Another part of international social work involves advancing the efforts of developing countries in regard to social welfare policy, instituting voluntary agencies, and providing technical assistance and research and information exchange. Social workers in the United States also offer their expertise to assist newly democratized countries establish social welfare systems and develop educational programs to train social workers. Here, examples include the assistance provided by social work faculty at the University of Connecticut's School of Social Work to a university in Armenia to establish a social work program. Six social workers attended a conference held by the Soviet National Academy for Social Pedagogy and Social Work to review experimental community projects and explore the development of social services and social work. Another group of U.S. social workers joined their counterparts in Russia at a seminar to train people in family therapy and work with organizations (Hiratsuka, 1991).

In recent years, interest in international social work among Americans has been on the upswing. In 1989 NASW established the Office of Peace and International Affairs to respond to the growing number of social workers involved in international exchange, consultation, and education. NASW received funding from the U.S. Agency for International Development to educate social workers about the relevance of international development to the everyday concerns of social workers and to train and provide technical assistance related to the development of the social work profession in former Soviet countries (Eileen Kelly, Director of International Affairs, personal communication, August 30, 1995). This "Global Family Ties Initiative" emphasized how poverty, child welfare, health, hunger, AIDS, and other social problems in developing countries affect American families and how U.S. policies, in turn, affect life in developing countries ("A.I.D. Grant," 1991). The NASW effort focused on training development–education specialists in selected states to use the news media to disseminate the message of global interdependence.

In July 1992, NASW and the International Federation of Social Workers cohosted World Assembly in Washington, DC, a conference cosponsored by six organizations from around the world (Battle, 1992). In addition, the membership of NASW was represented at the Fourth World Conference on Women in Beijing, China, in summer 1995.

The interests of social workers in international social work are represented through NASW's International Committee and the 15 state-based international committees of NASW chapters. The efforts of these committees are visible in the conduct of three national public information campaigns about international issues; in the publication of materials on international social work; and in the dissemination of information on innovative international programs and practice that might be adapted in the United States (Eileen Kelley, Director of International Affairs, personal comunication, August 30, 1995). The Council on Social Work Education also has an active international commission that seeks to improve social work education around the world.

In 1991 NASW reported that involvement of social workers in international activities was steadily increasing. Efforts cited include the work of Phillip "Skip" Kindy to resettle 100 Tibetans in the Madison, Wisconsin, area. A program called Project Kesher, based in Evanston, Illinois, and directed by social worker Sallie Gratch, provides assistance to Jews in the former Soviet Union republics as they work to maintain their culture and identity (Hiratsuka, 1991). These and other efforts by individual social workers, educational institutions, and agencies provide important links and practical assistance in developing social welfare services around the globe. At least 21 NASW chapters have initiated "twinning" projects with colleagues in developing countries to promote intercultural understanding and mutual learning ("International Efforts Up," 1991).

The level of international social work activity is likely to continue to increase with the growing realization that cooperation is needed to solve social problems affecting all people no matter where they live. In addition, there is recognition that migration patterns, which are changing the character of many nations and creating new social welfare issues, require cross-national solutions. Food, shelter, health care, and education needs worldwide also require global responses. Advances in communications technology mean increased opportunities for international activity and mutual problem solving and enhanced roles for social workers interested in international social work practice (Healy, 1995).

References

A.I.D. grant to assist "global family ties." (1991, October). *NASW News*, p. 4.

Battle, M. G. (1992). Foreword. In M. C. Hokenstad, S. K. Kinduka, & J. Midgley (Eds.), *Profiles in international social work* (pp. xiii–xiv). Washington, DC: NASW Press.

Gibelman, M., & Schervish, P. (1993). *Who we are: The social work labor force as reflected in the NASW membership*. Washington, DC: NASW Press.

Healy, L. M. (1995). International social welfare: Organizations and activities. In R.L. Edwards (Ed.-in-Chief). *Encyclopedia of social work* (19th ed., Vol. 2, pp. 1499–1510). Washington, DC: NASW Press.

Hiratsuka, J. (1991, November). Social work born in Soviets' motherland. *NASW News*, pp. 3, 5.

Hokenstad, M. C., Khinduka, S. K., & Midgley, J. (1992). The world of international social work. In M. C. Hokenstad, S. K. Khinduka, & J. Midgley, (Eds.), *Profiles in international social work* (pp. 1–11). Washington, DC: NASW Press.

International efforts up. (1991, October). *NASW News*, p. 4.

Midgley, J. (1995). International and comparative social welfare. In R. L. Edwards (Ed.-in-Chief), *Encyclopedia of social work* (19th ed., Vol. 2, pp. 1490–1499). Washington, DC: NASW Press.

public welfare

Public welfare as an area of practice is extremely broad, reflecting the fact that it represents the largest social welfare system in the United States. Ginsberg (1983) defined *public welfare* as "welfare that is organized, directed, and financed by government, rather than by voluntary contributions or activities" (p. 3). It includes programs of financial assistance, such as Aid to Families with Dependent Children, medical assistance (such as Medicaid), food stamps, and social services, a large portion of which are now purchased from private and other public providers of services (Ginsberg, 1983).

Twenty-five years ago, a discussion of social workers in public welfare would have occupied its own chapter. In the late 1960s and early 1970s, however, a number of factors coalesced to deprofessionalize public welfare functions. In part, this deprofessionalization resulted from the separation of income maintenance (cash assistance) and service provision mandated under the 1967 amendments to the Social Security Act. At about the same time, the declassification of social services positions was also occurring in public agencies throughout the country. The result was that those positions still designated as professional (requiring a BSW or MSW) tended to be within the "soft" services areas, such as child protective services or adoption. Positions related to income maintenance tended to be relegated to a new category of income maintenance workers and clerks, for whom professional qualifications were not required. Public welfare agencies, then, have focused extensively on their responsibilities to provide cash assistance to those who qualify, using nonprofessionals to make determinations of eligibility (Hagen & Wang, 1993).

In the 1960s, social workers headed most welfare departments (Snowden, 1987). But in the late 1960s and early 1970s, after public welfare costs had soared, management experts took over the stewardship of these agencies, believing that they were just another kind of business operation, like an insurance company or private business operation. These management experts didn't succeed either, according to the prevailing political definition of "success" (reducing welfare costs), and the next phase was to bring in public administrators whose expertise was in the business of government (Snowden, 1987).

As discussed in Part II, social workers still occupy positions in the child welfare system, including jobs associated with the planning and delivery of foster care, adoption, and child protection services but are far less represented in public assistance. In 1991 only 0.9 percent of responding NASW members indicated a primary area of practice in public assistance (Gibelman & Schervish, 1993). Roles include commissioners and directors of state and local departments, direct services providers, supervisors, research, training, hearing officers, fraud investigators, fiscal planners, and unit directors (Ginsberg, 1983). However, although "social work" is the most common profession among personnel in public welfare, most employees have not studied social work, nor do they hold a degree in this field (Ginsberg, 1983). The title of "social worker" may be bestowed on the basis of the position classification rather than the qualifications of those holding the position. Another view of the diminishing career opportunities for social workers in public welfare has been offered by Breslow (1993), who wrote that "social work became 'endangered' in public welfare not because social workers didn't want to work in welfare, but because welfare didn't want to hire social workers" (p. 503).

The "look" of public child welfare and public assistance offices seems to reflect their lack of status within state and local governments, perhaps a reflection of the lack of status afforded by citizens to this type of work. Some public offices have been called "downright dreadful" in appearance (Lewis, 1994), uninviting both to their clients and to their professional workforce.

The nature of the work in public welfare may also dissuade social workers from practicing in these settings. There has been an increased emphasis on the function of case management in the public sector. Welfare reform efforts have embraced the concept of case management as a means to tighten accountability and move clients through the service system. The premise is that the assignment of a caseworker or team of caseworkers to individuals and families will aid in coordinating the provision of all needed services to promote family growth and self-sufficiency (Harris, 1987).

However, in the words of a social worker holding the position of budget director for a state social services department, public welfare work is certainly diverse. Following is a description of one day in the social worker's schedule:

> Met with the youth parole and review board to mediate corrections/social service issues related to the lives of 3,000 children for whom my department has responsibility. Met with state legislators in a vain attempt to resolve an impasse resulting in two months' nonpayment of Medicaid bills. . . . Met with other department administrators on the final steps toward a substantial redirection in information systems. Met with state cabinet officials on economic projections and to present our projected welfare caseload estimates, which, as in any state, will drive the decisions with respect to all other state spending. Delivered a speech on national welfare before a statewide association vitally concerned with our role in national

issues. Met with our department's lawyers to try to convince them that we must participate in a national lawsuit on an issue so arcane even they don't understand it. And these are only the highlights. (Snowden, 1987, p. 4)

Dealing with the System on Behalf of a Client

Amy Holden is a supervisor in the Lakeland County Department of Public Assistance. She first came to the department as an eligibility worker 10 years ago. Through a scholarship program made available by the agency, she obtained her MSW four years ago and was quickly promoted to the position of supervisor. In this position, she supervises 25 eligibility workers.

The state in which Lakeland County is located recently applied for and received a waiver to implement a "two years and you're out" program for certain recipients of Aid to Families with Dependent Children (AFDC). Under this waiver program, mothers of children over the age of three are required to enroll in work training, a component of which includes placement in a job once the training is completed. If the recipient is not employed after two years, he or she becomes ineligible for AFDC.

Jennifer, who holds a BSW, is one of the eligibility workers Amy supervises. In a recent case conference, Jennifer told Amy about one of her clients, Ms. Allen, whose AFDC benefits were scheduled to be terminated next month. Ms. Allen is one of the successful graduates of the job training program. She has learned word processing and has recently been offered a job. However, in her last visit with her, Jennifer learned of the Ms. Allen's concerns about her financial situation; she had figured out that her financial situation would actually worsen once she started working because she would no longer be eligible for food stamps and Medicaid, and the subsidy she would receive for child care still required a copayment. As a new employee earning the minimum wage, Ms. Allen would not be eligible for the company's health insurance benefits for six months. She would thus either have to pay for any medical expenses for her three children or purchase private health insurance. With rent, utilities, transportation, food, and clothing expenses, Ms. Allen simply did not know how she could do it.

Jennifer agreed with Ms. Allen's assessment of the pending financial situation. She asked Amy about the possibility of obtaining an exception for Ms. Allen, whereby her Medicaid and food stamp benefits would continue for the first six months of her employment. Amy knows that exceptions are not often granted, but she feels that Ms. Allen's case warrants intervention. Amy wrote a memo to the department's commissioner asking for the waiver. She indicated the merits of the situation and the need for a timely decision before benefits are terminated. Once Ms. Allen is terminated from benefits, it would take a lot of time and paperwork to get her back on should the exception be granted.

Three weeks have gone by and Amy has not heard from the commissioner. She prepared another memo, again urging that the exception be granted. A copy of the original memo was attached. Ms. Allen's benefits were scheduled to be terminated the following week.

Working in a bureaucracy can be frustrating. The waiver program is intended to save the state money by getting people off the welfare rolls as quickly as possible. Although the workfare component of the program has merit, most recipients get jobs that initially pay only the minimum wage or a little more, often equal to less than they received on AFDC when food stamps, Medicaid, and child care benefits are considered.

Jennifer determined that the waiver program rules created a barrier to her client's financial independence, an assessment with which Amy agreed. Both Amy and Jennifer engaged in advocating for the client to obtain an exception to the rules. Advocacy is targeted to the specific situation of the client, but has policy implications for others who may be in similar circumstances now or in the future. Amy carried out the function of mediating between the interests of the client and the administrator of the department who is responsible for granting any exception. Her negotiating position, however, was stymied, at least for the moment, by the failure of the commissioner to respond in a timely way. Amy continued her advocacy role by preparing a follow-up memo, while Jennifer continued to work with Ms. Allen on budgeting and self-sufficiency issues, and together they explored community resources.

References

Breslow, D. B. (1993). Welfare doesn't want social workers [letters]. *Social Work*, *38*, 503.

Gibelman, M., & Schervish, P. H. (1993). *Who we are: The social work labor force as reflected in the NASW membership*. Washington, DC: NASW Press.

Ginsberg, L. H. (1983). *The practice of social work in public welfare*. New York: Free Press.

Hagen, J. L., & Wang, L. (1993). Roles and functions of public welfare workers. *Administration in Social Work, 17*, 81–103.

Harris, D. V. (1987, April). Case management is gaining popularity in the public sector. *NASW News*, p. 2.

Lewis, R. K. (1994, September 17). Government workplaces often lack aesthetic appeal of private businesses. *Washington Post*, pp. F1, F12.

Snowden, J. M. (1987, November). Former caseworker reflects on first job. *NASW News*, p. 4.

career
opportunities

Assistant Director

Statewide, growth-oriented, nonprofit corporation providing services/advocacy to people with disabilities, seeks to fill a new position of assistant director. The corporation stresses quality services, revenue growth, board/membership sensitivity, and strong business approach to liability, financial, and general management issues. Successful candidate will have strong organizational, financial, and interpersonal skills and program experience.

Community Resource Consultant

Challenging opportunity for individual experienced in human services program administration/development to represent the office of mental retardation services in the provision of community Medicaid services within a comprehensive mental retardation delivery system. The selected candidate will provide assistance to local community service boards and service provider agencies in developing programs to address the needs of people with developmental disabilities; monitor, review, and evaluate services delivered to specific individuals; assist in program planning; and provide community services to people with severe disabilities through Medicaid State Plan Option and Community Based Waiver funding. Qualifications: Familiarity with human services, working knowledge of the field of mental retardation/developmental disabilities and the resources, programs, and logistics needed to deliver person-centered services to consumers; demonstrated ability to work independently and make decisions about the need, appropriateness, and efficacy of services specific to individual needs; ability to interpret state and federal regulations and communicate effectively with local, state, and federal officials and consumers; ability to use computer software programs and analyze data. Degree in human services or related field preferred.

Community Services Specialist

Opportunity for experienced professional to work in department of housing/ human services. You will provide intake and referral services for various groups of clients; housing counseling and tenant/landlord informational outreach services to groups in the community; administrative and special project assistance. Must have Spanish fluency; familiarity with Latino culture; experience working with diverse clientele. Required: degree in social work plus excellent verbal communication skills in both languages.

Coordinator, Parent Education Infant Development Program
Coordinates, manages, provides direct early intervention services to developmentally delayed and/or physically handicapped infants (age birth to $2^{1}/_{2}$) and related parental educational services at Community Services Board and surrounding counties. Responsibilities: program coordination and administration, transdisciplinary team assessments; staff supervision; direct services. Qualifications: Advanced knowledge of infant/child development, associated abnormalities, treatment interventions, knowledge of P.L. 99-457, experience with early intervention and transdisciplinary service delivery, treatment precautions related to medical condition.

Correctional Social Work
Due to a rapidly expanding organization, there are several highly responsible correctional clinical social work positions available within our mental health and social work services branch at various adult correctional facilities statewide. Services will be provided to offenders who are experiencing problems of a personal, social, emotional, family, addictions, or adjustment nature. Varied programming will be focused toward general counseling services, alcohol and drug abuse services, services to younger offenders, services to long-term offenders, personal growth and development workshops, clinical services to sex offenders, mental health–related services, and institutional prerelease services. Desire mature, creative, enthusiastic, and skilled individuals. Excellent clinical and administrative career potential. Position minimally requires an MSW and one year of social work experience.

Criminal Justice/Substance Abuse Treatment Specialist
Professional services firm has an immediate opening for a criminal justice/substance abuse treatment specialist. The successful candidate will provide leadership in developing strategic approaches to delivering technical assistance and organizational linkages among the state's substance abuse treatment systems, criminal/juvenile justice systems, and the public health systems. Responsible for new business development in the criminal justice/substance abuse treatment areas. Master's degree preferred; seven or more years' experience managing and delivering criminal justice/substance abuse treatment projects. Strong group facilitation experience needed. Excellent report writing skills and oral presentation skills.

Director, Vocational Services
Seeking an experienced human services professional to manage a comprehensive vocational division consisting of assessment, training, and employment of

individuals with disabilities. This is a key management position that will be responsible for program development, quality assurance and program evaluation, budget management, staff supervision and development, division marketing efforts, as well as ensuring compliance with various regulatory bodies. Requirements: a master's degree from an accredited college or university with emphasis in rehabilitation or a human services–related field, plus three years' experience in a rehabilitation setting. Supervisory/administrative experience required.

Eligibility Worker
Interview individuals and families to determine their eligibility for public assistance programs, such as Aid to Families with Dependent Children, Medicaid, and food stamps. Secure necessary information and make recommendations in accordance with policies and procedures regarding eligibility for assistance. Prepare reports and maintain case records. Requirements include a GED issued by a state department of education plus four years of related employment or college graduation. Prefer degree in sociology, social work, public administration, business, or related field.

Management, Gun Violence Prevention
Leading gun violence prevention organization seeks creative, highly experienced professional to manage innovative national youth program. Minimum requirements include a master's degree, five years' experience developing youth programs and curricula, staff supervision, and success creating and leading public service projects. Fluency in Spanish a plus.

Mental Health/Intensive Probation Counselor
Provide intensive probation supervision and counseling as part of youth and family services team to high-risk delinquent youths placed on probation. Incumbent develops service plans, documents progress, provides data/reports, and coordinates services provided to youths through other agencies, that is, schools, counselors, employers, vocational rehabilitation/job corps. Position requires knowledge of the juvenile criminal justice system; child/adolescent growth and development; ability to maintain effective working relations with clients, treatment personnel, community agencies, and others; ability to maximize the potential for positive behavioral change while maintaining the authority and integrity of the court. Relevant bachelor's degree preferred. Must be available to respond to emergencies 24 hours a day.

Project Director
Nation's leading nonprofit crime prevention agency specializing in crime prevention, youth service, and community development seeks experienced person to direct exciting new project that combines successful youth–community service program with public housing communities. Individuals must have initiative and ability to work autonomously; excellent management and supervisory skills; ability to relate well to young people; adaptability to different

environments; sensitivity to ethnically and culturally diverse people; and desire to work with growing socially responsible organization focused on social justice. Qualifications include five years in management position; two to five years' experience with design and delivery of training and technical assistance. Experience with public housing community; working with youth programs.

Social Work Consultant
Licensed, certified social worker needed to provide services to developmentally disabled people. Experience in working with SSI/Medicaid funding, training staff, writing goals and objectives, and working with teenagers.

Vocational Specialist
Full-time position to manage a day program for adults with severe disabilities. Develop curricula for systematic instruction of clients in personal care, daily living, and other activities. Coordinate community access, events. Supervise four staff. BA degree required, plus two or more years of experience working with individuals with disabilities in an educational or day program setting. Prefer bilingual (Spanish–English) or sign language fluency.

macro practice

introduction
to part VIII

Because the social work functions of social planning, community organization, and advocacy span all areas of practice, I have devoted a separate chapter to them. The proportion of social workers engaged in "macro" social work—interventions with larger systems to effect change in those agencies designed to serve people, communities, and society—is relatively small, but these activities constitute an important component of the profession's history and mission. Macro practice has also been referred to as *indirect social work practice*: "those professional social work activities, such as administration, research, policy development, and education, that do not involve immediate or personal contact with the clients being served. Indirect practice makes direct practice possible and more efficient; as such it is considered essential and of equal importance to the mission of the profession" (Barker, 1995, p. 185).

Netting, Kettner, and McMurtry (1993) defined *macro practice* as

> professionally directed intervention designed to bring about planned change in organizations and communities. Macro practice, as all social work practice, is built on theoretical foundations, proceeds within the framework of a practice model, and operates within the boundaries of professional values and ethics. Typically, macro social workers occupy positions in social agencies and are involved in the agency's functioning. The unifying concern of macro workers is how the agency relates to its environment and the forces that shape that environment. (pp. 3–4)

Gibelman and Schervish (1993) found that policy, consultation, research, and planning functions combined were primary practice areas of only 2.7 percent of NASW members in 1991 and 3 percent in 1988. Specialists in community organization and planning are disproportionately those who have doctoral degrees. The ratio of men to women working in community organization and planning is also higher than it is in the NASW membership as a whole; 39 percent of the labor force in this area of practice are men, whereas 22.7 percent of the NASW members in 1991 were men (Gibelman & Schervish, 1993). These same trends are manifest for those social workers engaged in policy, consultation, and research functions—they are concentrated at the DSW–PhD level, and there are disproportionately more men.

The involvement of social workers in macro practice has waxed and waned throughout the profession's history. Policy practice, including legislative advocacy, social action, and social policy analysis, has been called the "neglected side of social work intervention" (Figueira-McDonough, 1993, p. 179). Mobilization for macro interventions tends to occur when there is an impetus from external events—for example, when the government offers program and financial incentives for macro practice, such as during the War on Poverty, or there is a perceived assault on social programs, such as during the Reagan Administration. A more recent example is when the Republicans gained control of Congress in 1995 and promised substantial changes that are antithetical to the values and interests of the social welfare community. At such times, social workers seek to protect their own status and programs as well as the services and benefits received by their clients.

Conclusion

Although social work is often thought of as a predominantly clinical profession, the macro functions of social work are equally important. Administration, program development, supervision, policy analysis and development, planning, evaluation, community organization, and consultation are all means by which social workers can use their knowledge and skills to have a larger role in shaping the programs and policies that guide our nation's attitudes and actions toward the most vulnerable in our society.

References

Barker, R. L. (1995). Social work dictionary (3rd ed.). Washington, DC: NASW Press.

Figueira-McDonough, J. (1993). Policy practice: The neglected side of social work intervention. Social Work, 38, 179–188.

Gibelman, M., & Schervish, P. H. (1993). Who we are: The social work labor force as reflected in the NASW membership. Washington, DC: NASW Press.

Netting, F. E., Kettner, P. M., & McMurtry, S. L. (1993). Social work macro practice. New York: Longman.

advocacy

Advocacy refers to the act of directly representing or defending others and seeks to champion the rights of individual or communities through direct intervention or through empowerment. The *NASW Code of Ethics* (NASW, 1994) identifies advocacy as a basic obligation of the profession and its members.

Legislative advocacy activity is centered on influencing the course or content of a legislative or regulatory measure. Efforts can be targeted to preventing harmful government actions or initiating or expanding new legislation, and may occur directly by using specific legislative advocacy tactics or indirectly by mobilizing community groups (Barker, 1995). Advocacy can be undertaken by one agency or in concert with other individuals, organizations, or coalitions. Mickelson (1995) offered a more complete definition of *advocacy*: "In social work, advocacy can be defined as the act of directly representing, defending, intervening, supporting, or recommending a course of action on behalf of one or more individuals, groups, or communities, with the goal of securing or retaining social justice" (p. 95).

Advocacy has been a part of social work from the time of the charity movements in the 1870s and 1880s (Burghardt, 1987). Throughout the years, various skills have been identified as essential to the advocacy process. Several of these skills are presented below, along with the relevant social work function:

- *Data collection and research skills.* To effect change, advocates must gather facts and information about the issue that they wish to change. In addition, they must plan for future advocacy campaigns (Burghardt, 1987). The social work functions that correspond to these skills are policy analysis, policy advocacy, and planning.

- *Effective public relations and media skills.* Working with the press is extremely important in advocacy and involves writing press releases, organizing press conferences, and maintaining relationships with journalists and reporters (Burghardt, 1987). The corresponding social work functions are coordination and policy advocacy.

- *Knowledge of the legislative process.* Advocates must know how political forums operate, which subcommittees are important, and where decisions are made in a legislative body (Burghardt, 1987). The necessary social work functions include policy analysis, coordination, policy development, and policy advocacy.

- *Fundraising.* To run productive grassroots organizations, advocates must know how to write grant proposals, approach funding agents, and develop effective promotional efforts (Burghardt, 1987). The necessary social work functions include planning, review, and policy advocacy.

Effectiveness in social work practice means working with as well as for clients (Kinoy, 1984). Before any social work advocacy is attempted, it is essential to determine that the environment is obstructing a client's self-determination or causing a social injustice (Mickelson, 1995). Social workers are in a unique position to document and quantify human conditions, determine service needs of individuals and groups, and identify ways that community social welfare systems can be improved to better meet human needs. Front-line social workers count the people who arrive at soup kitchens and the people who are turned away from shelters because they are filled. This information can be provided to decision makers. Social workers also give voice to the human impact of fiscal cutbacks or the frustrations experienced by families who get the runaround from an agency.

Social work advocacy also includes helping organize and participate in community groups formed around a specific problem or issue, such as threats to close a senior citizens center or concerns about the potential impact of locating a homeless center in the community. Social workers can help such community groups make effective presentations and collaborate to develop their testimony (Kinoy, 1984).

Like the social work profession, advocacy can be defined as either micro or macro intervention. *Case advocacy* (micro level) is intervention with the client and his or her interaction with the environment, whereas *class advocacy* (macro level) refers to intervention to change the environment through social policy (Mickelson, 1995). However, the distinction between case and class can become blurred when working with a small group. Furthermore, it is not always obvious which type of advocacy to use when a decision made on behalf of an individual affects others (Sosin & Caulum, 1983). There are three levels of classification for advocacy: individual, administrative, and policy (Sosin & Caulum, 1983), and social workers must assess the situation and clarify the level of their advocacy interventions to determine the most effective strategies (Sosin & Caulum, 1983).

Regardless of the setting and the level of advocacy, social workers continually confront unmet needs, social problems and injustices, and barriers to service (Mickelson, 1995). Advocacy for and on behalf of clients is a function that runs through most social work practice, irrespective of practice or setting. A component of this function is client empowerment, although this component may be more highly embraced in theory than practice (Hartman, 1993). Indeed, there is a debate as to whether students in social work should necessarily be educated for social change (Abramovitz, 1993a, 1993b; Bardill, 1993a, 1993b). Advocacy may also take the form of political lobbying or employing organized demonstrations, as the vignettes below illustrate. In addition, policy analysis can also be seen as a form of advocacy, as such analyses are used to influence the dialogue about social policy issues, development, and impact.

There have been some real constraints on social work advocacy. For more than 50 years, the political activity of social workers working within the public sector has been restricted by federal and state laws governing political activity. On the federal level, the Hatch Act has prohibited substantial political involvement. The result has been a general passivity among social workers employed by the federal government in the areas of advocacy and social reform (Thompson, 1994). However, the Hatch Act and similar state laws have not precluded all advocacy, particularly at the case level, and social workers employed in the voluntary and proprietary sectors generally do not have such limitations imposed on them.

Professional and advocacy organizations at the national and state level, such as the National Association of Social Workers and its chapters and the Child Welfare League of America and Family Services America and their affiliates, include advocacy for the profession and the clientele it represents to be a prime focus of activity. However, the role, commitment, and legitimacy of most social workers in the political arena is less evident (Ewalt, 1994).

Also at issue in the practice of advocacy is the influence the social work agency maintains over the level of advocacy of the individual social worker. This issue has been succinctly summed up in the question "Does social work have a distinct expertise and frame of reference or are our expertise and professional role dictated and limited by the organization for which we work? Is the social work frame of reference something we follow in all settings or only when social workers are the primary professionals in the organizational setting?" (Ashford, Macht, & Mylym, 1987, p. 199).

Although advocacy is one of the centerpieces of the profession, it is not without its own ethical dilemmas. For example, self-determination is a key social work value. However, young children, some elderly people, emotionally disturbed clients, and people with developmental disabilities are often most in need of advocacy assistance and yet are unable to practice self-determination. In such cases social workers must assume the responsibility of deciding the best advocacy method (Mickelson, 1995).

As political and economic trends shift in the coming years, social workers must learn to effectively compete for public and legislative attention to be successful in long-term advocacy for social justice (Mickelson, 1995). To maintain their unique and influential role, social workers must continue to practice and coordinate advocacy efforts on both the macro and the micro level (Mickelson, 1995).

Lobbying

Either as individual citizens committed to social justice and social change, or as part of their job responsibilities, many social workers engage in lobbying at the local, state, or federal level. Representative Gary Ackerman (D-NY), in an NASW videotape *Lobbying Tips for Social Workers* (NASW, 1989) told social workers how to engage in this essential activity. According to Ackerman:

> Anybody who has an idea, anybody who has an opinion, anybody who will want to affect the way government performs, to change some of the laws and to make their feelings known, is a lobbyist. And each and every one of you should be seriously considering yourself lobbyists if you want to put in place the kind of changes that you feel are necessary, especially for your profession and for other things that you may find of importance. ("Techniques of Lobbying," 1989, p. 6)

The purpose of lobbying is to influence the opinion of decision makers. It can take many forms, including petitions, telegrams, telephone calls, and face-to-face meetings. Social workers are effective lobbyists because they can talk about issues from personal experience, and social workers' expertise in fact-finding, communicating, negotiating, and mediating can help national, state, and local leaders make important decisions.

Government Relations at NASW

[Note: This vignette describes an actual person who currently occupies the position discussed.]

Susan Hoechstetter is director of the government relations office at NASW's national office. Susan has worked at NASW for 11 years and has participated in the growth of this department (from one lobbyist to six) over the years.

Susan describes the dual agenda of NASW in government relations: to influence the social policy agenda in a manner consistent with the profession's commitment to vulnerable populations, and to protect and improve the status of the social work profession and its membership. This dual agenda, Susan notes, almost always overlaps in regard to the office's policy objectives. For example, efforts to improve access to health care services for poor people include attention to requirements that social workers be recognized as independent mental health providers in underserved areas.

Currently, the dual focus in regard to welfare reform is apparent in the efforts to maintain child welfare training and, concurrently, to promote the types of programs that will provide people with the supports they need to get jobs and to meet their basic needs. The objective is to balance efforts to promote the general welfare with a more specific focus on issues of concern to the social work profession.

The NASW lobbyists find themselves working differently in 1995 than in past years as the 104th Congress has been vigorously attacking social programs. In past years, NASW has focused on proactive legislative work, such as the association's initiative to draft a health care reform bill which was introduced by Senator Daniel K. Inouye (D-HI). NASW took a leadership role in the recent national health care reform policy debate. However, with the 104th Congress, NASW is focusing on protecting rather than advancing programs.

As the "Contract with America," the Republican's congressional platform, plays out on Capitol Hill, the staff of the NASW Government Relations Office have been monitoring developments daily and working to influence the final legislation. The work of the Republican-dominated Congress in regard to social welfare policy is on a fast track, with efforts to enact new policies and modify existing laws in ways often detrimental to social work and the populations it serves.

One example Susan cited is welfare reform and proposals to collapse existing federal programs, such as AFDC and Titles IV-B and IV-E of the Social Security Act, into block grants. For years, the child welfare training programs under these titles have provided financial support and incentives to train social workers for child welfare practice. Block grant programs would mean the elimination of federal protection for these programs through loss of entitlement status. States could opt to use their lump sum block grants for purposes they deem to be a priority, and a block grant program would likely mean a reduction of financial resources for benefits, service delivery, and child welfare training, areas already considered to be deficient in allocations.

The House of Representatives has already passed its version of welfare reform, which would turn over to the states primary control of welfare programs. This House bill includes five block grants that combine a vast array of federal programs ("House Gives States Welfare Control," 1995). The matter is currently under consideration by the Senate. NASW staff have been focusing their efforts on garnering congressional support to keep these titles separate federal programs ("Protection Urged," 1995). Thus far, in important Senate proposals, the child welfare titles have remained separate from block grant program proposals. But NASW staff learned, through informal discussions with Republican staffers that an amendment to collapse Titles IV-B and IV-E into the proposed block grant may be offered when welfare reform goes to the Senate floor for debate. Government relations' relationship-building efforts have paid off.

New developments emerge daily. With the new Congress, Susan and her staff have worked hard to form relationships with newly elected officials and congressional staff of both parties and to strengthen relationships with returning members who have new roles. In fact, Susan describes this relationship-building for networking purposes to be a major component of NASW's lobbying effort. Information gathering from congressional and other sources, particularly other national organizations, is an ongoing task.

The government relations staff use a number of strategies to influence the decision-making process. Staff frequently meet to discuss strategy in light of new information gathered. For example, one day Susan and her staff met twice to discuss strategies with Congress, including consideration of which senators to influence, what the message should be, when to bring in the NASW network, which senators to target for an NASW amendment, and how to get one Republican senator to write a letter to his colleagues about protecting the child welfare programs. The membership has already been activated in several ways. An *NASW News* article, "Child Welfare Block Grants Seen a Threat" (1995), urged social workers to inform senators about the importance of preserving the many child welfare programs that would be eliminated under the welfare reform bill based by the House of Representatives in March 1995.

Within NASW, Susan coordinates efforts with PACE staff to support decision makers who might be amenable to influencing their colleagues on the subject of welfare reform or who have stood up for an NASW position. Susan and her staff frequently attend political fundraising events to meet politicians. Member contacts are also used. For example, if a social worker in Kansas is known to have been active in campaigning for a senator from that state, or is in a key position with a legislative issue, when that member visits Washington, a meeting with the member, the senator, and NASW might be arranged. Face-to-face contact of constituents with members of Congress and lobbyists is an effective tool of influence (Richan, 1991).

Current efforts also focus on the appropriations process. As the Senate Finance Committee deals with the 1996 budget, budget cuts in child welfare, health care, and health professions training are being considered in an effort to reduce the deficit and curtail federal spending ("NASW Urges Hill," 1995).

Multiple strategies are implemented concurrently. Susan and her staff have just finished preparing a letter to the deans and directors of social work education programs regarding child welfare training programs. The goal is educate them about current developments and motivate them to write letters urging their legislators to keep the child welfare programs, including the training components of the Social Security Act, out of the block grant. The deans and directors were urged to call, fax, and write to legislators, and to do so quickly.

On the same day, Susan initiated a conference call with leaders of social work education organizations, such as the Council on Social Work Education and the National Association of Deans and Directors of Schools of Social Work. The purpose of the call was to share new information from Congress and to determine which senators should be the recipients of the organizations' lobbying activities. Susan feels that the combined impact of interorganizational collaboration is extremely important. When it is time to mobilize their constituencies, Susan and her colleagues will prepare materials to send to legislators. Part of the message must be to document the positive outcomes that have resulted from the child welfare training programs.

Susan and her staff also work on developing and refining position papers as changes in Congress occur. These papers are a form of policy analysis in which a position is taken on an issue—they are not value-free. They are intended to provide facts in such a way as to persuade, inform, and motivate. Each position statement is oriented toward a particular group, and facts and statistics are organized with that specific audience in mind.

Susan and her staff have a tall agenda. The functions they perform on any given day may vary but all relate to the goal of influencing the course of social policy development. A lot of time is spent in meetings, on the telephone, and writing letters and action alerts. Much time is also spent on Capitol Hill meeting with members of Congress or their staffs and then back in the NASW offices following up on these visits.

The social work functions involved in the lobbying process include monitoring the legislative process, information gathering and information dissemination, mobilizing the membership, working collaboratively with other national organizations on a shared agenda, preparing policy analysis and position statements, drafting legislative language, dealing with the media, visiting with congressional staff and others for face-to-face contacts, participating in coalition meetings, devising and redevising strategies in light of emerging developments, and preparing written materials that may be used to influence decision making. These tasks have taken on increased urgency with the swift-moving pace of the Republican Congress and the anti-social-welfare sentiments associated with many of the legislative proposals.

Susan has counterparts in other national organizations, such as the American Public Welfare Association and the Child Welfare League of America. In these national organizations and in state agencies that represent groups of agencies or individuals, social workers' interests are always kept in mind. Some practitioners may concentrate on one or two of the components of macro practice, where as others run the gamut.

A small proportion of social workers have a primary work function related to policy analysis, although a much larger number of social workers may conduct such analyses as a component of their job. Barker (1995) defined *policy analysis* as "systematic evaluations of a policy and the process by which it was formulated. Those who conduct such analyses consider whether the process and result were rational, clear, explicit, equitable, legal, politically feasible, compatible with social values, cost-effective, and superior to all the alternatives, in the short term and in the long run" (p. 285).

Many other social workers perform advocacy, lobbying, testifying, and mobilizing roles as a component of their job rather than the primary function. Clearly, in this sociopolitical environment, such functions have taken on renewed importance.

Policy and the Media

Negative public attitudes toward social welfare policy and programs in the United States suggest that social workers must constantly look for opportunities to engage in dialogue with relevant community groups. The shift in human services funding decisions from Capitol Hill to states and localities means that social workers can have an impact on the community decision-making agenda (Stoesz, 1993).

There are many ways that social workers can influence human services decisions. Writing op-ed pieces for the local newspaper is one way to communicate ideas about human needs and alternative ways of meeting them. Social workers can undertake this role at any level of practice, representing themselves as individuals or their agencies. Op-ed pieces offer an immediate response to a community problem to a wide audience. Photocopies of the op-ed pieces can be used by the agency to illustrate their concerns about and commitment to alleviating community problems (Stoesz, 1993).

Letters to the editor are another way to continue a dialogue begun in the press. For example, in response to an "indictment of social workers" by William Raspberry, a nationally syndicated columnist and commentator on social issues, NASW Executive Director Sheldon R. Goldstein (1993b) wrote a letter to the editor of the Washington Post:

"Indict the Social Helper"

William Raspberry's fingering social workers as the cause of the decline of city neighborhoods is spurious. . . . Gosh, if professional social workers had only stayed away, our cities wouldn't be in the mess they are in now.

Almost every aspect of social work practiced in community development is concerned with strengthening resources and empowering communities, especially leaders and programs that spring naturally from the neighborhood. There are clergy members in the District, for instance, who head large churches with excellent aid programs and would be surprised to hear that they had been displaced by the work of "certified experts."

There have been demonstrations and pilot programs sufficient to show that when people get education, training, job skills, employment, transportation, day care and opportunities, they fix their own problems.

Frustration often causes people to lash out a convenient target. So we have "shoot the messenger" (every journalist knows that one) and "blame the victim." Mr. Raspberry seems to have invented a new one: "Indict the helper." (p. A30)

This letter, in addition to responding directly to Mr. Raspberry, also serves to educate the public about what social workers do and current social issues.

An op-ed piece authored by NASW members Mimi Abramovitz and Frances Fox Piven, "Scapegoating Women on Welfare," was published in the *New York Times* on September 2, 1993. This article challenged proposals to force women to go to work and to "shape up" by reducing the welfare checks of mothers whose children are truant from school or who did not receive their health checkups or immunizations ("People in the News," 1993). Irwin Garfinkel, professor of social work at Columbia University, and coauthor Sara McLanahan, also contributed an op-ed piece to the *New York Times* in 1994 on welfare. Their article faulted those who "demonize single mothers and the institutions that help them" (quoted in "People in the News," 1994). They argued that welfare reform should include the requirement that government guarantee a minimum benefit and universal health care to all children and subsidized child care to all working parents, regardless of marital status.

As a class assignment, MSW student Jennifer Stallbaumer Rouyer (1994) responded to a *Washington Post* front page story about proposals to revive orphanages:

Families, Not Orphanages

I would like to clarify some possible misconceptions about the revival of orphanages ["As At-Risk Children Overwhelm Foster Care, Illinois Considers Orphanages," front page, March 1]. Charles Murray has such contempt for the welfare system that now he wants to eliminate welfare benefits to single mothers and use the money to take children from their "welfare-dependent biological mothers" and put them in institutions, excuse me, orphanages.

First, let us not mix entitlement programs. Government economic support to families, primarily through the Aid to Families with Dependent Children program, is not child welfare. AFDC is an income-support program that provides temporary assistance to legitimate families.

Child welfare services, on the other hand, are designed to protect children from abuse and neglect, improve opportunities for child development, help establish and fortify family structures and improve family functioning. While a family may participate simultaneously in both programs, AFDC and child welfare have separate and distinct goals—they are not interchangeable.

Second, most families want to care for their children, but not all families have the necessary skills and resources to do so effectively. Orphanages do not meet the intended goals of child welfare services. For vulnerable children, a placement in an orphanage ignites feelings of abandonment and confusion—experiences which make for a precarious beginning to child and adult development.

As for those of us social workers, child psychologists and others who "prattle" about keeping children with their biological families, we know what we are talking about. The biological family, be it biological mothers or fathers, is almost always the best place for a child to live. We know that the family is the best environment for the healthy growth and development of all children, bar none.

However, as was stated so eloquently in the article, "Not every home is the best place." When this is the case, the foster care system, while not perfect, provides a temporary family-type environment that is essential to a child's health and well-being. When the child cannot be reunited with the biological family, every effort is made to ensure a permanent adoption. The adoptive family serves as the best substitute for the biological family. An orphanage cannot provide the loving and supportive care that a human family environment will.

Ultimately, the best solution for children is to provide a comprehensive national policy that supports families, not be taking from the needy to give to the needy but by focusing on prevention and family support, which would help many children avoid entering the child welfare system in the first place.

The commitment of resources that builds upon family strengths and helps families who are in crisis would establish homes that provide an environment that is far better than any orphanage. (p. A22)

In this letter, the social worker provided concrete, factual information that corrects faulty statements; she argued a point of view that seeks to influence the opinion of others; she identified herself as a social worker and informed the public about a professional social worker's point of view; she identified social work as one of the disciplines concerned and knowledgeable about the welfare of children; and she offered specific suggestions about how improvements in the current situation can be brought about.

Demonstrations

One method of achieving social change is by organizing group action to call public or political attention to a problem or issue. Examples include organizing marches or sit-ins in highly visible settings or picketing the entrances of buildings. Social workers have long used confrontational methods to call attention to issues of social justice and social welfare. An example of such strategies follows.

Confrontational Techniques

Kettlebrook is a low-income housing project in Chicago. The complex has 25 separate housing units, but only 10 of them are still occupied. After the other 15 units were vacated, the landlord simply refused to rent them. The 10 remaining units are in complete disrepair: Neither the heat nor electricity works regularly, paint is peeling from the ceilings and walls, and termites have begun destroying the floors.

Kelsey Green is a social worker with the department of social services and she has a client who lives at Kettlebrook. Kelsey is disgusted at the deterioration of Kettlebrook, and she begins to talk and work with the tenants. They first attempt to meet with the landlord, but this fails to produce results. Kelsey then helps the tenants organize themselves.

The following week, all of the tenants gather to picket on the street in front of the landlord's home. The landlord never leaves his house and the tenants come back every day for a week. Kelsey arranges for the media to be present, and the press coverage brings the support of the surrounding community. Finally, the landlord agrees to have the necessary repairs made.

Social workers may be motivated to engage in macro-level interventions when they perceive a threat to themselves or those they represent. One tactic that has been employed is the job action, which includes workplace organizing, lobbying, education, protesting, and sometimes striking (Hiratsuka, 1992a).

There are no hard and fast rules concerning when to initiate a job action, but the time has come, in general, when a group of social workers identify conditions that endanger the lives of clients and employees or when it becomes impossible to provide quality services (Hiratsuka, 1992a). Sometimes services may be disrupted in the short run, but the intended outcome is long-term improvements, which are often the result of calling public attention to problems. In turn, pressure is brought on administrators or legislators to act.

Some social workers belong to unions, such as the American Federation of State, County and Municipal Employees (AFSCME). In 1992, social work members of District Council 1707 of the AFSCME staged part-day and full-day walkouts, held "work-ins" (during which they attended to paperwork but did not see clients), and picketed agency board meetings. Most job actions are held during contract negotiations. Issues may concern salaries, caseload size, supervisory issues, and worker safety.

Social workers in the public child welfare system in Washington, DC, frustrated by the failure to institute changes in the system despite a court ruling ordering massive improvements, stayed off the job for one day in February 1992. These social workers held a public vigil to bring attention to the issues of large caseloads, unfilled staff vacancies, and other conditions affecting their ability to adequately protect children (Hiratsuka, 1992a). In Los Angeles County, social workers have used demonstrations, workplace protests, and threats of a strike to gain limits on child welfare caseloads. Following their use of a variety of confrontational techniques, social workers in the county child welfare system obtained a "caseload cap" in their contract.

Community Organizing

Social work began in the communities with the goal of bridging the gap between an increasingly industrialized society and its citizens. Although the profession has gone through many different eras of change, it has never lost its community roots (Martinez-Brawley, 1995).

Community organization has been defined as "an intervention process used by social workers and other professionals to help individuals, groups, and collectives of people with common interests or from the same geographic areas to deal with social problems and to enhance social well-being through planned collective action" (Barker, 1995, p. 69). A social worker in community organization may assist a community group by acting as a facilitator to help the group recruit members, define problems, and develop advocacy strategies (Weil & Gamble, 1995). In addition, social workers are increasingly becoming mobilizers of community resources in an effort to meet local needs during times of scarcity (Martinez-Brawley, 1995).

The primary practice areas of community organizing and planning are largely held by members who received their highest social work degree during the 1960s and early 1970s. The high proportion of earlier graduates in community organization and planning is consistent with the tendency for social workers to move from direct practice to macro practice as their careers progress (Gibelman & Schervish, 1993).

During the 1960s, community organization was a more visible form of social work practice. Although community organization may have faded from the center spotlight, its methods have become more sophisticated in the ensuing years, new issues are being addressed, and a more diversified range of tactics are being employed (Hiratsuka, 1990b). Community organizing is often carried on outside the social work profession, but many social work activities still incorporate the principles and methods of community organization, including planning and implementing community-based services, networking, outreach, coalition building, and grant writing. Community organizing is evident in the efforts of social workers to bring people together to solve problems or improve services. They may occupy positions as social planners, grassroots program developers, or social activists (Hiratsuka, 1990b).

In the wake of the 1992 Los Angeles riots, social workers mobilized to help heal affected communities. The violence exploded after a jury acquitted four white police officers of nearly all charges in the beating of Rodney King, a black motorist (Hiratsuka, 1992b). Virtually the entire country had watched, countless times, the videotape of that beating and held strong opinions about it.

The University of California at Los Angeles School of Social Work, in conjunction with public television station KCET, initiated a call-in line staffed by social workers and other trained professionals on a volunteer basis for people seeking emotional support. The hot line took more than 2,000 calls during a 10-day period from Korean-, Spanish-, and English-speaking residents. The hot line was disbanded when the county community health department established its own hot line (Hiratsuka, 1992b).

Many social workers responded in the aftermath of the Los Angeles riots, visiting schools, disaster centers, and communities to provide crisis counseling; delivering food and clothing; and mediating ethnic tensions, racism, and bigotry. Attempting to soothe racial tensions, these social workers performed crisis counseling in affected neighborhoods. For instance, the Korean–American Social Workers' Association sent bilingual social workers into the hardest-hit areas to soothe racial tensions and minimize the violence.

Helping to Heal a Community

Leslie Dang, a 34-year-old Korean American social worker, works as a community outreach worker for the Los Amigos Multi-Cultural Service Center in Los Angeles. In the aftermath of the Los Angeles riots, Leslie and her colleagues visit the stricken area of the city and find themselves knee-deep in rubble and the ruins of peoples' businesses and lives. The primary questions she hears from members of the Asian American community are "Why me? Why us? Why do they (African Americans) hate us so much?" Her job, over the long run, is to work with community residents to answer and resolve these questions. The immediate agenda is to assess individual and family needs and link residents of the community with assistance in the form of housing, food, and clothing. Soon, there will be the need to help residents apply for business loans to rebuild their businesses, and to work with local banks and unaffected businesses to revitalize the community.

Leslie spends the first day on the streets, talking with residents and assessing the types of services they will need. She then returns to the office and begins the networking process of contacting community agencies to arrange for necessary services and to coordinate the efforts of the concerned neighborhood agencies.

Within the heart of the Asian community, Leslie organizes a "town meeting," encouraging everyone in the community to attend, not just the affected merchants. Three police officers, functioning as a crisis-response team, also attend in an attempt to reassure residents that the police will step up efforts to protect Asian American businesses should any more violence occur. The residents are angry; they want to know why the police did not do more. With Leslie's help facilitating the discussion, police are able to answer residents' questions and address their concerns.

Following the town meeting, Leslie invites social workers from the Association of Black Social Workers of Greater Los Angeles to attend a separate meeting. Out of this combined effort, participants shape a task force, which includes Asian American business owners, the three police officers, and leaders of the black community, as well as black, Asian American, and white social workers. The job of this task force is to open up channels of communications among the various ethnic communities in Los Angeles to facilitate a better understanding among people who need to live and work together. Regular meetings are scheduled, with the location of the meeting shifting from one ethnic community to another to allow everyone equal participation. Various city officials attend to show their concern and involvement in efforts to stem the rising tide of violence among divergent ethnic communities. Leslie acts as the facilitator during the formation of this task force, and she helps eligible residents obtain federal assistance.

Leslie also holds special group meetings for adolescents in the Asian American community in an attempt to minimize any organized, violent response. Leslie particularly reaches out to the Asian American gangs through her community connections and is successful in opening channels for dialogue with this volatile segment of her target population. Having established one task force, Leslie works with other social workers to address the adolescent population, including gang members. Although she helps initiate several programs, other social workers and civic leaders perform the necessary follow-up tasks. Through Leslie's efforts, a permanent coalition of ethnic leaders carries on the work of healing wounds and building networks in the stricken communities.

When she began her work in Los Angeles, Leslie engaged in the functions of assessment and identification to determine what problems needed to be addressed. She then used her information and referral skills to help needy residents access necessary services. Organization and coordination functions also were important in Leslie's efforts to facilitate communication among community groups. Communities are only one arena in which organizing skills are used. Others include unions, places of employment, and educational facilities.

Union Organizing

[Note: The information for this vignette is drawn from "Social Worker Helps Chavez with Boycott." (1987, March). *NASW News*, p. 12.]

Social worker Arturo Rodriguez is a long-time employee of the United Farmworkers, working with union president Cesar Chavez. He signed on with the UFW in 1973 when he graduated from the University of Michigan School of Social Work. In May 1993, he was named president of the union, succeeding Cesar Chavez who died earlier that year.

Earlier in his career, as mid-Atlantic director of the table-grape boycott and a member of the union's national board, Rodriguez used a variety of techniques to achieve the union's goals, including the application of social marketing techniques for social causes. Mr. Rodriguez says that his social work skills, including organizational skills, research, and ability to assess a community and target efforts, have served him well in his job.

The Grapes of Wrath campaign and table-grape boycott began in July 1984 and received more than 1,000 endorsements from politicians, labor leaders, and organizations. The campaign focused on free and fair organizing of elections, a ban on the use of specific pesticides that can cause cancer and birth defects, and the instituting of tests to determine pesticide residue on fruits and vegetables. Although union members engaged in picketing, this was only one of many strategies employed. The importance of augmenting direct confrontation techniques, such as picketing, with other strategies was accentuated by the conservative national mood.

In planning public education campaigns, Rodriguez targeted audiences that were likely to be sympathetic to the cause, such as labor, Chicanos and other racial and ethnic groups, and religious and academic communities. The campaign focused on the hazards to consumers as well as farmworkers, thus broadening its appeal to and participation of consumer and environmental groups. To raise funds and engage in public education strategies, Rodriguez has overseen the implementation of direct mail, films, sales, and other fundraising solicitation techniques.

Part of community organizing is to help communities help themselves. Here, the focus is on involving volunteers and other citizens in a community in decision making, human services planning, and coordinating with agencies and professionals. The process, according to Barker (1995), includes decentralizing responsibility and control from national, state, or local agencies to individuals and community groups. Methods used include identifying problem areas, analyzing causes, formulating plans, developing strategies, mobilizing necessary resources, identifying and recruiting community leaders, and encouraging interrelationships between them to facilitate their efforts.

Rothman, Erlich, and Tropman (1995) detailed three basic models of community intervention—locality development, social planning, and social action. Locality development attempts to correct a problematic situation or achieve social progress with the participation of the entire community. For effective locality development, social workers must perform needs assessments and research to determine realistic development goals (Weil & Gamble, 1995). Social planning usually addresses long-term goals of the community and emphasizes a technical process of problem solving for substantive social issues. At this level of community intervention, social workers must be able to identify necessary community resources and plan, manage, and negotiate to best achieve the desired social changes (Weil & Gamble, 1995). Finally, social action presupposes the existence of a disadvantaged segment of the population that must be organized to make demands on the larger community for fair and equal treatment. Social action practitioners frequently focus on challenging the existing power structures in society and exercise the functions of advocacy, education, and organizing (Martinez-Brawley, 1995; Rothman et al., 1995; Weil & Gamble, 1995).

Many social workers in this field today believe that the face of community organization has changed. They cite a pragmatic trend that emphasizes politics, consensus building, data collection and research, and the use of administrative channels. The confrontational tactics of the past may occasionally be used, but they are generally considered ineffective because administrators and officials have learned how to defuse them (Hiratsuka, 1990b).

Because of the individuality of communities, there is no one correct method of community organization. However, to meet the growing needs in areas of child welfare, youth services, and elder care, social workers in this field must be able to coordinate formal and informal systems of care in the community (Martinez-Brawley, 1995). Community organization work emphasizes the creation of an egalitarian environment where community services are as much a result of attitude as a collection of techniques. In working to organize formal and informal resources to achieve such a society, social workers must be able to effectively use the functions of advocacy and enabling as well as referral, planning, organizing, and coordination (Martinez-Brawley, 1995). As formal resources continue to diminish, social workers' ability to organize and mobilize community and informal resources will become increasingly important.

Perhaps one of the most important functions of social workers in this arena is that of mobilization and empowerment. "In mobilizing, people who have been disempowered and dispossessed begin to find their voices, to discover confidence, to feel that they actually have a chance of changing the conditions of their lives and communities" (Kahn, 1995, p. 571). Mobilization, although important, usually takes place as a means of attacking a specific problem or issue. However, organization is what is needed to sustain the community activism and involvement over time (Kahn, 1995). Social workers involved in community organization must be able to help people discover their own strengths so they may become self-sufficient. Si Kahn (1995), one of the most well-known and respected community organizers, explained the challenge facing social workers in this field: "To reach, teach, and organize people in ways that transform their understanding of power and their relationship to power—not just individually, but collectively" (Kahn, 1995, pp. 575–576).

References

Abramovitz, M. (1993a). Response to Dean Bardill. *Journal of Social Work Education, 29*, 17–18.

Abramovitz, M. (1993b). Should all social work students be educated for social change? Pro. *Journal of Social Work Education, 29*(1), 6–11.

Ashford, J. B., Macht, M. W., & Mylym, M. (1987). Advocacy by social workers in the public defender's office. *Social Work, 32*, 199–204.

Bardill, D. R. (1993a). Response to Dr. Abramovitz. *Journal of Social Work Education, 29*(1), 11–13.

Bardill, D. R. (1993b). Should all social work students be educated for social change? Con. *Journal of Social Work Education, 29*(1), 13–17.

Barker, R. L. (1995). *Social work dictionary* (3rd ed.). Washington, DC: NASW Press.

Burghardt, S. (1987). Community-based social action. In A. Minahan (Ed.-in-Chief), *Encyclopedia of social work* (18th ed., Vol. 1, pp. 292–299). Silver Spring, MD: National Association of Social Workers.

Child welfare block grants seen a threat. (1995, May). *NASW News*, p. 7.

Ewalt, P. L. (1994). Federal legislation and the social work profession. *Social Work, 39*, 341–343.

Gibelman, M., & Schervish, P. H. (1993). *Who we are: The social work labor force as reflected in the NASW membership.* Washington, DC: NASW Press.

Goldstein, S. R. (1993b, October 10). Indict the social helper [Letter to the editor]. *Washington Post*, p. A30.

Hartman, A. (1993). The professional is political. *Social Work, 38*, 365–366, 504.

Hiratsuka, J. (1990b, September). Community organization: Assembling power. *NASW News*, p. 3.

Hiratsuka, J. (1992a, May). Social work puts it on the picket line. *NASW News*, p. 3.

Hiratsuka, J. (1992b, July). L.A. burning: Social workers respond. *NASW News*, p. 3.

House gives states welfare control. (1995, May). *NASW News*, pp. 1, 8.

Kahn, S. (1995). Community organization. In R. L. Edwards (Ed.-in-Chief), *Encyclopedia of social work* (19th ed., Vol. 1, pp. 569–576). Washington, DC: NASW Press.

Kinoy, S. K. (1984, November). Advocacy: A potent antidote to burnout. *NASW News*, p. 9.

Martinez-Brawley, E. E. (1995). Community. In R. L. Edwards (Ed.-in-Chief), *Encyclopedia of social work* (19th ed., Vol. 1, pp. 539–548). Washington, DC: NASW Press.

Mickelson, J. S. (1995). Advocacy. In R. L. Edwards (Ed.-in-Chief), *Encyclopedia of social work* (19th ed., Vol. 1, pp. 95–100). Washington, DC: NASW Press.

NASW urges Hill to fund '96 programs. (1995, May). *NASW News*, pp. 1, 10.

National Association of Social Workers. (1989). *Lobbying tips for social workers* [video]. Silver Spring, MD: Author.

National Association of Social Workers. (1994). *NASW code of ethics*. Washington, DC: Author.

People in the news. (1993, November). *NASW News*, p. 15.

People in the news. (1994, September). *NASW News*, p. 17.

Protection urged for key programs. (1995, April). *NASW News*, pp. 1, 12.

Richan, W. C. (1991). *Lobbying for social change*. New York: Haworth Press.

Rothman, J., Erlich, J. L., & Tropman, J. E. (1995). *Strategies of community intervention: Macro practice* (5th ed.). Itasca, IL: F. E. Peacock.

Rouyer, J. S. (1994, March 25). Families, not orphanages [Letter to the editor]. *Washington Post*, p. A22.

Social worker helps Chavez with boycott. (1987, March). *NASW News*, p. 12.

Sosin, M., & Caulum, S. (1983). Advocacy: A conceptualization for social work practice. *Social Work, 28*, 12–17.

Stoesz, D. (1993). Communicating with the public. *Social Work, 38*, 367–368.

Thompson, J. J. (1994). Social workers and politics: Beyond the Hatch Act. *Social Work, 39*, 457–465.

Weil, M. O., & Gamble, D. N. (1995). Community practice models. In R. L. Edwards (Ed.-in-Chief), *Encyclopedia of social work* (19th ed., Vol. 1, pp. 577–594). Washington, DC: NASW Press.

consulting

Social work consultation refers to a problem-solving process in which advice and other helping activities are offered to an individual, group, organization, or community. Consultation differs from supervision in that it occurs more on an ad hoc or temporary basis than on a continuous basis and is focused on a specific goal or situation (Shulman, 1987). The social work consultant often does not work for the organization that is experiencing the problem or which seeks advice, but rather is retained because of his or her special expertise to solve a specific problem (Barker, 1995).

The role of the consultant in human services organizations is broad and is limited only by the resources and constraints of those who hire them. Consultants are hired to contribute their knowledge and experience on topics ranging from interior decorating to crisis programs, fund raising, and staff training (Walsh & Moynihan, 1990). The process by which the need for a consultant is recognized and acted on deserves attention, as board support of this decision can make all the difference in how well the consultant is received and the recommendations followed.

An Agency in Trouble: Looking for Direction

The Children's Center, a nonprofit residential treatment center serving emotionally disturbed youth, has fallen on difficult times. For the past 10 years, the largest portion of the center's funding (70 percent) was derived from a contract with the state Department of Human Resources. The state, in turn, was the main source of referrals to the program. But in 1994, a new governor was elected with a twofold agenda: (1) to pare down the size of government, and (2) to cut taxes. The governor immediately announced that he would review all existing contracts and that none should be considered "safe."

The Children's Center's executive director, Nancy Aimes, who recently received a doctorate in social welfare, realizes that the very existence of the agency is in jeopardy. Despite discussions at board meetings over the years about the need to diversify sources of center funding, the priority given to the day-to-day management of the agency and the false security of the 10-year history of state funding meant that a long-range funding plan had never evolved.

In consultation with the board president, an ad hoc committee on fiscal development is immediately convened. At the first meeting of the committee, Nancy is charged with locating a consultant who can help devise a fund development plan. The committee also realizes the importance of coordinating with other service providers facing the same threat of contract termination and to activate the agency's constituency (parents of the children served, other public and voluntary community agencies, government officials "friendly" to the agency, and influential community residents who have donated funds in the past). Within a few days, Nancy is able to obtain information about existing and newly forming coalitions in the state and in the community who are mobilizing to fight the cutbacks in contract funds. Several of these groups include the families of the clients served by family and children's agencies. Several committee members volunteer to serve as agency liaisons to these coalitions.

Nancy has also been on the phone to her colleagues at other agencies to obtain a list of potential consultants with expertise in fund development. Based on the recommendations she receives, Nancy develops a "short list" of three names. Nancy explains the situation to each one and arranges appointments to meet with them individually. In preparation for these meetings, Nancy asks the potential consultants to prepare a brief proposal outlining their initial thoughts on possible directions and cost estimates for their time.

Within a week, Nancy meets with the three consultants. The selection is relatively easy. Monica Smith stands out as a person with experience helping agencies in similar circumstances. Monica has an MSW degree, but her career path has been nontraditional. She also obtained an MBA and developed expertise in fundraising and fiscal development. In recent years, she has worked as a consultant to nonprofit organizations, mostly those concerned with health and human services.

Nancy is comfortable with Monica's style and approach and thinks that she will work easily with the committee. Monica, however, makes clear that she cannot "solve" the agency's problem. Her job, as she explains it, is to guide the agency's decision makers to identify alternatives and make decisions. Monica's proposal also emphasizes the decision-making responsibility of the committee and, ultimately, the board of directors. Her proposal details a highly interactive process in which Monica will engage with the agency and its elected and staff leadership.

Resource mobilization and development is a concern of all social welfare agencies. In this case, Nancy identifies the problem and seeks to institute a process that will result in mobilization of resources. Resource mobilization is "the process of bringing together and making available the organization's assets including existing funds, funds to be raised from the constituency and other sources, information base, personnel and volunteers, and the knowledge and talents of board members and others who can be called on for assistance. This process depends on the organization's making clear its needs and mission, identifying the population to be served, and communicating this information to the public" (Barker, 1995, p. 324).

Nancy and her board, however, are also aware that they need outside assistance in developing short- and long-term fiscal development plans. This issue has been on the "back burner" for so long that a crisis has developed. Outside assistance is seen as an important way to get the agency moving in the right direction. Nancy is confident that an outside perspective can help overcome past obstacles to strategy development and establish an accountability system to keep up the momentum. She also recognizes her own limitations in regard to fund development expertise and looks forward to help in learning new skills.

Monica begins her consultation assignment by spending two days in the office reviewing financial records, past proposals, fundraising and public relations materials, and interviewing staff responsible for income-generating activities. A meeting with the ad hoc resource development committee is set for the following week.

As Monica reviews the agency's financial history and current status, she realizes that the current financial crisis should have been anticipated and that the agency made a common mistake: it had grown dependent on government contracts and had not considered that this funding stream might someday "dry up." Creating a more diversified and secure funding base is the long-range goal, but a crisis plan needs to be developed immediately to deal with cash flow problems.

Monica develops a series of options for presentation to the ad hoc committee. She knows that some of the options will not be popular, particularly those that concern laying off some of the staff. Other cost-saving strategies will be proposed, including curtailment of some non–revenue-producing programs and cancellation of recently ordered computer equipment. Cost savings is only part of the picture. Monica will also propose that the entire board, many of whom are well connected in the business community, engage in face-to-face fundraising with their associates. Perhaps a "challenge" program could be set up, with each board member responsible for soliciting contributions of $25,000.

Monica discusses each of these ideas with Nancy in terms of their implications for the agency and the likely reaction from the ad hoc committee and board members. This type of strategizing is important to assess the potential climate of the meeting and to anticipate the issues that will be raised. She hopes to elicit additional ideas from the ad hoc committee before meeting with the full board. The following weeks and months will involve the active participation of the board and staff; although it will be a rough road, it is possible to turn the financial situation around.

In this vignette, there were two social workers. Nancy, as executive director, used her administrative skills, including those of fiscal management, to identify the agency's troubles. She then engaged in consultation with her board of directors, communicating to them the nature and scope of the problem in a timely way and identifying the initial steps that will be taken to address the problem. Nancy then mobilized her personal and agency resources to identify and select an appropriate consultant and negotiated the terms of consultation. Collaboration between Nancy and the consultant, Monica, was planned to occur on an ongoing basis.

Monica conducted a type of needs assessment by reviewing past records and proposals and interviewing staff. She then engaged in planning, organizing, and program development to identify several action plans for meeting the agency's crisis. Finally, Monica carried out the function of coordination and review to discuss all issues with Nancy in preliminary strategy sessions. Ultimately, the Board of Directors, with facilitation from Nancy and Monica, will develop a plan of action, for which Nancy will have implementation responsibility.

References

Barker, R. L. (1995). *Social work dictionary* (3rd ed.). Washington, DC: NASW Press.

Shulman, L. (1987). Consultation. In A. Minahan (Ed.-in-Chief), *Encyclopedia of social work* (18th ed., Vol. 1, pp. 326–331). Silver Spring, MD: National Association of Social Workers.

Walsh, J. A., & Moynihan, F. M. (1990). Using external consultants in social service agencies. *Families in Society: Journal of Contemporary Human Services, 71*, 291–295.

political involvement of social workers

Speaking before the 1984 NASW Symposium, Barbara Mikulski, then U.S. Representative from Maryland and a social worker, asserted that the Reagan administration's assaults on social programs have sent "social workers back to our roots, the roots of advocacy, activism, and politics—raw, pure politics" ("Social Work Skills," 1984, p. 8). She further urged that this involvement in politics be "direct, it must be specific, it must be immediate, and it must be realizable" (p. 8). She urged social workers to become involved with "nitty gritty" campaigns, going door to door, stuffing envelopes, working on fundraisers, taking people to the polls on election day, and working with people to register to vote. She also posed the challenge of social workers themselves running for office. "I am trying to change the political landscape, and I encourage you to do the same" (p. 8).

Consistent with Mikulski's vision of a politically active social work profession, there is evidence of significant growth in the political involvement of social workers during the Reagan years (Ezell, 1993). Politics and macro practice are not synonymous, although the boundaries certainly overlap. The involvement of social workers in the political realm has been inconsistent and ambivalent (Mahaffey, 1987). Their involvement generally has been motivated either by a supportive presidential administration, such Lyndon Johnson's, or by an adverse political climate, exemplified by Presidents Reagan and Bush, who placed both the profession and those it serves at risk.

Social workers evidence their political activity largely by writing letters to public officials, discussing political issues with friends, attending political meetings, and joining politically active organizations (Ezell, 1993). A substantial proportion of social workers also make campaign contributions and campaign for candidates. Others participate on an ad hoc basis, depending on the issue and its importance to them. For example, faculty and students from about 250 schools of social work across the nation joined in an 1993 "Teach-In On Women, Welfare and Children" to protest cuts in welfare programs and dispel misconceptions about people on welfare. The teach-in was initiated by the ad hoc

Committee for a National Social Work Teach-In and was endorsed by NASW and other social work organizations. The teach-in included campus and community events, meetings, demonstrations, and other activities designed to affect public attitudes ("Teach-Ins," 1993).

Many social workers, however, believe that politics is out of their purview and that policies are made somewhere "out there," removed from the day-to-day practice world. Scholars and activists argue, however, that policy practice is a legitimate and essential component of social work that ranges from direct work with individuals, in which the emphasis is on matters such as empowerment and change, to interventions in larger-scale systems (Flynn, 1992). Policy practice, then, emphasizes the "environment" in the person-in-environment paradigm.

Ginsberg (1988) addressed the salience of political involvement:

> It would be difficult to overstate the importance of political activity to large numbers of people, including the profession of social work and those it serves. Few arena have more potential for benefiting or harming people. The distinctive culture of politics is the backdrop before which the major decisions about social welfare in the latter part of the twentieth century are made and implemented. (p. 247)

Political Action

Political action refers to "coordinated efforts to influence legislation, election of candidates, and social causes. Social workers engage in political action by running for elective office, organizing campaigns in support of other candidates or issues, fundraising, and mobilizing voters and public opinion. Political action also includes lobbying, testifying before legislative committees, and monitoring the work of officeholders and government workers" (Barker, 1995, p. 286).

A small proportion of social workers have job responsibilities within the political action realm. An example is NASW's government affairs and political action for candidate election (PACE) divisions. More frequently, political action is a component of community organization activities in which social workers engage as independent citizens based on their personal convictions and commitment to social change. Examples in this latter category include participation in demonstrations. In Minnesota, social workers participated in peace activities to persuade the Honeywell Corporation to stop doing defense work and convert to peacetime production. A small number of the 50-plus social workers who demonstrated against the company also engaged in civil disobedience, joining more than 2,000 people arrested at the work site since 1982 ("Honeywell Protest," 1987). Social workers were also among a crowd of 6,000 people rallying in support of peace and disarmament at the Mercury, Nevada, nuclear test site in 1988 ("Social Workers Arrested," 1988).

Social workers possess the qualities needed for effective political intervention. According to Goldstein (1993):

> In addition to being educated in sound social policy development and having seen firsthand the terrible impact of inadequate policies on individuals and society, social workers possess natural at-

tributes—an innate concern for others, a desire to see justice done—that suit us well for both politics and policy making. These activities, at their best, are simply logical extensions of our efforts to help people one to one. Also, many of us have learned the principles of persuasion and organizing, along with the skills of mediation—all vital in the world of politics. (p. 2)

Many of the political interventions in which social workers engage are carried out on an individual basis, independent of the employment situation; others are carried out on behalf of agencies as part of the social worker's job. The involvement of social workers in the political process has given the profession greater recognition and influence and has resulted in tangible gains in public policy of benefit to clients. NASW and schools of social work have long encouraged social workers to be active in politics either professionally or voluntarily, the justification of which goes back to ancient Greek civilization. When Thucydides was asked when justice would come to Athens, the philosopher replied: "Justice will not come to Athens until those who are not injured are as indignant as those who are injured" (as cited in Dworak-Peck & Battle, 1988, p. 2).

NASW has always included the exercise of influence in social policymaking among its priorities. In this respect, NASW speaks for and represents its full membership, although not all members always agree with all the positions taken. In 1993–94, for example, NASW became involved in advocating for passage of health care reform, offering its own legislative proposal. Introduced in the 102nd Congress by Senator Daniel K. Inouye (D-HI), the NASW plan, known as the National Health Care Act, became the most comprehensive single-payer health reform proposal (Abbott, 1993; Mizrahi, 1995).

Throughout the years, NASW has also endorsed and campaigned for political candidates. In 1984, NASW took a great risk by declaring its endorsement, before the primaries, of Walter Mondale to be the Democratic nominee for president (Stewart, 1984). In the following years, NASW, through PACE, endorsed and actively campaigned for presidential candidates Dukakis and Clinton ("PACE Endorses," 1988; Hiratsuka, 1992c).

PACE, formed in 1976, takes an active stand in electoral politics at the national level, including financial contributions. Endorsements are based on the priority-issue preferences of members (as determined by periodic surveys conducted by PACE), and the consistency of candidates' views with member preferences (Dworak-Peck & Battle, 1988; "PACE's Donors," 1990).

Social workers have served as delegates to the Democratic National Convention over the years. In 1984, 24 delegates represented social work (Stewart, 1984), and in 1988 NASW cosponsored the Women's Caucus and more than a dozen social workers served as convention delegates or on committees ("Social Workers' Presence," 1988).

Social workers have also been a major force in voter registration drives (Stewart, 1984) and have joined with other groups in large-scale demonstrations. Examples of the diversity of social concerns around which social workers demonstrate include the following:

- the 1987 National Mobilization for Peace and Justice in Central America and Southern Africa ("Social Workers Among 75,000," 1987)

- the 1987 American–Soviet Walk to demonstrate bilateral citizen opposition to the arms race ("Members Join," 1987)

- the 1987 Gay Rights March calling for federal action to ensure civil rights for lesbian and gay men and to strengthen the nation's response to AIDS ("Over 200,000 March," 1987)

- the March 1989 rally for Women's Equality/Women's Lives to extend women's constitutional rights through passage of the Equal Rights Amendment and to protect women's existing rights to safe and legal birth control and abortion ("NASW Backs Rally," 1989)

- the April 1992 March for Women's Lives in support of abortion rights ("In the News," 1992)

- the 1993 National March on Washington for Lesbian, Gay, and Bi Equal Rights and Liberation which included a protest against the military ban on lesbians and gays and lobbying for stepped up efforts in the fight against AIDS (Moss, 1993).

Acting through NASW's state chapters, social workers have also devoted time and resources to policy issues. In recent years, a major focus of chapters' attention has been on state legal regulation and vendorship laws for social workers, the latter of which require insurance reimbursement for clinical social work services. These efforts are often undertaken in concert with other organizations with shared concerns. For example, the North Carolina Chapter teamed with the North Carolina Society for Clinical Social Work to push successfully for legislation adding "certified social workers" to the state's list of reimbursable service providers ("People in the News," 1993c). A grassroots lobbying network helped gain active support for the bill.

Also in 1993, the Oregon Chapter created a Committee on Human Dignity to encourage social workers' involvement in human rights issues, and the Massachusetts Chapter, as a member of that state's Human Services Coalition, joined many other organizations to launch a Campaign for Real Welfare Reform ("Chapter News," 1993). The New York City Chapter mounted a campaign to fight social services budget cuts proposed (and eventually implemented) by the city council and Mayor Rudolph Giuliani. Members testified at a city council committee hearing about the role of social workers in delivering public services ("Chapter News," 1994).

Social workers also take individual or collective action within the political system independent of an organizational base. The issues addressed may be personal, professional, societal, or all three. For example, 16 clinical social workers in Maryland sued Prince George's County and the state health department demanding equal pay for equal work. The issue: Even though they performed the same tasks, the social workers earned about $5,000 less per year than psychiatric nurses and $15,000 less than psychologists. They were asking for back pay to July 1984, payment of their legal expenses, and a pay scale adjustment that would put them on par with nurses (Hiratsuka, 1991). (This six-year struggle met with defeat when the Maryland Court of Appeals ruled that social workers may be paid less than psychiatric nurses performing the same tasks. The court held that there was a rational basis for the state's classification and, therefore, no violation of equal protection principles had occurred ["Court Rejects Equal Pay," 1991].)

Other state and national groups include policy development and policy advocacy among their primarily goals. Such organizations include the Child Welfare League of America, American Public Welfare Association, Children's Defense Fund, National Assembly of Voluntary Health and Social Welfare Organizations, and Family Services America. These organizations rely on social workers to implement their programs.

Seeking and Holding Political Office

In 1916, Jeannette Rankin, at the age of 36, became the first woman and the first social worker to be elected to the U.S. House of Representatives. As a suffragist, pacifist, and Republican, her early experiences in working in agencies concerned with children led her to wonder if she was doing enough. During her political career, Rankin supported legislation to benefit underrepresented and vulnerable populations. She supported national women's suffrage, the extension of child welfare reform, legislation to provide loans to farmers, and tariff legislation that benefited workers (Harris, 1986; Weismiller & Rome, 1995).

PACE determined that, in 1993, 165 social workers held national, state, or local offices—nearly a 50 percent increase from 1991. Results of a survey show that nearly two-thirds of the elected social workers are women and more than 25 percent are from racial and ethnic groups. Approximately 60 social workers hold office in state legislatures, about 90 on local bodies such as city and county governments or school boards, and, in 1993, three served in the U.S. Congress—Senator Barbara Mikulski (D-MD) and Representatives Ron Dellums (D-CA) and Edolphus Towns (D-NY) ("165 Social Workers Elected," 1993). Examples of social workers who have held or now hold elected or appointed political office follow:

- Social worker Barbara Mikulski, a 12-year veteran of the House of Representatives, was elected senator in 1986 ("PACE Candidates Romp," 1987) and reelected in 1994 by an overwhelming majority. Edolphus Towns was reelected to the House of Representatives in 1994 by a wide margin, as was social worker Ronald Dellums ("PACE Scores," 1995). In 1991 Representative Towns was elected chairman of the Congressional Black Caucus ("Social Worker Is Elected," 1991).

- In 1986, social worker Wilma Mankiller was the first woman to be elected chief of the Cherokee Nation of Oklahoma ("Cherokees Elect Female," 1986) and was reelected in 1991 ("People in the News," 1993a). Also in 1986, social worker Sidney Barthelemy was elected mayor of the city of New Orleans, Louisiana ("Barthelemy Is Orleans Mayor," 1986); he was reelected in 1990 to serve a second four-year term ("People in the News," 1990b).

- In 1987, Sol Gothard, a former juvenile court judge and a social worker, was elected to the Fifth Circuit Court of Appeals in Louisiana ("People in the News," 1987a). That year also saw the election of social worker Art Agnos as mayor of the City of San Francisco. He began his term in January 1988 ("San Francisco," 1988).

- Social worker Ruth Messinger was elected borough president of Manhattan in 1989, a position she continues to hold. Earlier, Ms. Messinger represented Manhattan's upper west side on the New York City Council ("People in the News," 1990a). Also in 1989, Maryann Mahaffey, a former NASW president, after serving on the elected City Council since 1978, was named president-elect of the Detroit City Council ("People in the News," 1990b). In 1988, both Messinger and Mahaffey were elected to positions in the National League of Cities, an organization representing local elected officials. Mahaffey was elected to the board of Women in Municipal Government and Messinger was elected second vice president ("People in the News," 1988).

- Social worker Pamela Carter was the first black woman elected to the post of Indiana's attorney general ("Social Worker Named," 1993).

Social workers have also held prominent appointed positions. For example, in 1989 social worker Patricia Rodgers was named director of VISTA (Volunteers in Service to America), where she supervised the activities of 2,800 volunteers serving in 605 community projects throughout the United States (Hiratsuka, 1990a; "People in the News," 1989a). In that same year, Ruth Brandwein was named commissioner of social services for Suffolk County, New York, becoming the first social worker appointed to lead this department ("People in the News," 1989b). And in 1990, social worker Eddie F. Brown was confirmed as the U.S. Interior Department's assistant secretary for Indian Affairs. Prior to this appointment, Brown served as director of Arizona's Department of Economic Security, the state's largest public agency ("Brown Heads Indian Affairs," 1990).

In April 1993, the U.S. Senate confirmed the appointment of Fernando Torres-Gil, a social work professor and former staff director for the House Select Committee on Aging, as assistant secretary for aging for the Department of Health and Human Services (Hiratsuka, 1993a). Also assuming appointed positions in the Clinton administration are Wardell Townsend, assistant secretary of agriculture and Wendy Sherman, assistant secretary of state (Hiratsuka, 1993b). Former NASW Wisconsin Chapter President Ada Deer was confirmed in 1993 as assistant secretary for Indian Affairs at the Department of the Interior, and Augusta Kappner was confirmed as assistant secretary for vocational and adult education at the Department of Education (Hiratsuka, 1993c). Thomas P. Glynn was named deputy secretary of labor in the Clinton administration, where he oversees the day-to-day operations of a department with 18,000 employees, a $35 billion budget, and major responsibility for implementing the Clinton administration's "Reinventing Government" initiative (Hiratsuka, 1993d).

On the state level, recent examples of social workers appointed to positions include Irene Lapidez, Jacqueline Morgan, and Marjorie Shuart, all named commissioners of three departments in Nassau County, New York, one of the largest suburban areas in the country. Lapidez was named commissioner of social services and mental health and oversees 800 employees, a budget of $277 million, and service provision to 80,000 people a year. Morgan was appointed commissioner of drug and alcohol addiction and is responsible for the largest network of drug and alcohol-related programs in New York State, with an annual budget of $40 million. Under her jurisdiction are about 175 chemical dependency programs that provide treatment to more than 25,000 people and the operation of prevention and education programs in 46 county school districts. Shuart was appointed to oversee the system of mental health and mental retardation contract agencies including a variety of voluntary agencies. She is responsible for a budget of $67 million and for program operations of agencies with annual expenditures of nearly $110 million ("People in the News," 1993b).

This partial list of social workers who have held or are now holding elected or appointed political positions suggests that the body politic is an important, albeit nontraditional, arena of practice.

References

Abbott, A. A. (1993, November). In tune with the times of reform. *NASW News*, p. 2.

Barker, R. L. (1995). *Social work dictionary* (3rd ed.). Washington, DC: NASW Press.

Barthelemy is Orleans mayor. (1986, April). *NASW News*, p. 17.

Brown heads Indian affairs at Interior. (1990, February). *NASW News*, p. 13.

Chapter news. (1993, April). *NASW News*, p. 11.

Chapter news. (1994, September). *NASW News*, p. 15.

Cherokees elect female as chief. (1986, January). *NASW News*, p. 19.

Court rejects equal pay for social workers. (1991, November). *NASW News*, p. 13.

Dworak-Peck, S., & Battle, M. G. (1988, January). Perspectives. *NASW News*, p. 2.

Ezell, M. (1993). The political activity of social workers: A post-Reagan update. *Journal of Sociology & Social Welfare, 20*, 81–97.

Flynn, J. (1992). *Social agency policy.* Chicago: Nelson-Hall.

Ginsberg, L. (1988). Social workers and politics: Lessons from practice. *Social Work, 33*, 245–247.

Goldstein, S. R. (1993, January). Best way to sway policy? Make it! *NASW News*, p. 2.

Harris, D. V. (1986, October). Social workers urged to follow profession's activist tradition. *NASW News*, p. 2.

Hiratsuka, J. (1990a, January). VISTA chief boosting voluntarism. *NASW News*, p. 3.

Hiratsuka, J. (1991, January). Social workers persevering for equal pay. *NASW News*, p. 3.

Hiratsuka, J. (1992c, September). NASW's PACE backing Clinton–Gore campaign. *NASW News*, pp. 1, 8.

Hiratsuka, J. (1993a, June). Social worker named to HHS post on aging. *NASW News*, pp. 1, 10.

Hiratsuka, J. (1993b, July). More colleagues take high posts. *NASW News, pp.* 1, 8.

Hiratsuka, J. (1993c, September). Deer, Kappner tapped. *NASW News*, pp. 1, 14.

Hiratsuka, J. (1993d, October). Glynn takes number-two post at Labor. *NASW News*, pp. 1, 4.

Honeywell protest: Social work dilemma. (1987, April). *NASW News*, p. 5.

In the news. (1992, May). *NASW News*, p. 6.

Mahaffey, M. (1987). Political action in social work. In A. Minahan, (Ed.-in-Chief), *Encyclopedia of social work* (18th ed., Vol. 2, pp. 283–293). Silver Spring, MD: National Association of Social Workers.

Members join in U.S.–Soviet peace march. (1987, September). *NASW News*, p. 11.

Mizrahi, T. (1995). Health care: Reform initiatives. In R. L. Edwards (Ed.-in-Chief), *Encyclopedia of social work* (19th ed., Vol. 2, pp. 1185–1198). Washington, DC: NASW Press.

Moss, M. S. (1993, June). Members join half million gay-rights marchers. *NASW News*, p. 1.

NASW backs rally urging equal rights. (1989, March). *NASW News*, p. 13.

165 social workers elected. (1993, June). *NASW News*, p. 9.

Over 200,000 march in gay rights rally. (1987, November). *NASW News*, p. 9.

PACE candidates romp in House, Senate races. (1987, January). *NASW News*, pp. 1, 17.

PACE endorses Michael Dukakis. (1988, July). *NASW News*, pp. 1, 10.

PACE scores 65% wins despite GOP sweep. (1995, January). *NASW News*, p. 10.

PACE's donors pick top issues for 1990 action. (1990, April). *NASW News*, p. 8.

People in the news. (1987a, January). NASW News, p. 20.

People in the news. (1987b, February). *NASW News*, p. 18.

People in the news. (1987c, March). *NASW News*, p. 17.

People in the news. (1988, May). *NASW News*, p. 15.

People in the news. (1989a, April). *NASW News*, p. 17.

People in the news. (1989b, May). *NASW News*, p. 15.

People in the news. (1990a, January). *NASW News*, p. 21.

People in the news. (1990b, April). *NASW News*, p. 17.

People in the news. (1993a, January). *NASW News*, p. 17.

People in the news. (1993b, September). *NASW News*, p. 17.

People in the news. (1993c, November). *NASW News*, p. 15.

San Francisco social worker elected mayor. (1988, February). *NASW News*, p. 8.

Social work skills and political action make a potent mix, Mikulski asserts. (1984, January). *NASW News*, p. 8.

Social worker is elected Hill's black caucus chief. (1991, February). *NASW News*, p. 10.

Social worker named to HHS post on aging. (1993, June). *NASW News*, pp. 1, 10.

Social workers among 75,000 marchers in mobilization for peace and justice. (1987, June). *NASW News*, p. 13.

Social workers arrested during nuclear protest. (1988, May). *NASW News*, p. 11.

Social workers' presence felt at convention. (1988, September). *NASW News*, p. 13.

Stewart, R. (1984, October). From the president. *NASW News*, p. 2.

"Teach-ins" bash welfare misconceptions. (1993, January). *NASW News*, p. 10.

Techniques of lobbying revealed in new video. (1989, February). *NASW News*, pp. 6–7.

Weismiller, T., & Rome, S. H. (1995). Social workers in politics. In R. L. Edwards (Ed.-in-Chief), *Encyclopedia of social work* (19th ed., Vol. 3, pp. 2305–2313). Washington, DC: NASW Press.

program planning

Social workers engaged in macro practice use their knowledge of organizational and community development processes to establish new programs to meet recognized needs of individuals, groups, and communities. One such example concerns the development of "clean needle" programs to stem the spread of AIDS.

Injection drug users (IDUs) today constitute the majority of new AIDS cases reported in the United States (Ruscavage & Jones, 1994). The Centers for Disease Control (CDC) have reported that, of all known cases of AIDS in the United States, IDUs make up 29 percent, sexual partners of IDUs 3 percent, and children born to IDUs or to partners of IDUs 1 percent (Lurie et al., 1993). Communities of color are particularly hard-hit: 52 percent of cases among African Americans and 45 percent of cases among Latinos are injection drug–related, versus 19 percent among white people (Lurie et al., 1993). New York City, for example, has an estimated 200,000 IDUs, 50 percent of whom are HIV positive (National Commission on AIDS, 1991).

The public has been generally unsympathetic about this group of people. Concern has typically had more to do with the public cost of care and fear of discarded contaminated needles than with the suffering of those within the IDU population. Elected officials, with widespread backing, have endorsed the use of the policy and criminal justice system to punish IDUs (Blansfield, 1994). Even methadone maintenance programs are generally implemented judgmentally (Springer, 1991). This approach may result in premature termination of treatment, followed by relapse into drug use, with the continued risk of HIV infection (Blansfield, 1994). The National Commission on AIDS (1991) concluded that the government's strategy of interdiction and increased prison sentences has not worked to halt the spread of drug use or of HIV.

What can be done? Social workers have helped reframe the terms of the public debate in ways that justify HIV prevention efforts for IDUs. Social workers have been proponents of the harm reduction model, a strategy intended to minimize the harmful consequences of drug-taking behavior for the individual and society (Kayman, 1995; Springer, 1991). Here, the prevention of drug use takes a back seat to the prevention of HIV infection because AIDS is seen as the greater threat. Preventing HIV infection improves the addict's chance to stay healthy until such time as he or she enters drug treatment (Lurie et al., 1993). Needle exchange programs are a logical outgrowth of the harm reduction model. And, indeed, studies have shown that needle exchange programs decrease HIV infection rates and serve as a bridge to drug treatment and other medical and social services (Heimer, Kaplan, O'Keefe, Knoshnood, & Altice, 1994).

Needle exchange programs are defined by the CDC as "any establishment at which injecting drug users can exchange an old needle or syringe for a new one" (Lurie et al., 1993, p. ii). Needle exchange seeks to encourage the use of sterile injection equipment and discourage the sharing of such equipment. However, needle exchange is controversial because of fears that it may increase drug use, attract drug-related activity, and divert resources that could be better spent on drug treatment (Kayman, 1995; Sanchez, 1994). How, then, can social workers help allay fears and set up needle exchange programs in inner-city communities?

A Needle Exchange Program

When social worker Patrick Green became the director of the publicly sponsored New Hope AIDS Project, he faced a rising tide of AIDS cases, primarily because of intravenous drug injecting. Before accepting this position, Patrick worked as the director of the San Francisco alcohol and drug treatment office where he was involved in developing a program that used former addicts as educational counselors. They would walk the streets in areas of high drug use and distribute information about the risk of HIV transmission.

After coming to New Hope, located on the East Coast in a major urban center, Patrick worked to implement a similar information campaign. However, after one and a half years of operation, the evaluation results showed little change in behavior or rates of HIV infection from intravenous drug use.

Patrick was concerned. He continued to do research on the topic and talk with seasoned professionals as well as addicts in treatment facilities. Many of the addicts told him that they knew the risks of HIV, but because of their addiction they injected anyway—with any needle they could find. Through information gathering, Patrick became convinced that education about the risks of HIV infection would not be enough to generate widespread, lasting behavioral change. He concluded that drug users must be provided with a way to make the desired behavior changes, such as clean needles or bleach to sterilize needles.

Patrick attended meetings at the Centers for Disease Control and Prevention (CDC) in Atlanta, and he actively participated in the HIV Information Network (HIN) to obtain additional information about working effectively with IDUs. Patrick continued to pursue his ideas with his staff at the New Hope AIDS office as well as professionals at CDC, HIN, and his colleagues at the Whitman-Walker Clinic in Washington, DC, which experienced some success in its prevention campaigns. The staff at the New Hope AIDS office worked aggressively under Patrick's direction to design a needle exchange program to submit to the state Department of Health for partial funding. At the time, there were very few such programs anywhere in the United States, and the staff knew that it may be a controversial proposal.

Indeed it was controversial. Many members of the state council said that such a program did not deal with the real problem of drug use, but rather helped addicts continue their self-destructive behavior by giving them new needles. Patrick and his colleagues presented arguments backed by national studies about the need to do more than simply educate. Unfortunately, after all was said and done, the state council denied funding and the New Hope AIDS office went back to the drawing board.

Patrick was determined not to give up, so he began developing a coalition that included two other local AIDS clinics, a drug treatment facility, the CDC, the HIN Advisory Committee, and the Whitman-Walker Clinic. He also met with the local homelessness advocacy group and several church leaders. They held open public meetings and distributed information to the community about the current rate of HIV infection due to intravenous drug use and the potential effectiveness of needle exchange services.

One year later, the New Hope AIDS Office resubmitted its application for funding for a needle exchange program. Patrick and his colleagues appeared at the hearing to determine funding, but they also invited key participants from the coalition organizations, including former addicts and those currently in treatment facilities. Funding was granted, with the contingency that regular evaluations must prove effectiveness of the program. Four years later health workers say the percentage of AIDS cases due to intravenous drug use has dropped. In addition, more than 500 of the 1,643 addicts who have participated in the exchange sought and were placed in treatment.

In this case Patrick performed several different social work functions. First, he had to identify the social problem of IDUs and increasing HIV rates. He then began to organize and mobilize to get community groups interested and active in the issue. The social work function of exchange was used when community networks were identified in order to share information and resources. Patrick engaged in program development when he studied community needs and possible solutions. He used coordination in his work to develop the coalition of interested agencies, and the review function was used to determine the effectiveness of the program. Finally, as a director, Patrick used the social work functions of management, supervision, and planning to foster communication and cooperation among the staff at the New Hope AIDS office and to monitor the program's implications on future policy development.

References

Blansfield, H. N. (1994). Oral methadone and HIV. *AIDS & Public Policy Journal, 9*, 75–77.

Heimer, R., Kaplan, E. H., O'Keefe, E., Knoshnood, K., & Altice, F. (1994). Three years of needle exchange in New Haven: What have we learned? *AIDS & Public Policy Journal, 9*, 59–74.

Kayman, D. J. (1995). Needle exchange: A strategy for preventing HIV infection. Unpublished manuscript, Yeshiva University, New York.

Lurie, P., Reingold, A. L., Bowser, B., Foley, J., Gudydish, J., Kahn, J. G., Lane, S., Sorensen, J., DeParlo, P., Harris, N., & Jones, T. S. (1993). *The public health impact of needle exchange programs in the United States and abroad: Summary, conclusions, and recommendations.* Atlanta: Centers for Disease Control and Prevention.

National Commission on AIDS. (1991). *The twin epidemics of substance abuse and HIV: Executive summary* (Report No. 5). Washington, DC: Author.

Ruscavage, D., & Jones, P. M. (1994). *Needle exchange: Moving beyond the controversy.* Washington, DC: U.S. Conference of Mayors.

Sanchez, R. (1994, April 18). Scarcely a dent in the AIDS menace: Needle exchange reaches few drug addicts in D.C. Washington *Post,* pp. A1, A8.

Springer, E. (1991). Effective AIDS prevention with active drug users: The harm reduction model. *Journal of Chemical Dependency Treatment, 4,* 141–157.

career
opportunities

A brief sampling of career opportunities in macro social work are listed in this chapter. (These listings are adapted from recent classified advertisements but do not constitute current job offerings.) However, these selections only scratch the surface of the rich array of opportunities for creative, professional growth in this field of practice.

Community Organizer

Requires energetic, outgoing person to recruit, develop, and license foster families. Applicants must have a BA degree with two to three years of human services case management or community outreach experience. Must also have excellent interpersonal and communication skills.

Community Resource Consultant

Challenging opportunities are available to two individuals experienced in human services program administration/development. The selected candidate will provide assistance to local Community Services Boards and service provider agencies in developing programs to address the needs of persons with developmental disabilities; monitor, review, and evaluate services delivered to specific individuals; assist in program planning, provider incentives, and in providing community services to persons with severe disabilities through Medicaid State Plan Option and Community Based Waiver funding. Qualifications include familiarity with human services; working knowledge of the field of mental retardation/developmental disabilities and the resources, programs, and logistics needed to deliver person-centered services to consumers; demonstrated ability to work independently and make decisions about the need, appropriateness, and efficacy of services specific to individual needs; ability to interpret state and federal regulations and communicate effectively with local, state, and federal officials as well as consumers; ability to use computer software programs and analyze data. Degree in human services program or a related field preferred.

Deputy Project Director

National project to prevent HIV and sexually transmitted diseases (STDs) in Hispanic communities. Master's degree in social work, health education, or related field preferred; at least two years' experience with a community-based organization; knowledge and experience in the prevention of HIV and STDs in Hispanic communities and in management of nonprofits. Bilingual English/Spanish. Excellent writing and organizing skills, excellent knowledge of Word and Excel for Macintosh. Will assist the project director with the overall implementation of the project, including providing technical assistance and training in HIV/STD prevention and nonprofit management.

Director

Rapidly growing consulting firm seeks individual to manage project, contract, and staff activities. Must have experience in public health and/or health promotion and disease-prevention–related areas (cancer, HIV/AIDS, drug abuse, and child abuse); eight years' demonstrated experience in management of multitask contracts; and five years' experience in logistical/conference coordination, scheduling, and planning. Federal contracting experience preferred. Qualifications: BA/BS in a related field, graduate school preferred; supervisory experience; excellent writing and verbal communication skills and problem-solving ability.

Executive Director

Visionary leader sought for a community development association, a nonprofit planning and community action agency serving several communities. Agency has excellent local reputation for innovations in health, education, housing, child care, employment, and integrated family services. Experience in community planning and administration in human services required. Master's degree in social work with a major in community organization; or a similar graduate degree with four years' experience in planning, community organizations, and administration of a nonprofit entity. Demonstrated leadership, experience with volunteers and community leaders, management skills, communication skills, and fundraising.

Executive Director

National organization seeks an executive director to serve as chief executive officer of the association. The executive director is responsible to the executive committee for the effective conduct of the affairs of the association. The successful candidate should be a licensed social worker with an advanced degree. Candidates should have at least 10 years of executive level experience, with skills in planning, policy, program development, and administration. Preference will be given to individuals with association or state licensing board management experience, office management skills, knowledge of test development and administration, and facility with computer technology.

Human Services Program Analyst

The city's mental health division seeks an outstanding professional to perform analytical and evaluative work identifying problems, improvement needs, and effectiveness of program operations in relation to program goals. Minimum requirements include at least three years of experience in human services program evaluation, program analysis, and policy development. Excellent analytic and writing skills are essential.

Policy Associate

National human services organization seeks a policy associate with proven program and regulatory knowledge of public child welfare services to conduct analyses and to represent association positions. Strong technical writing and oral skills as must. Graduate degree in social work or related field, plus two to three years in public welfare programs and state or federal legislative experience.

Policy Associate

Provides staff support on a variety of federal legislative issues, concentrating on issues of health and human services. Bachelor's degree plus three years' relevant work experience is required. One year of legislative or state government experience preferred, as is knowledge of health and human services issues. Competence in writing and good oral communication skills required. High degree of initiative and ability to work independently, handling a variety of tasks concurrently is a must.

Program Developer

Grant and proposal writer needed for national human services organization set to expand its mission of helping at-risk youth enter the workforce and become self-reliant adults. Requirements include bachelor's degree, knowledge of human services, and excellent writing/research skills. Position could lead to a full-time program manager/director position.

Program Development, Social Services

Neighborhood organization seeks human services professional to assist in design of family/community development center. Tasks: identify/assess providers, overall center program design, funding–financial plan. Experience with integrated services systems, excellent management, and proposal writing skills.

Project Associate

Full-time opportunity for seasoned professional to participate in a dynamic new service for a national information clearinghouse. Must have command of human/social services prevention programs. Expertise in child abuse and neglect preferred. Strong writing, networking, and organizational skills required. Must be computer literate and have knowledge of database management. Master's degree and minimum of three years' experience preferred.

Research Analyst

National human service organization seeks candidates for senior research analyst. Must have master's degree plus several years of social research experience with knowledge of aging services and proven skills in research design, data analysis, and report writing.

Research Associate/Writer

Human services consulting firm seeks research associate with strong technical writing skills to include the development of research designs, development of psychological assessment instruments, and report writing. Must have prior grant and proposal writing experience, research publications and excellent writing skills. PhD preferred with knowledge of addictions and HIV fields.

Research Specialist

National religious nonprofit organization seeks individual to conduct research on current evolving refugee and immigration policy issues. Duties will include but not be limited to preparation of reports, position papers, and correspondence; maintaining databases and reference information; monitoring legislative, executive, and judicial information sources for policy changes; monitoring on-line computer services; and answering requests for information. Qualified candidates should possess a bachelor's degree in a related field and have a minimum of five years' research experience. Knowledge of immigration and refugee issues and Catholic social teaching required. Excellent oral and written communication skills required.

Senior Policy Associate

A national nonprofit organization seeks senior policy associate for state and federal policy analysis in the areas of welfare reform, employment and training, and federal benefit programs. Position requires at least five years of related experience in state/federal government or Hill legislative experience. Master's degree in social work, social policy, or public administration; computer, writing, and editing skills necessary.

the future

the future
of social work

What do social workers do? Many social work functions have been identified in this book However, the profession is closely intertwined with the society of which it is a part. Therefore, what social workers do very much depends on the context of the times—the prevailing economic, political, and social climate. It is this larger context that defines the circumstances in which social workers practice—with whom, where, for how long, and with what types of problems. This dynamic interaction of the profession with its environment was aptly expressed by Stewart (1984):

> Social work was born of a mixture of idealism and pragmatism, lofty altruism and earthy problem-solving. Religious motivation, humanistic commitments, and political radicalism combined in an unlikely blend to drive social workers to become personally involved in neighborhoods, families, and individual lives in order to find solutions to human problems. Those same forces have caused social workers to take to the streets, enter the halls of justice, and lobby legislative bodies on behalf of human well-being. The continued dynamism of social work, through a myriad of societal climates, can only be explained by the strength, vitality, and integrity of its fundamental wellspring of professional motivation. (p. 2)

Contemporary society has grown sophisticated in its ability to predict the world of the future and the consequences of projected changes. Although there may be some surprises on the social scene, we have a pretty good idea about what the future holds for our society and for our profession. We know, for example, that the absolute and proportionate number of aging people in our society is increasing; many will require services ranging from those associated with the creative use of leisure time to those concerning the provision of home health care. The number of poor people will also continue to grow, especially children, as the middle class continues to shrink (Hopps & Collins, 1995). Biotechnology will continue to solve some of the mysteries of disease, elongating life but creating, in some instances, new ethical dilemmas about the quality of life. Violence as a means of conflict resolution—on the streets in the case of drug wars and in the home in the case of domestic violence—will continue to threaten our safety and humanity, until other ways of resolving conflicts are taught and accepted. Creating an ethnically and culturally diverse society that is able to live harmoniously will become an increasing challenge as demographic trends create an even more heterogeneous population.

With the identification of new social concerns or the compounding of existing social problems, the boundaries of the social work profession will continue to broaden and change. Some social workers will be at the forefront of identifying new arenas of practice, whereas others will respond to the social welfare agenda defined by others. Examples of these boundary-changing and boundary-spanning areas include the following:

- An important role for social work has been identified in relation to facilitating human adaptation to ecological change. A basis for this role is the articulation of values and purposes that encompass ecological concerns (Berger & Kelly, 1993).

- With rapid biomedical advances, new opportunities are afforded to couples facing infertility. Social workers are among those counseling infertile couples and helping them cope with the choices that become possible with advanced technology. With these advances, however, come an array of moral, ethical, and legal questions. For example, when eggs or sperm are donated, who are considered the "real" parents? Do payments to surrogate mothers unfairly take advantage of low-income women? What about custody disputes over embryos? (Hiratsuka, 1991). These and other questions will continue to emerge as we grapple with the long-term implications of the technological revolution.

- Satellite communications have made the world smaller; we get instant news, and social workers are among those who have extended the boundaries of their concern to events in other countries. Social workers have long been concerned with issues of peace and justice. With the efforts to introduce democracy into Eastern European countries, these nations are forced to grapple with a range of social problems. Increasingly, countries such as Hungary, Poland, and Romania are turning to social workers in the United States to help them establish social work education and training programs and formal social welfare systems (Edwards, 1991).

- Although some may lament the small role of social work in social policy, planning, and advocacy (see, for example, Specht & Courtney, 1994), others urge a more active role for social workers in the political realm (see, for example, Ewalt, 1994). This re-activation and furtherance of social advocacy may be rekindled by the anti–social welfare sentiment that is pervasive in the mid-1990s.

- The third sector of social welfare—for-profit enterprises—is expanding. Although for-profit social welfare activities have been carried out in private for-profit hospitals, in nursing homes, and in child care for some time, the growth in for-profit social welfare in recent years has been explosive (Macarov, 1991). Given that for-profits have a "bottom line" of making a profit, services may be modified to ensure financial success.. To what extent clients may receive different, less-effective, or perhaps better services is as yet unclear. The debate on privatization, in fact, includes consideration of the ultimate impact on the quality and quantity of services.

- Despite a dramatic downward trend in the proportion of social workers employed by government at any level over the past 30 years, the involvement of social workers in government is on the increase (Gibelman & Schervish, 1993). Most social services in this country are provided by voluntary agencies under purchase-of-service arrangements; government remains the chief financer of services (Gibelman, 1995). In addition, many private practitioners depend on third-party payments, such as Medicaid, for their income (Ginsberg, 1988).

Social Workers and Technology

Technological change deserves special mention, as its speed and range of influence is pervasive in our society and in our profession. The development of an "information superhighway" has had a profound effect on society, including the frequency, speed, and nature of communications between people. Technological change has led to improvements in products and services, growth of new industries, and the need to retool and re-educate people for a changing work environment (Macarov, 1991).

Technology has also, directly and indirectly, affected what social workers do and how they do it. These impacts range from enhanced research capability to new and emerging forms of agency and case management.

Social work agencies and social work practitioners have embraced technology as a way to enhance professional work. However, acceptance of new computer resources has met with varied reactions among social services organizations throughout the country. Some view the new technology with trepidation, whereas others see it as an exciting advance (Hopps & Collins, 1995).

Initially, computer technology was used in social services agencies only to provide information to administrators, through management information systems and data processing, and by researchers to evaluate programs ("Social Workers Harnessing Technology," 1984). Agencies have increasingly adopted standardized data collection formats to meet the demands of funding sources for accurate and detailed information about service provision.

Computerized information systems have become indispensable to many social services organizations for recording, storing, analyzing, evaluating, and consolidating information (Hopps & Collins, 1995). Agencies are also using computers to monitor the performance of workers, which raises questions about the implications for the rights of individual workers (Butterfield, 1986).

The application of computer technology in direct services to clients is also evolving. Examples include self-administered psychiatric diagnostic interviews;

self-administered programs dealing with assertiveness, self-esteem, and stress; and clinical mental health assessments (Macarov, 1991). Computer-conducted interviews are also used to collect case history data and to screen clients at risk of suicide. Counseling via computer is another example of the clinical application of this technology (Butterfield, 1986). In addition, computer-assisted instructional programs can be useful for practitioners to learn skills such as making a diagnosis, keeping an interview focused, and engaging in crisis counseling (Hopps & Collins, 1995).

Within the field of child welfare, state agencies have developed sophisticated management information systems to provide information on case status and types of clients as a basis for monitoring and evaluation (Hiratsuka, 1990). Some agencies use lap-top computers and cellular telephones so that workers in the field can obtain information stored in a central computer. Easy access to information on child abuse cases, including family history and related offenses, facilitates decision making based on accurate and up-to-date information.

Telecomputing, in which telephone lines are used to transmit information between computers, is also revolutionizing the way social workers practice. Examples of social services telecomputing include the National Adoption Exchange in Washington, DC, which makes available to adoption agencies the case summarizes on all children and prospective parents listed in its exchange (Butterfield, 1987a). This technology, which is becoming more sophisticated each day, allows agencies to share information, locate resources to help clients, conduct research, hold electronic conferences, and obtain information on grants, among other uses (Hiratsuka, 1995). And E-mail makes it possible to communicate with many destinations simultaneously, reducing mail and telephone costs while hastening the speed of communication (Butterfield, 1987b).

Technology is also being harnessed to reach distance learners. Electronic conferences and training sessions are being used by schools of social work and training institutions to reach students on branch campuses or those who live far from training locations. And computer bulletin boards are being used to exchange information, post notices and advertisements, access and copy files and software, or send cost-effective and speedy messages (Butterfield, 1987a). These bulletin boards have also been initiated for the wider social services community, such as the National CUSSnet (Computer Users in the Social Services) (Hiratsuka, 1995).

Social workers are using computers to communicate with each other. Bulletin boards enable users to hook up with a range of support groups, including those concerned with adoptees, battered women, and people with AIDS. Internet, for example, allows for ongoing dialogue among colleagues on issues that range from stress management to ways to forestall pending budget cuts. "Therapist" is an information exchange network initiated by a social worker, Mark Young, and a psychologist colleague, which practitioners can use to tap into discussions on treatment strategies, ethics, and practice issues (Landers, 1993).

Changing Context of Practice

As always, the sociopolitical environment will serve either to constrain or expand the boundaries of social work practice. We can forecast the future by examining the problems emerging now and ones that are taking on different dimensions. These problems include AIDS; societal violence, particularly violence among youths; inner-city decay; continued feminization of poverty and child poverty; industrial downsizing; and the growth in the proportion of elderly people in our society.

Social workers may find themselves addressing new or worsening psychosocial problems within an expanding number of practice settings. For example, as discussed in Part 5, social workers are now practicing in concert with veterinarians on issues of loss and grief. Social workers are also working across practice settings with people who have eating disorders, such as bulimia and anorexia nervosa, and those who are trying to kick their nicotine addiction. Although these problems may not be new, social workers until now have played only a minor role in the provision of related services. The boundaries continue to expand.

We can anticipate that social workers will play a continuing and growing role in working with people with AIDs as the affected population increases numerically and across gender, racial, and socioeconomic lines. New and expanding social work roles are reflected in curriculum changes within schools of social work. In recent years, we have seen an increasing array of courses offered in specialty areas such as homelessness, AIDS, pharmacology, gerontology, and occupational social work.

Ewalt (1994) suggested that social workers can and should transform the profession in those areas identified as needing change. Several of these "weak spots" in the profession have already been identified: multicultural practice, social work research, school and agency partnerships, and participation in government affairs. The question becomes whether there is sufficient investment to achieve the degree of change required. Any effort to redefine the domain of social work runs the risk of resistance from some segments of the profession. However, social work is committed to and incorporates within its agency context the concept and practice of planning. Anticipating the future enables the profession to engage in longer-term planning and to devise strategies to meet projected needs. According to Ewalt (1994) "the profession must not only be sensitive to change but must also be able to identify and measure it" (p. 2). This planning process is critical if social work is to influence as well as respond to the changing world and its place within it.

The preference of people in the United States and their elected leaders have to "privatize" as many public functions as possible has been evident for some time, and political and societal support for this movement is increasing. An important impetus to privatization has been the reduction in government funding for social welfare programs and the preference of government to purchase services for nonpublic agencies rather than provide services directly (Gibelman, 1995). This movement suggests that social services increasingly will be delivered by nonprofit and for-profit agencies. However, government responsibility for planning, evaluating, and financing services will probably not be delegated, at least not to the same degree as service provision (Gibelman & Demone, 1989).

The Republican domination of the U.S. Congress after the 1994 midterm elections and the promises of the new leadership to severely curtail social welfare programs raise questions about the immediate and longer-term future of government-sponsored programs. Reminiscent of the Reagan era, House Speaker Newt Gingrich is calling for less government spending, greater charitable giving, more self-reliance, and more time-limited help. In this atmosphere, the values, commitments, and work of social workers may once again be looked on with disfavor.

Social workers continue to become more sophisticated about the world of politics. The increased involvement of social workers in the political realm is evident, as discussed in Part 8, in the growing number of social workers who are elected and appointed to official positions at the national, state, and local levels and the increasingly active participation of social workers in political campaigns (Ginsberg, 1988).

Closely intertwined with the political scene is the health care reform movement and its potential impact on what social workers do. Although Congress did not act on President Clinton's health care reform plan, which would have recognized clinical social workers as care providers, new proposals will surface. A key question is whether and to what extent social workers will be included as care providers in the final legislation. What is clear is that health care reform will impose limitations on the nature and extent of health and mental health practice. For example, among the considerations in the array of health care proposals in 1994 was a limit on outpatient psychotherapy and higher copayments for psychotherapy. Limitations on inpatient and residential treatment coverage were also considered (Hiratsuka, 1994).

There is justifiable concern about the evolution of managed care systems and their impact on health and mental health services. Edwards (1990) observed that

> While it is hoped that such arrangements will balance service quality with costs, there are inherent risks in using fiscal criteria to determine who gets services, what service method is used and how resources will be allocated for the services. These risks become even greater when nonclinicians make the decisions. (p. 2)

The risks in managed care thus concern both potential limitations to the role of social workers within this system and the quality and quantity of services that will be available to the clients. The issues of service quality and of assuring the adequacy and appropriateness of services will continue to occupy the profession. The need to document the effectiveness of social work services has never been more important; social workers must continue and expand research efforts about the outcomes of different types of interventions. Also on the research agenda are questions concerning what criteria are used to select different treatment methods, how effectiveness can best be determined, and what impact managed care has on the provision of health and mental health services (Edwards, 1990).

The mandate for all social workers to incorporate research into their practice is underscored by the increasing influence of research-based knowledge on the development of and debate about public policy. To date, Inouye, Ell, and Ewalt (1994) noted, there has been a pronounced lack of rigorous research to shed light on the most effective way to prevent or resolve human problems, and they aptly stated the centrality of research in informing public policy:

> Policy formulation and debate in the areas of health care reform, crime, welfare reform, and child and family welfare have drawn on relevant research when it was available, but all too often these discussions have revealed critical gaps in convincing research-based knowledge. Advocacy for an enhanced mental health benefits package in health care reform, for example, was hampered, according to Clinton administration officials and their opponents, by limited knowledge about the use of these services by varied socioeconomic and ethnic groups. (p. 629)

The New Professionals

The shape of the social work profession of the future can also be discerned from data on the primary fields of practice and social problem concentrations selected by master's students currently enrolled in social work education programs. The fields of practice or social problem concentrations identified on the basis of self-reports by schools of social work to the Council on Social Work Education are shown in Table 64-1.

Although there is a large proportion of students in the "not yet determined" or "none, methods concentration only" categories, data on the declared areas of practice of MSW students are remarkably consistent with the statistical profile of the NASW membership in 1991 (Gibelman & Schervish, 1993). Family services and child welfare as a combined category ranks first among primary fields of practice, followed closely by mental health and then by health, which is lagging behind but still a major area. The dearth of social workers concentrating in aging, substance abuse, community planning, occupational social work, public welfare, and mental retardation shows a consistent pattern with the proportion of social workers represented in these areas among the NASW membership (Gibelman & Schervish, 1993).

Visions of the Future

Social workers have an important role to play in defining the social work profession of the future. The profession is not only affected by the environment in which it functions, but by the directions it sets for itself. As Macarov (1991) noted: "Without forecasting there is no freedom of decision. Only insofar as we try to influence the direction that the future will take are we exercising choice, rather than resigning ourselves to the inevitable or—to be more precise—to capriciousness" (p. 3).

Table 64-1

Fields of Practice or Social Problem Concentrations, Schools of Social Work, 1993–94

Aging/gerontological social work	670
Alcohol, drug, or substance abuse	517
Child welfare	2,172
Community planning	325
Corrections/criminal justice	183
Family services	2,600
Group services	181
Health	2,243
Mental health or community mental health	4,133
Mental retardation	151
Occupational/industrial social work	184
Public assistance/public welfare	208
Rehabilitation	94
School social work	696
Other fields of practice/social problems	1,165
Combinations	331
Not yet determined	6,792
None (methods concentration only)	9,405
Total	32,050

Source: Lennon, T. M. (1994). *Statistics on social work education in the United States: 1993*. Alexandria, VA: Council on Social Work Education.

Social work can initiate its own transformation, based on the preferences of its labor force and in response to the identification of conditions in need of change, both societal and professional. For example, one area in which change is required was identified by Ewalt (1994): multicultural practice. The populations social workers serve are often composed of disenfranchised people, including immigrants, ethnic and racial groups, women, and poor people. As a predominantly white profession (88 percent of the NASW membership in 1991), social work needs to develop and perfect the theories and tools that multicultural practice requires.

Practice Implications

For social workers, these changes have important practice implications. New methods of practicing and of learning to practice social work may be required (Macarov, 1991).

First, as government reduces its financial support for social programs, social workers in the nonprofit sector will need to develop and fine-tune their fundraising skills. The result may be that social workers will be able to devote less time to direct practice or, alternatively, that schools of social work will need to prepare a larger cadre of social workers with the requisite fundraising knowledge and skills. Transferring social welfare functions to nonprofit and for-profit organizations may also affect the characteristics of the client groups served (Gibelman, 1995; Macarov, 1991).

The practice of social work will increasingly emphasize accountability to funding sources and to the general taxpaying public. The use of management information systems and quality assurance mechanisms in practice will become more standardized and far-reaching.

Similar developments are occurring in the private practice of social work. Although students maintain their interest in independent practice, the realities of the health care industry suggest a less lucrative field for social workers in this field. A full-page advertisement in a 1995 issue of the *NASW News* asked, "Is managed care threatening the survival of your practice?"

Managed care, in fact, raises fundamental issues for the profession that go far beyond its impact on independent practice. Social services agencies are being forced to review and, often, revamp their style of operations, modes of service delivery, and even their mission to adapt to the changing health care system. United Charities, an agency in Chicago, adopted a proactive stance on managed care by forming a task force, composed of board members and staff, to explore its implications. The question quickly centered not on whether the agency would get into managed care, but what the nature of its participation would and should be (Council on Accreditation, 1994). The agency hired a consultant to help address the array of programmatic, technical, and philosophical issues.

Some agencies are less optimistic. Sal Ambrosino, executive director, Nassau County Family Service Association in New York, put it this way:

> Managed care is a very special kind of nightmare these days because one is caught in a situation with little control. One either goes along or opts out. We've been told by managed care outfits that we can only provide 3–6 sessions. So it means all you can provide is emergency brief treatment. The literature has a lot to say about the positives of brief treatment, and workers skilled at brief treatment can get good results. However, brief treatment forces counselors to use one modality for all clients, when many clients may require a more sustained period of counseling.
>
> Managed care can be a very onerous arrangement. The preapproval process can take hours of clerical time, with each managed care organization having a different set of rules. We're also concerned about undermining the standard of confidentiality that is so essential to social work practice. . . . We have a serious concern that, with managed care, we may no longer be in control of our treatment plan. The professional standards we've worked so hard to maintain are being undermined by the new system. (quoted in Council on Accreditation, 1994, p. 3)

The Job Market

For those considering a career in social work or those already in social work but contemplating a change in what they do, an inevitable concern is about the status of the job market. How "open" is the market and in what areas? The current political climate and promises of deep budget cuts cause understandable worry.

Social work was prominently featured by U.S. News & World Report in its tally of "best jobs for the future." Singled out were employee assistance counseling (listed as one of the 20 best bets for the future), private practice psychotherapy, family counseling, and gerontology as "other hot tracks" in the social work field ("Best Jobs for the Future," 1993; "20 Hot Job Tracks," 1994).

And in the October 31, 1994, issue of U.S. News & World Report, featuring its annual career guide, social work was again listed as one of the 20 best "hot tracks." Given particular mention as a burgeoning career area in social work was the specialty of home health. The need for home health care has emerged as the number of inpatient hospital days has decreased. Home health social workers, employed by the hospital or home health agencies, evaluate the client's living conditions and medical and psychological care needs and arrange for or refer for needed care ("Home Health Social Work," 1995).

Forecasts of gloom for social work careers are thus offset by some positive predictions. The best prognosis, however, comes from the proven resilience of the profession in unfavorable political times. Social work continues to expand and adapt its boundaries to fit the circumstances of time.

A review of the classified advertisements for the period 1993 through 1995 reveals some interesting insights about the job market.

Growth in For-Profit Opportunities

Ten years ago, a classified advertisement for a social work position in a for-profit corporation would have been a rarity. In fact, a review of the NASW News classified section for January 1985 revealed only one such ad for a social worker for Mental Health Management, Inc., "a nationwide firm specializing in the management of psychiatric and alcoholism inpatient facilities. . . ." In 1995 such ads have become commonplace. For example, the January 1995 issue of NASW News advertised the following for-profit opportunities, among others:

- A provider of geriatric mental health services in locations across the country seeks clinical social workers to provide geriatric mental health services.

- A private (for-profit) health and human services organization headquartered in Washington, DC, is recruiting for social workers in locations in the Midwest and Northeast to provide case management, day treatment, foster care, and/or mental health services.

- A provider of supports and services to persons with developmental disabilities through supported living programs; group homes; contract management for state and local governments, nonprofit agencies, and private owners, has management opportunities available for senior administrators and area directors. Requirements include five years of management experience in the field of providing community residential services to persons with developmental disabilities.

- A professional recruiting firm that, under contract with employers, recruits social workers for full-time positions across the country seeks social workers to fill a variety of positions.

- A national company that is locally managed seeks multidisciplinary teams of clinical social workers and psychologists to provide mental health services at the direct or management levels.

- A health care corporation specializing in military health care has a need for a social worker/therapist to provide clinical services to child abuse and spouse abuse victims.

The most frequent form of for-profit, or proprietary, practice in social work is independent or private clinical practice. But proprietary practice also extends to macro areas, such as consultation, organizing of special interest groups, and work in agencies targeted to meet the needs of special populations, such as home care combined with social services for elderly people (Barker, 1995). The privatization of human services has led to the creation of a new and growing network of proprietary agencies that are ready and willing to compete for contract dollars. An example is PHP Healthcare Corporation, cited above, a private firm providing military social services on a military base.

Specialization

Given the enormous breadth of the field of social work, it is both logical and necessary that a system of specialization develop within it. Although beginning social workers may seek and hold more generalist-type positions, in which they work with diverse demographic populations with a range of situations and problems, typically social workers begin to focus their growing knowledge and skills on a specific type of problem area (such as homelessness, chronic mental illness, or juvenile delinquency); target population (children and youth, senior citizens, or couples); or objectives of services (providing housing for runaway youths, preventing child abuse, rehabilitating drug-addicted people). A *social work specialist* is "a practitioner whose orientation and knowledge are focused on a specific problem or goal or whose technical expertise and skill in specific activities are highly developed and refined" (Barker, 1995, p. 362). Specialization is both efficient and expedient for the individual social worker and for employers as it reduces the amount of on-the-job training and learning that is necessary and provides for a higher level of experience.

Social workers develop their specialist expertise through on-the-job experience and continuing education. Continuing education is now frequently required by state licensing boards as a condition of maintaining one's license; a specific number of continuing education units (CEUs) must be taken within specified time periods (Barker, 1995).

Part-Time Employment

Another emerging trend in the social work labor market is the increasing use of part-time employees. The motive seems clear in this era of cutback management: keep employer costs down. Hiring two part-time employees is substantially less expensive than hiring one full-time worker if the employer does not provide the same level of fringe benefits for part-time employees as they do for full-time employees, which, including pension plan and health and disability benefits, can total 27 percent or more of salary. This trend in social work employment mirrors trends in the overall employment market. The U.S. Department of Labor determined that the percentage of workers receiving health insurance from employers has declined significantly in recent years (as cited in "In Brief," 1994). In 1993, 61 percent of workers were covered by their employer for health insurance, down from 65 percent in 1988. Those who fared the worst were low-paid and part-time workers, and very young and very old workers.

Another advantage, from the employer's perspective, is that the agency can recruit and retain a more specialized labor force. For example, the January 1995 issue of *NASW News* included a classified advertisement for two part-time openings at Kaiser Permanente Medical Center in Hayward, California. One of these positions called for a specialization in adult psychotherapy, the other in child, adolescent, and family psychotherapy. In the past, one social worker might have been responsible for a generic mental health caseload. By splitting jobs, employers can gain a higher level of expertise, which may have public relations as well as cost value.

Another variation in the labor market is the use of per diem (or per contracted job) employment. Social workers may be hired by an adoption agency to do home studies, and be paid on the basis of each completed home study. Or a social worker may be retained to provide in-home services on a case-by-case basis.

Degree and Experience Requirements

Classified advertisements often specify the absolute requirement that applicants be licensed or license-eligible. In addition, frequently cited "buzzwords" appearing in classifieds include experiential requirements in total quality management, case management, clinical *and* administrative supervision, grant writing, and contract management. Many jobs now require a combination of clinical and administrative skills, and designated job functions reflect this multiple dimensional emphasis. Requirements are emphasized and often form the major portion of classifieds.

Social workers are often in competition with other human services professionals, such as psychologists, counselors, marriage and family therapists, public administrators, and even business administrators for direct service, supervisory, and administrative positions. In 1985, the classified ads under such categories as "social work," "mental health," and "counselor" generally specified the MSW degree as a requirement. Today, it is not unusual for social work to be one of several eligible professions for jobs that heretofore required a social work degree. Counseling, psychology, psychiatric nursing, and marriage and family therapy are sometimes listed as acceptable specialties. Similarly, there is a growing tendency for a degree in business or public administration to be listed as a qualification for a management position, combined with clinical or supervisory experience. The terminology used in the classifieds shows this trend: "human services or related degree"; "social worker or psychologist."

In a similar vein, many ads list the bachelor's degree as the baseline requirement, with a master's degree cited as "desirable" or "preferred." Sometimes no degree requirement is specified, a trend that may relate to several phenomena:

- By not listing a degree as a requirement, employers have greater flexibility in their hiring decisions.

- The hiring of less experienced or less educated personnel may be a way to control agency costs.

- Declassification has downplayed degree requirements within certain agencies, particularly those in the public sector.

The current fiscal constraints felt by most human services agencies may lead to pressure to hire social workers who cost less: those holding a BSW rather than an MSW, or those with less experience. A recent study of the differential work assignments of social work practitioners in Canadian hospitals (Levin & Herbert, 1995) suggests that administrators differentiated social workers on the basis of knowledge and skills, but nevertheless made few distinctions between BSWs and MSWs in regard to actual task assignment. The implications raise concerns about the lack of differentiating criteria for levels of practice. To the extent that the BSW-level social worker is perceived to be doing the job as effectively as the more educated and expensive MSW, hiring patterns may tend to favor the less trained worker or lead to competency expectations that could compromise patient care (Levin & Herbert, 1995).

On the other hand, there are now certain "imperatives" that appear frequently in classified advertisements for social workers. Prominent in this category are the need for computer skills and a strong preference for bilingualism. Proposal-writing skills are also frequently listed as desirable. And licensing is no longer optional; virtually all positions for which a social work degree is required mandate that the successful applicant be licensed in the applicable state or be eligible for licensure.

Social workers need to look beyond the social work section of the classifieds and search for related opportunities that draw on and require the skills social workers possess. These include positions under such headings as mental health, mental retardation, health, administration, coordination, advocacy, management, and education. There is also an increasing number of opportunities for social workers in nontraditional settings. National health agencies, for example, are expanding their range of services to include professional assistance as well as self-help and patient education.

The current employment scene holds both opportunities and challenges. Competition is keen. Changes and emerging patterns in the job market for social workers is accompanied by and occurs within the context of a growing pool of social workers. Lennon (1994) reported that in 1967–68, 4,614 MSWs and 67 doctoral degrees in social work were awarded; in 1987–88, the numbers were up to 9,891 MSW degrees and 332 doctoral degrees; in 1992–93, the numbers reached 12,583 MSWs and 229 doctoral degrees. Also in 1993, 10,288 baccalaureate degrees in social work were awarded (Lennon, 1994).

Enrollments in schools of social work tend to fluctuate slightly, depending on the perceived place of social work in society at any given period of time. For example, the annual number of MSW graduates, a reflection of the number of enrollees, for the periods 1983–84 and 1986–87 were down significantly from 1982–83 and in the years following the Reagan era. Prospective students may be dissuaded from pursuing social work education because the media message is that human services are on the chopping block. This constriction in the number of newly entering social workers may, in fact, be an important self-regulation of the size of the labor force. But, as we have experienced before, the job market bounces back, although perhaps in somewhat modified form.

Conclusion

What do social workers do? The following letter, which appeared in the July 1994 issue of *Social Work* (Wolfe, 1994) provides a heart-felt perspective on the role of social workers.

Dad, You'd Be Proud

When I think about the degree I am about to receive, I cannot help but revisit those times when I sat down with my father and spoke about the art and craft of social work.

Dad had received his master's degree in social work from Case Western Reserve University in 1959. It was a time, he said, when becoming a social worker meant making a commitment to serve humanity. Being a social worker meant taking a disadvantaged youth under your arm and into your heart and making his world a little less painful. And maybe, if you were skilled enough, you could give that child a glance through a window of opportunity, a chance to realize some of his hopes and dreams.

Being a social worker, he said, was helping the parents of that underprivileged child cope with the frustration and hopelessness of living a life entrenched in poverty. It meant assisting a disabled person through the maze of government bureaucracy to secure the financial aid necessary to eat for another day or to stay warm for another night.

Dad said a social worker provided case management and advocacy for clients who otherwise would be left to survive by means that guaranteed social isolation and enlistment in an often unfair and prejudiced correctional system.

My father said to me that social work was accepting that our society, despite its claim of plurality and declarations of democracy and equality, often leaves the young, the old, and the poor to swim alone in a turbulent ocean of social and economic inequity. The social worker is the lifeline to these people. He said that the catastrophe of a sinking ocean liner, during which many lives are miraculously saved but scores more are lost, reminds us that the key to professional survival means accepting the losses and keeping our desire and commitment to serve our fellow human.

As I am on the threshold of accepting the degree that will provide an entree into the profession of serving humanity, advocating for the disenfranchised and socially underprivileged, serving the victim and offender, and helping young and old, I realize I am devoted to social work as an art and science.

Clearly the professional advances that social work has developed over past decades have made their presence felt in a myriad of institutions, corporations, small business, government bureaucracies, and unions. The social worker is used not only as therapist for resolving individual and interpersonal dysfunction, but also as facilitator of increased productivity and sustained participation in the global marketplace.

It has been a decade since my father passed away, and many values have changed in our world. But certainly the profession which he, like many before and since, chose to practice, is needed. The single teenage mother, the developmentally disabled youth, the dysfunctional family, and the isolated elderly person will all continue to exist over time. The powerless, even in their powerlessness, remain an indelible mark on our society. The needy, through their need, remain a mark on our consciences and our spirits.

So as I embark on my term of serving humanity, I can feel proud of my profession and my fellow professionals. And I can say, Dad, you would be proud.

John C. Wolfe
Portland, OR

References

Barker, R. L. (1995). *Social work dictionary* (3rd ed.). Washington, DC: NASW Press.

Berger, R. M., & Kelly, J. J. (1993). Social work in the ecological crisis. *Social Work, 38*, 521–526.

Best jobs for the future. (1993, November 1). *U.S. News & World Report*, p. 112.

Butterfield, W. (1986, November). Computers changing social work practice. *NASW News*, p. 3.

Butterfield, W. (1987a, January). Compute, reach out and "CUSS" someone. *NASW News*, pp. 5, 18.

Butterfield, W. (1987b, February). E-mail: The intrepid electronic carrier. *NASW News*, p. 5.

Council on Accreditation of Services for Families and Children. (1994). Responding to managed care. *A Voice for Quality, 1*(2), 3.

Edwards, R. L. (1990, January). Benefits, pitfalls seen in managed care. *NASW News*, p. 2.

Edwards, R. L. (1991, April). Eastern Europe sees help in social work. *NASW News*, p. 2.

Ewalt, P. L. (1994, January). Visions of ourselves. *Social Work, 39*, 5–7.

Gibelman, M. (1995). Purchasing social services. In R. L. Edwards (Ed.-in-Chief), *Encyclopedia of social work* (19th ed., Vol. 2, pp. 1998–2007). Washington, DC: NASW Press.

Gibelman, M., & Demone, H. W. (1989). The evolving contract state. In H. W. Demone & M. Gibelman (Eds.), *Services for sale: Purchasing health and human services* (pp. 17–57). New Brunswick, NJ: Rutgers University Press.

Gibelman, M., & Schervish, P. H. (1993). *Who we are: The social work labor force as reflected in the NASW membership*. Washington, DC: NASW Press.

Ginsberg, L. (1988). Social workers and politics: Lessons from practice. *Social Work, 33*, 245–247.

Hiratsuka, J. (1990, November). Computer power comes to child welfare. *NASW News*, p. 3.

Hiratsuka, J. (1991, February). Life crisis, loss plague infertile couples. *NASW News*, p. 3.

Hiratsuka, J. (1994, July). Health reform moving. *NASW News*, pp. 1, 10.

Hiratsuka, J. (1995, February). Computerizing: A calculated approach. *NASW News*, p. 3.

Home health social work called "hot track." (1995, January). *NASW News*, p. 10.

Hopps, J. G., & Collins, P. M. (1995). Social work profession overview. In R. L. Edwards (Ed.-in-Chief), *Encyclopedia of social work* (19th ed., Vol. 3, pp. 2266–2282). Washington, DC: NASW Press.

In brief. (1994, September). *NASW News*, p. 10.

Inouye, D. K., Ell, K., & Ewalt, P. L. (1994). Social work research and social policy. *Social Work, 39,* 629–631.

Landers, S. (1993, January). Colleagues connect for high-tech talks. *NASW News,* p. 5.

Lennon, T. M. (1994). *Statistics on social work education in the United States: 1993.* Alexandria, VA: Council on Social Work Education.

Levin, R., & Herbert, M. (1995). Differential work assignments of social work practitioners in hospitals. *Health & Social Work, 20,* 21–30.

Macarov, D. (1991). *Certain change: Social work practice in the future.* Silver Spring, MD: NASW Press.

Social workers harnessing technology. (1984, January). *NASW News,* pp. 3–4.

Specht, H., & Courtney, M. (1994). *Unfaithful angels: How social work has abandoned its mission.* New York: Free Press.

Stewart, R. (1984, November). From the president. *NASW News,* p. 2.

20 hot job tracks. (1994, October 31). *U.S. News & World Report,* p. 110.

Wolfe, J. C. (1994, July). Dad, you'd be proud. *Social Work, 39,* 478.

index

AIDS (acquired immune deficiency syndrome), 83, 88, 149–157, 168–169, 179–180, 352–354, 367

Aid to Families with Dependent Children (AFDC), 7, 102, 310

Airplane crashes and crisis interventions, 37

Alcohol abuse, 83–84, 179, 258–261

Alone, elderly preferring to live, 233

Alternative drug programs, 262–263

Alternative educational programs for students
    in special circumstances, 186–187

Alzheimer's disease, 240–242

Ambivalence of society hampering social work, 16, 258

Ambrosino, Sal, 371

American Association for Counseling and Development, 182

American Board of Examiners in Clinical Social Work (ABE), xxv

American Federation of State, County and Municipal Employees (AFSCME), 330

American Hospice Movement, 243

American Hospital Association, 132

American Psychological Association (APA), 26

American Public Welfare Association, 96, 327, 346

American School Counselors Association, 182

American–Soviet Walk (1987), 345

Americans with Disabilities Act of 1990 (P.L. 101-336), 10

Animal–human bond, 226–229

Anorexia nervosa, 134–135

Antidepressant medications, 225

Anti-Drug Abuse Act Amendments of 1988 (P.L. 100-690), 10

Armenia, 305

Ashkinazy, Steve, 186

Assessment and referral teams, 74. *See also* Functions carried out by social workers

Association of Gerontology in Higher Education, 207

Association programs, EAP, 42

Atlanta VA Medical Center, 72

At-risk behavior, 153

Attacks against social work profession, 10–12

Attention-deficit hyperactivity disorder (ADHD), 178, 196–197

Auspice of practice, xviii–xx, 132

Automobile accidents, 188–190

AZT (antiviral drug), 151

B

Baby boom generation, 216

Baccalaureate degree (BSW), xii
    Academy of Certified Baccalaureate Social Workers, xxiv, xxv–xxvi
    aging, field of, 207
    career opportunities, xxiii, 126, 171, 273, 356, 357
    corrections, field of, 279
    future, the, 375–376
    mental health practice, 23

Banks, Ebie, 255

Bennett, William J., 142

Bereavement process, 228, 246

Binge-eating disorder (BED), 135–136

Biomedical technology, 146, 160–161, 210, 294, 363–366

Birth control, 141, 142

Bisexuals, 150

Blended families, 81

(DSW); Master's degree (MSW)

Education for All Handicapped Children Act of 1975 (P.L. 94-142), 176, 178

Elderly people, 45, 131, 220–221, 299. *See also* Aging, field of

Elders, Joycelyn, 142

Electroconvulsive shock therapy, 225

Elementary School Counseling Demonstration Act, 177

Emergency medical workers, 37, 77, 170

Emotional and physiological problems, interplay between, 132

Empathic communication, 107, 145

Employee assistance programs (EAPs), 42–48, 74–75

Empowerment, 108, 322–323

Encyclopedia of Social Work, xv

End-of-life decisions, 247

Enhancement function, 99

Environmental disasters, 37

Environmental factors influencing mental health, 1–2

Ethnicity, 208–209, 299

Experience influencing what social workers do, xxiv, 374–376. *See also* Vignettes, case

External programs, EAP, 42

Exxon Valdez, 38–39

F

Families, 50, 105–108, 139–143, 155. *See also* Child and family services

Families and Schools Together (Fast), 254

Family and Medical Leave Act of 1993 (P.L. 103-3), 10

Family and Primary Associations Commission, 96

Family Assessment Project, 287

Family Services America, 323, 346

Farmers, 66–69, 117

Federal Employee Health Benefits Program (FEHBP), 55

Federal government, xix, 365, 367–368. *See also* Legislation influencing social work; Political ideology and social work

Federal Social Work Consortium, 14

Fee-for-service in the private sector, 57, 63, 108, 217, 365, 372–373

Flooding and crisis interventions, 38

Flying, fear of, 60–61

Forensic social work, 289–290

Foster care, adult, 234–235

Foster care for children, 109–113, 127, 156

Frail elderly, 209

Full-risk capitation arrangements, 63

Functions carried out by social workers, xxi–xxii, 11–12. *See also* Direct practice; Macro functions of social work

aging, field of, 210–211

alcohol abuse, 261

attention-deficit hyperactivity disorder, 197

case management, 217

community organization, 335

consultation, 340–341

corrections, field of, 282–283

crisis interventions, 190, 192

depression, 224, 225

developmental disabilities, 295

dropout problem, school, 196

HIV/AIDS, 155

home-based programs, 232

homeless population, 118

hospice care, 245–246

hospital social workers, 161–163

the
author

Margaret Gibelman, DSW, ACSW, is professor, Wurzweiler School of Social Work, Yeshiva University, New York. She has worked in the human services as a clinician, supervisor, educator, and manager. In the latter category, she has served as executive director of the National Association of School Psychologists and, earlier, of the Lupus Foundation of America. She was also associate executive director, Council on Social Work Education.

Dr. Gibelman frequently consults with nonprofit organizations and is the author of numerous articles on nonprofit management, privatization, social work education, social policy, and service delivery systems.

What Social Workers Do

Designed by The Watermark Design Office.

Composed by Sheila Holzberger, Wolf Publications, Inc., in Bodoni, Futura, and Goudy.

Printed by BookCrafters, Inc., on 60# Lakewood.